In Search of Christopher Marlowe

The Archbishop's throne ('*Peter's chair*') in Canterbury Cathedral.

Albeit the world think Machiavel is dead,
Yet was his soul but flown beyond the Alps;
And, now the Guise is dead, is come from France,
To view this land, and frolic with his friends.
To some perhaps my name is odious;
But such as love me, guard me from their tongues,
And let them know that I am Machiavel,
And weigh not men, and therefore not men's words.
Admir'd I am of those that hate me most:
Though some speak openly against my books,
Yet will they read me, and thereby attain
To Peter's chair; and, when they cast me off,
Are poison'd by my climbing followers.
I count religion but a childish toy,
And hold there is no sin but ignorance.

Prologue to THE JEW OF MALTA.

In Search of
CHRISTOPHER
MARLOWE

A PICTORIAL BIOGRAPHY

Text by A. D. Wraight

Photography by Virginia F. Stern

Adam Hart (Publishers) Ltd
CHICHESTER, SUSSEX, ENGLAND

By the same authors

CHRISTOPHER MARLOWE AND EDWARD ALLEYN
by A.D. Wraight

GABRIEL HARVEY
A Study of His Life, Marginalia
and Library
by Virginia F. Stern

SIR STEPHEN POWLE
OF COURT AND COUNTRY
Memorabilia of a Government Agent
for Queen Elizabeth I, Chancery Official,
and English Country Gentleman
by Virginia F. Stern

First Published in 1965 by
Macdonald & Co. (Publishers) Ltd.
This edition first published by
Adam Hart (Publishers) Ltd
Chichester, Sussex, England

Contents

Credits

All photographs in this book are by Virginia F. Stern unless otherwise noted. Unfortunately, on the following pages some credits were omitted, and the authors gratefully acknowledge permission to use these illustrations:

Cover picture: The putative portrait of Christopher Marlowe courtesy of the Master and Fellows of Corpus Christi College, Cambridge.

(p. 2) Distant view of Canterbury, Wm. Somner. *Antiquities of Canterbury,* 1703: N.Y. Public Library. (p. 3) Cobbler's shop, from *Roxburghe Ballads:* British Museum. (p. 21) Canterbury in 1580, Wm. Smith. *Particular Description of England,* 1588: British Museum. (p. 30) Pilgrims leaving Canterbury, from Prologue to Lydgate's *Siege of Thebes:* British Museum, Dept. of MSS. (p. 43) Dr. Matthew Parker. Photo by Edward Leigh from painting at Corpus Christi College. (p. 48) Discipline in an Elizabethan schoolroom, from *Roxburghe Ballads:* British Museum. (p. 49) List of King's School scholars: MS. from Canterbury Chapter Library. (p. 54) Extract from Admission Book (1581): Corpus Christi College. (p. 65) "Marlowe" portrait. Photo by Edward Leigh from Corpus Christi painting. (p. 88) Privy Council letter of 29th June, 1587, P.R.O. PC 2/14, p. 381. Crown copyright; reproduced by permission of H.M. Stationery Office. (p. 89) Northern France: British Museum, Dept. of Maps. (p. 97) Letter from Anthony Babington to Robert Poly: British Museum. Lansdowne MS. 49, f.63. (p. 103) 1593 Map of London from Norden's *Speculum Britanniae:* Folger Shakespeare Library. (pp. 106 – 7) Map of Moorfields: London Museum; Crown copyright. (p. 108) Tavern Courtyard, drawing from H. T. Stephenson's *Shakespeare's London,* 1906. (p. 110) Sir Philip Sidney's funeral, from a roll drawn by Thomas Lant, Windsor Herald: British Museum, Dept. of Prints & Drawings. (p. 115) Ortelius' map of Africa (1579): N.Y. Public Library. (p. 118) Section of London showing Hog Lane: London Museum. (p. 119) Newgate Prison, engraving from Stephenson's *Shakespeare's London,* 1906. (p. 124) Thomas Watson. *Madrigal!s,* 1590: British Museum. (p. 128) Thomas Watson. *Amintae Gaudia,* 1592: British Museum. (p. 130) MS. copy of "The Passionate Shepherd": Folger Shakespeare Library. (p. 146) George Carey, Baron Hunsdon: from a miniature in the collection of the Duke of Buccleuch. (p. 154) Edmund Spenser: British Museum, Dept. of Prints & Drawings. (p. 159) Title page of Thomas Lodge's *Rosalynde,* 1592: British Museum. (p. 161) George Chapman: British Museum, Dept. of Prints & Drawings. (p. 163) Ferdinando Stanley, Lord Strange: John Rylands Library. (p. 185) Caricature of Robert Greene, from John Dickenson's *Greene in Conceipt,* 1598: British Museum. (pp. 188 – 9) Greene's *Groatsworth of Wit,* 1592: British Museum. (p. 216) Head of the "Marlowe" portrait before retouching. Photo by Edward Leigh from painting at Corpus Christi College. (p. 216) Head of retouched portrait (complete portrait showing details of costume is on p. 65). (p. 222) *Hero and Leander,* 1598: British Museum. (p. 225) "Massacre at Paris" entry in Henslowe's Diary: Dulwich College. (p. 228) Collier forgery of an Elizabethan manuscript: British Museum, Additional MS. 32,380. (p. 229) Marlowe's signature on a 1585 will, courtesy of Archives Comm., Kent County Council. (p. 240) Woodcuts depicting the plague, from *Roxburghe Ballads:* British Museum. (p. 263) Initials on beech tree, noted by Mr. Calvin Hoffman in 1952 – 3. (p. 280) Pedigree of Walsingham, Webb, Miller, & Beckwith. *History of Chislehurst,* 1899: British Museum. (p. 284) Warrants of Arrest and of Marlowe's Appearance in Star Chamber: Public Record Office PC. 2/20, p. 374. (p. 292) Coroner's Inquisition: P.R.O. Chancery Miscellanea 64, 8, 241b. (p. 294) Archbishop John Whitgift, from painting at National Portrait Gallery. (p. 299) Lower House of Convocation, an ecclesiastical assembly: British Museum, Dept. of Prints & Drawings. (pp. 308 – 9) Richard Baines' note: British Museum, Harleian MS. 6848 f.185/186. (p. 314) Kyd's signed letter to Sir John Puckering: British Museum, Harleian MS. 6849 f.218/218v. (p. 316) Kyd's second letter to Puckering: British Museum, Harleian MS. 6848 f.154. (p. 321) Title page of *Doctor Faustus,* 1628: British Museum. (pp. 324 – 5) Accusation against Cholmley: British Museum, Harleian MS. 6848 f.190/190v.

Errata

The reader's indulgence is requested for the following error:

(p. 61) Second page of Cambridge manuscript, f.84v., has been printed instead of f.85. The latter is the page described and from which the enlargement (p. 60) containing Marlowe's name is taken.

Foreword

In the reign of Elizabeth I, Canterbury was a little community of about 4,000 people. Everyone knew everyone else, and the atmosphere was much like that of a large village. But the population if small in numbers comprehended all sorts and conditions of men and women. At the head stood the Archbishop of Canterbury, by virtue of his office first nobleman of the realm. In Canterbury there were clergymen of every rank, from the Primate to the semi-literate curates whom the Archbishop was compelled to use to man his churches in the first generation of the Elizabethan settlement, until a better-trained race of ministers grew up. There were lawyers in and around the city, like Sir Roger Manwood, Chief Baron of the Exchequer, or William Lovelace, Serjeant-at-Law, who occupied in the public eye a position much like that of an eminent Q.C. today, and (at the other extreme) squabbling petty attorneys like John Smith, who defended Christopher Marlowe in a case of assault and battery in 1592, just seven months before the poet's death. At one end of the economic scale stood wealthy merchants like Alderman Rose, the woollen draper, and at the other very minor industrialists such as 'Alice that maketh straw hats' up in St. Paul's parish. Many of the populace were of old Canterbury stock, like the valiant soldier Ancient Prowd, but many were immigrants like Mr. Pistol at the Spittal. There was a steady drift of population from the north, and some of it reached Canterbury. Kit Marlowe's brother-in-law, Thomas Graddell, came from Lancashire, and John Marlowe's crony, Plessington the baker, came from Cheshire. One man came from the other end of England, from 'Carlisle in Yorkshire', as a Canterbury clerk put it, with the usual local vagueness about northern geography. Some inhabitants came from even further afield, like a man from Scotland, who had two wives, one in Canterbury and another in 'Dunfermlyne'. There were Welshmen in the city, talking in their native tongue to the bewilderment of the Canterburians.

As the reign of Elizabeth progressed, crowds of refugees flying from persecution and death in the Low Countries and France came flooding up the Dover Road in such numbers that they packed out the great Cathedral Crypt assigned to them as a church. Even the ordinary casual conversation of neighbours must have been an exchange of ideas and information from all over the British Isles and North-West Europe. Moreover, since Canterbury stands astride the main road from Dover to London, there was a constant procession of travellers, broken soldiers from the wars, beggars, merchants, ambassadors, noblemen, some of the great men of Europe (Sir Philip Sidney met Prince John Casimir, leader of the Protestant armies on the Continent, at Canterbury in 1578). Some travellers provoked the Canterbury citizens to wonder, like 'the man from the land of Babylon', who came into Canterbury one day in 1564 when Kit was a tiny baby.

It is a commonplace that the sights and sounds of early childhood are the most formative influence undergone by any man or woman. In the case of a sensitive and receptive mind such as that of a great poet, the influence is bound to be proportionately sharper, and no one therefore can claim to know Christopher Marlowe who does not know something of the surroundings where his mind was first shaped and made aware. When four hundred years have passed away, it might be thought difficult to recover much of a childhood background, but at Canterbury this is easier than it might be elsewhere. To begin with, the local scenery in terms of great monuments of the past was, and still is, of a remarkable character. If the greater part of the city's gates have disappeared, and if much of the fortifications have been swept away, if the monstrous hall of the Archbishop's Palace exists only in a ghostly outline, yet the great cathedral still stands, despite narrow escapes in the Civil War three hundred years ago, and in World War II in our own day. Churches frequented by Christopher's kinsfolk and acquaintances still exist in weekly use, while despite slow erosion by rebuilding over the centuries, or sudden destruction in air-raids, a considerable proportion of the houses and shops known to him still flanks the streets. St. Augustine's Abbey was already a ruin when little boys from the local parishes like St. Paul's or St. George's played there in the 1560's, and stands in much the same condition today, apart from a tidying-up by the Ministry of Works. Beyond the city walls, out in the countryside, the meadows, cherry orchards and primrose-lined lanes are as yet very beautiful, despite the occasional intrusion of a coal mine or giant power station.

It is perhaps poetic justice that the most immediate surroundings of Marlowe's early childhood, the parish of St. George, should have been annihilated by the 20th-century Tamburlaine, who indeed made a great deal of Canterbury to 'caper in the air'. The St. George's area was the worst hit in the raids, and Christopher's church, where he was baptised, and where he was sent (I say sent advisedly, since John Marlowe the shoemaker did not always attend church regularly himself) to listen every week to the Rev. William Sweeting groaning out the sermons, was gutted in the air-raid of 1 June 1942. The tower, as thoroughly burnt out as any of those in Ilium, has happily survived, and now, well-restored, presides with its great clock above the new shops at the upper end of the High Street. One tragic loss must be alluded to here. A dominating sound from Christopher's youth can no longer be recalled. The bells of St. George's, including the splendid mediæval bell *Sanctus Georgius*, were destroyed

viii

when they fell from their burning bellframes about 2 a.m. in the night of the raid. The great bell of St. George's was very well known to citizens of Elizabethan Canterbury, since early every morning it was rung as a waking bell for the whole city.

Virginia Stern's studies of the Canterbury and Kentish scene thoroughly contradict the affirmation made more than once, that Christopher Marlowe, in contrast to Shakespeare, discloses in his works little of his own origins and background. There is the strongest biographical element in some of Marlowe's plays, very strong indeed in the case of *The Jew of Malta*. Without the exercise of very great ingenuity a description of much of Elizabethan Canterbury can be extracted from this play. A case can even be made for the presence of biographical material in such an improbable item as *Tamburlaine*.

Despite long sojourns at Cambridge and in London, despite meddling in the secret service, despite mixing with advanced thinkers and atheists, despite a dozen years of danger, adventure and excitement, Christopher Marlowe had perhaps by the date of his death moved very little distance away from the shoemaker's shop and the narrow streets of Canterbury.

*William Urry**

**William Urry, Ph.D., F.S.A., F.R.Hist.S., is Archivist to the City of Canterbury, Keeper of MSS. for the Dean and Chapter of the Cathedral.*

Acknowledgements

No one attempting a critical biography of Marlowe can fail to owe a considerable debt to the already formidable spade work done by previous researchers in this field. The authors wish especially to make grateful acknowledgement to the now famous researches of Dr. Hotson published in *The Death of Christopher Marlowe* (1925) and of Dr. Eccles in his *Christopher Marlowe in London* (1934); and to Dr. Boas' *Christopher Marlowe* (1940) and Professor Bakeless' two-volume classic *The Tragicall History of Christopher Marlowe* (1942). Dr. Charles Norman's evocative biography *The Muses Darling* (1960) affords documentation for the proceedings at Cerne Abbas, not given by other authorities. Dr. William Urry, Archivist to the City of Canterbury, Keeper of the MSS for the Dean and Chapter of the Cathedral, has most generously allowed us to publish new facts about Marlowe's Canterbury existence, and to him we owe a very special debt of gratitude, both for his encouragement and for his generous help.

Our thanks are due to the many authors and publishers who have granted permission to quote from copyrighted works to which full acknowledgements are given in the Notes and References.

In addition, we would like to express our sincere appreciation and gratitude to many who have assisted in the compilation of this volume. The list is far too long to make it possible to include all who have helped us in so many different ways, but particular mention must be made of the following for their considerable assistance: the British Museum, John Ryland Library, Folger Shakespeare Library, Chapter Office of Canterbury Cathedral, Master and Fellows of Corpus Christi College, Cambridge; Mr. W. S. Wright, Librarian of Dulwich College; Major Marsham Townshend, Sir Giles Isham, Mr. Henry Robinson, the Marlowe Society, especially Mr. Thomas Miles and Miss Elizabeth Vann; to Dewitt Stern for kindly translating the Walsingham tomb inscription, and Jack Waterhouse for his valuable assistance in reading and editing the text.

A. D. Wraight, Virginia F. Stern

Preface

In recent years no name in literature has aroused greater controversy than that of Christopher Marlowe, the Elizabethan poet and dramatist. Born the son of a humble Canterbury cobbler, his natural gifts raised him to the circles of the greatest in the land, noblemen of Queen Elizabeth's court, intellectuals, university wits, poets, and the aristocracy of the Inns of Court. By virtue of his education and his genius he became the premier poet and dramatist of England and delved headlong into the fiercely probing intellectual climate of the great spirits of his day; at the same time he was sucked into the vortex of the political stratagems of statesmen. His life was as compact of intrigue and drama as any play he wrote; his death, cutting short a brilliant career at the age of twenty-nine, is still surrounded with mystery.

J. E. Morpurgo writes in his Introduction to an edition of Marlowe's historical tragedy *Edward II*:

'Few great writers are as interesting as their works, the stern thrust of biography topples many of them from the hero's pedestal and sets them back: hard-working, earnest labourers who have chosen a study-desk instead of an office-table, a pen instead of a plough. But Christopher Marlowe, even had he written nothing, would make the wonderful, swashbuckling hero-villain of an exciting, blood-filled and frequently sordid romance.'

While we may disagree with Morpurgo's conclusions regarding the character of the man, and would emphasise the 'hero' rather than the 'villain' in one who is, perhaps, the most widely misunderstood genius of them all, we can otherwise endorse his statement. Marlowe's life-story is the antithesis of dullness, and as we celebrate the Quatercentenary of his birth few historical figures can command so much fascination as this son of Kent holds for us today, when the laurel wreath on his head is once more stirred by the winds of contrary opinions.

Marlowe was the epitome of Renaissance Man, who aspires to grasp all knowledge and all experience within the compass of his brief and all too hazardous life. He has been aptly described as 'the morning star' of the great literary effulgence that took place in the Renaissance England of Queen Elizabeth's reign, and at his end, like a shooting star, he fell. The unjust stigma on his name, together with the dazzling brilliance of Shakespeare and the constellation of dramatists who followed Marlowe—these have obscured him from us. His works remain as deathless commentary on his genius, a happy hunting-ground for literary scholars who have testified that it was he, and only he, who provided the pattern and the mould in which Shakespeare's works were cast. But it is the story of the man himself which it is mainly our task to attempt to tell here.

Genius is a phenomenon of human existence, and those to whom it is granted are rarely easy to understand. So it is in our search for Christopher Marlowe that the man often eludes us in the apparent contradictions of his many-sided and enigmatic personality. But the historical documentation of his short and eventful life is more plentiful and precise than that afforded by any other Elizabethan poet, and this made our task rewarding.

In compiling a pictorial background of Marlowe's life our researches took us first to Canterbury and Cambridge, two cities of incredible architectural beauty and antiquity that had been the cradle and nurse of his formative years, and finally to London and its environs, the scene of his triumph and his downfall. The ensuing photographs and accompanying text tell his story.

Part I

Canterbury 1564-1580

Canterbury, 1564–1580

The mediæval city of Canterbury has nurtured many men of genius, but with the capricious perversity of the great she has reserved all her enthusiasm for her adopted favourites whose illustrious names still draw visitors to this ancient city of pilgrimage: London-born Becket, Chaucer, and the Black Prince whose magnificent tomb, surmounted by his helmet, gauntlets and surcoat, is one of the sights of the cathedral. Somewhat obscurely, in the little parish church of St. George the Martyr, almost under the shadow of the great cathedral, was registered in the year 1564 the baptismal entry of a true son of Canterbury, destined to be her greatest. It reads simply:

> 'The 26th day of ffebruary was Christened
> Christofer the sonne of John Marlow.'[1]

There had been Marlowes in Canterbury for over a hundred years before Christopher was born. The Canterbury city records testify to men of that name from 1414 onwards, recording them with a nonchalant disregard for any uniformity in spelling as Marlo, Marloe, Marlow, Marley, Morley, Morle, Marlye, Marlen, Marlin, Merlin, and even Marlynge.[2] They followed the trades of fuller, vintner, roper, and finally a tanner emerges, also one John Marlowe by name, admitted a freeman to the city in 1467. From this line sprang the first Christopher

2

Marlowe, likewise a tanner, who has been suggested by Professor Tucker Brooke as the probable grandfather of our poet. He died in 1540 bequeathing certain properties to his widow Joan and her unborn child 'if hitt be a man child' for his inheritance, and it is generally assumed that his hopes were presently realised in the birth of a son, John Marlowe. This John Marlowe adopted the allied trade of shoemaker, tanners and shoemakers being under one guild in Canterbury. Professor Bakeless has added to our information from the Canterbury records by proving that John Marlowe was enrolled as an apprentice to a shoemaker and freeman of Canterbury, one Gerard Richardson, in 1559 60. Later we find 'John Marlyn, shoemaker' admitted as a freeman of the City on payment of 4s. 1d. in 1564, the birthyear of his son Christopher.[3]

On May 22, 1561, John Marlowe had married Katherine Arthur, a Dover girl of yeoman stock, as has been established by the researches of Dr. William Urry.[4] Their marriage was registered at the same church of St. George the Martyr where eight of their nine children were christened. Just a year after the marriage came a daughter, Mary, followed next by their first son, Christopher, and in due course a succession of two more sons and four daughters. Several of the Marlowe children died young and Christopher was their eldest surviving child and only son until many years later when a younger brother, Thomas, makes his appearance. He grew up therefore as the eldest, a boy, in a family of girls, and it would appear from the number of times that John Marlowe had to move house (because

Cobbler's shop. *Old wood block showing 16th-century shoemaker's shop similar to that of John Marlowe. Kit Marlowe is often spoken of, even in later life, as 'the cobbler's son'. Business seems to have done well enough, despite John Marlowe's apparent pecuniary difficulties from time to time. In 1564, when his son Christopher was born, we know that he already employed two apprentices.*

Anno Dm̄i, 1564

MONTAGE OF RELICS OF
MARLOWE'S BIRTH

1. *The 12th-century Tower of St. George the Martyr, only remaining relic of the church in which Christopher Marlowe was christened. Demolished by bombing in 1942, it stands only a stone's throw from the great Cathedral at which the destruction was aimed. The Church Register also lists the marriage of Marlowe's parents.*

2. *Entry in the Birth Register of St. George the Martyr recording baptism of Christopher Marlowe in 1564.*

3. *Baptismal Font (base). The base of the Early English octagonal font at which Christopher Marlowe was baptised. This relic was salvaged from the ruins of St. George's Church after the bombing of Canterbury on the terrible night of June 1st, 1942. Dr. Urry, the Archivist to the City of Canterbury, himself carted the broken pieces in a wheelbarrow and deposited them in the Chapter Library of the Cathedral, where they can still be seen. This night saw the destruction of so much of Marlowe's Canterbury, including also the Tudor house on the corner of St. George's Street and St. George's Lane which was reputedly his birthplace.*

4

he could not pay his rent) that the family were not as well off as in former days. John Marlowe, the shoemaker, is best described in the words of Dr. Urry as a 'busy, active, pugnacious fellow, clearly very fond of the limelight, prone to go to law at the slightest excuse, ready to perform public office, and probably rather neglectful of his business'. He features constantly in Canterbury records of the time in a professional capacity as bondsman on behalf of couples seeking marriage licences. On one occasion he stood surety for £100, while at the opposite end of the scale he is sued with almost equal frequency for non-payment of his rent.

In plying his trade as cobbler of Canterbury, John Marlowe must have come into personal contact with people in all walks of life, including the local gentry. His son Christopher, if we are to judge by his presumptive portrait painted when aged twenty-one, must have been a strikingly beautiful bright-eyed boy, intelligent beyond the usual, who might readily have attracted the attention of a patron amongst his father's wealthier clients. A likely benefactor has been suggested in the person of Sir Roger Manwood, a Kentish nobleman dwelling just without the West Gate of Canterbury at Hackington, who might have put in a good word to further the lad to the scholarship which he was awarded to the King's School. This, however, was not until his fifteenth year. We do not know where he had acquired the grounding in reading, writing and grammar which qualified him for this scholarship, but it is probable that he attended one of the small local schools which abounded in Elizabethan Canterbury, a city in which literacy would appear a most desirable acquisition. This was a natural result of its all-important position lying directly on the trade route from Dover to London.

As mother-city of the Church of England, the seat of the Primate and centre of national ecclesiastical affairs of state, Canterbury had for centuries been a place of pilgrimage as well as commerce, and held a position of political pre-eminence second only to London. The to-ing and fro-ing of travellers from the Continent, sojourning in the famous city in one of its many hostelries, must have made Christopher's childhood experience more varied and stimulating than that to be had in any other city of the time with the possible exception of the metropolis. Here he could meet soldiers returned from the wars, and sailors with tales of overseas and enough yarns to stuff his imagination for a dozen plays. With his own eyes he could witness sights of impressive pomp and splendour in the ceremonies connected with the great cathedral, and observe human behaviour in all its manifold facets: comic, terrible, and magnificent. What an experience in terms of human contact for a future dramatist! Above all, Canterbury was a city with a great tradition, immensely rich in historic memories that crowd in upon the receptive mind at every turn. The world and his wife, from the highest to the lowest, came here trapped in holiday finery and in mourning weeds, in armour and in chains, and here much that had a stirring dramatic impact on the nation's life was enacted. Indeed, the Dramatic Muse herself might have chosen this city of all others in the world in which to place her 'darling', for in his brief hour of glory he was to be dubbed, immortally, 'Marley, the Muses darling'.

The West Gate, *Canterbury*

'Two lofty turrets that command the town,
I wonder how it could be conquered thus.'

THE JEW OF MALTA

The ancient bastions of the West Gate remind us that Marlowe's boyhood was lived out in a walled city. These massive sentinels still guard the only remaining gateway to the city. It was rebuilt by Archbishop Simon of Sudbury in the reign of Richard II, replacing a structure on the same site which was possibly of Roman antiquity. Leland, writing in the reign of Henry VIII, tells us that 'Sudbury builded the West Gate, and made new and repaired to gither fro thens to the North gate, and wolde have done lykewise abowt al the town, yf he had lyved. The mayr of the town and aldermen, ons a yere cum solemply to his tumbe, to pray for his sowle, yn memory of his good deade'.[5]

The highway to London passes through this gate and on it the ghosts of such a cavalcade of history as might fire the imagination of less than a poet. Here

6

came the Canterbury Pilgrims, celebrated by Chaucer, whose *Canterbury Tales* were available to Marlowe in several editions from Caxton's first imprint in 1475 to Stowe's edition of 1561. Their annual offerings are reckoned to have poured £20,000 a year into the coffers of the cathedral, a trail of gold following down the years in the wake of the penitent figure of King Henry II, who had walked this way 'barefoot and weeping' on July 12th, 1174, to do penance for the murder of the sainted Thomas à Becket by suffering scourging in the cathedral crypt. In brilliant contrast, gorgeous in the trappings of their pomp and ceremony, had been the endless processions of kings, queens and princes from every reign of Plantagenet and Tudor, going to the Cathedral to give devotion or to lay their royal offerings at the Shrine of St. Thomas; or to solemnise a wedding, as that of Edward I to Margaret of France; or to give thanks to God, amid popular rejoicing, for victories won in the Holy Land or

Within the West Gate the Condemned Cell *can still be seen, with the arm and leg irons by which prisoners were chained to the floor or walls. On the ground floor of the South Tower there appears to have been a circular iron cage in which the more favoured prisoners were allowed to beg for alms and food from the public. In the time of the Catholic Mary Tudor, Protestant martyrs awaited death at the stake in this prison. In later life Marlowe himself was to engage in espionage work against the Catholic plots aimed at Mary's Protestant successor and half-sister, the great Elizabeth. The drama of political intrigue and religious antagonism was destined to be a part of his life. Of these things the West Gate stands as a grim reminder.*

7

Drawing by A. E. Henderson

A drawing of the south side of Canterbury Cathedral *shows its immensity. It must have seemed particularly imposing to the Canterbury residents of Marlowe's day. The tall central tower is known as 'Bell Harry' after a bell originally given by Prior Henry of Eastry. The bell (recast in 1635) sounds the curfew and the knell on the death of a member of the Royal Family or an archbishop.*

on the fields of France. Or again, to hold their court at Canterbury for a season, with great solemnity at Christmas as had been done by King John in 1204, or with tournament and joust as preferred by Edward III.

It is impossible to recount all that has passed here, but one event nearer to Marlowe's time may serve to give us a glimpse of the sights and sounds that Canterburians were used to witness. In 1520 King Henry VIII received the newly-elected emperor Charles V at Dover, and on Whit Sunday the two monarchs proceeded to Canterbury with regal pomp, riding together under one canopy, with Cardinal Wolsey riding next, and the nobility of England and Spain in attendance. They entered the city at St. George's Gate which stood in Marlowe's parish, and 'on both sides of the streets stood all the clerks and priests that were within twenty miles of Canterbury with long censers, crosses, surplices, and copes of the richest sort'.[6] All this company, we are told, attended service at the cathedral, and a day or two after were entertained at the Archbishop's palace with a ball and a sumptuous banquet. No other city in England except London could boast such a tradition of splendour.

8

In sombre magnificence passed also the funerals of primates and princes. Long remembered would be the torch-lit procession of the beloved Black Prince, accompanied by black-clad horses and general mourning as they laid him to rest beneath his splendid effigy in the cathedral; the entombment of Henry IV; and the stay en route of the body of Henry V, brought back from France for burial in Westminster Abbey.

Strife and terror have their place. In 1381 these very towers, then newly erected, witnessed the Great Peasants' Revolt when the rebels, having seized Canterbury, surged through the gates to march on London and presently returned bearing the headless body of their Archbishop slain on Tower Hill; and again in 1500 the clash of the secular and the religious broke out in riots around the gate between the monks and the citizens, while from within came the cries of the prisoners, for since 1400 the West Gate had been used as a prison. Under the shadow of such traditions Marlowe grew up.

★   ★   ★

' The appearance of the city of Canterbury is beautiful, from whatever part you approach it, and equals the most sanguine expectation, lying as it does in the valley of the River Stour meandering through the fertile meads '.

Hasted's KENT.

Mercery Lane, *leading towards the Christchurch Gate of the Cathedral, still has something of the mediaeval aspect it presented in Marlowe's day, with the overhanging upper storeys of the houses leaning towards each other across its narrow passage. Marlowe's uncle (by marriage) lived in a house on the right-hand side of the lane, where he plied his trade cs a draper or mercer, the name Mercery Lane being derived from the business carried on there. These houses are among the oldest remaining in Canterbury.*

10

The Christchurch Gate *entrance to the Cathedral Precincts from Mercery Lane. This magnificent portal, erected by Prior Goldstone in 1517, must have been passed almost daily by the young Kit Marlowe from earliest childhood as he attended a service in the Cathedral, or visited his uncle in Mercery Lane, or when later, as a scholar, he went to the King's School to learn his lessons in company with the sons of the Kentish aristocracy, some of whose family armorial bearings are carved above the gate. The fourth shield from the left shows the arms of the Fineaux family (three golden eagles on a green ground with a chevron of gold) from whom Richard Marley, Christopher's great-grandfather, had leased twenty acres of land. Christopher himself became intimate with Thomas Fineaux, who followed Marlowe to Corpus Christi College in Cambridge and was said to have been converted by him to Atheism. Of Marlowe's alleged 'atheistic' beliefs we shall hear more later.*

BEAUTY both of sight and sound environed Marlowe in his most impressionable years.

The magnificent vaulted Cathedral, a symphony in stone, as peerless an example of Gothic architecture at its most harmonious and inspired as one could find in the world, enriched with stained glass of iridescent splendour, feasted his eyes daily; the swelling music of the organ and sweet singing of the choirboys re-echoed in his soul.

The distillations of these choirboy experiences seem to find expression in this exquisite mourning paean from *Tamburlaine* uttered at the death-bed of his beloved Zenocrate:

> *Black is the beauty of the brightest day;*
> *The golden ball of heaven's eternal fire,*
> *That danc'd with glory on the silver waves,*
> *Now wants the fuel that inflam'd his beams;*
>
> .   .   .   .
>
> *Now walk the angels on the walls of heaven,*
> *As sentinels to warn th' immortal souls*
> *To entertain divine Zenocrate:*
> *Apollo, Cynthia, and the ceaseless lamps*
> *That gently look'd upon this loathsome earth,*
> *Shine downwards now no more, but deck the heavens*
> *To entertain divine Zenocrate:*
> *The crystal springs, whose taste illuminates*
> *Refinèd eyes with an eternal sight,*
> *Like tried silver run through Paradise*
> *To entertain divine Zenocrate:*
> *The cherubins and holy seraphins,*
> *That sing and play before the King of Kings,*
> *Use all their voices and their instruments*
> *To entertain divine Zenocrate;*
> *And, in this sweet and curious harmony,*
> *The god that tunes this music to our souls*
> *Holds out his hand in highest majesty*
> *To entertain divine Zenocrate.*
> *Then let some holy trance convey my thoughts*
> *Up to the palace of th' empyreal heaven*
> *That this my life may be as short to me*
> *As are the days of sweet Zenocrate.—*
> *Physicians, will no physic do her good?*

TAMBURLAINE THE GREAT, Part II, Act II, Sc. iv.

How poignantly that last line strikes us in its pathetic human frailty after the splendour of the poetic vision that has gone before. This is the magic of Marlowe.[7]

Opposite: The Choir of Canterbury (1175–1200). *In* 1174 '*the glorious Choir of Conrad' was destroyed by fire, and out of its ashes, like the Phoenix, rose the no less glorious choir of the two Williams, William of Sens, the Frenchman, and William the Englishman. It was completed in about* 1200.

Here Kit Marlowe as a King's scholar attended High Mass every morning, and on festivals and Sundays, in addition, Matins and Vespers. An important part of the King's School curriculum was the musical education of the boys, and those with good voices were especially favoured. According to the Statutes of Henry VIII the King's scholars were expected to assist the choristers under the direction of the Precentor. There is no doubt that Marlowe would have been a choirboy, since he later won a scholarship to Cambridge which specified the possession of musical ability, and the records testify that his younger brother Thomas became a chorister here.

The sublime architecture of the great cathedral, under whose shadow Marlowe was born and lived out his boyhood, must have had a profound influence on the awakening consciousness of one whose nature was so responsive to beauty. Inevitably he was drawn to worship at the shrine

'Where Beauty, mother to the Muses sits
And comments volumes with her ivory pen.'

TAMBURLAINE THE GREAT, Part I, Act V, Sc. I.

14

Tomb of King Henry IV. *The effigies of kings and princes and great ones laid to rest in the Cathedral were a present reminder to the boy Marlowe of England's history. Later he was to write the first great historical tragedy our stage had seen,* Edward II, *which foreshadowed the tremendous cycle of history plays of the English kings by Shakespeare.*

The Tomb of Edward, the Black Prince, *showing his 'achievements' hanging in replica above the magnificent canopy. Eldest son of the tournament-loving King Edward III and Queen Philippa, he was born at Woodstock on June 15, 1330. He won his knighthood at the battle of Crécy at the age of sixteen and through a lifetime of victorious campaigning earned a reputation as the 'Soul of Chivalry'. He had married Joan of Kent, and their son Richard II next ascended the throne, which his father might have occupied somewhat more fittingly. Edward died of dysentery at the age of forty-six and was buried with great state at Canterbury on September 29, 1376, in the Cathedral for which he seems to have had a special affection.*

16

St. Augustine's Chair *in which Archbishops of Canterbury have been enthroned for the past*
700 years. The marble throne dates probably from the early 13th *century and stands today*
in the corona of the cathedral, its mellowed stone lit by the splendour of 13th-century
stained glass.

The Cloisters at Canterbury. *Marlowe's way to school would probably have taken him daily through the cloisters of the cathedral. On the vaulted ceiling is sculpted one of the finest collections of coats of arms in the world.*

These peaceful Cloisters *associate the cathedral with the great monastery which formerly adjoined it. The monks served both the cathedral and the school, which at the dissolution of 1541 was re-endowed by Henry VIII as the King's School, and today incorporates what remains of the monastic buildings.*

The warrior Tamburlaine teaches his sons the rudiments of war:

I'll have you learn to sleep upon the ground,
March in your armour thorough watery fens,

.   .   .   .

And, after this, to scale a castle-wall,
Besiege a fort, to undermine a town;
And make whole cities caper in the air:
Then next, the way to fortify your men;
In champion grounds that figure serves you best
For which the quinque-angle form is meet,
Because the corners there may fall more flat
Whereas the fort may fittest be assail'd,
And sharpest where th' assault is desperate:
The ditches must be deep; the counterscarps
Narrow and steep; the walls made high and broad;
The bulwarks and the rampires large and strong,
With cavalieros and thick counterforts,
And room within to lodge six thousand men;
It must have privy ditches, countermines,
And secret issuings to defend the ditch;
It must have argins and cover'd ways
To keep the bulwark-fronts from battery,
And parapets to hide the musketeers,
Casemates to place the great artillery,
And store of ordinance, that from every flank
May scour the outward curtains of the fort,
Dismount the cannon of the adverse part,
Murder the foe, and save the walls from breach.

TAMBURLAINE THE GREAT, Part II, Act III. Sc. II.

Bastion of the old Roman Walls *which encircled the city of Canterbury completely in Marlowe's time. Doubtless these fired his boyhood imagination and perhaps inspired that intense interest in methods of fortification and battle tactics evidenced in his plays.*

CANTERBVRY.

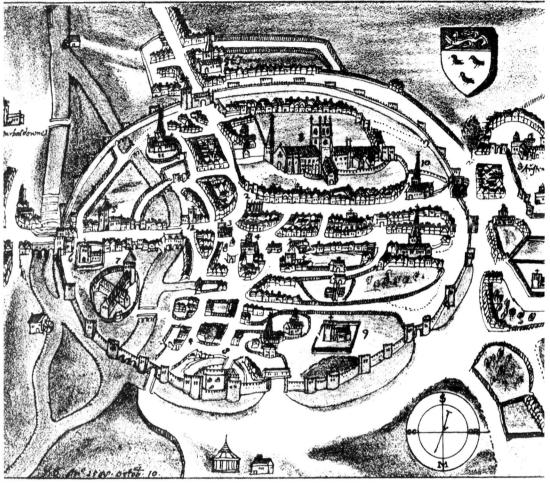

1. Chriftschurch.
2. ỹ market Place.
3. our Lady.
4. St. Andrewes.

5. St. Peter.
6. westgate church.
7. St. mildred.
8. The Caftell.

9. our Lady.
10. St. george.
11. The freeres.
12. Alhalows.

View of Canterbury *in* 1580, *showing old city walls.*

From William Smith's A PARTICULAR DESCRIPTION OF ENGLAND

'*What is beauty, saith my sufferings, then?*
If all the pens that ever poets held
Had fed the feeling of their masters' thoughts,
And every sweetness that inspir'd their hearts,
Their minds, and muses on admired themes;
If all the heavenly quintessence they still
From their immortal flowers of poesy,
Wherein, as in a mirror, we perceive
The highest reaches of a human wit;
If these had made one poem's period,
And all combin'd in beauty's worthiness,
Yet should there hover in their restless heads
One thought, one grace, one wonder, at the least,
Which into words no virtue can digest.'

TAMBURLAINE THE GREAT, Part I, Act V, Sc. I.

The Marlowe Memorial. *Standing rather forlornly in a corner of Canterbury's public park, the Gardens of the Dane John, is a statue of the Muse of Poetry (by Onslow Ford) as memorial to Marlowe. The blast of the bombs, which threatened the great cathedral and destroyed all but the tower of Marlowe's parish church of St. George-the-Martyr, blew the Muse off her pedestal, and she was replaced facing the wrong way. The Quatercentenary celebrations have seen her restored the proper way round, but not to her original place in the centre of the Butter Market. It was felt that her semi-nude figure facing the august portal to the cathedral was too shocking a sight and Victorian morality banished her to the groves of the Dane John, where she has lingered under something of the disgrace of her poet.*

The original committee which sponsored the Marlowe memorial was headed by such illustrious names as Alfred, Lord Tennyson, Sir Henry Irving and Sir Sidney Lee. The Muse has already been twice unveiled: first in her unfinished state by Sir Henry Irving, and later, when completed, by Sir Hugh Walpole, who, like Marlowe, was educated at the King's School and wrote: 'No boy who lives for a number of years under the protecting wing of one of the loveliest cathedrals in the world is likely to be quite unaffected. Something of that grey stone, of those towering pinnacles, of the music and green lawns and the flowering May, will be a gift to him . . . for all his life after.'

East of the city of Canterbury, and only just outside the old Roman Wall, are the remains of St. Augustine's Abbey, the great monastic foundation placed here in deference to the Roman regulation that no burials might be permitted within the town circuit. St. Augustine erected the original abbey partly as a burial place for himself and the kings of Kent. It was dedicated to the blessed apostles Peter and Paul and over the centuries grew up a great ecclesiastical establishment famed for its learning, vying in splendour with the monastery of the Cathedral of Christ Church, and having many great and extraordinary privileges conferred upon it, both by royal charters and by papal bulls.

Hasted writes: 'Between this monastery and that of Christ Church there was ever an apparent jealousy and emulation; though no episcopal chair had been placed in it, yet the abbot had the privilege of the mitre and other ensigns of episcopacy, and that the abbey might not seem second to any, or inferior to Christ Church itself, they put themselves under immediate subjection to the Pope.'[8]

These two great rival monastic houses for centuries dominated the life of Canterbury, as their towers and spires dominated the city itself. It was Elizabeth's father, Henry VIII, who changed all that. The Abbey of St. Augustine without the city walls possessed the tomb of the founder of English Christendom, while the Cathedral Church of Christ within the walls boasted the Shrine of St. Thomas the Martyr, and Henry stripped them both.

The crash of falling masonry, as the once glorious spires were toppled to the ground, was to be a familiar sound to Canterbury citizens for many years after. By the time Marlowe was born the wind of the Reformation, personified by Henry VIII, had accomplished this phase of its work with relentless thoroughness and left little more than a heap of ruins for the children to play amongst. The Abbot, John Essex, or Foche as he was also called, had surrendered the Abbey on July 30, 1538. The systematic destruction of the buildings, including the Norman church of SS. Peter and Paul, almost as large as the cathedral, and most of the monastic buildings, was given to the charge of the King's surveyor of works, James Needham, who was also entrusted with the conversion and rebuilding in part of the former abbot's lodging for the purposes of the King's use as a private palace, thereafter called the King's Lodging. Mary Tudor had bestowed the King's Lodging on Cardinal Pole in 1553, and when Queen Elizabeth came to the throne she granted it to William Brooke, Lord Cobham, in the year of Marlowe's birth, 1564.

When Marlowe was nine years old, in the September of 1573, Elizabeth came on one of her many royal Progresses to Canterbury and kept her Court at this palace without the wall. It stands a bare three minutes' walk from the house at which the Marlowe family were probably then living in the parish of St. George.

The Queen made it her policy to allow herself to be seen by her subjects and it may be assumed that Kit had his first glimpse at this tender age of the fabulous Virgin Queen whom he was later to serve as a political agent.

23

The Ruins of St. Augustine's Abbey *much as they were left after the demolition hammers brought into play by Henry VIII's decree of dissolution had done their work. This once great pile housed the splendour of a proud and mighty prelate who owed his allegiance to the Pope in the face of Henry's elevation of himself as the supreme head of the English Church. It was brought low long before Marlowe's time, but the ruins in which he probably played as a child had made a deep impression. Reflections of this are seen all too clearly in his expressions of iconoclasm:*

> 'I'll fire his crazed buildings, and enforce
> The papal towers to kiss the lowly earth'

cries the smitten King Henry III as he lies dying in The Massacre at Paris, *and again the same angry outburst comes from King Edward II—an instance of Marlowe's occasional tendency to repeat himself word for word when his characters are involved in similar emotional situations (possibly evidence that these feelings were in some way deeply grounded in his own childhood experiences):*

> 'Why should a king be subject to a priest?
> Proud Rome, that hatchest such imperial grooms,
> With these thy superstitions taper-lights,
> Wherewith thy antichristian churches blaze,
> I'll fire thy crazed buildings, and enforce
> The papal towers to kiss the lowly ground.'
>
> EDWARD THE SECOND.

Opposite

The Gateway to St. Augustine's Abbey.

> 'Know Selim, that there is a monastery
> Which standeth as an out-house to the town;
> There will we banquet them.'
>
> THE JEW OF MALTA, Act V.

24

During her stay Elizabeth was magnificently entertained by Archbishop Parker at his palace of Canterbury, which he had just renovated to the tune of £1,400. He had prepared for her coming with extraordinary attention to every detail, ordering wine and beer and provisions to be stored in the cellars and looking up precedent for such ceremonial reception in previous reigns. By the middle of July the Queen was about to commence her Progress when 'in this nick' Lord Cobham, the Lord Lieutenant of Kent, came in all haste to warn the Queen that smallpox and measles were abroad in the county. She therefore postponed her journey until the end of the month, when, although the weather proved very cold and wet, she nevertheless set forward.⁹

Progressing through Kent, the Queen reached Dover on August 25th, where she was received by Archbishop Parker and dignitaries of Kent and conducted

The countryside around Canterbury *was young Marlowe's playground. Here he probably observed the ways of the partridge:*

> 'he hides and buries it up, as partridges do their eggs, under the earth.'

Boylike he marked it. And with a poet's eye he noted the beauties of his native Kent:

> 'where painted carpets o'er the meads are hurl'd'
>
> .   .   .   .
>
> 'the meads, the orchards, and the primrose lanes.'
>
> THE JEW OF MALTA, Act IV.

26

to the castle 'amidst the ringing of bells and roaring of heavy ordnance'. Here she was entertained for six days by the Constable of the castle, Lord Cobham, the Archbishop meanwhile hurrying back to Canterbury to see that all was in readiness for her there. He has left his own inimitable account of the Queen's visit in a letter to his brother prelate, Archbishop Grindall of York, who was so delighted to hear about it all that he wrote back to Parker:

'Your Grace's large description of the Entertainment at Canterbury did so lively set forth the matter, that, in reading thereof, I almost thought myself to be one of your guests there.'

Leaving the entertainments at Dover, Parker writes how he

'went to Canterbury to receive her Majesty there, which I did, with the Bishops of Lincoln and Rochester, and my Suffragan, at the West door: where, after the Grammarian had made his Oration to her upon her horseback, she

Ruins of St. James' Parish Church in Dover, *where Marlowe's mother was baptised. Katherine Arthur, who married John Marley, or Marlowe, the Canterbury shoemaker, was not, as previous biographers have claimed, the daughter of the Reverend Arthur of Canterbury, but in fact a Dover girl of yeoman stock from the parish of St. James. This has been established by the latest researches of Dr. William Urry, the Archivist of Canterbury.*

The 'Shakespeare Cliffs' at Dover. *What boy having the spirit of adventure that Kit obviously had, and having grandparents by the sea at Dover, would not have escaped as often as he could to visit this fascinating little port?—in those days one of the most important in England. If Katherine Arthur did not take her son often enough to see his grandfather William Arthur, who was still alive in 1574 when Kit was ten years old, we may be sure that the boy would have found means of cadging a lift on a passing wagon, riding pillion on some kindly traveller's horse on occasion, or simply walking the fifteen miles from Canterbury for the excitement of seeing the ships at anchor in the harbour, and listening to the sailors' talk of distant lands, fights at sea, storms overpassed, and the noisy argument of commerce. These memories he stored to be used later in his dramatic writings. One such ship riding at anchor at Dover during Kit's boyhood was 'The Flying Dragon' which later appears as one of the argosy of* The Jew of Malta.[10]

Lying belly-wise on top of the sheer cliffs, he must often have noted the scene as Shakespeare, who evidently also knew these cliffs, described it so vividly in his Kentish play King Lear.

> ' *How fearful*
> *And dizzy 'tis to cast one's eyes so low!*
> *The crows and choughs that wing the mid-way air*

28

Show scarce so gross as beetles. Half-way down
Hangs one that gathers samphire—dreadful trade!
Methinks he seems no bigger than his head.
The fishermen that walk the beach
Appear like mice; and yond tall anchoring bark
Diminish'd to her cock; her cock, a buoy
Almost too small for sight. The murmuring surge
That on th' unnumb'red idle pebbles chafes
Cannot be heard so high. I'll look no more.'

KING LEAR, Act IV, Scene vi.

Ospringe, *near Faversham, lying on the Roman road of Watling Street from London through Canterbury to Dover, the highway of pilgrims and travellers, was the birth-place of John Marlowe, Christopher's father.*

Although only a small village, Ospringe was notable for its Maison Dieu or God's House, the Hospital of Blessèd Mary of Ospringe, formerly a mediæval hospital which offered shelter to the pilgrims en route to and from Canterbury. This had been a royal foundation of Henry III, and its Camera Regis or King's Chamber had provided a resting-place for the king and his suite whenever they passed this way.

The Hospital had gradually suffered a decline through mismanagement and other troubles, and finally in 1516 it was dissolved, and its revenues added to the new college of St. John's at Cambridge. But the obligation to pray for the souls of benefactors still remained, and John Marlowe, or Marley as he always preferred to sign himself, probably owed his literacy to the chantry priest who was appointed for this spiritual function and also acted as the village schoolmaster.

Pilgrims leaving Canterbury *from prologue to John Lydgate's* Siege of Thebes.

Pilgrims' Footbath: *A stream flows through this room below the ground floor of the Maison Dieu at Ospringe. Here the Canterbury pilgrims washed their feet after a hard day's journey.*

alighted. We then kneeled down, and said the Psalm *Deus misereatur* in English, with certain other Collects briefly; and that in our chimers and rochets.* The Quire, with the Dean and Prebendaries, stood on either side of the Church, and brought her Majesty up with a Square-song, she going under a canopy, born by four of her Temporal Knights, to her traverse, placed by the Communion board; where she heard Even-song, and after departed to her lodging at St. Austin's, whither I waited upon her. From thence I brought certain of the Council, and divers of the Court, to my house to supper, and gave them fourteen or fifteen dishes, furnished with two mess at my long table, whereat sat about twenty. And in the same Chamber a third mess, at a separate table, whereat sat ten or twelve; my less Hall having three long tables well furnished, with my Officers, and with the Guard, and others of the Court. And so her Majesty came every Sunday to Church, to hear the Sermon; and upon one Monday it pleased her Highness to dine in my great Hall, thoroughly furnished, with the Council, Frenchmen, Ladies, Gentlemen, and the Mayor of the Town, with his Brethren, &c., her Highness sitting in the midst, having two French Ambassadors at one end of the table, and four Ladies of Honour at the other end. And so three mess were served by her Nobility at washing, her Gentlemen and Guard bringing her dishes, &c.'[11]

For this 'splendid and solemn' entertainment which he conducted with 'so much order and decency' the Archbishop gained 'extraordinary praise' from

---

* Chimer—*a loose upper robe, especially as worn by a bishop, to which the lawn sleeves are attached. Until Elizabeth's time it was always of scarlet silk, but Bishop Hooper thought it too light and gay for episcopal gravity and had it changed for a 'chimere of black satin'. The under garment was a white linen rochet.*

Rochet—*an ecclesiastical vestment of linen of the nature of a surplice, usually worn by bishops and abbots.*

the Queen and all her nobles. No doubt the royal visit must have made an impression on even such a lad as Kit Marlowe, and would have been talked about in Canterbury for long after.

*　　*　　*

'The city of Canterbury is of an oval shape. It is within its walls about half a mile from east to west, and somewhat more from north to south. The circumference of its walls is not quite a mile and three-quarters; it has four large suburbs situated at the four cardinal points. The western part of the city may be called an island, being encircled by two branches of the river Stour, which divides just above it, and unites again at a small distance below it, the road through the city passing over two bridges, the one at Westgate, the other at Kingsbridge. Here are several corn and other mills on the river.'[12]

This description written in 1799 finds the city substantially the same as in Marlowe's day. The wall gave it a martial aspect with its six imposing twin-towered gates and its more than twenty watch-towers. From the portcullised and machicollated battlements of the West Gate the bodies of condemned prisoners were sometimes hanged when the three gibbets in the town were occupied. Grisly sights and public executions with all the sadistic refinements of Elizabethan popular taste were a commonplace. Bull-baiting was another popular Canterbury sport and the Burghmote decreed that no meat might be sold unless the animal had first been subjected to public baiting. The stake at which the bulls were tied, while dogs were set on them, stood in the centre of the city. When Marlowe was ten years old the family removed to a house in the town centre, quite near to the bull stake, in St. Andrew's parish.

Life in Canterbury was a lively rumbustious affair; Canterburians, according to the records, were as quarrelsome, as litigious, as ready with tongue and fist and dagger-thrust as any Elizabethans anywhere. Among these John Marlowe, Christopher's father, was entirely at home, transacting business: whether it was making footgear to be worn out on the cobblestones, or acting as bondsman for couples desiring marriage licences, or as church clerk witnessing wills, or doing his turn as town constable, or serving 'vittels', wine and food, or sallying forth as a freeman of his city armed with a pike to repel the expected landing force of the dreaded Armada; for he did all this.

A fair had been granted to Canterbury by charter of Henry VI which was held annually on the 4th of August and the two days following. Besides this, in the days when the pilgrims 'gadded to St. Thomas for help' their coming and going had been a constant source of income, but after the removal of the shrine and the suppression of the religious foundations (the two great monasteries as well as the friaries of the Grey and Black Friars) Canterbury had suffered a period of decline. But the Reformation, which robbed Canterbury of one source of wealth, gave it back presently with the other hand, for with the persecution of the Protestants by the Duke of Alva and the forces of the Counter-Reformation on the Continent, new life and trade began to flow back to

32

The houses of the Weavers, *relic of the Huguenot settlement in Canterbury during the 16th century, when they were driven to seek protection from the Protestant persecution in France and the Low Countries. The weavers 'made choice of Canterbury for their habitation, where they might have the benefit of the river and an easy communication with the metropolis'. Amongst other privileges granted them by the Mayor and aldermen was the right 'that their schoolmaster might be permitted to instruct their children and such others as desired to learn the French language'.[13] Kit Marlowe could have acquired his knowledge of French in his native Canterbury.*

33

Tomb of Sir Roger Manwood, *Knight of Kent, probably Marlowe's first patron. The coloured alabaster bust on his tomb in the little 12th-century church of St. Stephen, one of the original churches built by St. Anselm, at Hawe or Hackington just two miles out of Canterbury, shows him in his robes as the first Chief Baron of the Exchequer to be allowed the use of a gold chain of the 'S' collar type. This fine portrait bust is the work of Maximilian Colt or Coult (alias Poutrain), a famous Huguenot from Arras who also made Queen Elizabeth's monument and Lord Salisbury's at Hatfield. The materials here used are English, the alabaster from Nottingham, and the pillars of Bethesden marble quarried near Ashford, Kent.*

Canterbury with the immigration of craftsmen from abroad. Queen Elizabeth received these Protestant immigrants kindly and settled them in various parts of the country. Weavers of 'silk and stuffs' settled in Canterbury where they could make use of the river and have easy communication with markets abroad and with the metropolis. At first those permitted to settle in Canterbury comprised only eighteen 'housekeepers' besides their children and servants. By and by they obtained certain concessions from the mayor and aldermen, and in 1568 Queen Elizabeth granted the Huguenots the use of the undercroft of the cathedral as a place of worship for themselves and their heirs. By 1665, a century later, there were 126 master weavers in Canterbury alone, and, altogether, 1,300 Walloons, employing 759 English, instructing them in the arts of weaving silk, cotton and woollen goods, combing, spinning and making yarns.[14] This influx of immigrants was stimulated by the dreadful massacre of the Huguenots in Paris on St. Bartholomew's Eve in 1572. The presence of Huguenot refugees in Canterbury during Marlowe's boyhood may have inspired his dramatisation of this gruesome event in one of the last works he wrote for the London stage, *The Massacre at Paris*. His Huguenot sympathies are evident in the play, and may have stemmed from recollections of the Canterbury Huguenots who helped to bring prosperity to his native city.

*   *   *

Among Canterbury notables was *Sir Roger Manwood*, well known for his philanthropy in and around Canterbury, who has been suggested as Marlowe's first patron. It is possible that the bright lad attracted Sir Roger's attention and that he recommended him to the scholarship he gained at the King's School. Benign patronage to the people of his home town is typical of Manwood's attitude, although completely at variance with his public career on the Queen's Bench where he had 'acquired a well deserved reputation for oppression and the taking of bribes'. Sir Thomas Perrot charged him as 'guilty of covinous pleading and corrupt compact',[15] so that it is perhaps just as well for Marlowe that he was on good terms with this formidable Kentish gentleman, for the day was to come when he would find himself face to face in the dock with Sir Roger Manwood as one of his judges. Manwood was also among the judges who passed sentence on Mary Stuart at Fotheringay, while Marlowe, in his capacity as a political agent, may have been in part responsible for uncovering the evidence that marked her doom. It is certain that Marlowe became the intimate of another noble Kentish family, the Walsinghams, with whom Sir Roger Manwood also had connections, and to whom he may possibly have introduced Marlowe in the first instance. The connection makes a fairly tightly knit circle. Sir Francis Walsingham, Queen Elizabeth's Secretary of State, organised her spy service and employed Christopher Marlowe as an espionage agent; his younger cousin, Thomas Walsingham, who inherited a splendid estate at Chislehurst in Kent, became Marlowe's intimate friend and patron, and his son, also named Thomas Walsingham, married Sir Roger Manwood's grand-daughter, Elizabeth.

Sir Roger's country seat was the splendid manor house at Hackington, formerly called Hawe, a couple of miles without the West Gate of Canterbury, which had been granted him by Queen Elizabeth and which he rebuilt in a 'very handsome manner, in size and grandeur equal to his rank and fortune in life'.[16] Here he died in 1592, making amends for such wickedness as his life had contained by providing in his will for a row of almshouses 'with a cloister, conduit, gardens &c. all built of brick', and for a 'double-house' at the west corner which 'should be for the dwelling of the parish clerk forever, and for the safe custody of the wool, hemp and other stuff for the parish stock, to set the poor to work from time to time for ever'. Further bequests of 12*d.* in money every Friday, a one penny wheaten loaf every Wednesday and Sunday, and Sunday dinner in the hall of his chief house, plus 'four cartloads of fuel' to each house, not to mention new gowns and shoes and caps every third year against the feast of St. Andrew, kept his memory green, salved his conscience, and ensured that the necessary prayers for his soul would be said. Christopher Marlowe contributed a Latin epitaph extolling Manwood's virtues, and on the evidence of this it is suggested that he was probably his early patron and benefactor.[17]

★　　　★　　　★

In making his attack on the institution of the Priory of Christ Church, which administered the cathedral, Henry VIII moved with caution. The dissolution was not brought about 'by one sudden blow, but by slow degrees, lest, from the veneration and sanctity in which it was held . . . the fall of it might have raised a public tumult'.[18] First he ordered the abrogation of certain festivals, including the high festival of the Translation of St. Thomas on July 7 with its shew of lights, rich vestments, etc. Two years later all observance of the Saint's day was forbidden and Archbishop Cranmer himself 'gave precedent by supping on flesh in his parlour with his domestics instead of fasting'.[19] Finally, Becket was declared to have been a stubborn rebel and not a saint, and his images and pictures commanded to be pulled down. Next his shrine was stripped and the relics and bones taken away to be burnt to ashes by order of Lord Cromwell in September, 1538.

Henry doubtless had his sights fixed on the enormous wealth enshrined in this religious stronghold. Describing the high altar of the cathedral, Erasmus had been moved to remark 'we should think the richest monarchs mere beggars in comparison of the abundance of silver and gold which belonged to the furniture of it'. This was easily surpassed by the richness of the Shrine of St. Thomas, the goal of every pilgrim. The shrine consisted of a coffin of gold protected by a carved wooden cover which was drawn up to disclose invaluable treasure, 'gold being the meanest thing to be seen there; all shined and glittered with the rarest and most precious jewels of an extraordinary bigness, some being larger than a goose's egg. When this sight was shewn, the prior, who was always present, touched every jewel with a white wand, one by one, telling the name, the value, and the donor of it'.[20] The legend of the shrine which so 'shined and glittered' may well have excited Marlowe's interest in rich jewels,

THE SHRINE OF ST. THOMAS was demolished long before Marlowe's day by the royal arch-iconoclast, Henry VIII, but Marlowe as a boy could have seen its replica in miniature depicted in the gorgeous stained glass of the 'Miracle' windows in the aisles of the Trinity Chapel of the cathedral. These twelve superbly beautiful windows illustrate the stories of the miracles of healing performed at St. Thomas' shrine and tomb. Contemporary representations of both shrine and tomb abound amongst the medallions, crescents, diamonds and trefoils of curious design set in their intricate stone tracery. The fabulous riches of the shrine itself must have been an oft-recounted legend in Canterbury during Marlowe's childhood, and reflections of the impression all this made on him are seen in his lingering over the recounting of jewels, each by name, and rare and costly metals, which recurs so frequently in his writings. The Jew of Malta, telling over his wealth, in his counting house, gives him a splendid opportunity to indulge this opulent vein:

> Give me the merchants of the Indian mines,
> That trade in metal of the purest mould;
> The wealthy Moor, that in the eastern rocks
> Without control can pick his riches up,
> And in his house heap pearl like pebble stones,
> Receive them free, and sell them by the weight!
> Bags of fiery opals, sapphires, amethysts,
> Jacinths, hard topaz, grass-green emeralds,
> Beauteous rubies, sparkling diamonds,
> And seld-seen costly stones of great price,
> As one of them, indifferently rated,
> And of a carat of this quantity,
> May serve, in peril of calamity,
> To ransom great kings from captivity.

But not only in *The Jew*, here happily engrossed with his 'infinite riches in a little room' —a description that would aptly fit the shrine itself—but throughout Marlowe's writings such phrases as 'rocks of pearl', 'the coffin and the sheet of gold', 'spangled with diamonds', 'a golden canopy enchas'd with precious stones', 'enchas'd with precious jewels' ad infinitum, betray the Canterbury boy whose eyes were dazzled by the jewelled windows of the cathedral and whose mind ravished by the stories of its past splendours.

orient pearl, and precious stones so lovingly dwelt on in his plays and poems, detailed descriptions of which he could have had as a boy from many an old Canterbury beldame who remembered the shrine in all its glory. The spoils from the shrine alone, in gold and jewels, filled two great chests which eight strong men could hardly carry out of the cathedral. All this was taken for the King's use. The dissolution of the monastery thus prepared, the surrendry was finally signed on April 4 in the chapter-house by the prior and twenty-four other members of the convent and sealed with their common seal.

To quiet the people and convince them of the necessity of these measures the monks were libelled and accused of every shameful vice. We thus see in Marlowe's own city a precedent for his iconoclasm. When Barabas the Jew sneers at 'religious caterpillars' and Marlowe makes ribald fun of monks and friars, representing their religious pretensions as a cloak for hypocrisy, he is expressing the critical spirit of the Reformation of which he himself was a child.

Henry stripped the shrines and appropriated the wealth accumulated in the religious houses, carting it away to the jewel-house of the Tower of London in twenty-six cartloads, but he left the Archbishop's Throne intact and compensated the monks with yearly pensions. Many were, in fact, retained in the new foundation which also embraced the ancient grammar school formerly administered by the monks, and tracing its lineal descent from the scholastic institution founded here by St. Augustine in the 6th century. This was now re-endowed by him as the *King's School.*

The King's School

By his charter of 1541 Henry VIII granted to the dean and chapter provisions for a school consisting of a master, an usher, and fifty scholars who were to eat at the common table. The stipend of the scholars was to be £4 per annum to be held for five years, the age limits for entry being between nine and fifteen years, the treble singing years of a normal boy's development, for these youngsters were destined to be employed in the cathedral choir.

It was to this school, the most ancient in England, that Christopher Marlowe was admitted in the Michaelmas term of 1578/9, upon having been awarded a scholarship under the terms of the capitular statutes which specifically make provision for the education of 'fifty poor boys, both destitute of the help of friends, and endowed with minds apt for learning, who shall be called scholars of the grammar school, and shall be sustained out of the funds of our Church'.[1]

Despite this specific and well-intentioned statement, first place in the grammar school went not to the poor man's son but to the sons of gentlemen. Only if there was a vacancy not to be filled by the latter would a poor man's son with

The Dark Entry *is the name given to this passage leading from the cathedral cloisters
through Prior Sellingegate to the King's School.*

> 'There's a dark entry where they take it in,
> Where they must neither see the messenger,
> Nor make inquiry who hath sent it them.'

THE JEW OF MALTA

Thus *Barabas, the Jew, bids his servant take a pot of poisoned broth to the nuns in the
nearby nunnery. Marlowe was no doubt thinking of the Dark Entry familiar to his childhood (later also to have sinister associations with poisoning, for according to the* Ingoldsby
Legends *the monks buried Nell Cook here after she had served her master, the Canon, a
poisoned pie).*

'mind apt for learning' be given such a chance as occurred for the cobbler's son. He would of necessity already have had to prove himself proficient in reading and writing, and must in addition have impressed the selection committee with his brilliance to have been admitted at so late a date, for he was almost fifteen and therefore only two weeks within the upper age limit.

Although Marlowe's entry into the King's School under the scholarship he obtained is dated 14 January, 1578 9, it is not improbable that he may have been already a fee-paying commoner at the school before this. It was the practice to admit some of these, their payments no doubt helping to augment the meagre salaries of the masters, but unfortunately the names of such scholars are not often recorded. If John Marlowe, or Mistress Katherine his wife, had ambitions for their son, and the lad's promise seemed to warrant it, they would obviously have wished to send him here in preference to any of the other local schools. John Marlowe's financial position at this time, when he kept two apprentices and a maid for his wife, suggests that he could well have managed it. The fact that Christopher was granted his scholarship so late rather suggests that he was already a pupil here, and that his progress had been such as to attract attention and gain the good offices of his masters in pressing for his continuance under a scholarship grant. With only two years to go it seems unlikely that this would have been awarded to an outsider. Instances of the kindly patronage of masters for their most promising pupils are not rare. Dean Wotton had sent the promising young Anthony Rushe (later a head-master of King's) to Oxford at his own charges in the absence of any scholarship to help him. Exceptions of any kind were usually made to ex-choristers of the Canterbury Cathedral Choir or the Chapel Royal, and the favours accorded to Marlowe once again argue musical talent and a good voice. As has been mentioned before, Sir Roger Manwood might also have had a hand in it.

According to the Statutes of 1541 governing the curriculum, by the time a boy reached the Fourth Form (and Marlowe would have gone into this straight away at least, or probably into a higher grade) he would have been required to know his Latin syntax thoroughly, and there he would be 'practised in poetic tales, the familiar letters of learned men, and other literature of that sort'.[2] In the Fifth Form Latin oratory and classical rules of verse-making were taught, and here Christopher would have made a beginning in 'translating the most chaste Poets and the best Historians'. In the Sixth and highest form he would cope with Erasmus and 'learn to vary speech in every mood' in Latin. Here the boys would be given the opportunity to 'taste Horace, Cicero and other authors of that class, and shall compete with one another in declamations, that the competition may encourage them in their studies'.[3]

The entire school of fifty boys underwent examination by the headmaster once a week, and those who had shown themselves proficient might expect to be upgraded at any of the three yearly periods when this was done.

Although school lessons concluded at 5 p.m., there was 'prep' to be done between 6 and 7 p.m. under the supervision of the masters. This took the form

Canterbury Cathedral, *north aspect, as seen from the King's School.*

of repeating the lessons they had learnt 'to their fellow pupils who have become ripe in learning'. It may be assumed that Kit was usually one of the latter since he was later favoured with a second scholarship, which is hardly likely to have been granted to the shoemaker's son if he had been lazy at his work.

As implied by its name, and evidenced by the curriculum, one of the main functions of the grammar school was to impart a thorough grounding in Latin grammar and speech, with Greek as a second language. To encourage fluency in this the favoured teaching method of the Renaissance was the performance of plays in these languages. The records of the King's School for the year 1562–3 show that the headmaster, Anthony Rushe, received £14 6s. 8d. from the Cathedral Chapter for 'settynge out of his plays at Christmas'[1]—quite a goodly sum wherewith to finance a school production! But perhaps this included capital expenditure of some kind, for the next Christmas he received only

£2 16s. 8d. for the school's productions of 'Tragedies, Comedyes and inter- ludes'. John Gresshop and Nicholas Goldsborough, successively headmasters in Christopher's time, probably maintained the school tradition of putting on plays at Christmas, and of instruction through the drama, although unfor- tunately no records existing for this period afford similar evidence. But it may be assumed that early contact with the drama proved a formative influence in the life of Marlowe, who was destined to create an entirely new dramatic form for the English stage and call into being a dramatic literature unsurpassed in the history of the world.

But for the time being he was to sit on the hard benches of the King's School and think himself lucky to share his board and his learning with the sons of Kentish gentlemen whose feet his father shod. Taunts of 'cobbler's son' were to be flung at him even after he had gained fame in London, though this was to come from envious contemporary playwrights rather than from the aristocrats who befriended him. But brilliance is not always welcome to fellow scholars, and that arrogance of mind, conscious of its own genius, striving after an out-topping power, so typical of many of Marlowe's heroes, Tamburlaine, Faustus, the Guise, and even Barabas, is perhaps a reflection of his youthful experience as a gifted commoner thrown amongst young aristocrats.

DR. MATTHEW PARKER, Archbishop of Canterbury from 1558 to 1575.

Dr. Parker had been Master of Corpus Christi College at Cambridge (from 1544 to 1553) before his promotion to the Episcopal Throne at Canterbury, and fortunately for Marlowe he remembered his old college in his will made on April 5, 1575. By this he added to the already generous endowments granted to Corpus Christi three further scholarships to the value of £3 6s. 8d. per annum each, of which he stipulated that the first was to be awarded to a native of Canterbury who was a scholar of the King's School. The nomination of these awards was expressly reserved to his son, John Parker, to whom posterity may be grateful in that he selected Christopher Marlowe as the beneficiary of the scholarship from the King's School. Again Marlowe had caught the patron's eye and was furthered along the next step of his career.

The terms of the scholarship to Corpus Christi stipulate proficiency in the following skills which supply evidence of Marlowe's musical ability:

'All which schollers shall and must at the time of their election be so entred into the skill of song as that they shall at the first sight solf and sing plaine song. And that they shalbe of the best and aptest schollers well instructed in their gramer and if it may be such as can make a verse.'

43

The King's School, Canterbury. *The superb Norman staircase with its adjoining great hall, formerly known as the Strangers' Hall, is a splendid survival from the original monastery. For those who seek Marlowe this represents undoubtedly 'haunted ground', for in 1559 the school had removed from its former quarters above the Mint into this building and the adjacent Almonry Chapel (now demolished). Kit was formally entered on January 14, 1578–9.*

The school day began at 6 a.m. with prayers and a psalm taken by the Lower Master (in Kit's day Master Robert Rose) and closed with a service at 5 p.m.

Over the years the expansion of the King's School has gradually absorbed almost all that has survived of the monastic buildings. 'Marlowe' House, appropriately named for the day boys, occupies part of the present Deanery, built by Prior Goldstone (1495–1517). Lattergate also dates from c. 1541, and a considerable part of the tremendous rebuilding carried out under Prior Chillenden (1391–1411) is today incorporated into the school. Of these Priory Classrooms were formerly the monastery's bakery and brewhouse.

44

Marlowe's Books. *A shelf of 16th-century editions of books which Christopher Marlowe might have used, as assembled by Dr. Urry from the Chapter Library of Canterbury Cathedral.*

From left to right: Two large volumes of Holinshed's Chronicles, which Marlowe was the first dramatist to use before Shakespeare resorted to Holinshed as a source book for his historical dramas.

Lying on top: A beautifully illustrated edition of Ovid, *favourite poet of both Marlowe and Shakespeare.*

Bale's Acts of the English Votaries, 1550; The Apology of J. Bale, 1541; *and the* New Testament, 1544. *All books Marlowe would have used for his studies in Divinity.*

Fortescue's Foreste, or Collection of Histories, 1571, *used by Marlowe as a source book for* Tamburlaine the Great.

Tindal's translation of the Bible, 1551. *Echoes of the magnificent language of this translation are manifest in Marlowe's works.*

Book of Common Prayer, 1552, *exemplar of the English Reformation.*

T. More's Miscellany, 1556.

Munster's Cosmography, *a geography used as a source for* Tamburlaine the Great.

Chronica Turcica *by Loniceros, also used as a source for* Tamburlaine.

The Works of Machiavel.

The influence of Machiavelli's ideas is reflected in Marlowe's heroes, and he himself was nicknamed 'Machevil' by his contemporaries.

46

JOHN BOYS' TOMB in Canterbury Cathedral bears the effigy of the man who was Marlowe's schoolmate both in Canterbury and at Cambridge. Boys was born in 1571 at Eythorne, near Canterbury, and attended the King's School at the same time as Marlowe, although in a lower class. Marlowe had matriculated at Cambridge in 1580/1; Boys followed him in 1585, also entering Corpus Christi under a Matthew Parker scholarship. After obtaining his M.A. at Corpus he became a Fellow of Clare Hall in 1593. Archbishop Whitgift subsequently appointed him Master of Eastbridge Hospital, and later instated him as Dean of Canterbury Cathedral.

In later years he gained fame as a great preacher; at the time of the Essex Rebellion many heard him preaching at St. Paul's Cross. His published sermons and theological and liturgical works became very widely read in his day.

Boys was one of the great collectors of books of his time, and his writings contain frequent and varied quotes from these works, testifying to his omnivorous reading of contemporary writers. His works are interesting because of his many allusions to the manners and customs of his time, of his use of homely proverbs, and of quaint words and expressions. The following is a sample of his pungent style from his *Exposition of the Dominicall Epistles and Gospels*, containing a tract dealing with 'The Paines of Hell':

'Feasts appointed at unseasonable hours and continued longer than ordinary time, seeme tedious to the guests, and therefore the lazie Frier sweating at his fat commons and large dinner, cryed out "*heu quantum patimur*, alas how much do we suffer which are Friers!" O then I beseech you consider, what the damned suffer at the devils supper, where time without end is the very sauce of every dish at the table: for their darkness is an everlasting night; their bonds everlasting chaines; their fire, everlasting burning; their worme, never dying; their woe never ending; their paines diversity is great, their paines universitie greater, but their paines eternitie greatest of all.'

Boys died in 1625 at the age of fifty-four while seated in his study surrounded by his extensive library. In these times books were frequently shelved with their pages instead of their covers to the front, the titles being written across the page-edges. This portrait monument erected by his wife portrays the bibliophile meditating among his books.

Discipline in an Elizabethan School-room. *The emphasis of education in Elizabethan grammar schools was on Latin to the exclusion of almost everything else. The authorized Latin grammar used was written by William Lilly, the first headmaster of St. Paul's Cathedral School. The boys were expected to learn their lessons by heart and repeat them to the master. If they were slow or disobedient they might be beaten.*

Elizabethan Canterbury was famous for its learning and Marlowe was lucky to have come to this school which opened its doors to the artificer's son in accordance with the wishes of the Archbishop that 'if the Gentleman's Son be apt to Learning let him be admitted; if not apt, let the poor Man's Child apt enter his Room'.

1578–1579

[The names for the period Christmas 1578–Michaelmas 1579 are to be found in the fair copy of the Chapter Accounts (Accounts, Post Reformation, Treasurer, No. 9). The heading is missing but dates occurring among the entries show that the period covered is that indicated above. The H.M. and Usher for the year are named as John Greshop and Robert Rose. The names of boys appearing at all four terms, Christmas, Ladyday, Midsummer and Michaelmas, are given in the list immediately below.]

Thomas Russell	Edward Partridge	Richard Reader	Peter Olyver
Richard Betham	Henry Lovelace	William Playse	Christopher Stretesley
Stephen Nevinson	Bartholomew Kettell	Henry Jacobs	Thomas Colwell
Samuel Kennett	(Kevell)	William Potter	Thomas Hammon
Sidrac Kemesley	Reginald Stafferton	Henry Drewry	(Hammonde)
Robert Groves	Thomas Taylor	Thomas Wyn	Roper Blundell
William Playfer	Henry Bromerick	Jesse Gilbart	John Wilforde
Richard Parrett (Perott)	William Bolton	Richard Purefrey	Nicholas Wilder
Josias Snow	Leonard Swetinge	Clement Perret	Alexander Clyfford
Isaac Clerke	Nicholas Elmyston	(Perrot)	Bartholomew Godwyn
Christopher Duckytt	Richard Lecknor	Caleb Smythe	
John Marshall	(Lewknor)	William Lyllye	

[The names of scholars which do not appear at all four terms (1578–1579) are given below, with indication as to which terms they do in fact appear at. It will be noticed that one distinguished name makes a first appearance at Ladyday, 1579. The surname is rendered in the contemporary records with a great number of variations: Marlow, Marlo, Marley, Marle, etc.]

John Emeley	Christmas			
Edward Bradford	Christmas,	Ladyday,	Midsummer	
Ralph Groves	Christmas,	Ladyday,	Midsummer	
Thomas Stales (Scales?)	Christmas,	Ladyday		
Christopher Marley		Ladyday,	Midsummer,	Michaelmas
*John Edwyn }			Midsummer	
*John Gwyn }				Michaelmas
Bartholomew Beseley				Michaelmas
Barnabas Pownall				Michaelmas
John Reynarde				Michaelmas
Nathaniel Bull				Michaelmas
Samuel White				Michaelmas
Nicholas Parker	Christmas,	Ladyday,	Midsummer	
George Hawkes	Christmas,	Ladyday,	Midsummer	
Philemon Pownall	Christmas,	Ladyday,	Midsummer	

*John Edwyn and John Gwyn are probably identical, one name being a mistranscription by the Chapter clerk.

List of Scholars at the King's School, 1578–9, *showing entry of Christopher Marlowe. (Reprinted from the Magazine of the King's School as prepared by Dr. Urry from the document in the Chapter Accounts shown in the photograph opposite.)*

Fifty-six names appear (fifty-five boys being represented if there is in fact one duplication as suggested in the note). The statutes provided that each scholar receive a yearly stipend of £1 8s. 4d., which, together with the allowances for 'commons' (i.e. food and money to pay for two and a half yards of cloth for a new gown at Christmas), made a total annual payment of £4. 'Christopher Marley' is listed in the accounts of the Treasurer of the Cathedral for 1578–9 as one who received his quarterly allowance of £1.

Lessons began at six in the morning with a psalm, and ended, again with a psalm, at five in the afternoon.

48

List of Scholars of the King's School, 1578–1579. *Marlowe's name is in the 22nd line.*

Part II

Cambridge 1580-1587

52

Cambridge, 1580–1587

In the winter of 1580, some three weeks before Christmas, Christopher Marlowe said farewell to Canterbury, to humbler family ties and childhood associations, and set his face towards Cambridge, there to present himself as the new Archbishop Parker scholar at Corpus Christi College, also known as Bene't College (see map opposite), one of the oldest colleges of the University, situated between the ancient churches of St. Bene't and St. Botolph, just off Trumpington Street, the main thoroughfare into Cambridge. Here he would read Divinity, ostensibly in preparation for a life in Holy Orders.

Emblem of Corpus Christi College.

The average age of university entrants in those days was fourteen years, so that at seventeen Marlowe was considerably older than the normal freshman. He was soon to discover that he had exchanged the stiff curriculum of his school days for an even more ascetic existence, at least on the face of things. The regulations were strict. In college the students were supposed to converse with one another only in Latin or Hebrew. They rose at four, prayed, listened to lectures, and studied by candlelight in unheated rooms. The reading of books other than those prescribed was frowned upon. The students were not permitted to leave the college precincts unless accompanied by a member of the college, and taverns, fairs, and places of public entertainment were strictly out of bounds. The regulation garment to be worn was an ankle-length straight woollen gown of black or brown or 'other sad colour'; as for 'Barilled Hosen' or 'great Ruffs', they were definitely out. In fact, however, these academic strictures were openly disregarded by the sons of the rich who paraded in ruffs and velvets, wore their swords, and indulged in such extra-curricular pastimes as dicing, card-playing, cock-fighting and bear-baiting and, of course, drinking and such other 'lewdness'.

Similarly, although the religious atmosphere set out to be as intense as anything Marlowe had experienced under the shadow of the Ecclesia Anglicana at Canterbury, the ebullient spirit of youth prevailed. The Reformation had found some of its readiest disciples amongst the students. The authorities were already concerned over the spread of the more advanced ideas of Calvinism, and, even worse, of 'atheism'. This last loosely defined term comprised any kind of questioning of the accepted religious dogmas. Dr. Parker himself had been a staunch Protestant, forced into retirement during the brief reign of Queen Mary, but he discountenanced the more rabid forms of Puritanism which were gaining such ground on the Continent and in Scotland. Amongst the young, ever ready to scent out the hypocrisies of their elders, could also be

Opposite
Elizabethan Cambridge. *This is part of an engraving by Richard Lyne, 1574, for insertion in John Caius'* Historiae Cantabrigiensis Acadamiae, 1574. *(Folger Shakespeare Library.)*

53

1580–81: *Christopher Marlowe is admitted to Cambridge.*

In the Admission Book *extract above, Marlowe is listed as 'Marlin'. During his Cambridge career he is also variously known as 'Marlor', 'Marlen', and even 'Merling'.*

detected a certain irreligious attitude most disconcerting to the authorities. The students, they complained, 'fooled about in chapel, made up nonsensical prayers, and turned in the wrong direction during the Creed'.[1]

Into this stimulating atmosphere strode young Christopher Marlowe. His new quarters were to be a converted store-room on the ground floor, with a window looking out on to the Old Court at Corpus Christi. Dr. Parker had given precise instructions for his reception:

'*Item*, I wish my Executors to make ready a chamber in that college, now called *A Storehouse*, for three other of my scholars to inhabit. . . . Of which scholars I wish the first to be chosen from Canterbury School, and to be a native of that place.'[2]

He was to receive his 'barber and his launder freely without anything paying there fore'. His barber would see to it that his head was kept suitably 'polled, notted or rounded' and that he did not wear any unpermitted 'long lockes of Hayre uppon his heade'. When in residence Kit qualified for a weekly allowance of one shilling, but if absent from college he forfeited this. The students resided in their colleges during vacations as well as in term time, the permitted absence being limited to one month in a year, unless due to sickness or college business. It did not seem to matter to Marlowe that he forfeited quite a few shillings during his last two years at the university, for the college Buttery books show that he spent considerably more than that amount from time to time.[3] He apparently had other means of supplementing his income.

His room in the Old Court was furnished in reasonable comfort by Elizabethan standards. Details from the college archives listing furniture for the

54

rooms set aside for the use of Parker's Norwich students give a picture of how Marlowe's room might have looked:

'Implements to remain within the under chambers of the IXth, Xth, and XIth chambers on the east side for the use of certaine Norwich scholars now founded in C.C.C. in Cambridge:[1]

ffirst ii several bedstedes corded	v˙		
item ii matresses for the same	xiii˙ iiiid		
ii bolsters of Fethers	xiii˙ iiiid		
ii coverlets of Tapistry	vi˙ viiid	ffor the	
ii chaires of iii feete	xxd	first	
a Table & iii Tressels	ii˙	2 Chambers'	
ii formes to the same	viiid		

Such clothes and personal possessions as the students had would presumably have been kept in chests of their own providing.

Christopher's day of study at Corpus Christi began with the tolling bell calling him before five from his trundle bed to the chapel for an hour's service; this was followed by breakfast at six, and a morning of college studies: lectures by college tutors in the subjects of the students' studies, Latin, Greek, Hebrew, Logic, Mathematics, Philosophy, Divinity, Dialectics, &c. Dinner was at twelve noon, 'whenas they be content with a penny piece of beef among four, having a pottage made of the broth of the same beef, with salt and oatmeal, and nothing else'.[5] After this repast Kit might devote the next two hours to attendance at disputations in the public schools between contending graduates, or similar exercises in his own college. And then he would be free to study alone, or divert himself perhaps in reading what he should not.

'You cannot step into a scholar's study but (ten to one) you shall likely find open either Bodin de Republica or Leroy's Exposition upon Aristotle's Politics or some other like French or Italian political discourses. And I warrant you some good fellows amongst us begin now to be pretty well acquainted with a certain parlous book called, as I remember me, Il Principe di Nicolo Machiavelli, and I can peradventure name you an odd crew or two that are as cunning in his Discorsi, in his Historia Fiorentina, and in his Dialogues della arte della Guerra too, and in certain gallant Turkish discourses . . .'[6]

According to Gabriel Harvey, the Cambridge don who thus reported on the university scene to his friend, Edmund Spenser, this rot had set in the year before Marlowe arrived, and there is no doubt that he would soon have made one of this cunning crew. Machiavellian policy was something Christopher was well able to expound. Archbishop Parker had solicitously provided a small chained library of theological books for the use of his Norwich and Parker scholars, consisting of Greek and Latin Bibles, Erasmus' New Testament (Latin version in two volumes), a Latin Bible concordance, classical lexicons and *thesauri* and a history of Cambridge. If Marlowe resorted to this little library it was but to sharpen his critical faculty, and he was soon weaned on to

55

other literature, browsing particularly happily among the Latin classical authors, Virgil and Ovid claiming him as disciple. Aristotle and Ramus he also read. The controversy over these two was the pivot of much Cambridge disputation. Echoes of this are found in Marlowe's works. As at Canterbury, so now at Cambridge, his genius was to receive, to some extent, the stamp of his environment and be enriched by it.

At Corpus Christi Marlowe alighted in a predominantly young, though

His new lodgings *were to be a room with a window looking out on to the Old Court at Corpus Christi.*

'And this the man that in his study sits.'

DR. FAUSTUS

Marlowe's precise room has not been identified, but it was doubtless very similar to this one, as the Old Court rooms have been almost unaltered externally. However, considerably more comfort has been added within, both in the furnishings and in the heating, which latter was non-existent in Marlowe's day.*

The Elizabethan student's life was not a 'bed of roses': up before five, when the clanging bell called them to service in the college chapel (lasting about one hour), breakfast at six o'clock, and a long day of study and lectures to follow in unheated rooms. It is no wonder that the frozen students were 'fayne to walk or runne up and downe halfe an hour to gette a heate on their feet whan they go to bed'.

* According to H. P. Stokes, Corpus Christi, 1898 (University of Cambridge College Histories series), Marlowe 'kept in the ground floor room on the right-hand side of the old-court staircase now lettered R; this room had long been used as "the store house" but it had lately been fitted up as a chamber where three of the Parker scholars might live'. This has now been questioned.

57

The north side of the Old Court at Corpus Christi *showing the memorial plaque to Marlowe (at left) and at right the sundial bearing Matthew Parker's motto: 'Mundus transit et concupiscentia eius.' The Old Court dates from the 14th century and is almost unchanged since Marlowe lived here. The quadrangle, of which this is one side, was all that existed of the college; it comprised Fellows' sets on the upper storey and students' rooms below, the Master's Lodge, hall, Elizabethan chapel (just completed before Marlowe entered), the kitchens, and outhouses.*

There were three classes of students in Marlowe's day. The first were the fellow-commoners (the sons of gentry); next came the 'pensioners', of which Marlowe was one and lucky to be so as a mere tradesman's son, for these were usually in the third class, the poor 'sizars', whose task it was to act as 'fags' cleaning boots, rousing their masters in time for prayers and waiting on them at high table. It was compulsory to attend evensong in the chapel before supper in Hall at seven p.m. This was 'not much better than the dinner' of a pottage of salted beef and oatmeal. Entries in the buttery books show that Kit frequently betook himself to the buttery bar for a snack to eke out this meagre fare, and fortunately he seems to have been able to afford it.

heterogeneous community. Although he was a good two years older than most in his year, there would have been others nearing the end of their six years' study who would have been his seniors. The college had just passed through a period of enormous expansion, almost trebling its numbers in the previous ten years. In all, there were about ninety members, thirteen of these being Fellows, twenty scholars, four Bible-clerks, and fifty-four in the student body of fellow commoners, pensioners, and sizars, including young Lord Stafford and others of gentle birth. To accommodate all these 'every available part of the College was inhabited', writes Stokes. Attics were furnished and brought into use; Marlowe's room was a recently converted store-room; and the Fellows who

58

occupied the first-floor rooms in the Old Court probably each had a student or two billeted on them. Some students were accommodated in a nearby hostel called 'The Christopher' for lack of room in the buildings of the quadrangle.

Among the more eccentric of the residents was Francis Kett, who had been a Fellow of the college from 1573 to 1580, and was still at Corpus Christi for a short while after Marlowe was admitted. He was charged with holding heretical opinions and was burnt at Norwich eight years later; but, as Boas points out, it is most unlikely that Marlowe as a young freshman would have come into contact with so much older a man who was no longer there in the capacity of tutor to the students. Marlowe had plenty of opportunity to develop his own unorthodox religious ideas from other sources, and it is likely that poor Kett was a religious fanatic and slightly insane. According to an eye-witness account of his martyrdom, 'he went to the fire clothed in sackcloth, and went leaping and dauncing. Being in the fire, above twenty times together, clapping his hands, he cried nothing but *blessed bee God*; . . . and so continued untill the fire had consumed all his neather partes, and untill he was stifled with the smoke'.[7]

Memorial Plaque *to Marlowe and Fletcher on the wall of the Old Court at Corpus Christi. John Fletcher was a notable collaborator in playmaking among the younger dramatists who followed in the new tradition established by Marlowe. Francis Beaumont became his most constant partner in collaboration, and they wrote many successful plays together. He may also have collaborated with Shakespeare in writing* Henry VIII *which is said to bear marked traces of Fletcher's hand. Like all those who followed Marlowe he was undoubtedly influenced by him, and perhaps in the first instance because he went to Marlowe's college when the dramatist's fame was at its height in London and his name fast becoming a legend at Corpus Christi.*

An amusing piece of documentation tells us that one undergraduate at Corpus had become such an ardent Marlowe fan that he 'learnd all Marlo by heart', and not content to stop there decided one night to try to emulate Dr. Faustus by conjuring the devil. Unfortunately for him, his magic incantations only succeeded in rousing some rather angry dons. His name was Thomas Fineaux, a Canterbury boy of good family, who was said to have been later converted to atheism by Marlowe—quite a step from conjuring the devil for our young Marlovian apostle to have taken. It would seem from this that Marlowe's name had some significance at this time for at least the younger members of his old college.

59

A greater than Kett was to influence Marlowe, not through any direct contact, but through his writings and ideas: Giordano Bruno, whose life was also to end at the stake.

Because of the general youthfulness of the students, rules of discipline were strict. No one under the status of a B.A. in his second year might venture abroad unaccompanied, and all students had to be in college by nine o'clock from Michaelmas to Easter, and by ten o'clock from Easter to Michaelmas. The status of B.A. raised a student automatically to the level of 'adult', if he was not already considered so on account of having attained his eighteenth birthday. Graduates were exempted from the indignity of corporal punishment. At Corpus Christi this was administered to the miscreants due for it on Thursdays at seven p.m. in the Hall before the assembled undergraduates. The university punishments in order of severity were fines, flogging, imprisonment, rustication or expulsion.

We do not hear of Marlowe being in any kind of trouble during his six and a half years' residence (apart from the false rumours concerning his government

A CAMBRIDGE UNIVERSITY document dated October 29, 1581, which lists the names of its professors, readers, and students subdivided into areas of study and classified as to colleges. This document, now in the British Museum (Lansdowne MS. 33, ff. 84–85), consists of three oversized pages, on the last of which is a total of 1,862 names.

The top of the listing is entitled *Nomina Professorum et Auditorum omnium artium et scientarum in Universitate Cantabrigia* (The Names of the Professors and Auditors of all the arts and sciences in the University of Cambridge). Then follow the various areas of study, commencing with the graduate fields and working downward. The list is headed by the Regius Professor of Theology, M. Whitiker; then the Lady Margaret Professor of Theology, D(ominus) Baror. The latter is evidently Peter Baro of Trinity, who in 1574 was elected to the professorship of Divinity and whose ideas provoked so much opposition within the university that there were several efforts to oust him. Under each of the professors are listed the names of auditors grouped according to their respective colleges. Next follows the Professor of Hebrew, M. Lyler, the Professor of Civil Law, D. Bing, then Medicine, Philosophy, and Mathematics.

Following the above are the fields of study required for the Bachelor of Arts degree: Greek with Professor Wilkenson and a very large number of auditors classified thereunder. On the last of the three pages of the document (as shown at left) is the heading *Professor lecturae Dialecticae* followed by a listing of his auditors. M. Johnes is the Professor of Dialectic and one of his students in the Corpus Christi group is Christopher Marlowe, here listed as 'Merling', the 29th of the 31 Corpus Christi students. Grouped with him are three schoolmates: Burman, Walford, and Bennett, who, like Marlowe, entered Corpus Christi in 1580 as scholarship holders. Dialectic (logic) was studied in a student's second and third years at Cambridge, the first year towards the B.A. being spent on Rhetoric. As an undergraduate one also studied Greek, arithmetic and elements of astronomy, but, after obtaining the Bachelor's degree, one continued with the more advanced courses in astronomy, mathematics, and philosophy. Divinity, medicine, and law were undertaken only after receiving an M.A.

The remainder of this document covers the Professor and auditors of Rhetoric, again with subdivision into colleges, of which in 1581 there were fourteen: King's, Queens', Corpus Christi, Clare Hall, Trinity Hall, Catherine Hall, St. John's, Jesus, Gonville and Caius, Peterhouse, Christs, Pembroke Hall, Magdalene, and Trinity.

At right is the complete third page of the 1581 report and, at left, is an enlargement of the Corpus Christi group containing the name 'Merling'.

60

The south-east corner of the Old Court, Corpus Christi, *showing the Old Master's Lodge where Matthew Parker resided. A collection of 16th- and early 17th-century panel portraits are in the possession of the college and now hang in the New Master's Lodge in the New Court, presumably having been removed thence from the Old Master's Lodge. The 'Marlowe Portrait' is believed to have been one of this set, but for some reason was not hung with the others but hidden away, perhaps because it was broken, perhaps because Marlowe's name had fallen into odium. The story of its discovery is still something of a mystery.*

service at the end), as, for instance, we hear of Richard Harvey. Nashe reported of him 'Thou hadst thy hood turned over thy ears when thou wert a Bachelor, for abusing of Aristotle, and setting him upon the school-gates painted with ass's ears on his head'. This makes Harvey sound more human. Nashe himself was probably 'sent down' from the university, if the story be correct, presumably for some scandalous play he had written. Marlowe, as a sensitive youth, was perhaps a more serious and reticent character than we have credited him. Being too brilliant, thinking too deeply, and trying to cause others to think got him into trouble. But at Cambridge he kept out of it. And if he broke the rules he did it with discretion, or got away with it by the disarming use of his personal charm.

Corpus Christi must have been fairly comfortable compared to some of the other colleges. The benign ghost of Matthew Parker hovered over his old college, for he saw to it that they were supplied with certain amenities and comforts in the form of regular gifts of firing and food, including an annual feast. He had also had the walks paved so that one could go relatively dry-shod around the building. And he donated valuable books and manuscripts to the library together with costly plate, with the proviso that the plate was only to be retained as long as the manuscripts were kept safe from damage and loss—a sure sign of the old man's worldly wisdom. His precious manuscripts have remained intact until this day. Despite this solicitude for the welfare of the college, trouble was brewing. Dr. Norgate was Master in Marlowe's day. He seems to have been an extraordinarily inefficient and easy-going head, for at his death in 1587, the year that Marlowe completed his studies, the college was found to be so much in debt, and the finances generally in such a ruinous state, that it was shaken to its foundations. The years that followed were beset with insecurity. Kit had enjoyed the best of its history for a time.

'Quod me Nutrit me Destruit'

One of the most exciting discoveries of recent years in Cambridge was the finding of a portrait believed to be a likeness of Christopher Marlowe. This magnificent painting came to light in 1953. Its two broken panels were found in a heap of rubble left by workmen who were making repairs to the Master's Lodge at Corpus Christi College in preparation for the residence of the then recently appointed Master, Sir George Thomson.

It had been raining heavily for some days when an undergraduate passing the heap of débris saw two pieces of broken wood with some painting on them partly projecting from the heap, and upon closer inspection found them to be two sections of a portrait of a young man dressed in Elizabethan costume. Thinking this to be of interest, he brought his find to the attention of Dr. J. P. T. Bury, at that time Librarian to Corpus Christi. After being photographed by Mr. Edward Leigh in its original state, it was sent to the National Portrait Gallery in London in an attempt to identify the subject. The Gallery authenticated it as a genuine portrait of the Elizabethan period, but could give no clue as to its subject since it was not similar to any previously identified portrait; and since no known portrait of Marlowe is in existence, this negative conclusion leaves the matter open.

As the picture was in very poor condition, the colours in particular being much obscured, it was decided to send it to a firm of London art dealers, Messrs. W. Holder & Sons of Brook Street, London, for restoration at the hands of an expert. Restored and framed, it now hangs in the dining hall at Corpus Christi.

The painting is about eighteen by twenty-four inches in size, and in the upper left corner bears the inscription 'Ætatis suæ 21 1585' (aged 21, 1585), which age and date are correct for Marlowe in the year in which, having obtained his

B.A., he commenced studies for his M.A. degree.* As one of the oldest of the college graduates, he may well have been the only graduate of this age in that year, his scholarship under the Matthew Parker bequest having been granted to him unusually late. Marlowe was admitted as a pensioner in December 1580/1 when he was seventeen. According to Elizabethan practice, students were commonly not more than fourteen or fifteen when they entered Cambridge. John Harvey (younger brother of Gabriel) was born in the same year as Marlowe but he had matriculated at Queens' College in June, 1578 at the age of fourteen; Thomas Nashe matriculated at St. John's in 1582 at the age of fifteen; Richard Proud, a probable classmate of Marlowe's, was admitted pensioner at the age of fifteen. The dates of admission as shown in the *University of Cambridge Book of Matriculation and Degrees, 1544–1659* (Cambridge 1913) give evidence that the vast majority of entrants in the 1575–1590 period were not more than fifteen.

The sitter for this portrait must have been a Corpus Christi student because it is highly improbable that at the age of twenty-one, or shortly thereafter, any outsider would have been deemed of sufficient interest to Cambridge authorities to have had his portrait hung in the Master's Lodge, and it can be assumed that the portrait must have come from the Lodge since it was found as part of the débris from this structure.

The work is executed on a wooden panel which may originally have been inset in a panelled wall, or possibly in some kind of wooden box-fender around the fireplace.[1] An example of this treatment of a similar portrait can be found at Madingley Hall, Cambridge (formerly the residence of the Hynde family). Here a wood panel portrait of about the same size (inscribed 'Ætatis suæ 18 1607') is inserted above the mantel so that, except for the frame, it is flush with the wood panelling of the room.

Evidence suggests that the Master's Lodge at Corpus Christi traditionally constituted a miniature portrait gallery. A partial listing in an 1884 *Catalogue of the First Exhibition of University and College Portraits Held in the FitzWilliam Museum* (the university's art museum), subdivided according to the rooms of the colleges from which they came, includes the following portraits as submitted for this exhibition from Corpus Christi Master's Lodge:

Thomas More	John Foxe
Thomas Cromwell	Robert Cecil, 1st Earl of Salisbury
Queen Mary	John Jegon, Master of Corpus
Matthew Parker (two portraits)	Christi, 1590–1603
Portrait of a young man (inscribed	Portrait of a man
'1579 Ætatis suæ 23')	

* *The suggested identity of Christopher Marlowe was first put forward by Calvin Hoffman in his book* The Murder of the Man who was Shakespeare, Methuen, *1955.*

64

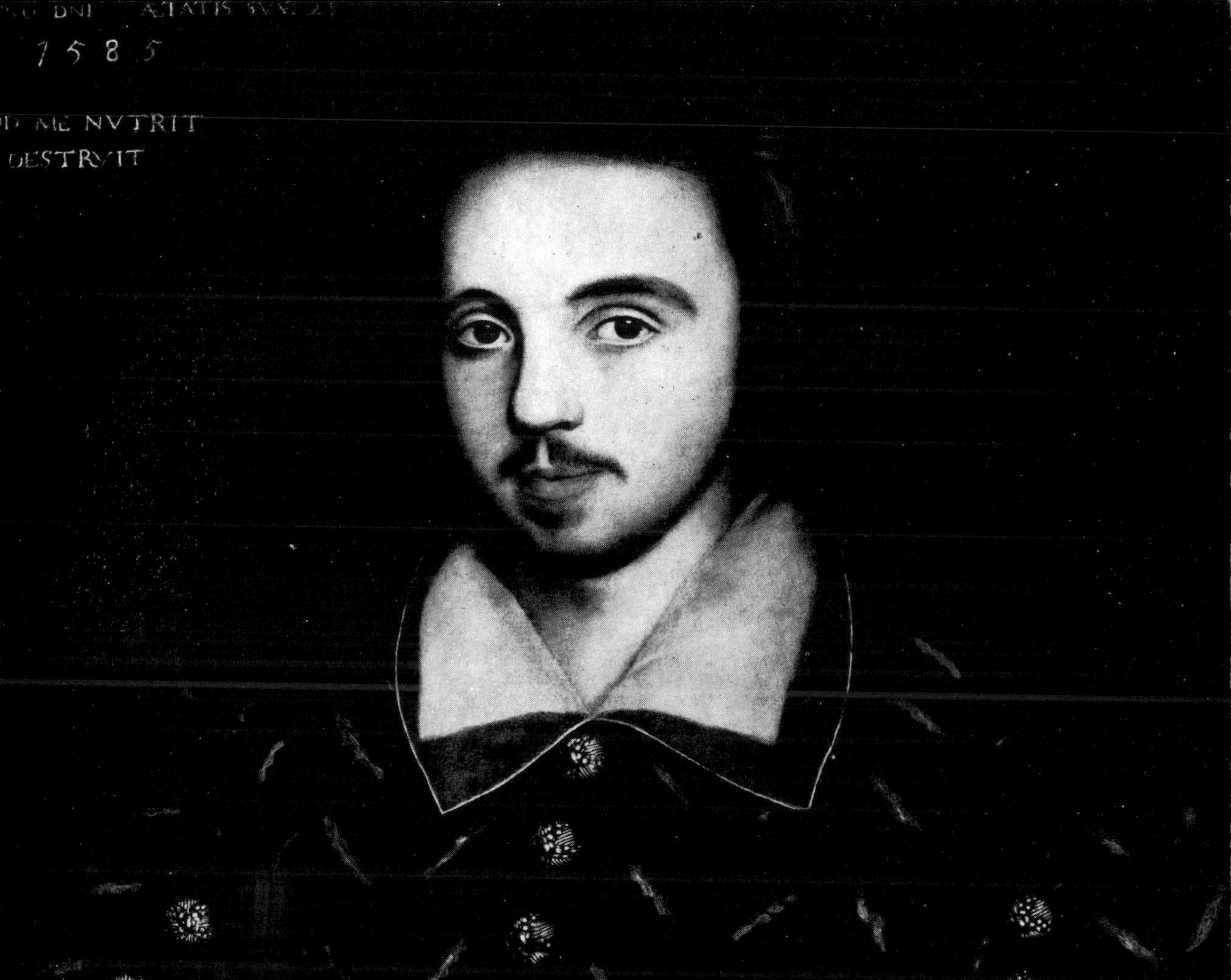
DNI ÆTATIS SVÆ 21
1585
ME NVTRIT
DESTRVIT

There is no indication that the 'Marlowe' portrait was amongst these, or that its existence was known at this time. The present Master's Lodge in the New Court is not an old house, having been built in the 1820s, but it still contains a large collection of 16th- and early 17th-century panel portraits which presumably came from the old Master's Lodge (formerly the residence of Matthew Parker). It is believed that the 'Marlowe' portrait belonged to this set, and perhaps some accident befell it and it was put away in a cupboard and forgotten. It is believed that the two panels which formed the portrait had been known to be in the Lodge before, although no one had ever recognised them for what they were until they were found in the heap of rubble of materials removed from the Lodge during the renovations. The circumstances of its discovery are, in fact, shrouded in mystery which, despite the closest enquiries, it has not been possible to resolve with certainty.[2]

A possible explanation is that the portrait had originally hung for a few years in a place of honour in the Master's Lodge, and was thrust into obscurity as a result of Marlowe's disgrace and death in 1593. A precedent for this may be cited in the case of the portrait of a Corpus Christi master, Henry Butts, D.D., Master in 1632. Butts did valiant relief work at the time of the plague and so overtaxed himself that he subsequently lost his reason. His portrait, which had hung in the dining hall at Corpus Christi, was removed after his 'disgrace', although it was restored to view in a later century. Similarly, the 'Marlowe' portrait might have been taken from its place of honour and hidden as a result of the universal condemnation in which Marlowe's name was held immediately after 1593, especially by the Puritans, who were well represented at Corpus Christi. The fact that this genuine Elizabethan portrait remained in obscurity and was not reinstated tallies with the identification of Marlowe as the subject, since Corpus Christi is unlikely to have displayed the portrait of one believed to have been a notorious atheist. The memorial plaque was not erected until the arrival of a more enlightened age, by which time the existence of the portrait had doubtless been long since forgotten.

Returning again to the portrait on the previous page, we find an interesting Latin inscription directly under the date, 'Quod me nutrit me destruit' ('That which nourishes me destroys me'). This would appear to be just the kind of motto such a young man as Marlowe would have chosen for himself; he liked to say the startling thing with subtle effect. Moreover he was a poet, and the motto chosen is significant. 'That which nourishes me destroys me' would seem to be a reference to the sitter's poetic muse, which both inspired and nourished him, and yet consumed him with its fiery genius. There is a certain affinity in this idea to the expressions of languishment for love found in the writings of the mediæval and Elizabethan lyric poets, and in some heraldic mottoes of the 14th and early 15th centuries. If this is indeed Marlowe, we may be sure that he was not expressing his love for any mortal being, but was referring to his Muse, that goddess so constantly invoked by the Elizabethan poets, and it has been remarked that the motto has an Ovidian ring, though

St. Bene't's Churchyard *adjoins the Old Court at Corpus Christi. In the background can be seen the gallery which was constructed to connect St. Bene't's Church with the north-east corner of the quadrangle. Windows from the back of the Old Court overlook this quiet plot.*

apparently original and individual to the sitter. According to Professor Gilbert Highet, the American classicist, its exact parallel has not so far been traced in the writings of any Latin or Greek writer of antiquity which Marlowe might have used as a source; nor has it been traced in the works of English writers prior to Marlowe.[3] Strikingly, its first reappearance is found in the works of Shakespeare at a somewhat later date; first, in Sonnet LXXIII in an English rendering, '*consum'd with that which it was nourish'd by*', and in a variant Latin version in *Pericles*, Act II, scene 2, line 33, when the fourth knight, who bears the device of an upturned torch being consumed by its own fire, has the motto '*Quod me alit me extinguit*'.[4] Marlowe alone of his contemporaries exerted any deep and lasting influence on Shakespeare; that he did so is undeniable, and this fact argues in favour of the identification of the sitter as none other than Marlowe, for whom else would Shakespeare be so likely to re-echo? Marlowe is the only one from whom Shakespeare quotes directly, and the closeness of their minds may here once more be evidenced in the chosen motto on the portrait of Marlowe's college, and a line in an autobiographical sonnet by Shakespeare:[5]

> *That time of year thou mayest in me behold,*
> *When yellow leaves, or none, or few do hang*
> *Upon those boughs which shake against the cold,*
> *Bare ruin'd choirs, where late the sweet birds sang.*
> *In me thou seest the twilight of such day,*
> *As after sunset fadeth in the West,*
> *Which by and by black night doth take away,*
> *Death's second self that seals up all in rest.*
> *In me thou seest the glowing of such fire,*
> *That on the ashes of his youth doth lie,*
> *As the death-bed, whereon it must expire,*
> *Consum'd with that which it was nourish'd by.*
> > *This thou perceiv'st, which makes thy love more strong,*
> > *To love that well, which thou must leave ere long.*

Let us now turn to consider the appearance of the sitter (which is further discussed in the comparison of two portraits, see pp. 214–222). The face is at once arresting; the eyes, with their searching, fearless look, have the character that, though here calmly observant, yet betrays a certain passionate intensity. He might well be a poet, and something of an intellectual. His motto he has written there for all to mark: 'Quod me nutrit me destruit.'

The costume of the sitter is a rather elegant one of black Elizabethan velvet profusely slitted to show a touch of gold beneath. An unusual touch, however, is the simple collar of 'cobweb lawn'; lace collars were far more frequent in this period. Here again a certain individuality is bespoken in the sitter.

The objection has been raised recently at Corpus Christi College that the clothing worn by the subject of the portrait was too aristocratic to fit the cobbler's son. Under the legislation of the Statute of Apparel, brought in by Mary Tudor and still in force until its repeal in the reign of James I, anyone under the rank of knight of the realm was forbidden to wear silk or velvet, and the doublet of the sitter is undoubtedly of the latter. However, abundant contemporary evidence shows that the rulings of the Statute were almost completely ignored, to the annoyance and remark of some, and it can also be argued that there were

68

certain persons exempted from this prohibition, and these included servants of the Queen, of which Marlowe, as one of Her Majesty's secret agents, most definitely was one. We know from documentary evidence that he was so employed in 1586–7. This portrait is dated 1585, and the inference must in this case be that Marlowe was first engaged in espionage work in this year when he was aged twenty-one and already a B.A.

Such a suggestion is borne out by the records of Marlowe's periods of residence and of absence from college, as shown in the entries against his name for payments in the college accounts. Details of these are given in Professor Boas' *Christopher Marlowe*, 1940 (see pp. 13–14). Marlowe as a Parker scholar was to receive one shilling weekly when in residence, but this sum was forfeited if he was absent from college, and the following table quoted from Professor Boas' book presents an interesting study:

	1ᵃ Trim.	2ᵃ Trim.	3ᵃ Trim.	4ᵃ Trim.
1580–1		Marlin xijˢ	Marlen xiijˢ	Marlen xijˢ
1581–2	Marlin xiijˢ	Marlin xiijˢ	Marlin xiijˢ	Marlin vijˢ
1582–3	Marlyn xijˢ	Marlin xiijˢ	Marlin vjˢ	Marlin xiiijˢ
1583–4	D Marlyn xijˢ	D Marlyn xiijˢ	D Marlyn xiijˢ	D Marlin xjˢ vjᵈ
1584–5	Ds Marlin iijˢ	Ds Marlin vijˢ	Ds Marlin iiijˢ	Ds Marlin vˢ
1585–6	(Accounts missing)			
1586–7	Ds Marly ixˢ	Ds Marlye vˢ vjᵈ		

Three terms of thirteen weeks each and one of fourteen weeks add up to fifty-three shillings in the year as against fifty-two weeks, so presumably the odd shilling was some kind of Christmas bonus so that the students could have a binge in the buttery bar! As has been noted elsewhere, the Elizabethan student was expected to remain in residence at his college for the entire time, vacations included, with a maximum of one month's leave per year (with permission) and only extra leave with special dispensation. On this basis these entries tabulated by Prof. Boas from the Corpus Christi scholarship accounts books show Marlowe's record of attendance as good, and apparently comparable to the attendance records of other students, for the first four years of his university career.

Prof. Boas remarks: 'In his fifth year, 1584–5, the scholarship payments suggest an abrupt change.' Three shillings, seven shillings, four shillings, and five shillings, amount to exactly half of the year in absence. However, as Prof. Boas points out, there is some discrepancy between Marlowe's apparent absence in his non-receipt of his weekly shilling residence bonus, and the expenditures listed against his name in the Buttery book. In the Michaelmas term of this year he received three shillings representing three weeks' residence, but he spent money at the buttery in the second, third, fourth, seventh, tenth, eleventh, and twelfth weeks of that term. Was he perhaps dropping in for the odd meal only?

And if he was in regular residence why did he not trouble to collect the scholarship payments due to him? Again in the second term he received only seven shillings but buttery entries against his name are spread into nine weeks. In the third and fourth terms the entries pretty well agree, and he seems to have been absent (totally) from the fifth to the twelfth week in the third term, and in the fourth term from the fourth to the twelfth weeks inclusive. There is indication here of an unusually long absence. Professor Boas draws a conclusion we would like to endorse:

'Presumably the Government service upon which Marlowe was for a time employed before taking his M.A. degree was after he had become "Dominus". If so, on the evidence of the Buttery books his only lengthy periods of absence from Cambridge, if this was involved, were in the third or fourth terms of 1584–5, or the third of 1585–6.'

He adds:

'Can it have any bearing on this question that Marlowe's weekly expenditure in 1585–6 seems to have been in excess of any previous period, items of xviiid. to xxid. being not infrequent, though even from the first he had by no means always kept within his scholarship allowance of one shilling and must have had it supplemented in some way? Though he began with the humble payment of *1d.*, his life at Corpus was far from one of penury.'[6]

The evidence of Marlowe's unexplained absences and affluence combine to underline the conclusion that his government service commenced during the year in which the 'Marlowe' portrait was painted. In that case the objection to the aristocratic clothing of the sitter would be completely answered, irrespective of whether Marlowe would in any case have abided by the strictures laid down. He would at this time have had a double incentive, and a possible opportunity, for having his portrait painted: he had just gained his B.A., and he had become a servant of the Queen and probably completed some mission of importance, receiving payment for it. He may possibly also have made his first acquaintance with young Thomas Walsingham through the connection of his employer, Sir Francis Walsingham.

It is a tantalising thought to imagine Kit delighting in his new-found status and being so taken with his appearance in his first velvet doublet, which he would now be fully qualified to wear, that he decided to have his portrait painted in it. Perhaps it was Thomas Walsingham, admiring his poet's fine new look, who suggested it to him, and at whose home the portrait might have been executed. Spanish artists came to London to do work for patrons from time to time. The style of the painting with its dramatic chiaroscuro, or heavy shadowing, has been likened to the work of the artists of the Toledo school. Another possible alternative, but a very much less likely one, is that

Marlowe might have had the portrait painted in Spain, since his government work could well have taken him there.

That Marlowe came to have a rather special status during his time at Corpus Christi is indicated not only by the Privy Council letter to the Cambridge authorities requesting that he be given his degree despite certain unfounded rumours about him, but it is also suggested further by the Buttery book entries as remarked by Professor Bakeless (*The Tragicall History of Christopher Marlowe*, 1942). In 1580 (as Marlen) the entries in the Corpus Christi Buttery book show various purchases made by Marlowe and his fellow students and at the right of each entry is a notation of their having been paid. In the later entries, although the procedure for his classmates is the same, Marlin's (*sic*) purchases are entered without any notation of payment for same. Did Marlowe perhaps have a patron by then who subsidized him, or was the cobbler's son for some other reason a favoured customer?

By 1585 Marlowe had written his translations of *Ovid*, we may confidently assume, and possibly also of *Lucan*, and probably also the dramatisation of *Dido*. It was only two years after that the brilliant success of the production of *Tamburlaine the Great* in London established Marlowe's reputation. Although the portrait was painted in 1585, it probably would not have been presented to the college until his departure from Cambridge in 1587, when the eminence of its subject was well established. Professor Bakeless believes that the granting of Marlowe's M.A. degree was the final result of an intramural struggle between Dr. Norgate, Master of Corpus Christi, who was evidently annoyed at Marlowe's absences from college and chiefly instrumental in withholding the degree, and Dr. Copcott, Vice-Chancellor of the University, an appointee of Lord Burghley's and therefore pro-Marlowe. In November 1587 Norgate died, and was succeeded as Master of Corpus Christi by Copcott. Since Marlowe was ultimately granted the degree, it seems likely that he would have felt some gratitude to the man who had taken up the cudgels on his behalf, and possibly he gave his portrait to Dr. Copcott as a gift upon the latter's accession to the Mastership of his old college. The fact that it was evidently hanging in the Master's Lodge, which was Copcott's residence, is suggestive of such a conclusion.[7]

That a poet was considered fit subject for portraiture is evidenced by the many portraits of Marlowe's literary contemporaries. Edmund Spenser was considered sufficiently illustrious to have his portrait hung in the university library. If Marlowe had never had his portrait painted it would be a matter of surprise, rather than the contrary, and the place where one would have expected to find it would be in his old college, Corpus Christi.

*   *   *

The Backs *between King's College and St. John's.*

A place 'of nestling green for poets made'.

In Elizabethan times it was strictly forbidden to swim in the river. Needless to say this rule was frequently broken.

While at the university Marlowe began (necessarily in secret as these were not the prescribed books for student reading) to translate some of the Latin poems of Ovid, whose influence was ever after to pervade his work. They were love poems.

> *In summer's heat and mid-time of the day*
> *To rest my limbs upon a bed I lay;*
> *One window shut, the other open stood,*
> *Which gave such light as twinkles in a wood,*
> *Like twilight glimpse at setting of the sun,*
> *Or night being past, and yet not day begun.*
> *Such light to shamefast maidens must be shown,*
> *Where they may sport, and seem to be unknown.*
> *Then came Corinna in a long loose gown,*
> *Her white neck hid with tresses hanging down,*
> *Resembling fair Semiramis going to bed*
> *Or Laïs of a thousand wooers sped.*
> *I snatch'd her gown; being thin, the harm was small,*
> *Yet striv'd she to be cover'd therewithal.*
> *And striving thus as one that would be cast*
> *Betray'd herself, and yielded at the last.*
> *Stark naked as she stood before mine eye,*
> *Not one wen on her body could I spy.*
> *What arms and shoulders did I touch and see,*
> *How apt her breasts were to be press'd by me!*
> *How smooth a belly under her waist saw I!*
> *How large a leg, and what a lusty thigh!*
> *To leave the rest, all lik'd me passing well;*
> *I cling'd her naked body, down she fell;*
> *Judge you the rest; being tir'd she bade me kiss;*
> *Jove send me more such afternoons as this.*
>
> *Elegy V, Ovid's* A M O R E S

It was hardly the sort of poetry the authorities would approve. They did not. Marlowe's translations of Ovid's *Elegies* or 'Amores' achieved the distinction of being publicly burned by order of the Archbishop of Canterbury and the Bishop of London. This was not until June, 1599, although we cannot be sure when they first appeared in print as the printer cautiously left his edition undated and marked 'At Middlebourgh' in Holland, where prohibited literature was habitually printed and smuggled into the country, but doubtless the poems were circulating in manuscript among the students even in Marlowe's day. His other essay in translation, Lucan's *Pharsalia*, is on a warlike theme and finds its echoes in the thunderous, exulting hexameters of *Tamburlaine* that were to take London audiences by storm and put the seal on his success.

Marlowe's translations from Ovid and from Lucan are the work of an immature genius, but they are important for the influence exerted on his creative mind in its formative period. With Ovid and Lucan Marlowe went to school. When the young man we are considering is later going to become a great poet, even his stumbling beginnings are of interest. His line-by-line translations, though occasionally inaccurate, owing either to a corrupted printed text or his own imperfect mastery of Latin (and these gaps were not always helped by the lexicons available), have yet a charm and vigour of their own. Ovid, whom he especially loved, drew sweetness from him, and these elegies represent the rosy dawn from which the golden sunlight of his *Hero and Leander* later emerged; his Lucan foreshadows the martial clang and thunder of *Tamburlaine*.

> *The soldiers, having won the market place,*
> *There spread the colours, with confused noise*
> *Of trumpets' clang, shrill cornets, whistling fifes.*
> *The people started; young men left their beds,*
> *And snatch'd arms near their household gods hung up*
> *Such as peace yields; worm-eaten leathern targets,*
> *Through the wood peer'd, headless darts, old swords*
> *With ugly teeth of black rust foully scarr'd:*
> *But seeing White Eagles, and Rome's flags well known,*
> *And lofty Caesar in the thickest throng,*
> *They shook for fear, and cold benumb'd their limbs,*
>
> . . . .
>
> *The pilot from the helm leaps in the sea;*
> *And mariners, albeit the keel be sound,*
> *Shipwreck themselves; even so the city left*

ALL

OVIDS ELEGIES:

3. BOOKES.

By C. M.

Epigrams by J. D.

[***]
[***]

At Middlebourgh.

LVCANS
FIRST BOOKE
TRANSLATED LINE
FOR LINE, BY CHR.
MARLOW.

AT LONDON,
Printed by P. Short, and are to be sold by Walter Burre at the Signe of the Flower de Luce in Paules Churchyard, 1600.

Title pages of Marlowe's first works. *The translation of Lucan's* Pharsalia, *and of Ovid's* Amores, *both written by Marlowe while at the university. Ovid especially was to exert a lasting influence on him.*

All rise in arms; nor could the bed-rid parents
Keep back their sons, or women's tears their husbands;
They stay'd not either to pray or sacrifice,
Their household gods restrain them not, none lingered
As loth to leave Rome whom they held so dear:
The irrevocable people fly in troops.
O gods that easy grant men great estates,
But hardly grace to keep them! Rome that flows
With citizens and captives, and would hold
The world (were it together) is by cowards
Left as a prey now Caesar doth approach:

.   .   .   .

Strange sights appear'd, the angry threat'ning gods
Fill'd both the earth and seas with prodigies;
Great store of strange and unknown stars were seen
Wandering about the North, and rings of fire
Fly in the air, and dreadful bearded stars,
And comets that presage the fall of kingdoms.
The flattering sky glitter'd in often flames,
And sundry fiery meteors blaz'd in heaven:
Now spearlike, long; now like a spreading torch
Lightning in silence stole forth without clouds,
And from the northern climate snatching fire
Blasted the Capitol.
                    Marlowe's translation of Lucan's PHARSALIA.

Now o'er the sea from her old love comes she
That draws the day from heaven's cold axletree.
Aurora, whither slid'st thou? down again,
And birds of Memnon *yearly shall be slain.*
Now in her tender arms I sweetly bide;
If ever, now well lies she by my side.
The air is cold, and sleep is sweetest now,
And birds send forth shrill notes from every bough:
Whither run'st thou, that men, and women, love not?
Hold in thy rosy horses that they move not.
Ere thou rise, stars teach seamen where to sail,
But when thou com'st they of their courses fail.
Poor travailers, though tir'd, rise at thy sight,
And soldiers make them ready to the fight.
The painful hind by thee to field is sent,
Slow oxen early in the yoke are pent.
Thou cozen'st boys of sleep, and dost betray them
To pedants that with cruel lashes pay them.
                    Elegy XIII, Ovid's AMORES

The courtyard of The Eagle *in Bene't Street, opposite the old entrance to Corpus Christi College in Bene't Street which has been an inn since mediæval times. In such taverns the more daring of the Cambridge 'wags' would 'ruffle and roist it out, exceeding in apparel and haunting riotous company, which draweth them from their books unto another trade. And for excuse, when they are charged with breach of all good order, think it sufficient to say they are gentlemen, which grieveth many not a little'.*[8]

Doubtless Marlowe, once established, would have thrown caution to the winds and set foot here too on occasion.

> *Envy, why carp'st thou my time is spent so ill,*
> *And term'st my works fruits of an idle quill?*
> *Or that unlike the line from whence I come*
> *War's dusty honours are refus'd being young?*
> *Nor that I study not the brawling laws,*
> *Nor set my voice to sale in every cause?*
> *Thy scope is mortal, mine eternal fame,*
> *That all the world may ever chant my name.*
>
> *Elegy XV, Ovid's* AMORES

King's Chapel *was one of the beauties of Cambridge in Marlowe's day, as in ours, rearing its spires in exquisite symmetry a bare two minutes' stroll from his lodgings at Corpus Christi.*

'By shallow rivers, to whose falls
Melodious birds sing madrigals.'

Beside the Cam, flowing sweetly past, Marlowe found inspiration for a poet, bringing him
compensation, with its dawn bird chorus, for the early rising imposed on the drowsy students.
A little further down-stream there is a waterfall where formerly a mill stood.

Come live with me and be my love;
And we will all the pleasures prove
That hills and valleys, dales and fields,
Woods or steepy mountains yields.

And we will sit upon the rocks,
Seeing the shepherds feed their flocks
By shallow rivers, to whose falls
Melodious birds sing madrigals.

And I will make thee beds of roses,
And a thousand fragrant posies;
A cap of flowers, and a kirtle
Embroider'd all with leaves of myrtle;

A gown made of the finest wool
Which from our pretty lambs we pull;
Fair-lined slippers for the cold,
With buckles of the purest gold;

A belt of straw and ivy-buds,
With coral clasps and amber studs:
An if these pleasures may thee move,
Come live with me, and be my love.

The shepherd-swains shall dance and sing
For thy delight each May morning:
If these delights thy mind may move,
Then live with me, and be my love.

It is not known at what date *The Passionate Shepherd* was written but it strongly reflects Cambridge influences and makes play with customs connected with the May Week festivities in Elizabethan times. Nor do we know when Sir Walter Raleigh penned his famous 'Reply' to Marlowe's poem. Later in London Marlowe was to become one of Raleigh's intimate circle, yet we know that Raleigh was also present in Cambridge during Marlowe's residence, not as a student himself but in connection with troubles that had arisen over the granting of a licence to a Cambridge vinter, of which licensing Sir Walter had been given the monopoly by the Queen as one of her many marks of favour. This had conflicted with the university's own privileges in the matter and riots by townsfolk and students had resulted. Possibly he first met young Christopher Marlowe at the time of the sorting out of those troubles.

The tradition for play-acting at the universities goes back to Elizabethan times:

'Do not the Vniuersities, the fountaines and well springs of all good Arts, Learning and Documents, admit the like in their Colledges? . . . In the time of my residence in *Cambridge*, I haue seene Tragedyes, Comedyes, Historyes, Pastorals and Shewes, publickly acted, in which the Graduates of good place and reputation haue bene specially parted: this is held necessary for the emboldening of their *Iunior* schollers, to arme them with audacity, against they come to bee imployed in any publicke exercise, as in the reading of the Dialecticke, Rhetoricke, Ethicke, Mathematick, the Physicke, or Metaphysicke Lectures. It teacheth audacity to the bashfull Grammarian, beeing newly admitted into the priuate Colledge, and after matriculated and entred as a member of the Vniuersity, and makes him a bold Sophister.'

Thomas Heywood's APOLOGY FOR ACTORS, 1612

In 1583 there is a record of a play performance at Corpus Christi at which a scholar named Evance from Pembroke Hall made a disturbance by throwing stones.[9] Evidently Evance was a stern critic, but unfortunately we have no record of the play to which he thus expressed his strong objection. Perhaps Kit acted in it. Probably it was some dull piece in Latin which aroused this reaction, as such dramatic exercises in the classical languages were particularly encouraged. Several of these survive anonymously, and it is possible that Marlowe might have tried his hand at them before turning to English drama.

The Cloister Court at Queens' College, *with its charming half-timbered gallery, is unique in being the only remaining college in Cambridge with this type of construction. At Corpus Christi there was formerly also a gallery built on to the Master's Lodge in Matthew Parker's time, which is believed to have resembled this Tudor gallery of Queens'. It was unfortunately demolished during the rebuilding and extensions of the 19th century.*
The Cloister Court at Queens' forms a delightful setting for the annual May Week dramatic performances by the Queens' under-graduates.

Marlowe undoubtedly wrote *Dido, Queen of Carthage*, his first essay in drama, while still at Cambridge. The university influence is apparent in his choice of a classical subject, Virgil's *Æneid*, which he follows closely. He may have collaborated with Thomas Nashe in writing it, as claimed by Nashe in his posthumous publication of the play in 1594; on the other hand, it has been suggested that Nashe probably only edited it for his deceased friend, as the writing bears no trace of Nashe's hand but reads throughout like pure early Marlowe. In this work from his student pen we can already see foreshadowed the 'mighty line' of the master dramatist.

The play was first performed in 1587 when it was 'Played by the Children of Her Maiesties Chappell' at Norwich and Ipswich—not too far from Cambridge for Marlowe to have ridden over to watch the performance, a première which would have been of special interest to him.

Scene from a production of Dido, Queen of Carthage.[10] *Here Aeneas, Achates and Ascanius stand before the walls of Carthage and are amazed to see sculpted thereon the story of the Fall of Troy, which Aeneas retells in his magnificent speech at the court of Dido:*

> '*Then he unlock'd the horse; and suddenly,*
> *From out his entrails, Neoptolemus,*
> *Setting his spear upon the ground, leapt forth,*
> *And, after him, a thousand Grecians more,*
> *In whose stern faces shin'd the quenchless fire*
> *That after burnt the pride of Asia.*
> *By this, the camp was come unto the walls,*
> *And through the breach did march into the streets,*
> *Where, meeting with the rest, "Kill, kill!" they cried.*'

SIR PHILIP SIDNEY (1554–1586), the most notable of Elizabeth's courtier poets, had been an early patron of Edmund Spenser, the Cambridge 'new Poete', whom he had met at London in the household of his uncle, the Earl of Leicester. Spenser had been helped to this post at Leicester's through the agency of his former tutor at Pembroke Hall, Gabriel Harvey, who was a prominent lecturer in the public schools at Cambridge in Marlowe's time there. Harvey, a pretentious literary critic who aspired to Court circles, had taken the talented young Spenser under his wing, and ever after prided himself no end on the connection. He was soon also to come across Kit Marlowe at Cambridge, and to take rather less kindly to this genius, who nevertheless managed to make his way without Harvey's help. Possibly that was one of the things Gabriel Harvey had against him. Despite all his fine criticism it was not Harvey but Spenser and the brilliant Sidney who exerted the greatest influence on the new generation of poets.

Sir Philip Sidney's family possessed a fair seat in Kent, Penshurst near Tonbridge, to which Philip brought as his bride Frances Walsingham, the daughter of Sir Francis Walsingham, the Queen's Secretary of State and employer of espionage agents in her service, such as Marlowe was to become before his university days were over. It is possible that through this mutual connection Marlowe, as an aspiring poet, might also have come to know Sir Philip Sidney, whose acquaintance he would undoubtedly have desired. Sidney had early gained a reputation that made him the idol of the land, a romantic figure, poet and soldier, whom the nation had taken to their hearts and whose death at the Battle of Zutphen in the November of 1586 plunged Court and people into deepest mourning. His untimely death, like Marlowe's, cut short a brilliant career of great promise for literature and politics.

82

Cambridge was to know him for six and a half years of his life, from seventeen to twenty-three, a significant time in which a man matures. And such aspiring spirits as Marlowe do not meekly follow the path laid down for them; he was beginning to sense what he wanted, viewing his humble origins with an arrogant eye as he listened to the music of his poetic Muse, and spreading the wings of his intellect found that he might soar on these to loftier heights.

At Cambridge there was already a tradition of new writers. The first of these, the 'new Poete', Edmund Spenser, had graduated from Pembroke Hall under the encouragement of the brilliant but pedantic don, Gabriel Harvey, and had gained the patronage of the admired Sir Philip Sidney, in whose circle he was experimenting with verse forms. New literary trends were in the air. The Cambridge curriculum encouraged the writing of original dramatic essays—in the classical form and in Latin to be sure; but it is therefore not surprising that the universities were also producing the nation's dramatists. Such redoubtable critics as Evance (see p. 80) might have finally persuaded Marlowe that the classical form of plays was too dull to bother with and started him off on experiments which were to lead him away from Senecan construction.

Sir Philip Sidney, however, deplored those plays which currently ignored the classical unities: 'where you shall haue *Asia* of the one side, and *Affricke* of the other, and so manie vnder Kingdomes, that the Player when he comes in, must euer begin with telling where he is, or else the tale will not be conceiued. Now you shall haue three Ladies walke to gather flowers, and then we must beleeue the stage to be a garden. By and by we heare newes of shipwrack in the same place, then we are to blame if we accept it not for a Rock. . . . Now of time, they are much more liberall. For ordinarie it is, that two yoong Princes fall in loue, after many trauerses she is got with childe, deliuered of a faire boy: he is lost, groweth a man, falleth in loue, and is readie to get an other childe, and all this in two houres space.'

Kit heard the voice of the people, and did not heed the aristocrat. He ignored the great Sir Philip's advice (which was then not yet published, but he might have read it in manuscript) and with his superlative genius created such inspired sense out of these disunities that one feels sure that even Sir Philip would have forgiven him and been won. His poetry he would certainly have applauded.

Casting around for a subject for his first real drama, Marlowe drew from a classical source, Virgil's *Æneid*, drawing a picture of the love-lorn Queen Dido which presages Shakespeare's glorious conception of Cleopatra. In this he may have collaborated in a first draft with Thomas Nashe of St. John's College, a young lad of high spirits and literary talent, who soon became the terror of the dons. From 1582 onwards he was at the university contemporaneously with Marlowe. Another dramatist with whom Kit might have first struck acquaintance in Cambridge was Robert Greene, who had taken his B.A., also at St. John's in 1580, and then left to make a tour of Italy and Spain. Returning to Cambridge from these sophisticating experiences to take his M.A. in 1583, he declared, 'I light among wags as lewd as myself, with whom I consumed the flower of my youth.' Kit was later to meet him again in London where they would be rival playwrights, and on one occasion probably also collaborators.

★   ★   ★

Marlowe was a long-term scholarship holder and would have to satisfy the requirements of his studies or risk forfeiture of his grant, and it is evident from his record that he studied creditably, despite his involvement in poetics and dramatic composition. The Order of Curriculum in the Faculty of Arts lasted over more than six years, and since Marlowe remained at Corpus Christi for this full time, drawing his weekly scholarship shilling whenever in residence, it is to be assumed that he gave it out as his intention that he would eventually take holy orders. The time of decision would have to be at the taking of his B.A.

In order to qualify for graduation as Bachelor of Arts, four years, or twelve full terms' residence, was required. In preparation for this, during the fourth year two 'Acts' or 'Responsios' and two 'Opponencies' in the public schools had to be made. At the beginning of the academic year one of the proctors announced the names of the students intending to compete for B.A. that year. Shortly after the commencement of the Lent term of 1584 Marlowe would have received notification that in approximately two weeks' time he would be required to appear as 'respondent' in the public schools, and must have prepared three propositions (these were usually of a moral or metaphysical nature) to defend in debate against three students from other colleges who would represent his 'opponents'.

This exercise took place before an undergraduate audience in the public school with a Master of Arts presiding. The 'respondent' read his Latin thesis on his chosen subject and was answered in turn by the 'opponents' in Latin. At the conclusion of the 'Act' the President or 'Moderator' made such comment as he saw fit and dismissed the assembly.

Every aspiring Bachelor had to pass two of these public trials to show his skill in disputation before he could present himself for further examination by the officials of his own college in the hope that he would be admitted for B.A. Those who passed these preliminary hurdles were then allowed to sit for the examinations in the public schools before the proctors and members of the university. These were usually held in the week preceding Ash Wednesday and continued for three days. Those who passed were then given their *supplicat* to the University's Vice-Chancellor and Senate formally requesting their admittance *ad respondendum quaestioni*. The now hopeful Bachelors then went along with the Fellows of their colleges to the public school to answer

An excerpt from the 1583–4 *Grace Book of the University of Cambridge showing the B.A. degrees of that year in the order of their seniority.* 'Marley' *is* 199th.

(*Courtesy of Corpus Christi College*)

> 'Make trial now of that philosophy
> That in our famous nurseries of arts
> Thou suck'st from Plato and from Aristotle.'

EDWARD II

84

The back door of St. John's College *as it was in the days of Nashe and Greene.*

questions fired at them from Aristotle's *Prior Analytics*; thereupon they were promoted to 'determiners'. In the next days further exercises continued until on Palm Sunday the coveted title of Bachelor of Arts was conferred.[11]

On Palm Sunday 1584 plain 'Christofer Marlyn' became 'Dominus Marlyn'. In the university Grace Book his name is second in the list of twelve Corpus Christi graduates for that year, and in order of seniority for the university 199th out of 231. 'Sweet Analytics, 'tis thou hast ravish'd me!' wrote Marlowe in *Dr. Faustus*, harking back to his days as an aspirant for Bachelor of Arts.

In the Buttery books at Corpus Christi 'D' is inexplicably prefixed to his name in the year before he achieved his 'Dominus'. Perhaps the Buttery bar accountant thought he was a Bachelor by reason of his age and bearing, and Kit didn't bother to disillusion him.

One hundred and ninety-ninth in order of seniority out of 231 graduates who became Bachelors that year is perhaps not a scintillating record, but it is a fairly well-established university tradition that those who brilliantly engage

85

in extra-curricular activities are not the ones who run away with the double firsts. Kit is in good company as far as this goes. However, he seems to have enjoyed an estimable reputation, for Simon Aldrich, a native of Canterbury who was a near contemporary of Marlowe's at Cambridge, reported to his neighbour, Henry Oxinden, that 'Marloe . . . was a rare scholar and made excellent verses in Latin'. This piece of hearsay Mr. Oxinden noted down in his Commonplace Book a long time after (February 10, 1640). If Aldrich spoke truly, and there is no reason to doubt it, it is unfortunate that none of Marlowe's Latin verse has survived except the Manwood Epitaph.

With his B.A. achieved, Marlowe felt at liberty to indulge his Muse. Ovid and Lucan had probably by now given him his first serious poetic exercises, and had helped him to a patron, aided perhaps by those excellent Latin verses which have perished. If he came into the service of Sir Francis Walsingham now, as has been suggested, his new employer was something of a connoisseur of Latin verse. Thomas Watson, currently the sweetest singer in that language, had been his protégé in Paris. His cousin, the young Thomas Walsingham, on the other hand, would doubtless have found Kit's translations of Ovid very much to his taste. Indications of patronage in the background at this period, together with possible government service, are present in Marlowe's long and apparently sanctioned absences from college in the following year, and bolstered by his accompanying happy financial security.

It was the Dramatic Muse he now courted. The next three years culminated in glorious fulfilment. This time he found his inspiration in 'Turkish affairs familiarly known', which Gabriel Harvey had reported to Spenser in 1580 as being already then the talk of the university. Sir Francis Walsingham kept spies as far distant as the Turkish Court. Perhaps Marlowe had been there on a mission, or had spoken to some that had. The martial thrum and blazing imagery of Lucan were still with him. The heady vicarious excitement of spilling blood on sheets of virgin paper possessed him:

'Clashing of arms was heard in untrod woods.'[12]

He transposed the scene of conquest and battle to Africa, Turkey and the Near East, steeped it in the exotic splendour of the Orient, and began to write his first great masterpiece, *Tamburlaine the Great*.

Boas writes regarding Marlowe's attendance at college after a period of spasmodic absences: 'somewhat surprisingly, he is shown in the fourth term to have been in attendance every one of the fourteen weeks, also in the first three weeks of the Michaelmas term, 1586, after which the Buttery book fails us'.[13] In this, his last full academic year, he was presumably catching up on his studies for his M.A. degree, which he gained at 'Commencement' in the following July. But not without some troubles which throw a sharp light on his many-sided activities and the distance this son of a Canterbury artisan had already travelled.

As a poet and a dramatist Marlowe had already made his mark at Cambridge

86

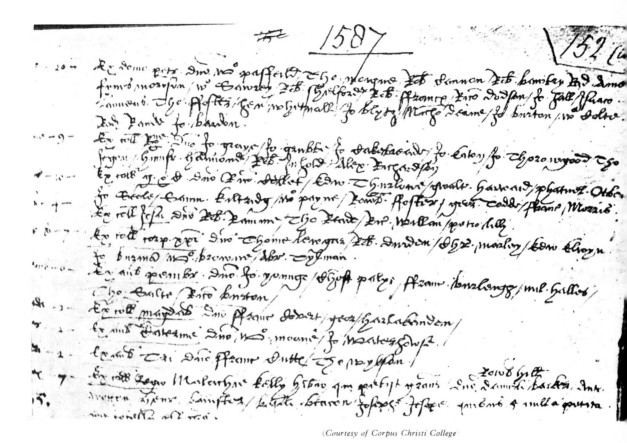

In 1587 Marlowe received his M.A. The Grace Book, which listed M.A.s in the order of their seniority, showed 'Chr. Marley' as fifth. It is the Grace Book which is being referred to in Dr. Faustus *when the chorus speaks of the protagonist as being 'grac'd with doctor's name'.*

by the time he entered his *supplicat* for proceeding to his Master's degree. He had written two plays besides his Latin translations in verse, the blank verse prototypes for Shakespearean drama henceforth, *Dido, Queen of Carthage* and *Tamburlaine the Great*. The latter was almost certainly begun if not completed before he left the university.

But Marlowe was destined to be a thorn in the side of the Cambridge authorities in more ways than by writing plays and translating Latin love poetry, both of which they would have disapproved of had they known (which perhaps they did not). He had also become engaged in espionage work of a dangerous nature on behalf of the Queen's government. This had involved him in unsanctioned absences from the university term and moreover rumour had been rife to the effect that he had been sojourning in Rheims, hotbed of Catholic intrigue and plots against Protestant Elizabeth, the inference being that Marlowe had himself turned traitor and had illicitly entered the Jesuit seminary at Rheims, there to hatch conspiracy. Upon his belated return to the university his explanations for his absence were apparently rejected and permission to proceed to his Master's degree was refused. Unable to move the Cambridge authorities from this decision, Marlowe apparently turned for help to someone high in the government, and we may assume that it would be none other than the Queen's Secretary of State, Sir Francis Walsingham, who was the organiser of her spy service.

Presently a letter arrived addressed to the Cambridge authorities and signed by the members of Her Majesty's Privy Council:[14]

'Whereas it was reported that Christopher Morley was determined to haue gone beyond the seas to Reames and there to remaine, Their Lordships thought good to certefie that he had no such intent, but that in all his accions he had behaued him selfe orderlie and discreetlie wherebie he had done her Majestie good service, & deserued to be rewarded for his faithfull dealinge: Their Lordships request was that the rumor thereof should be allaied by all possible meanes, and that he should be furthered in the degree he was to take this next Commencement: Because it was not her Majesties pleasure that anie one emploied as he had been in matters touching the benefitt of his Countrie should be defamed by those that are ignorant in th' affaires he went about.'

Their Lordships' request was duly granted. Marlowe, playwright, poet and government spy, became a newly-fledged Master of Arts. His term at Cambridge was ended.

Letter from the Privy Council:
'Whereas it was reported that Christopher Morley was determined to have gone beyond the seas to Reames, etc.'

A section of a 1574 map of France by Joane Joliveto enlarged to show area around Rheims. (Douay would have been north-west of it but does not seem to be indicated.)

From GALLIÆ REGNI POTENTISS (1574)

Part of the Jesuit seminary of Marlowe's day still stands behind the austere 17th-century façade on the Rue de Venise in Rheims. Within is a sizeable garden courtyard surrounded by a quadrangle of buildings, which in recent times have been used as a hospital. It is known as the Institution Libre Saint Joseph.

François Brulart, Archdeacon of Rheims and Chaplain to King Henry IV, helped the Jesuits establish their college here close to the priory of St. Maurice late in the 16th century. The seminary of English Catholic exiles was first set up at Douai (north-west of Rheims) but in 1578 it was moved to Rheims and remained there until 1593. During this period it provided a haven for teachers and students who had been driven out of Flanders by adherents of the Prince of Orange. The joint University of Douai-Rheims, the first English college established outside England, had as its original purpose the training of missionaries to England, many of whom, unsympathetic to the English Church, had escaped from England in order to work for its destruction and the overthrow

89

of Elizabeth and her political and ecclesiastical government. It also lured many temporary visitors who came mainly out of curiosity.

Douai had opened in 1568, with Dr. Richard Smith as first Chancellor. Among its students were Edward Campion and Cuthbert Mayne and, later, Thomas Watson, from whom Marlowe had probably heard life at Douai graphically described. The fare, both at Douai and later at Rheims, was frugal in the extreme, the Spartan regime being further augmented by compulsory fasting two days a week. Emphasis was on rigorous academic study—humanities, philosophy, and jurisprudence being among subjects taught. The graduates of Rheims were men of high academic and literary attainment, not all necessarily Catholics. The seminary at Rheims was evidently synonymous with high academic learning, for in *The Taming of the Shrew* Shakespeare introduces two young men and when wishing to emphasize the classical knowledge of one he designates him a Rheims alumnus:

'freely give unto this young scholar that hath been long studying at Rheims; as cunning in Greek, Latin and other languages, as the other in music and mathematics.'

Act 11, Scene ii

Marlowe had evidently engaged in some government service before June 1587, when the letter from the Privy Council to the Cambridge authorities is dated. According to Bakeless, it is likely that Marlowe had made a secret journey to Rheims acting on instructions from someone high in Elizabeth's affairs of state. This is most likely to have been Sir Francis Walsingham himself, who directed the Queen's secret service. His spies permeated everywhere, listening to tavern conversations, observing English Catholic students on the Continent, and reporting casual conversations of suspected Englishmen abroad. We do not know the exact purpose of Marlowe's mission, but there is convincing evidence that he was at the Jesuit seminary in Rheims.

Rheims Cathedral: *the northern portal. The fantastically profuse statuary and ornamentation covering a great part of the cathedral is of exquisite beauty and in perfect proportion to the whole. No wonder Soissons has called Rheims 'the most wondrous work of human activity'.*
The beauty of Catholic ritual in this magnificent setting evidently had its appeal for Marlowe; it would not have been difficult for him to enthuse over this aspect of Catholicism when posing as a Catholic convert. When Marlowe was later accused of atheism, his opinions were reported thus by the informer, Richard Baines:

'. . . that if there be any God or any good religion, then it is in the papists, because the service of God is performed with more ceremonies, as elevation of the Mass, organs, singing men, shaven crowns & cta . . .'

All this in its full splendour Marlowe must have witnessed at Rheims.

The Queen's Secret Agent

In the pattern of Marlowe's life we can now trace the shadowy figure of Sir Francis Walsingham, a Kentish nobleman who had risen to the position of Secretary of State by virtue of his undoubted ability and patriotism. The Queen, while recognising his qualities, made unashamed use of them without ever really rewarding him for his great services beyond appointing him to a post in which he shared with Lord Burghley the main burden of the administrative responsibilities of government. But that was the Queen's way, when she so pleased.

Walsingham's work was mainly concerned with foreign affairs, and the reports of his spies soon convinced him that the safety of the country was endangered by the continued existence of Mary, Queen of Scots, around whom active Catholic intrigue was centred and directed against the life of Elizabeth. Walsingham's answer was to advocate that conspirators who plotted assassination of their Queen should be dealt with as ordinary criminals. Henceforth he became Mary's implacable enemy.

'Knowledge is never too dear' was a favourite maxim which he proceeded to live up to. He made himself the architect of Elizabeth's spy service and set about building this up to proportions never known before, devoting his vast private fortune to financing it when the Queen was too parsimonious to provide the necessary cash. At one time he kept fifty-three paid agents in foreign courts, besides eighteen others who were engaged in capacities not officially defined. A list of the names of 'sundrie foren places from whence Mr. Secretary Walsingham was wont to receive his advertisements'[1] mentions thirteen towns in France, seven in the Low Countries, five each in Italy and Spain, nine in Germany, three in the United Provinces, and three in Turkey. From all parts of England, intelligence, usually in cipher messages, reached him almost daily, to be decoded by his expert decipherer, Thomas Phelippes. His methods were wily in the extreme:

> 'He would cherish a plot some years together, admitting the Conspirators to his own and the Queens presence familiarly, but dogging them out watchfully: his Spies waited on some men every hour for three years: and lest they could not keep counsel, he dispatched them to forraign parts, taking in new Servants.'[2]

It was by these methods that he uncovered the Babington Plot which at long last provided him with the evidence to convict Mary Stuart and obtain her death warrant from the reluctant hand of Elizabeth. There is no evidence to prove whether Marlowe's work was also connected with the exposing of this conspiracy, but we do know that he was in government service at this time by the testimony of the Privy Council's letter to the Cambridge authorities. It seems highly probable that he is the 'Morley' named in a later letter dated October 2, 1587, at Utrecht to Lord Burghley as the bearer of confidential dispatches from agents and ambassadors abroad.[3]

The austere 17th-century façade of the English Jesuit College *at Rheims.*

Did he not draw a sort of English priests
From Douay to the seminary at Rheims
To hatch forth treason 'gainst their natural queen?
THE MASSACRE AT PARIS

93

Agent for England, send thy mistress word
What this detested Jacobin hath done.
Tell her, for all this, that I hope to live;
Which if I do, the papal monarch goes
To wreck, and th' antichristian kingdom falls:
These bloody hands shall tear his triple crown,
And fire accursed Rome about his ears:
I'll fire his crazed buildings, and enforce
The papal towers to kiss the lowly earth.
Navarre, give me thy hand: I here do swear
To ruinate that wicked Church of Rome,
That hatcheth up such bloody practices;
And here protest eternal love to thee,
And to the Queen of England specially,
Whom God hath bless'd for hating papistry.

THE MASSACRE AT PARIS

Left, Elizabeth I (1558–1603), *from a medallion in the British Museum.*

Right, Francis Walsingham (1530?-1590) *from a portrait in the National Portrait Gallery. Sir Francis Walsingham was in charge of Queen Elizabeth's secret service and there is little doubt that it was he who employed Marlowe in the assignments of espionage of which documentary evidence remains, and possibly others of which we know nothing, for such a trusted man who had 'done good service', and on whose behalf the Privy Council had troubled to intervene, would surely have been retained. His younger cousin, Thomas Walsingham, whom he placed in charge of the espionage for Kent, became Marlowe's patron and intimate friend.*

94

Contemporary print of scene from The Massacre *based on eye-witness accounts.*

Sir Francis Walsingham had been resident in Paris at the Faubourg St. Germain as English Ambassador at this time, and had witnessed dreadful sights of which Marlowe might later have heard first-hand accounts from him. It was estimated that some 2,000 Huguenots had been murdered.

Henry III of France occupied a precarious throne in a country torn by Protestant and Catholic factions, in which he finally met his death at the hand of a Catholic assassin. Henry salutes the great Protestant Queen of England in the death-bed scene in Marlowe's play *The Massacre at Paris* which dramatizes the bloody massacre of St. Bartholomew's Eve in 1572. It was from plots such as this that Walsingham laboured to protect the Queen by enlisting in her service loyal and able young men like Christopher Marlowe. *The Massacre at Paris* was written after Henry's death in 1589, following the defeat of the Armada, when Marlowe was possibly still in government service. The 'Agent for England' might well be Marlowe himself, or one of his acquaintances, like Robert Poley, who combined the functions of court messenger and secret agent.

95

Another close associate of Marlowe deeply involved in the Babington intrigue was Robert Poley, who inveigled himself into the confidence of the unsuspecting and impetuous Anthony Babington and was chiefly responsible for drawing him into the net prepared with such infinite care by Walsingham. Poley, an experienced and subtle government agent, who seems to have known well how to live by his wits, was to have his name indelibly linked with Marlowe's in his death, and it is likely that they got to know each other at this time. Poley was also intimately linked with young Thomas Walsingham, who like him had been employed as a courier and confidential agent.[4] He was closely assisting his cousin, Sir Francis, in this affair and was later to become Marlowe's patron. He seems to have acted as intermediary between Poley and Sir Francis Walsingham as evidenced in a letter in which Poley refers to a meeting in Seething Lane, where the London residence of Sir Francis Walsingham was situated, 'where I attended Mr. Thomas Walsingham for my secret recourse to Mr. Secretary'.[5] Ballard, one of the chief conspirators who turned Queen's evidence at the final stages, was actually arrested at Poley's lodgings shortly after a visit by Thomas Walsingham and possibly on his orders. Poley was also regularly used as a court messenger in a similar capacity as the 'Morley' mentioned above, and it is possible to trace his government employment through the payments made to him for such journeys.[6]

Mr Babingtons Lre to polley
    befo his apprehension
Robyn, Sollicitae non possunt curae mutare, rati stamina fusi *I bee ready to endure whatsoev* shalbe inflicted.* Et facere et puti Romanorum est *what my course hath bene towarde m* Secretary yo* can wyttnes, what my love towarde yo* yo** self can best tell. Procedinge at my lodginge have bene very strainge. I am the same I allwayes pretended. I pray god yo* be, and ever so remayne towarde me. Take hede to yo** acomp** least of these my mysfortunes yo* beare the blame.* Est exilium inter malos viuere *ffarewell, Sweet Robyn, if as I take the, true to me. If not Adieu,* Omnium bipedum nequissimus *Retorne me thyne answere for my satisfaction and my dyamond & what els thow wilt. The fornace is prepared wherein ou* faithe muste be tryed. ffarewell till we mete, wich god knowes when.*

                    Thyne how farr tho knowest*
                    ANTHONY BABINGTON

Letter from Anthony Babington to Robert Poley.

Poley must have worked skilfully on Babington's impetuous and emotional nature to have obtained from him the incriminating account of the plot in detail which he wrote to Mary for her approval, eliciting the reply from her which marked her doom. He had Babington's complete trust and also appears to have gained the confidence of the Scots Queen. To the last Babington was unable to see through him, and could not believe that this was the man who had betrayed him.

THE BABINGTON PLOT. Francis Walsingham's secret service intercepted and read all letters that passed between the captive Mary, Queen of Scots, and Anthony Babington's Catholic conspirators, who had hatched a desperate plot to assassinate Elizabeth and place Mary on the throne. Walsingham himself was high on the list of those who would have been murdered, yet in order to entrap the conspirators he had entertained Babington to supper at his house only a few days before. His secret agents acted with stealth and efficiency. The letters, which were conveyed in beer barrels conveniently furnished by Walsingham for the purpose, were deciphered and then speeded on their way without arousing any suspicions.

The uncovery of the plot aroused violent anti-Catholic feeling in the country for a while. It ended in the ghastly public spectacle of the execution of the traitors on a scaffold erected in St. Giles fields near Holborn by hanging, drawing and quartering, before the assembled multitude on September 20, 1586. When Elizabeth heard of the dreadful suffering inflicted on the first seven to be executed, including Babington and the treacherous Ballard who, despite his duplicity in betraying his compatriots at the last, was not spared, she ordered greater mercy to be shown to the rest. Fourteen were executed altogether. And Mary's fair head was severed at Fotheringay the following February.

A translation of the Latin issuing from Babington's mouth:
  '*These are my companions whom danger itself led.*'

Over the scaffold is the ominous phrase:
  '*One is punished in that in which one sins.*'

Carleton's A THANKFULL REMEMBRANCE (1627)

98

Traitors' Gate *at the Tower of London was the entrance by which those accused of treason were brought into the Tower by barge upon the river after trial at Westminster. More often than not those so accused had been brought to book by the agency of Walsingham and his spies. Beheading was the penalty reserved for those of noble blood; the headsman would sit in the barge with the prisoner, the blade of his axe turned away if acquitted, and towards the victim if convicted. Babington and his conspirators were also housed here, and afterwards taken in hurdles from Tower Hill to St. Giles fields for execution by the more horrible death decreed for commoners.*

We can now see that Marlowe's career in government service would inevitably bring him to the notice and probably into the confidence of such gentlemen of the court as Thomas Walsingham, who were engaged in what would appear in these dangerous times as the commendable pursuit of safeguarding the Queen's life, even though to modern minds the profession of espionage is somewhat tainted.

Marlowe's entrée once achieved, it would not take long for his gifts as a poet and dramatist to endear him to the hearts of the sensuous, theatre-loving young bloods of Elizabeth's court. Add to this the fascination of his personality, bold yet enigmatic, which transmits itself from the dark eyes of his portrait, the 'passionate look' of the poet whose 'raptures were all ayre and fire', and we begin to realise why Marlowe could not fail to rise. Secret service proved a rung in the ladder, but the main impetus came from his self-revelation as a poet of undoubted genius. One of his earliest essays in poetry had been his translation of Ovid's *Amores*, in which he wrote:

> *Verse is immortal, and shall ne'er decay.*
> *To verse let kings give place, and kingly shows,*
> *And banks o'er which gold-bearing Tagus flows.*
> *Let base-conceited wits admire vile things,*
> *Fair Phoebus lead me to the Muse's springs.*
>
> ELEGY XV

Marlowe had drunk deep at those Ovidian springs, and the influence of that heady draught never left him. This it was set the seal on his decision:

To London—and 'Divinity, Adieu!'

Part III

London 1587-1593

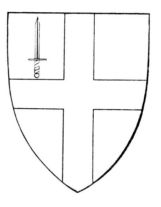

London, 1587-1593

Settle thy studies, Faustus, and begin
To sound the depth of that thou wilt profess:
Having commenc'd, be a divine in show,
Yet level at the end of every art,
And live and die in Aristotle's works.
Sweet Analytics, 'tis thou hast ravish'd me!
Bene disserere est, finis logices.
Is, to dispute well, logic's chiefest end?
Affords this art no greater miracle?
Then read no more; thou hast attain'd the end:
A greater subject fitteth Faustus' wit:

During his six and a half years of study at Corpus Christi there is no doubt that Marlowe had become steadily disillusioned by the limitations of such medieval learning as was offered by the schoolmen and university pundits, especially where theology was concerned. He had found it expedient to 'be a divine in show', and to seek his 'world of profit and delight' secretly in his reading of the classics and the pursuance of his art. Indeed, whether Marlowe had ever seriously considered becoming a churchman is open to question. His study of Machiavellian principles had early taught him to use such means as providence offered for his advancement. Archbishop Parker's grant was one of these.

The end of his study under Parker's scholarship grant was directed towards ordination and probably the acceptance of some country parish living. When the moment came, one feels that Marlowe would not have been at a loss for persuasive arguments as to why he should decline the offer of the cloth. Having excused himself to the Cambridge authorities as best he might, we may imagine that he packed up his belongings in his room at Corpus with a sigh of relief, and took horse to London, his spirit exultant, singing, perhaps, one of the lovely Elizabethan lyrics of which his friend Thomas Watson was such a connoisseur. ' 'Tis a pretty toy to be a poet' he had written when composing his first great dramatic work *Tamburlaine the Great*, which he had probably just completed at the university. The manuscript of this he would take to Edward Alleyn of the Lord Admiral's company of players, and receive payment for it, perhaps six pounds or so.

Marlowe was not without friends in London. Tom Watson, too, was a poet, and intimate with the Walsinghams. Not only government service but his literary efforts, though yet unpublished, had found him friends. In the more hectic atmosphere of the metropolis he was quickly to be drawn into the society of young literary men, who rather prided themselves on being slightly disreputable—the adventurous and high-spirited souls who, some of them of good family, and all of them well-educated, aspired to be the poet-laureates of England and did not scorn the drama for its excitement and the immediate

Birdseye view of London by Pieter Van Den Keere from Norden's Speculum Britanniae (1593)

Map of London in 1593, *showing Bankside, where the Rose Theatre stood (here called the Play House) at which many of Marlowe's plays would have been shown; Newgate Prison, where he was lodged for a space; and Norton Folgate where he had lodgings.*

> 'The sight of London to my exil'd eyes
> Is as Elysium to a new-come soul;
> Not that I love the city or the men,
> But that it harbours him I hold so dear.'   EDWARD II

These may have been Marlowe's own emotions when he returned to London, if it meant reunion with his young friend Thomas Walsingham, who, like Shakespeare's Southampton, was in a position to be a patron of poets at an early age.

In the will of Thomas' father, Sir Thomas Walsingham III, who died in 1584, leaving his estates in Kent to his eldest son Edmund, there is mention of my 'howse in London'. This is probably where Thomas would have been living for at any rate part of the year. Where exactly it stood is not known. Queen Elizabeth later granted him a splendid house in Whitehall, which was named Walsingham House. It was sold in King James' reign to the Duke of Buckingham. At the death of his brother Edmund without issue in 1589, Thomas came into the entire inheritance.

lucrative inducements it offered (though paltry enough), for most of them had trouble in keeping the wolf from the door. Of such were the University Wits, as this group of new dramatists fledged from the universities were called.

Among the University Wits were two from Cambridge with whom Marlowe was probably already acquainted, Robert Greene and Thomas Nashe, both from St. John's College, the former a few years older than Marlowe, the latter two or three years his junior. Others of their circle were George Peele, Thomas Lodge, John Marston, George Chapman, Matthew Royden, Michael Drayton, Samuel Daniel, William Warner, to mention only those we know were personally acquainted with Marlowe, or were closely associated with his friends. There was also Thomas Kyd, the son of a humble scrivener and not a university man, but a successful playwright who became a close associate of the cobbler's son.

Where Marlowe lodged upon first coming to London we do not know, but a record two years later, in September 1589, reveals him as having lodgings with Thomas Watson in the Liberty of Norton Folgate near the Curtain Theatre. Until the end of his Cambridge days Marlowe's record had been clear; more than that, it had been good. No less an authority than the Privy Council had testified to his good behaviour. London was to see him more often in trouble.

The City

'It is a very populous city, so that one can scarcely pass along the streets, on account of the throng. The inhabitants are magnificently apparelled, and are extremely proud and overbearing.'[1]

VISIT OF FREDERICK, DUKE OF WURTEMBERG, 1592 *(translated from the German)*

'In euery street, carts and Coaches make such a thundering as if the world ranne vpon wheeles: at euerie corner, men, women, and children meete in such shoales, that postes are sette vp of purpose to strengthen the houses, lest with iustling one another they should shoulder them downe. Besides, hammers are beating in one place, Tubs hooping in another, Pots clincking in a third, water-tankards running at tilt in a fourth: heere are Porters sweating vnder burdens, there Merchants-men bearing bags of money, Chapmen (as if they were at Leape-frog) skippe out of one shop into another: Trades-men (as if they were dauncing Galliards) are lusty at legges and neuer stand still!'

Thomas Dekker: THE SEVEN DEADLY SINNES OF LONDON, 1606

'London, a place both for the beauty of building, infinite riches, variety of all things, that excelleth all the cities of the world, insomuch that it may be called the storehouse and mart of all Europe. . . . It hath divers hospitals for the relieving of the poor, six-score fair churches for divine service, a glorious bourse which they call the Royal Exchange, for the meeting of merchants of all countries where any traffic is to be had. And among all the strange and beautiful shows me thinketh there is none so notable as the bridge which crosseth the Thames.'

John Lyly: EUPHUES AND HIS ENGLAND, 1581

'The manner of the most gentlemen and noblemen also is to house themselves (if possible they may) in the suburbs of the city, because most commonly the aire there beeinge somewhat at large, the place is healthy, and through the distance from the body of the town the noise not much, and so consequently quiet.'

From CYVILE AND UNCYVILE LIFE, 1579

Marlowe, not loving the city or the men, resided in the suburb of Norton Folgate with his friend Thomas Watson in 1589.

Opposite

The grim bastion of the Tower of London *brooding over the little city had its associations with Walsingham; his grandfather, Sir Edmund Walsingham, held the important post of Lieutenant of the Tower during Henry VIII's reign. Sir Edmund was responsible for a steep rise in the family fortunes. Knighted at the battle of Flodden Field, he had gradually won the King's special affection, receiving a grant of monastic lands and many other favours. The inscription on his tomb at Chistlehurst relates that he was:*

> '*A knight some tyme of worthie fame,*
>
> . . . . .
>
> *Sir Edmond Walsingham was his name,*
> *Lieutenant hee was of London Tower,*
> *Servinge therein 22 yeares space,*
> *Continually in his Princes good grace.*'

*In his office of Lieutenant he had great responsibility and was in direct charge of the many important prisoners admitted to the Tower: Thomas Cromwell, the Earl of Essex, Henry's two queens (Anne Boleyn and Catherine Howard), Bishop Fisher, and Sir Thomas More whose remark: '*I pray you Master Lieutenant, see me safe up, and for my coming down let me shift for myself,*' was addressed to Sir Edmund when attending him to his execution.*

MAP OF MOORFIELDS and its environs, *c.* 1559 believed to have been the work of Anthonis van den Wyngaerde and engraved by Franciscus Hogenborg.[2] 'Norton ffowlegate' (not named here), where Marlowe and Watson resided, was that part of Bishopsgate Street adjacent to the entrance of Hog Lane. R. M. Holmes, describing the map in his *Moorfields in* 1559, has noted that 'the engraver has taken care to indicate the presence of houses of some quality and size' at this point —the 'many faire houses' in which were lodged the 'worshipfull persons' mentioned by Stow. Probably Marlowe lodged in one of these. Note the well for drawing water in the main street, and the many ditches and watercourses with which the area is traversed. The windmills were evidently used for grinding corn denoted by the sacks, while Moorfields itself was a waste ground used by the laundresses—one has pegged her sheet out flat to dry, while two lads stagger under such a laundry basket as might have harboured Falstaff. The scene is enlivened by little figures and animals to give an amusing representation of the times that invites close study. Marlowe's way into the City lay through Bishopsgate, on the turreted top of which the heads of traitors and criminals were spitted as gruesome warning to passers-by. Hog Lane, where the Bradley-Marlowe-Watson duel was fought, is the lane leading from Bishopsgate Street to the windmills. The ditch mentioned in the Inquisition is shown flanking Hog Lane on either side, and there are many little bridges leading into 'Fynnesburie Field', which was a popular duelling ground. Archery was also practised here and in Spitalfields, while musketry resounded from the Artillery Ground next door. Just off the map to the north were the Theatre and Curtain playhouses.

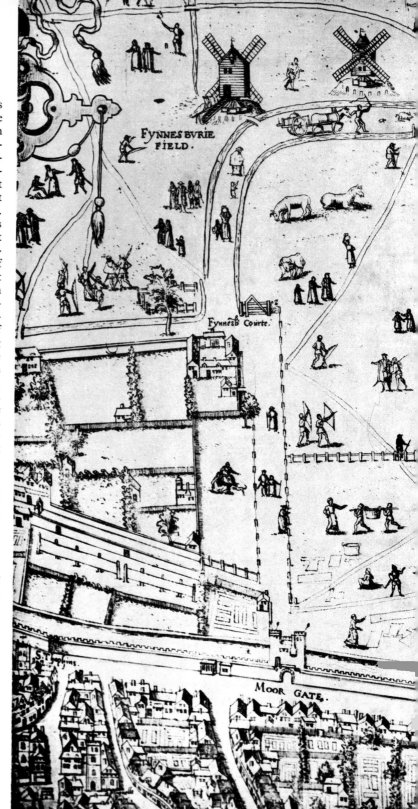

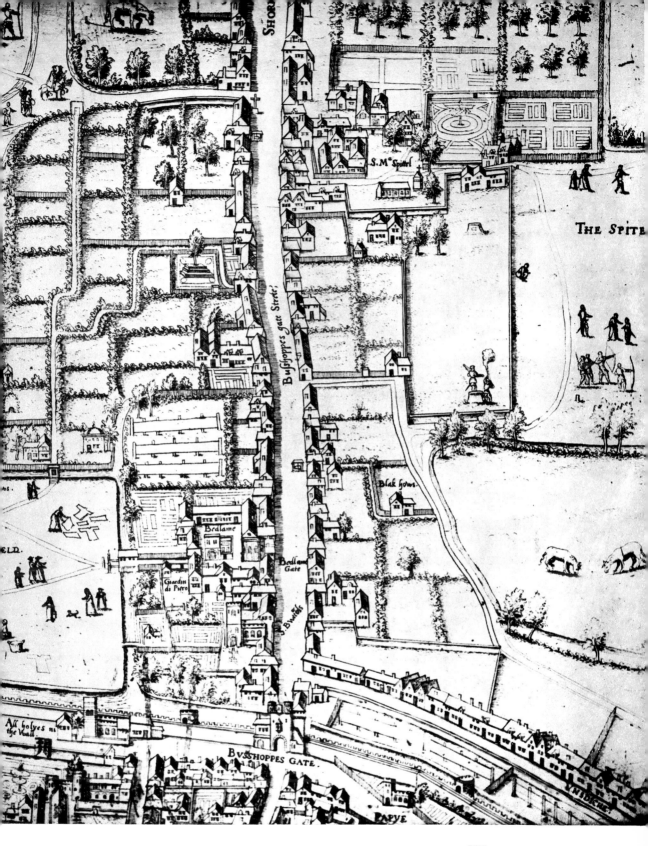

SHOR

S. M Spitel

THE SPITE

Busshoppes gatt Strete

Blak hows

Bedlame

Bedlam
Gate

Giardin
di Pietro

J. Busck

ELD.

All holyes ne
the Wall

BVSSHOPPES GATE.

PAPYE

VNDR

107

London was a city crowded with taverns of all types and sizes, well over fifty of them. At the larger inns, where an inner court-yard surrounded by galleries afforded a suitable setting, plays were regularly per-formed, beginning promptly at two o'clock in the afternoon to conform with the City regulations, thus allowing the spectators to get to their homes before dark. Such per-formances took place at Belle Savage's Inn on Ludgate Hill, the Bull in Bishopsgate Street, and the Bell and the Cross Keys in Gracechurch Street or at the Four Swans whose courtyard is shown here.

Drawing from H. T. Stephenson's SHAKESPEARE'S LONDON

'*Conversation:*

But I pray you tell me one thing, when saw you our friend mistresse C? now in good soothe, she is a kind creature, and a very gentle Peat: I promise you I saw her not since you and I drank a pinte of wine with her in the fish market. O gossip (saith the other) there is a great change since that time, for they haue bene faine to pawne all that euer they haue, and yet God knowes her husband lies still in prison. O the passion of my heart (saith another) is all their great and glorious shew come to nothing? good Lord what a world is this. Why gossip (saith another) it was neuer like to be otherwise, for they loued euer to goe fine and fare daintily, and by my fay gossip, this is not a world for those matters, and thereupon I drinke to you.'

Robert Tofte: THE BATCHELORS BANQUET, 1603

'In all our inns we have plenty of ale, beer and sundry kinds of wine ... Howbeit of all in England there are no worse inns than in London, and yet many are there far better than the best that I have heard of in any forren country, if all circumstances be duly considered ... And it is a world to see how each owner of them contendeth with other for goodness of entertainment of their guests, as about fineness and change of linen, furniture of bedding, beauty of rooms, service at the table, costliness of plate, strength of drink, variety of wines, or well using of horses. Finally there is not so much omitted among them as the gorgeousness of their very signs at their doors, wherein some do consume thirty or forty pounds, a mere vanity in mine opinion; but so vain will they needs be, and that not only to give some outward token of the innkeepers wealth, but also to procure good guests to the frequenting of their houses in hope there to be well used.'

William Harrison: DESCRIPTION OF ENGLAND, 1587

108

Street names of Marlowe's London *which still exist, superimposed on a picture of the narrow lane leading past the site of the old Clink prison, nearby the Rose Theatre on Bankside. This is a path Marlowe must often have trod on his way to the Rose, which stood in Rose Alley barely a hundred yards from here.*

William Sayer als Yorcke.   *Humfrey Hales als Blewmantle.*   *Nicholas Padsley als Rouge Dragon.*   *Richard Lea als Richmond.*   *Robert Glover als Somerset.*   *Robert Cooke als Clarenciulx Kinge of Armes.*

THE FUNERAL OF SIR PHILIP SIDNEY

Sir Philip Sidney, the admired poet and patron of poets, died a hero's death at the battle of Zutphen. The funeral took place amid general mourning on February 16, 1587. At this time Marlowe was probably already working as one of Walsingham's agents and as Sir Philip Sidney's father-in-law, Sir Francis Walsingham would have felt the loss keenly. The bereaved widow was the Lady Frances, Sir Francis Walsingham's only daughter. Thomas Walsingham's elder brother Edmund was one of the pall-bearers at the funeral, which was one of the most spectacular events of that year, no less than 700 mourners taking part. All of London seemed to have turned out (the press was so great) to watch the magnificently sombre procession and to mourn in sympathy.

At the head of the procession came 32 groomsmen, each representing one year of Sidney's life. These were followed by officers of his foot and horse regiments. Next his standard, embroidered with the Cross of St. George and porcupines with his device *Vix ea nostra voco*, and 60 gentlemen and yeomen, and behind these his chief physician and surgeon and his steward. Next squires and knights among his kinsfolk and friends, including Sir Francis Drake, followed by the preacher of the funeral sermon and two chaplains. Then came the bearer of a pennon with the Sidney arms followed by two of his horses, mounted by pages, one of whom trailed a broken lance, the other held a battle-axe reversed. Then came a standard bearer leading the *Heralds carrying the insignia of his Knighthood* (above) followed by Clarenceaux-King-at-Arms and a Gentleman Usher to the Corps. The five heralds carrying the 'hatchments and dignity' of Sidney's knighthood: his spurs, his gauntlets, his helmet surmounted by the wild boar which was an important part of the insignia of the Sidney crest, his shield, and his standard.

Behind the coffin with its velvet pall, the corners of which were held by Fulke Greville, Edward Dyer, Edward Wotton, and Thomas Dudley, walked the chief mourner, Sir Philip's younger brother, Robert Sidney, followed by his other kinsfolk. Gentlemen ushers and noblemen on horseback followed, including earls and the greatest in the realm. After them representatives of the States of Holland, where Sidney had died, and following, the Lord Mayor of London in his robes and officials of the City and members of the Company of Grocers, and last 300 London citizens bearing weapons reversed, marching three abreast. The Cathedral was hung in black, and after the funeral a double volley was fired by soldiers from the churchyard.

In the outpouring of elegiac verse which followed Sidney's death, in which the two universities vied to outdo each other, it seems unlikely that Marlowe would not have taken part, since in his close connection with the Walsinghams he could not have failed to mourn the loss of so great a poet, who was also their kinsman. Quite possibly he might have been introduced to Sir Philip through Walsingham, as Sidney's great interest in the encouragement of literary genius was well known. Further searches among the Latin verses contributed may yet produce something attributable to Marlowe.

110

BANKSIDE. 'The Anchor' on Bankside stands on the site of an old waterside tavern which in Elizabethan times was the inn of river pirates, smugglers, trollops from the houses of ill-fame nearby, workers and pleasure-seekers (from the gallants and ground-lings who comprised the theatre audiences to the actors themselves). Within a stone's throw, amid the maze of tiny cobbled medieval streets of this wharfside district of London, lie Rose Alley and Globe Alley where the Rose and the Globe theatres formerly stood. In Marlowe's day the Rose was the only theatre on Bankside, and there can be no doubt at all that he knew it and the inn here represented. The present structure recalls the 18th century rather than Elizabethan times, as the original inn was largely destroyed by the South Bank fire of 1676. An unconfirmed tradition survives, however, that a chamber in the original inn served as a 'tiring room' for the actors, i.e. for donning of their costumes, which were often of lavish splendour, costing as much as the poor playwright received for his script. It is a sobering thought that Edward Alleyn probably made far more money out of Marlowe's plays than their author, who had need to be employed in government service, or to seek generous patronage, in order to keep himself alive. The two posts in front of the door mark the boundaries of the Liberty of the Clink. Directly opposite stood the grim wills of the Clink prison within which Marlowe's friend and fellow playwright, Thomas Lodge, was languishing for non-payment of his tailor's bill in March 1587. Marlowe arrived in London in the summer of this year.

Further along Bankside were the brothels inhabited by the 'Winchester Geese', so called because the brothels were in the possession of the Bishop of Winchester.[3]

A BANKSIDE THEATRE. This view of a theatre somewhat similar to the Rose was drawn by Hollar in 1618–1620 (published in 1647). This structure has been variously identified as the Rose, the Hope, or the Globe, but, since contemporary maps are not noteworthy for their accuracy either as to locations or delineations of structure, one cannot be sure.

We do know that the Rose was built about 1588, and was probably of circular shape (although Adams thinks it may have been octagonal). Henslowe's accounts, especially those of 1592 and 1595, indicate that the building was set on a brick foundation but that the structure itself was of wood and plaster, open to the sky in the centre and with a thatched roof over the galleries. The tiring room would have been to the rear of the stage with another room above it and surmounting this a hut like that shown in de Witt's drawing of The Swan (see p. 199). Above this would have been a ceilinged box, topped by a flag. If this view of Hollar's is of the Rose, it has failed to include the turret-like superstructure built in 1591/2. Perhaps this was later demolished when plays were no longer presented here. There is no record of a play having been given here after 1603. Henslowe's lease expired in 1605 but his son-in-law, Edward Alleyn, evidently paid tithes on the property as late as 1622. It is thought that it may have had a renewed life for some sort of public use about 1618 1620. Prize fights were supposedly held here after 1620.

The Rose is clearly shown in Norden's 1593 map (page 103) but is here called 'The Playhouse'. It is known to have been situated on the north side of Maiden Lane at the corner of Rose Alley about 250 feet distant from the river. Its name was derived from the rose garden which had formerly occupied the site.

EDWARD ALLEYN was the son of a London innkeeper of some property who died when Edward was only four years old. His mother subsequently married a haberdasher named John Browne. The first appearance of Alleyn's name as an actor is on a list of the Earl of Worcester's players in 1586.

When Marlowe arrived in London with the manuscript of the First Part of *Tamburlaine the Great*, Alleyn was in his twenty-first year and ripe for great things. With the performance of this play the two men, actor and dramatist, rose to instant acclaim. Subsequently the partnership continued a close one, Alleyn in many cases retaining personal ownership of Marlowe's plays. It was Marlowe's great heroes, 'Tamburlaine', 'The Jew' and 'Faustus', that provided Alleyn with precisely the material best suited to his particular gifts, and his swift rise to fame was connected with Marlowe's success as a dramatist to such an extent that the title roles of Marlowe's plays became identifiable with Alleyn. Long after Marlowe's death he continued to play these roles to the delight of London audiences.

Alleyn was an astute business man, and in 1592 he married Joan Woodward, the stepdaughter of Philip Henslowe, proprietor of the Rose, then the only theatre on Bankside at which most of Marlowe's plays were performed. Thus started a theatrical partnership that made Alleyn's fortune. Besides interests in other theatres, Alleyn eventually also added the coarser amusements of the Bear Gardens, and in 1604 he and Henslowe became joint Masters of the Royal Game to James I.

Towards the end of his life he founded and endowed the college at Dulwich which commemorates his name. In the archives at Dulwich are preserved Alleyn's letters to his wife and other documents. Amongst these there is one reference to Shakespeare, an entry in his diary on June 19, 1609: 'Shakespers Sonnets 5d.' They were just off the press. Shakespeare and Alleyn were business rivals. Perhaps they did not care for each other. As far as we know, Alleyn never acted in any of the Shakespeare plays.

Edward Alleyn

'*Not Roscius, not Esope those tragedians admyred before Christ was borne, could ever performe more in action than famous Ned Allen,*' *wrote Thomas Nashe in his* Pierce Penilesse (1592) *by which time Alleyn had become established as the foremost tragedian in England, the interpreter of Marlowe's heroes. Doubtless it was to this connection that Robert Greene was referring when he hailed Marlowe as '*Thou famous gracer of Tragedians.*'

(*From the portrait at Dulwich College*)

Donald Wolfit in the title role first made famous
by Edward Alleyn in the Old Vic production of
Tamburlaine the Great, *directed by Tyrone
Guthrie in* 1951.

(Photographs by John Vickers Studio)

Tamburlaine the Great

MEANDER:
*Your majesty shall shortly have your wish,
And ride in triumph through Persepolis.*
TAMBURLAINE:
*And ride in triumph through Persepolis!
Is it not brave to be a king, Techelles!—
Usumcasane and Theridamas,
Is it not passing brave to be a king,
And ride in triumph through Persepolis?*
TECHELLES:
O, my lord, it is sweet and full of pomp!
USUMCASANE:
To be a king, is half to be a god.
THERIDAMAS:
*A god is not so glorious as a king:
I think the pleasure they enjoy in heaven,
Cannot compare with kingly joys in earth;—
To wear a crown enchas'd with pearl and gold,
Whose virtues carry with it life and death;
To ask and have, command and be obey'd;
When looks breed love, with looks to gain the prize,
Such power attractive shines in princes' eyes.*

PART I, Act II, Scene v.

TWO ASPECTS OF TAMBURLAINE.

TAMBURLAINE declares himself:
*I hold the Fates bound fast in iron chains,
And with my hand turn Fortune's wheel about;
And sooner shall the sun fall from his sphere
Than Tamburlaine be slain or overcome.
Draw forth thy sword thou mighty man-at-arms
Intending but to raze my charmed skin,
And Jove himself will stretch his hand from heaven
To ward the blow, and shield me safe from harm.
See, how he rains down heaps of gold in showers,
As if he meant to give my soldiers pay!*

PART I, Act I, Scene ii.

TAMBURLAINE in love:
*Zenocrate, lovelier than the love of Jove,
Brighter than the silver Rhodope,
Fairer than whitest snow on Scythian hills,
Thy person is more worth to Tamburlaine
Than the possession of the Persian crown,
Which gracious stars have promis'd at my birth.
A hundred Tartars shall attend on thee,
Mounted on steeds swifter than Pegasus;
Thy garments shall be made of Median silk,
Enchas'd with precious jewels of mine own,
More rich and valurous than Zenocrate's;
With milk-white harts upon an ivory sled
Thou shalt be drawn amidst the frozen pools,
And scale the icy mountains' lofty tops,
Which with thy beauty will be soon resolv'd:
My martial prizes, with five hundred men,
Won on the fifty-headed Volga's waves,
Shall we all offer to Zenocrate,
And then myself to fair Zenocrate.*
TECHELLES:
What now! in love?
TAMBURLAINE:
*Techelles, women must be flattered:
But this is she with whom I am in love.*

PART I, Act I, Scene ii.

Map from Abraham Ortelius' Theatrum Orbis Terrarum (1579). *Marlowe evidently used Ortelius' atlas as the source of his geography for the second part of* Tamburlaine the Great. *In the passage quoted we can discern Marlowe the thinker as well as Tamburlaine the conqueror. His prophetic utterances about the cutting of the Suez Canal and the discovery of Australia are remarkable.*

Give me a map; then let me see how much
Is left for me to conquer all the world.
That these, my boys, may finish all my wants.
Here I began to march towards Persia,
Along Armenia and the Caspian Sea,
And thence unto Bithynia, where I took
The Turk and his great empress prisoners.
Then march'd I into Egypt and Arabia;
And here, not far from Alexandria,
Whereas the Terene and the Red Sea meet,
Being distant less than full a hundred leagues,
I meant to cut a channel to them both,
That men might quickly sail to India.
From thence to Nubia near Borno-lake,
And so along the Æthiopian sea,
Cutting the tropic line of Capricorn,
I conquer'd all as far as Zanzibar.
Then by the northern part of Africa,

I came at last to Graecia, and from thence
To Asia, where I stay against my will;
Which is from Scythia, where I first began,
Backwards and forwards near five thousand leagues.
Look here, my boys; see, what a world of ground
Lies westward from the midst of Cancer's line
Unto the rising of this earthly globe,
Whereas the sun, declining from our sight,
Begins the day with our Antipodes!
And shall I die, and this unconquered?
Lo, here, my sons, are all the golden mines,
Inestimable drugs and precious stones,
More worth than Asia and the world beside;
And from th' Antarctic Pole eastward behold
As much more land, which never was descried,
Wherein are rocks of pearl that shine as bright
As all the lamps that beautify the sky!!
And shall I die, and this unconquered?

PART II, Act v, Scene iii.

The death of Cosroe.

COSROE:
The strangest men that ever nature made!
I know not how to take their tyrannies.
My bloodless body waxeth chill and cold,
And with my blood my life slides through my wound;
My soul begins to take her flight to hell,
And summons all my senses to depart:
The heat and moisture, which did feed each other,
For want of nourishment to feed them both,
Are dry and cold: and now doth ghastly Death
With greedy talons gripe my bleeding heart,
And like a harpy tires on my life.—
Theridamas and Tamburlaine, I die!
And fearful vengeance light upon you both!

PART I, Act II, Scene vii.

TAMBURLAINE:
'Now clear the triple region of the air,
And let the Majesty of Heaven behold
Their scourge and terror tread on emperors.
Smile, stars that reign'd at my nativity,
And dim the brightness of your neighbour lamps;
Disdain to borrow light of Cynthia!
For I, the chiefest lamp of all the earth,
First rising in the east with mild aspect,
But fixed now in the meridian line,
Will send up fire to your turning spheres,
And cause the sun to borrow light of you.
My sword struck fire from his coat of steel,
Even in Bithynia, when I took this Turk;
As when a fiery exhalation,
Wrapt in the bowels of a freezing cloud,
Fighting for passage, make[s] the welkin crack,
And casts a flash of lightning to the earth:
But, ere I march to wealthy Persia,
Or leave Damascus and th' Egyptian fields,
As was the fame of Clymene's brain-sick son
That almost brent the axle-tree of heaven,
So shall our swords, our lances, and our shot
Fill all the air with fiery meteors;
Then, when the sky shall wax as red as blood,
It shall be said I made it red myself,
To make me think of naught but blood and war.

PART I, Act IV, Scene ii.

The Bradley Affray

History is often silent, except when the law steps in to record and file for legal reference. So it is with Marlowe that nothing more is known of him personally for two years after his arrival in London, apart from what may be gleaned of the startling success of his career as a dramatist, until the dusty records of the Middlesex Sessions Rolls, No. 284, reveal that Christopher Marlowe and Thomas Watson were amongst prisoners delivered to the gaol at Newgate between September 9 and October 2, 1589. What can have been their crime? The researches of Professor Mark Eccles have established that the charge was one of homicide.[1]

The story unravelled in the Inquisition on one William Bradley, there lying dead and slain of a wound, six inches in depth and one inch in breadth, in the right side of his chest, from the sword of Thomas Watson, tells of a fatal duel. William Bradley, the twenty-six-year-old son of an innkeeper in Gray's Inn Lane, Holborn, had had a quarrel with Watson which had its origin in a debt of £14 that Bradley had incurred to another innkeeper, John Alleyn, the brother of Edward Alleyn, the actor. Bradley failing to settle the debt, Alleyn had threatened suit in the Court of Common Pleas through his attorney, Hugh Swift.

Bradley's reply had been to get a pal of his, George Orrell, who had a taste for such pastimes, to threaten Attorney Swift with a beating-up if he dared to take the matter to court. Whereupon Swift appealed to the Queen's Bench for securities of the peace 'against George Orrell being in fear of death &c'.[2] Swift happened to be Watson's brother-in-law, and, moved by these unpleasant threats, Watson apparently agreed to assist in giving Bradley a taste of his own medicine, and shortly thereafter Swift, with Watson and Alleyn, set out to take the belligerent Bradley to task. Bradley in turn now also lodged a petition for securities against 'Hugo Swift, & John Allen & Thomas Watson being in fear of death &c'.[3] Not content with this, Bradley, who had a record as a notable brawler, and apparently smarting under some insult or injury that Watson in particular had done him on the occasion of their last encounter, decided to seek him out for vengeance, and was lurking in the neighbourhood of Watson's lodgings in Norton Folgate on the afternoon of September 18, some time after dinner between two and three o'clock. No Watson appeared. However, he waited close by in Hog Lane, and presently Kit Marlowe sauntered forth. He was evidently known to Bradley as Watson's friend (possibly they actually shared lodgings, at any rate they were near neighbours) and he must have accosted Marlowe, saucily one assumes. Swords were drawn and a fight began. Their duel was only interrupted by the timely appearance of Watson himself, at whose advent Bradley now cries out in words that intimate clearly with whom his real quarrel lies: 'arte thowe nowe come then I will haue a boute with the',[1] and he turns on Watson. Marlowe withdraws, and the opponents fall to it. Bradley fights with both sword and dagger and means business.

London street map of 1799 *shows Hog Lane, which was part of present-day Worship Street and ran between 'The Curtain' (now Curtain Road) and Norton Folgate (now part of Shoreditch High Street). Present-day Folgate Street apparently was White Lion Yard. Marlowe and Watson resided presumably in one of the houses in Norton Folgate, opposite the entrance to Hog Lane, where Bradley was probably lurking in wait.*[5]

Up and down Hog Lane with thrust and parry they go, until Watson is driven to the edge of the ditch at the north end of Hog Lane and, turning at bay, in desperation gives Bradley the fatal thrust home. By this time a crowd has gathered, and both Watson and Marlowe know better than to flee. They stand their ground to plead homicide in self-defence. Watson has a wound to show for his part, and when Constable Stephen Wylde, tailor of Norton Folgate, arrives, they go submissively enough to make their statement before the justice of the district, who is Sir Owen Hopton, Lieutenant of the Tower. Their warrant of arrest being drawn up 'on suspicion of murder', they are duly lodged in Newgate Gaol, as dank and dismal a nurse for a wounded man as one could conceive.

*   *   *

NEWGATE PRISON
(now the site of the Old Bailey)

*A graphic description of the horrors to be
encountered in Newgate has been left on
record in* The Black Dog of Newgate *by
Luke Hutton, a contemporary prisoner with
Marlowe and Watson. In this dreadful place
of rat-infested cells starving men in irons
more often died of disease and fevers brought
on by overcrowding, filth and lack of sani-
tation, and bad food and water, than through
the execution of the law. Gentlemen with the
necessary means could buy their way to better
lodgings, and the gaolers grew rich on the
miseries of others. The condemned cell,
known as Limbo, a dark hole where no light
penetrated, was situated over the prison gate.*
(Picture from H. T. Stephenson: Shakespeare's London)

A Rat doth rob the candle from my handes,
And then a hundred Rats all sallie forth,
As if they would convoye their pryze of worth,
In vaine I strive to reobteyne whats lost.

. . . . .

Whilst thus I lay in irons under ground,
I heard a man that begged for releese:
And in a chaine of iron was he bound,
Whose clattering noise filde full my heart with griefe,
Begging one penny to buie a hundred bread
Hungerd and stervd, for want of food ny dead.

An other sorrye soule, without a ragge,
Hurckling for colde, in whom all want appeares,
At last gan speake, as if he ment to bragge,
And thus he sayes: Heare have I been nine years
Tell you of woes; when you my woes have seene,
And yet have many men more wofull beene.
Luke Hutton's THE BLACKE DOGGE OF NEWGATE, *pub. in* 1600

The next day, September 19, the Middlesex county coroner, Ion Chalkhill,
held the inquest on Bradley with a jury of twelve sworn men, and after hearing
and recording the evidence decided in their favour that Thomas Watson slew
William Bradley 'in self-defence' and 'not by felony', in the manner related
by the defendants. Coroner and jurors set their seals to the inquisition, and
Marlowe and Watson doubtless heaved a sigh of relief, for now it would be
only a matter of time before the Queen's official pardon would release them
free men.[6]

Marlowe, as one not involved in the actual homicide, was entitled to bail
which he presently procured from lawyer 'Richard Kytchine of Clifford's Inn,
gentleman, & Humfrey Rowland of East Smithfeilde, horner' on their sureties
of twenty pounds apiece, while he himself was bound over in the sum of forty
pounds on the undertaking that he would personally 'appear at the next Sessions

'*Art thowe nowe come? Then I will haue a boute with the.*'

Woodcut from the title page of Middleton and Rowley's play A FAIR QUARREL, 1617

of Newgate to answer everything that may be alleged against him on the part of the Queen, and shall not depart without the permission of the Court'.

The next Sessions, as it turned out, were held on December 3, and Marlowe duly appeared to find himself confronting the familiar face of Sir Roger Manwood, Chief Baron of the Exchequer, as one of the four judges on the Bench. This Kentish gentleman must have listened with some interest to the story of the activities of his former protégé, and perhaps found some gratification in dismissing him. When Sir Roger died almost exactly two years later, Marlowe acknowledged his debt to the great man, though for what other favours we do not know, by composing a Latin epitaph in his memory exhorting the innocent to mourn and evil-doers to rejoice (notwithstanding the reputation for corruption Manwood had acquired during his years of public office!).[7]

Also present was William Fleetwood, the Recorder of London, before whom Marlowe had been admitted to bail on the surities of Kitchen and Rowland, who seems to have taken a special interest in Marlowe, for he presently purchased one of the earliest editions of *Tamburlaine the Great*. Fleetwood was the busiest of all the Middlesex judges and had much to do in subduing the minor turmoils of the times in London, including disturbances at the playhouses. It was possibly in some such incident that Marlowe uttered threats against the constables of Holywell Street, the players' quarter of Shoreditch, as a result of which he was arraigned for disorderly conduct and once more brought before Sir Owen Hopton. This time, over two years later, on May 9, 1592, Sir Owen was content to bind him over to keep the peace on promise of payment of twenty pounds 'in good and lawful English money' which he would raise 'from his goods, and Chattle lands and tenements if he should fail in his promise'.⁸ This seems to indicate that Marlowe had achieved respectability and some property. He is now referred to as 'Christopher Marle of London, gentleman' instead of 'yoman', by which he was designated at the time of his being lodged in Newgate two years before. Presumably he may have changed his lodgings to an address within the City of London, but it is not stated where. He was specifically bound over to keep the peace towards the constable of Holywell Street, Allen Nicholls, and his underconstable, Nicholas Helliott, who had brought the charges. A proper couple of 'Dogberries' one would like to think.

⁹Considerable research around the identities of his two sureties, Richard Kitchen and Humphrey Rowland, has revealed some interesting connections. Kitchen practised law at Clifford's Inn, and came of a Yorkshire family with a long record of service with the Cliffords. His readiness to come to Marlowe's aid, though doubtless for a fee, may also have stemmed from personal friendship, for he was later to appear as Philip Henslowe's attorney. Many years later he gave evidence on behalf of the host of the Mermaid Tavern in Bread Street, 'William Wiliamson', in a Star Chamber case on June 1, 1600. This was the tavern frequented by Ralegh and his circle, of whom Marlowe was one. Kitchen seems to have been handy with a sword, too, and was not without troubles similar to Marlowe's Hog Lane affair himself. He would appear to have at least moved in the circle of Marlowe's associates, as testified by the record of his legal dealings with them.¹⁰

Humphrey Rowland, a much humbler man, is described as 'a very honest poore man' and a 'maker of Lanterne hornes' in an exchange of letters between the Lord Mayor and Lord Burghley concerning his admission into the Cutlers' Company in 1583. He fairly frequently stood surety for others, and that he did so for Marlowe on this occasion does not argue any close connection between them. He was for several years constable of East Smithfield where he dwelt.¹¹

Marlowe had been admitted to bail on October 1, so that he was under a fortnight in Newgate. Watson, however, only gained his final release on February 12, 1590, after five weary months in prison. We have no record as to how he passed his time; possibly trying to forget his misery by drinking in 'the Boozing Ken', the cellar frequented by the privileged prisoners who had gained lodgings on the 'masters' side' after proper remuneration to the gaoler, and not in the dismal underground 'Stone Hold' with the common prisoners. As for Marlowe, the story is repeated by Baines that he used his brief stay in Newgate learning how to make counterfeit coins from one 'poole a prisoner in newgate who hath greate Skill in mixture of mettals', and that he after-wards boasted that he had 'as good Right to Coine as the Queen of England . . . [and] ment through help of a Cunninge stamp maker to Coin ffrench Crownes pistolets and English shillinges'.¹² This sounds like reportage of Marlowe's table talk in ribald vein, and not like a boast that was intended to be taken seriously. Although he was probably an arrogant young man, and may well have considered that his verse entitled him to be a 'king' in the best Ovidian sense, yet it seems highly unlikely that he would have been willing to risk the penalty of boiling in oil for counterfeiting, and that he would have boasted of his intent to boot! Nor is there evidence of his need to resort to such desperate measures. The cobbler's son, as has often been remarked by his biographers, does not seem to have lacked money at any time in his career, probably because he had generous patronage. The startling remarks credited to him by the informer Richard Baines may be taken as another example of that mordant wit which led Marlowe into trouble when uttered in the presence of those liable to misunderstand him. However, one can well believe that his interest as a dramatist would have been aroused by such a character of low life as this Poole, who is not to be confused with Robert Poley, the government agent, but has been identified by Eccles as John Poole, a prisoner in Newgate on suspicion of coining, who remained there for several years from July 1587 onwards.[13]

A Summary

THE BRADLEY AFFRAY, one of those instances when Marlowe was in trouble with the law, has been seized upon by his biographers to present him in an unfavourable light as a man of violent temper. This not only ignores the testimony of the times in general, the Elizabethan way of life, but also the testimony of the time in particular, the context of the Bradley-Marlowe-Watson set-up. Of his biographers, Professor Bakeless and Charles Norman have both been swayed by the admittedly suspect evidence of Kyd and Baines, in connection with the later charges of Atheism against Marlowe, to launch forth into highly-coloured accounts of the Bradley Affray in order to argue that this incident is but one more 'proof' of Marlowe's violent nature, and, in the face of evidence to the contrary, have assumed that Marlowe must have been to blame in this quarrel. Let us allow the evidence to speak for itself.

To summarise: William Bradley, according to his record, was a man given to brawling. His temper may be evidenced from his action in engaging George Orrell as his accomplice to threaten Hugh Swift in the first place. It was Watson, and not Marlowe, who similarly visited Bradley in company with Swift and Alleyn, and it was against Watson *et al* that Bradley subsequently petitioned for securities of the peace. No mention so far of Marlowe.

We do not know how the fight in Hog Lane between Bradley and Marlowe began. What we do know is that it was Bradley who was lying in wait in this narrow lane far from his home, lurking there with obvious intent to do Watson an injury. He may have mistaken Marlowe for Watson originally, and so fallen upon him. Or, alternatively, the inference of the evidence is that it would be Bradley who rudely accosted Marlowe, knowing him to be a friend of his enemy, and that Marlowe in turn was not slow to defend himself or his friend from insult. We know, further, that when Watson arrived, Marlowe immediately withdrew (unlike Mercutio and Romeo, to whose three-cornered fight with Tybalt this has often been likened).

The quarrel was patently between Bradley and Watson, and all the evidence points to the conclusion that Bradley was the originator of the trouble. This is not to say that Marlowe was a saint, but to put matters in their proper perspective. Elizabethan London (and, for that matter, Elizabethan Canterbury, where he was bred) being what the times made them, handiness with a rapier was one of the elementary rules for survival which Kit must have learnt early. Through the researches of Dr. Urry we now know further that Marlowe also fought a duel with William Corkine, musician of the Cathedral at Canterbury in 1592. This duel did not prove fatal, but ended in a charming reconciliation between the two protagonists. This story provides one of the most revealing commentaries on the enigmatic Kit which has recently come to light.[11]

Tom Watson

Thomas Watson, born in 1557, was one of those educated Elizabethans whose spiritual brethren can be found gracing the benches of any institute of learning in any age for, according to Anthony à Wood, he had spent his time at the university 'not in logic and philosophy, as he ought to have done, but in the smooth and pleasant studies of poetry and romance'. This in itself would doubtless have commended him to Marlowe, who was five years his junior and probably found the company of this travelled gentleman of the world, musician, poet and Latinist, extremely congenial. A close friendship was soon cemented between them, and perhaps began in the first instance because they shared the same patronage.

Watson had for long been intimate with young Thomas Walsingham and his distinguished cousin, Sir Francis Walsingham. The latter he had met when in Paris in 1581 during Walsingham's period of ambassage there, and he may be said to have been Watson's first patron. As they passed the time pleasantly on the banks of the Seine together, Walsingham often delighted to listen to Watson's 'tunes' and admired his Latin poems, encouraging him to have his works published. This Watson did upon his return to London with the appearance of his Latin translation of Sophocles' *Antigone*, published by John Wolfe in 1581.

Eccles has shown the importance of Watson's Continental studies and travels 'in accounting for the unusual breadth of his reading in Italian, French and neo-Latin poetry, for the form his own poetry took, and for his high reputation and consequent influence upon his contemporaries in England'.[1] Watson's dedication to Philip Howard, Earl of Arundel, of his *Sophoclis Antigone* reveals

that his absence abroad had been a long one, and refers especially to Italy and France:

> 'while I altogether devoted my early years to study, and while far from my native land, I passed a lustrum and a half, learning to utter words of diverse sounds. At that time I was taking careful note of the tongues and manners of Italy, and of your language and manners, learned France. So far as I was able, I paid worship to the Muses, wherever I went. Justinian, too, was especially dear. But Mars often broke in upon reluctant Pallas, wars were often obstacles to my study.'[2]

This, as Eccles points out, suggests that Watson was a student of Roman Law, and not of English common law. He probably studied at one of the famous schools of Roman Law in Italy, at Padua or Bologna; the former in particular attracted many foreign visitors, including Sir Philip Sidney, who was there in 1573/4. In France he attended the English College at Douai, the famous Jesuit Seminary, renowned for its learning, which opened its doors to Catholic and non-Catholic alike, entering first on October 15, 1576, and again in May, 1577.[3]

124

Upon his return to England, Watson's decision was for a literary career rather than the law, although he continued to subscribe his Latin works 'Thomas Watsonus, I.V. studiosus', and he tells us he was at first 'not minded ever to have emboldened himself so far as to thrust a foot amongst our English poets'. But, encouraged by his admirers, he ventured from Latin poetry into the vernacular, and in 1582 published his *Passionate Century of Love*, a collection of one hundred sonnets derived from his study of the French and Italian sonneteers, which at once attained tremendous popularity. Watson may claim to be the originator of that great sonneteering vogue, ranging from the imitative to the deeply introspective, which enflamed his contemporaries and drew forth volumes of love poetry from the Elizabethan poets for the next decade. Probably this is what earned Shakespeare William Clerke's accolade as 'Watson's heir'.

Soon Watson was setting the fashion in London literary circles, for it was said that every 'balductum play' (worthless work) repeated that which was known to be but 'the froth of witty Tom Watson's jests'. William Cornwallis, to whose son Watson became tutor, claimed that writing plays had been Watson's 'daily practice and his living', but, so far as we know, none has survived. Still busy with Latin translations, he published his *Helenae Raptae*, the translation of Coluthus' *Rape of Helen*, in 1586, and dedicated it to Henry Percy, Earl of Northumberland. It was this poem that Marlowe is reputed to have Englished, which has since been lost. Watson also dedicated to the Earl his manuscript entitled *A learned Dialogue of Bernard Palessy; Concerning waters and fountaines, both naturall and artificiall: Translated Owt of French into English, by Thomas Watson*, thus establishing further his connection with the School of Night, to which he may have first introduced Marlowe.

Next to poetry, Watson's greatest love was music, and he counted several of the leading musicians of the day amongst his friends, including the famous William Bird, who composed madrigals in the Italian style for Watson's collection of Italian madrigals which he published in 1590 (see title page opposite).

In the same year, 1590, Sir Francis Walsingham died, worn out in the Queen's service and impoverished by the debts left by his son-in-law, Sir Philip Sidney, whose estates he had to settle after Zutphen, as well as his own continual expenditure on behalf of the burden he voluntarily assumed in his government duties.

Watson composed a memorial eclogue to Sir Francis entitled *Meliboeus*, written in Latin hexameters, and dedicated it to Thomas Walsingham. It is an Arcadian parable in verse consisting essentially of a dialogue between Watson (in the guise of Corydon) and Thomas Walsingham (as Tityrus) in which the latter is addressed as chief mourner for the death of Sir Francis (the shepherd, Meliboeus). Now that Meliboeus is dead 'flockes orespred the flowrie plaine'. Corydon attempts to console Tityrus and ease his 'burdened heart' by reminding him that Sir Francis will now be able to join Sir Philip Sidney (Astrophill), who was also 'by cruel Fates cut off before his daie', for Meliboeus's 'faith hath framed his spirit holie wings, to soare with Astrophill above the sun'.

England is represented as Arcadia and Queen Elizabeth as Diana, whose 'tempest' of grief for the loss of Sir Francis must be calmed, but Watson suggests that Edmund Spenser is better able to do this, since his 'never stooping quill can best set forth, such things of state as pass my muse and me'. Sir Francis' lady is represented as Dryas and his daughter (Philip Sidney's wife) as Hyall, but they are both minor characters in the parable.

Watson adds other words of comfort to Thomas Walsingham:

> *I must sorrow in a lower vaine, not like to thee,*
> *Whose words have wings at will:*
> *An humble stile befits a simple Swaine,*
> *My Muse shall pipe but on an oaten quill.*

This seems to imply that Thomas Walsingham was also an able poet, though the style of address is the exaggerated flattery of poet to patron.

At the same time Watson published an Englished version dedicated to Sir Francis' daughter, Lady Frances Sidney, being Sir Philip Sidney's widow. This was doubtless as a precautionary measure to forestall his former school-friend Abraham Fraunce, who had annoyed Watson by making capital out of Watson's Latin poem *Amyntas*. Fraunce produced an unauthorised English translation of the poem which found great favour, and was dedicated to that most desired of patronesses, Lady Mary Sidney, the Countess of Pembroke.

When Watson died two years later and was buried on September 26, 1592, in the little church of St. Bartholomew-the-Less, his fellow-poets mourned and hymned his praises, extolling him as the compeer of Spenser and Sidney. Harvey, Peele, Spenser, Nashe, Lodge, Fraunce, Daniel, and Clerke contributed verse and praise. To his friend Marlowe he had bequeathed the task of seeing his last Latin work *Amyntae Gaudia* through the press, which he did that same year, prefacing it with a choice Latin dedication on behalf of his deceased friend to his chosen patroness, the same Lady Sidney, Countess of Pembroke. It is the only known dedication Marlowe himself ever lived to write, for none of his own works were published in his lifetime except *Tamburlaine*, and that anonymously. Besides, it was not usual to dedicate plays, which were considered 'poor trifles', but with a poem or work of more serious matter a patron might be honoured.

Watson's sonnets, his Latin works, and his musical publications keep his name before us, and especially his association in his life and at his death with Marlowe, who addressed himself to Lady Mary Sidney on Watson's behalf, naming her the 'Muse of the Poets of our time, and of all most happily burgeoning wits', requesting her to 'Deign to be patron to this posthumous Amyntas, as to thine adoptive son: the rather that his dying father had most humbly bequeathed to thee his keeping'.

Mingled with his pleadings on behalf of Watson's work, Marlowe does not

When Sir Roger Manwood died in December 1592, Marlowe composed the following Latin epitaph:

> *In obitum honoratissimi Viri, Rogeri Manwood, Militis,*
> *Quaestorii Reginalis Capitalis Baronis.*
> *Noctivagi terror, ganeonis triste flagellum,*
> *Et Jovis Alcides, rigido vulturque latroni,*
> *Urna subtegitor. Scelerum, gaudete, nepotis!*
> *Insons, luctifica sparsis cervice capillis,*
> *Plange! fori lumen, venerandae gloria legis,*
> *Occidit: heu, secum effoetas Acherontis ad oras*
> *Multa abiit virtus. Pro tot virtutibus uni,*
> *Livor, parce viro; non audacissimus esto*
> *Illius in cineres, cuius tot millia vultus*
> *Mortalium attonuit: sic cum te nuntia Ditis*
> *Vulneret exsanguis, feliciter ossa quiescant,*
> *Famaque marmorei superet monumenta sepulchri!*

The Latin epitaph was discovered in a 1629 edition of *Hero and Leander* on the back of the title-page with Marlowe's name subscribed. It also appears twice in the Commonplace Book of Henry Oxinden, a younger contemporary and admirer of Marlowe's, who lived at Barham a few miles outside of Canterbury. A translation apparently never has been printed until now:

> Upon the death of a most honoured man, Roger Manwood, Knight,
> Lord Chief Baron of the Queen's Exchequer.
> The terror of the night prowler, the stern scourge of the profligate,
> Jove's Hercules and a destroyer of the obdurate brigand,
> Is buried within the funeral urn. Rejoice ye sons of iniquity!
> Weep, O Innocent One, with hair dishevelled on your sorrowful shoulder!
> The light of the courts, the glory of the respected law is dead:
> Alas, much virtue departed with him toward the worn-out shores
> Of the nether world. O envy, in the face of so much fortitude,
> Spare this man; be not too harsh upon his remains,
> On him who struck awe into the countenances of so many thousands
> Of mortals: thus, although the bloodless messenger of Death shall wound you,
> May your bones rest contentedly in peace, and may
> The fame of your statue transcend the monuments of the tomb!

---

neglect to add a word for himself, and at the end of the dedication makes a promise of future offerings of his own works to Lady Sidney's patronage:

> 'So shall I, whose slender wealth is but the seashore myrtle of Venus, and Daphne's evergreen laurel, on the foremost page of every poem invoke thee as Mistress of the Muses to my aid: to sum up all, thy virtue, which shall overcome virtue herself, shall likewise overcome even eternity.
>
> Most desirous to do thee honour,
>
> C.M.'[4]

Had he lived, he probably intended to keep his word. At the time, however, he had not yet conceived his poem *Hero and Leander* which Edward Blount dedicated posthumously to Thomas Walsingham; but in this case it would have been the only fitting dedication as Marlowe probably wrote the work at Scadbury, Walsingham's home in Kent. But it is interesting to note that he had also looked hopefully to the Countess of Pembroke as a future patroness for himself.

Illuſtriſsimæ Heroinæ omnibus & animi,& corporis dotibus ornatiſſimæ, Mariæ Penbrokiæ Comitiſſæ.

Aurigera ſtirpe prognata Delia, Sydnæi vatis Apollinei genuina ſoror; Alma literarū parēs, ad cuius immaculatos amplexus, confugit virtus, barbarici & ignorantiæ impetu violata, vt olim a Threicio Tyranno Philomela; Poetarum noſtri temporis, ingeniorumq; omnium fæliciſſime pullulantium, Muſa; Dia proles, quæ iam rudi calamo, ſpiritus infundis elati furoris, quibus ipſe miſellus, plus mihi videor præſtare poſſe, quam cruda noſtra indoles proferre ſolet: Dignare Poſthumo huic Amyntæ, vt tuo adoptiuo filio patrocinari: Ecque magis quòd moribundus pater, illius tutelam humil-

limè tibi legauerat. Et licet illuſtre nomen tuum non ſolùm apud nos, ſed exteras etiam nationes, latius propagatum eſt, quàm aut vnquàm poſſit æruginoſa Temporis vetuſtate aboleri, aut mortaliū encomijs augeri, (quomodò enim quicquā poſſit eſſe infinito plus?) multorum tamen camænis, quaſi ſiderum diademate redimita Ariadne, noli hunc purum Phœbi ſacerdotem, ſtellam alteram coronæ tuæ largientem, aſpernari: ſed animi candore, quem ſator hominum, atque deorū, Iupiter, prænobili familiæ tuæ quaſi hæreditarium alligauit, accipe, & tuere. Sic nos, quorum opes tenuiſſimæ, littorea ſunt Myrtus Veneris, Nymphæque Peneia ſemper virens coma, prima quaque poematis pagina, Te Muſarum dominam, in auxilium invocabimus: tua denique virtus, quæ virtutē ipſam, ipſam quoque æternitatem ſuperabit.

Honoris tui ſtudio-
ſiſsimus, C. M.

AMINTÆ
GAVDIA

Authore Thomâ VVatſono
Londinenſi, iuris
Studioſo.

LONDINI,
Impenſis Gulihelmi Ponſonbei.
1592.

Above: The dedication in memoriam for Watson to the Countess of Pembroke by Marlowe. It prefaces Watson's Amintæ Gaudia *which Marlowe saw through the press after his friend's death. A translation is given below.[5]*

Left: The title-page to Thomas Watson's Amintæ Gaudia, *posthumously published in 1592.*

To the Most Illustrious Noble Lady, adorned with all gifts both of mind and body, Mary Countess of Pembroke.

Delia born of a laurel-crowned race, true sister of Sidney the bard of Apollo; fostering parent of letters, to whose immaculate embrace virtue, outraged by the assault of barbarism and ignorance, flieth for refuge, as once Philomela from the Thracian tyrant; Muse of the Poets of our time, and of all most happily burgeoning wits; descendant of the gods, who impartest now to my rude pen breathings of a lofty rage, whereby my poor self hath, methinks, power to surpass what my unripe talent is wont to bring forth: Deign to be patron to this posthumous Amyntas, as to thine adoptive son: the rather that his dying father had most humbly bequeathed to thee his keeping. And though thy glorious name is spread abroad not only among us but even among foreign nations, too far ever to be destroyed by the rusty antiquity of Time, or added to by the praise of mortals (for how can anything be greater than what is infinite?), yet, crowned as thou art by the songs of many as by a starry diadem Ariadne, scorn not this pure priest of Phoebus bestowing another star upon thy crown: but with that sincerity of mind which Jove the father of men and of gods hath linked as hereditary to thy noble family, receive and watch over him. So shall I, whose slender wealth is but the seashore myrtle of Venus, and Daphne's evergreen laurel, on the foremost page of every poem invoke thee as Mistress of the Muses to my aid: to sum up all, thy virtue, which shall overcome virtue herself, shall likewise overcome even eternity.

Most desirous to do thee honour
C.M.

128

The Hall of the Middle Temple, *seat of legal learning in the heart of London, was built by the great 16th-century lawyer, Edmund Plowden. It is interesting that one of the last recorded appearances of Plowden as an advocate was in the Walsingham case (1578–1579 series of Plowden Reports) which concerned a dispute over lands belonging to the Walsinghams in Kent. During Elizabeth's reign this great hall with its magnificent hammerbeam roof and minstrels' gallery, was frequently used for theatrical performances. There is no record of any of Marlowe's plays having been performed here, although Shakespeare's certainly were. But we know that Marlowe had friends in the Middle Temple, the most notable being Sir Walter Ralegh.*

Manuscript copy *in an Elizabethan italic hand of Marlowe's poem* 'The Passionate Shepherd to His Love' *and Ralegh's* 'Reply' *in the Commonplace Book* entitled* Divers Divine Exhortations. *Its contents date from about 1580–1630 and a note on the last leaf suggests that the MS may have belonged to John Thornborough. Thornborough was Chaplain to the Earl of Pembroke at Wilton. It was for the Pembroke Players that Marlowe wrote his* Edward II. *There is also an intriguing connection between the Thornboroughs and Lady Audrey Walsingham, wife of Marlowe's patron. During the trial of the Earl and Countess of Somerset for the murder of Sir Thomas Overbury, one of the witnesses, Stephen Clapham, gave evidence asserting that Lady Walsingham was very intimate with Mrs. Thornborough. Perhaps it was through this association that Marlowe's and Ralegh's poems found their way into this Commonplace Book.*

*C. D. Bowen: 'It was the custom of the day for readers to copy out, in their commonplace books, whatever pleased them in other men's works.'

Sir Walter Ralegh, *upon first coming to court in* 1582 (*courtesy of Kunsthistorisches Museum, Vienna*).

SIR WALTER RALEGH (1552–1618)

Sir Walter Ralegh, Elizabeth's favourite, affectionately nicknamed her 'Water', was undoubtedly the most remarkable of all Marlowe's associates. His amazing success at Court had raised him from a plain Devonshire gentleman and captain in the Irish wars to one of the most powerful noblemen in the government. Elizabeth showered him with favours, savoured his fine intellect, adored his poetry, listened to his advice (it was feared he had the Queen's ear too much) and was even won over reluctantly to considering his schemes for colonization in America. Ralegh always cut a splendid figure at Court in his subtle satins and brocades, a single jewel in his ear, and Elizabeth loved him for his external graces. He gained an almost fabulous reputation for sartorial elegance which the records do not belie. An entry in the Middlesex Registers for April 26, 1583, when he was still plain Mr. Rawley, records the trial of one Hugh Pewe for the theft of 'a jewel worth 80 pounds, a hat band of pearls worth 30 pounds, and five yards of damask silk worth 3 pounds, goods and chattles of Walter Rawley, Esq., at Westminster'. He had a suit of silver armour made in which he stood at the Queen's chamber door as Captain of her Guard. However, such foibles should not obscure from us his true stature as a man, his undeniable greatness of spirit, which shines forth most clearly in his moments of greatest adversity. When King James had imprisoned him in the Tower, the young Prince Henry often visited him there and once exclaimed, 'Only my father would keep such a bird in a cage!' At his trial his contemporaries have left ample evidence of the power of Ralegh's eloquence and the magnetism of his personality to move even his enemies to his side. 'That great Lucifer' they called him. Like Christopher Marlowe, he was such another as was born to rise and fall.

The School of Night

All things that move between the quiet poles
Shall be at my command: emperors and kings
Are but obeyed in their several provinces,
Nor can they raise the wind, or rend the clouds;
But his dominion that exceeds in this,
Stretcheth as far as doth the mind of man.

DR. FAUSTUS

Marlowe's mind, keenly whetted with six years of cloistered university study, was never destined to be a blunted blade even if left to itself. Though disillusioned with Divinity, even that subject he did not let alone—an indication that in the first instance his intentions for the Church may have been serious. In another age he might yet have made a great churchman. It is a curious fact that there seems to be a hidden psychological link between the ecclesiastical and the theatrical professions, and a not infrequent migration from the latter to the former. For Marlowe, inevitably, it was the other way round. As Ingram has remarked:

> 'That Marlowe, a man of illimitable imagination and of the clearest intellect, would be bound by the rules and tenets of a creed defined by human law could not be expected.'[1]

It could not be expected. In this he shows himself once more a true son of the Renaissance which bred such gloriously rebellious, arrogant spirits, tormented with a desire to make all knowledge theirs.

After leaving Cambridge it was not long before he joined another kind of university, more exclusive, stimulating, and esoteric than any existing officially, Sir Walter Ralegh's 'little academie', the resort of free-thinkers like himself.

Ralegh was now at the crest of his ascendancy at Court, where he remained a dominant influence until his clandestine marriage to Elizabeth Throckmorton in 1592 brought the first wind of change in his fortunes—the rude blast of the Queen's violent displeasure which lodged him in the Tower for a space. But meanwhile, treading a courtly measure, and dabbling in politics in harness with the Queen's capricious humour, was never enough to satisfy his questing spirit. Prevented from adventuring abroad himself on journeys of discovery to the New World as was his dream, by the Queen's jealous hold over his person (too precious to her to allow him to risk on such madcap enterprises) he lavished instead his money, and that of others including the Queen's, on financing expeditions under his own band of sea-captains, not merely to explore, but to colonize. His 'plantings' of colonies failed, the Governor of the second Virginia expedition, John White, returning homeward in distress the year Kit came to London. Not so his planting of the tobacco weed in the garden of Durham House in the Strand, from which the Bishop of Durham had found

Title page to Ralegh's great work, The History of the World, *written during his long captivity in the Tower. It is a remarkable achievement. In it Ralegh's scientific scepticism is expressed, as when he states his belief that the antiquity of the Egyptians has been much exaggerated, but also his faith declared in the majestic opening words of his great work, which give the lie to the charge that he was an 'atheist'.*

'God, whom the wisest men acknowledge to be a power ineffable, and virtue infinite: a light by abundant clarity invisible; and understanding which only itself can comprehend: an essence eternal and spiritual, of absolute pureness and simplicity: was and is pleased to make himself known by the work of the world.'

(Courtesy of British Museum)

himself unceremoniously evicted to make room for Elizabeth's new courtier. Here Ralegh smoked his silver pipe in his delightful turret room overlooking the Thames. The 17th-century gossip, Aubrey, has described it:[2]

'I well remember his study, wch was on a little turret, that looked into and over the Thames, and had the prospect wch is pleasant, perhaps, as any in the world, and wch not only refreshes the eie-sight, but cheers the spirits, and (to speake my mind) I believe enlarges an ingeniose man's thoughts.'

Here Ralegh's ingenious thoughts, wreathed in clouds of tobacco smoke, swelled to encompass his dreams, and his restless energies sought out other fields for conquest. He gathered around him a group of men who were ready and eager to adventure with him on voyages of discovery in the realms of the mind. Courtiers and commoners were welcome alike, so long as they shared Ralegh's aristocracy of spirit. With him they studied, discussed, experimented, and earnestly sought to extend the bounds of scientific knowledge, then in its infancy and frowned upon as dangerous thinking. Meeting behind closed doors to discuss such subjects as were proscribed by the mediæval university curricula, their very secrecy excited suspicion which fed on the superstition of that age

133

and earned them the alternative more sinister title of 'The School of Night'. It was into this circle that Marlowe, probably shortly after his arrival in London, became drawn.

At the age of thirty-three Ralegh had achieved an astonishing pre-eminence that dazzled his contemporaries and gained him enemies as well as friends and admirers. Amongst the latter was Christopher Marlowe, for whom the brilliant figure of Sir Walter seemed obviously cut out to be the young man's hero. Ralegh was no mean poet himself, his verses being generally acclaimed the 'most lofty, insolent and passionate'. He would undoubtedly have recognised Marlowe's superlative gift and felt drawn to a spirit so much akin to his own. The matching of their verses in Marlowe's charming pastoral 'The Passionate Shepherd to his Love' and Ralegh's 'Reply' argues a degree of intimacy above mere acquaintance in the same circle, in which the participants were in any case closely drawn together by a common bond. But apart from this there is evidence to show that Marlowe had intended *Tamburlaine* in some measure as an over-life-size hero-portrait of 'that Great Lucifer' Ralegh.

The upstart Tamburlaine bears some striking resemblances to the upstart Ralegh, who came from country to Court 'a bare Gentleman' and had 'gotten the Queen's ear at a trice',[3] growing into a colossus before the very eyes of the amazed courtiers. She knighted him, showered him with rich emoluments, and, next herself, made him the most influential person at Court.

In his first great play Marlowe had written:

> *Nature, that fram'd us of four elements*
> *Warring within our breasts for regiment,*
> *Doth teach us all to have aspiring minds:*
> *Our souls, whose faculties can comprehend*
> *The wondrous architecture of the world,*
> *And measure every wandering planet's course*
> *Still climbing after knowledge infinite,*
> *And always moving as the restless spheres,*
> *Will us to wear ourselves, and never rest*

Of Ralegh it might truly be said he had an 'aspiring mind' that thirsted after 'knowledge infinite', but these words put into the mouth of the world-conquering Tamburlaine sound somewhat incongruous, yet they are obviously deliberate, for it is one of the most exquisite passages in the play. Of Ralegh it was written 'he had that awfulness and ascendency in his aspect over other mortalls' which Marlowe's description of his hero Tamburlaine immediately establishes in his idealised portrait of a man,

> *Of stature tall, and straightly fashioned*
> *Like his desire, lift upward and divine*

In other respects Ralegh had in recent years more nearly emulated the 'Scourge and Terror' of the world. In strange contrast to his later treatment of the Indians, and his remarkable humanity displayed in countless instances in dealing with his subordinates, Ralegh's campaigns in Ireland had been marked with a swift and relentless cruelty amounting to barbarism. Stories of his whole-sale massacres of prisoners had lent terror to his name, and excited such horror throughout Europe that the Queen, secretly approving, felt it expedient to let it be known that she was displeased at these extreme measures.

In December 1581 Ralegh arrived back in England figuratively dripping blood from the boggy fields of Ireland, with a reputation for ruthlessness relieved only by the stories of his equal recklessness and dare-devil courage, and at once won the Queen's love and favour. Six years later *Tamburlaine* burst upon the stage with speeches that might have reflected his own daring and ruthless exploits. Eleanor Grace Clark has pointed out the parallels between Tamburlaine's siege of Damascus and Ralegh's behaviour at the siege of Fort Del Ore. Hooker, in his continuation of Holinshed, describes the slaughter of 400 Spaniards and Italians who were assisting the Irish rebels, and who held out although repeatedly called to surrender until they

'began to fear, somewhat prophetically, that what they had built for a garrison would prove their monument, and they should be buried alive in the ruins of it. Therefore, finding no succours arrive, they beat a parley, and hung out the white flag, crying out, *Misericordia, misericordia*. But the lord deputy would not listen to any treaty with the confederates of traitors and rebels'.[1]

Ralegh, with Macworth, was placed by Lord Grey, then Lord Deputy of Ireland, in charge of the brutal massacre that followed, in which not even the women were spared. Similarly Tamburlaine, before the walls of Damascus, deals out a merciless retribution for the Damascans' stubborn rejection of his calls to surrender, and the pleas of the virgins sent to beg for mercy fall on deaf ears:

TAMBURLAINE:
What, are the turtles fray'd out of their nests?
Alas, poor fools, must you be first shall feel
The sworn destruction of Damascus?
They knew my custom; could they not as well
Have sent ye out when first my milk-white flags,
Through which sweet Mercy threw her gentle beams,
Reflexed them on their disdainful eyes,
As now when fury and incensed hate
Flings slaughtering terror from my coal-black tents,
And tell for truth submission comes too late?

. . . .

Virgins, in vain you labour to prevent
That which mine honour swears shall be perform'd.
Behold my sword; what see you at the point?

VIRGIN:

Nothing but fear and fatal steel, my lord.

TAMBURLAINE:

Your fearful minds are thick and misty then,
For there sits Death; there sits imperious Death,
Keeping his circuit by the slicing edge.
But I am pleas'd you shall not see him there;
He now is seated on my horsemen's spears,
And on their points his fleshless body feeds—
Techelles, straight go charge a few of them
To charge these dames, and shew my servant Death,
Sitting in scarlet on their armed spears.

VIRGINS:

O, pity us!

TAMBURLAINE:

Away with them, I say, and shew them Death!

It is a magnificent passage, lending an evocative beauty to deeds of horror, which must have fallen on Londoners' ears with a thrill of immediacy we cannot now recapture. Another point of resemblance is the same capacity for restless energy, ceaselessly striving after its goal, whether for knowledge or active enterprises, exemplified in both Tamburlaine and Ralegh, of whom Cecil was once moved to remark, 'he can toil terribly'. And, like Tamburlaine, who gloried in his 'golden armour like the sun', Ralegh delighted to stand at the Queen's door as Captain of Her Majesty's Yeomen of the Guard in the dazzling suit of silver armour he had had specially made.

However, if Marlowe admired Ralegh it was not because of the gory reputation he had acquired in Ireland. This phase of his career was not typical of the man and must be seen in the light of contemporary events. This applies also to Marlowe's writings. In presenting such a hero as Tamburlaine on the stage Marlowe was using the dramatic idioms of his day, playing to the gallery, or rather to the tastes of the groundlings, as did they all from Shakespeare to Webster. Marlowe uses the imagery of terror and cruelty to amaze and thrill his audience to cathartic effect, but it must not therefore be argued that there was something of a 'cruel heart' in him, as some critics have implied, any more than this can be argued of Shakespeare because he wrote *Titus Andronicus* or introduced such scenes as the putting out of Gloucester's eyes in *King Lear*. Much has been written of the 'humanity of Shakespeare', but Marlowe's critics have mostly failed to note that in his most blood-thirsty play *Tamburlaine* he also wrote:

Accurs'd be he that first invented war!
They knew not, ah, they knew not, simple men,
How those were hit by pelting cannon-shot
Stand staggering like a quivering aspen-leaf
Fearing the force of Boreas' boisterous blasts!

136

If there is an elaborately worked superficial resemblance as here shown between Marlowe's stage hero Tamburlaine and Ralegh, there was a more real and significant similarity between Ralegh and Marlowe. Ralegh, 'the best hated man of the world, in Court, City or country', had an inherent arrogance and scorn for what the world might think of him that was matched in Marlowe's make-up, and in each it was a trait that led them into trouble. Contemporary opinions of Ralegh are as contradictory as those we have of Marlowe; both men made fatal enemies amongst those who envied their success. Yet from Ralegh's more amply documented life the final picture of a man of outstanding humanity emerges through all the welter of conflicting evidence that surrounds him. When his enemies finally succeeded in bringing this 'atheist', the 'contemner and scorner' Ralegh to destruction, contemporary reports testify that he yet had the power to win even his opponents to his side. Roger Ashton, a witness at his trial, afterwards confessed that 'whereas, when he saw Sir Walter Ralegh first, he was so led with the common hatred that he would have gone a hundred miles to see him hanged, he would, ere they parted, have gone a thousand to save his life'. It was under the banner of this 'beautiful daemon' that Marlowe enlisted in the quenchless search for knowledge.

Ralegh's leadership of this group was shared with two other eminent noblemen: *Henry Percy, Earl of Northumberland,* and *Henry Brooke, eighth Baron Cobham.* Lord Henry Howard described these three as 'the infamous Triplicity that denies the Trinity', impugning them with atheism as the accepted corollary of all free thinking. This was the stigma with which all the members of the School of Night were constantly tarnished, whether commoners, such as Marlowe, or an hereditary earl of the realm, such as Northumberland.

Henry Percy, 'the Wizard Earl' as he was called, was a courageous, proud, and eccentric nobleman, the ninth earl in his line and the descendant of that famous Harry Hotspur immortalised by Shakespeare. This earl made study his chief pursuit, indeed his obsession. In his London residence at Blackfriars he closeted himself with his books, and set about systematically building up his grandfather's library with such additions as the works of Machiavelli, Guicciardini, Tasso, Holinshed, and many others, the records of his household accounts showing year by year a heavier expenditure for book binding and cataloguing. Here Marlowe might have read all he wished. The range was wide: architecture, archaeology, geography, military and political science, astronomy, chemistry, geometry, mathematics, navigation, gardening, history, medicine, philosophy, literature and poetry. To furnish himself the wherewithal to conduct scientific experiments he added a laboratory with crucibles, furnaces, alembics, and 'speculative glasses'.[5] No wonder he was nicknamed 'the Wizard Earl' while such names as 'conjurer' also clung to his associates and protégés.

As one of this accredited atheistical crew Marlowe's reputation was probably not helped by the appearance in due course of *Dr. Faustus* with its incantations and devil-raising. The story is told how on one occasion when *Dr. Faustus* was being performed the rumour spread that among the actors disguised as

HENRY PERCY, NINTH EARL OF NORTHUMBERLAND, 'THE WIZARD EARL' (*1564–1632*), *after a painting by William Dobson (courtesy of Frick Art Reference Library, N.Y.).*

Northumberland devoted his life and his resources to scientific study. He was a most courageous champion of free thought and religious toleration, and, like Marlowe, was consequently believed to be an atheist. He was imprisoned in the Tower in 1606 by King James I on suspicion of complicity in the Gunpowder Plot, and ironically one of the charges upheld against him was his persistent championship of the Catholics as a persecuted minority. Altogether he spent almost sixteen years in the Tower, much of it contemporaneously with Ralegh on whose behalf he had vigorously campaigned while yet free himself. While in the Tower he made his prison a study and laboratory in which he pursued his scientific experiments. Though his body was captive his mind was freer than most men's. Some of Marlowe's closest friends (Hariot, Warner, Roydon, Chapman, and Peele) were in his patronage, which in his case was no mere formal relationship but a genuine companionship based on shared interests.

devils the real Devil had made his appearance, and the panic-stricken audience rushed out praying aloud in terror as they went. This was typical of the age in which Marlowe lived. Superstition was rife amongst the ignorant as well as the educated, witch-hunting a terrible reality.

But those who carried out their investigations and studies in Ralegh's and Northumberland's circle dared all for the sake of knowledge, and it should surely count for something in our estimation of him that Marlowe belonged to this brilliant and courageous group. Northumberland himself was nothing lacking in courage, and the testimonial of this great free-thinker has been admirably written by Eleanor Grace Clark:

'Nothing could exceed the courage and candour with which he [Northumberland] defended the cause of religious toleration, in a period when to do so meant the risk of life and lands. Though not a Catholic himself, he wrenched from James VI, almost single-handed, a written pledge of leniency toward the persecuted Catholic tenantry of the North. He kept under liberal patronage persons of all religious persuasions, and his doors were ever open to welcome those who brought and sought knowledge. Though he was proud—some say arrogant—to those of his own social order, despising their tortuous intrigues with their grotesque alternation of pomp and servility, yet with men of genius he doffed his rank and worked and talked with them as equals, the only difference being that he usually paid all the costs.'[6]

When Northumberland later suffered imprisonment in the Tower, like Ralegh, he continued his scientific researches, particularly in chemistry, which fascinated him, assisted by the three men whom he liberally patronized, Robert Hues the geographer, Thomas Hariot the mathematician, and Walter Warner, a mathematician, philosopher and alchemist (the Elizabethan term for geological chemistry)—the Earl's 'three Magi' as Ralegh humorously dubbed them.[7] These three often visited him, dined at his table there, and worked, experimented and discussed with him, in which they were frequently joined also by Ralegh.

Hues was educated at Brasenose College, and subsequently at Magdalen Hall, Oxford, taking his B.A. in 1578. He was a scientific geographer and accompanied Thomas Cavendish on his voyage round the world. Northumberland later made him tutor to his son, and allowed him an annuity. His treatise *Tractus de Globis*, published in 1594, was written especially for use in connection with the set of globes made by Emery Molyneux, now in the Library of the Middle Temple. He dedicated this work to Ralegh, who was a member of the Middle Temple. Hues must have also been well known to Marlowe, for he shared a close friendship with two of Marlowe's most intimate friends, Hariot and George Chapman, the poet. Chapman refers to Hues in the preface of his Works of Homer (1616) as 'another right learned, honest and entirely loved friend of mine', after a similarly warm reference to Hariot.

HENRY BROOKE, NINTH BARON COBHAM
(d. 1619) was reputed more a courtier than a soldier, but nevertheless he was granted the coveted office of Warden of the Cinque Ports in succession to his father in preference to the Earl of Essex, who was his rival. Elizabeth showered him with many favours, but the accession of King James saw his undoing. He became involved in a plot allegedly to 'kill the King and his cubs' and place Arabella Stuart on the throne. At his accusation he attempted to implicate Ralegh as the originator of this pro-Spanish Catholic plot, which Ralegh repudiated. In contrast to Northumberland's loyalty, Cobham proved the Judas of the 'infamous Triplicity'. His trial revealed him as a base coward. When led to the block for execution he again accused Ralegh, and as a reward the sentence was commuted to life imprisonment. He died ignominiously of an illness when on his way to Bath to procure treatment for which his temporary release from prison had been granted.

(Courtesy of British Museum)

139

Thomas Hariot (1560–1621). Richard Hakluyt (1552?–1616). John White (*fl.*1585–1593). *Title page from the second edition of Thomas Hariot's report on* The New Found Land of Virginia, *published in folio by Theodor de Bry in Frankfurt. This 1590 volume incorporates the work of these three men, Hariot as author, Hakluyt as translator (from Hariot's Latin original) and White as artist. The book is illustrated with the beautiful engravings by de Bry based on John White's watercolour paintings of Indian life made while he was in Virginia with the first colony. The work is dedicated to Sir Walter Ralegh who organised the Virginia expedition. The first edition of Hariot's report was brought out in London in 1588 as a small quarto without illustration. Its publication is attributed to London printer Robert Robinson.*

140

Thomas Hariot was the most brilliant of the gifted mathematicians of this group, and a student of astronomy, in which he soon became pre-eminent. Almost contemporaneously with Galileo, Hariot was observing the heavens through his telescope, which had a magnification of fifty times, and was the first to see Halley's comet on 17 September 1607. He made observations and sketches of the moon, and recorded 199 observations of sun-spots. He also made a series of observations of Jupiter and its 'new-found' planets. He corresponded with Kepler on optical subjects, and prepared a treatise on the rainbow and colours. His manuscripts (now in the Egremont and Harleian Collections at the British Museum) include many sheets of miscellaneous calculations, tracts on mechanics, hydrostatics, specific gravity, magnetism, harmony, solid geometry, and astronomy. The dazzling scope of Hariot's papers reveal him as one of the greatest of early English scientists. As a mathematician he had no peer; his contributions to algebra, which he virtually created in its modern form, are among his most notable achievements.[8]

So incisive a mind as Hariot's would not have been inclined to accept contemporary theological dogma without questioning, and it seems likely that it was he who was, in fact, at the heart of the religious scepticism that struggled for expression within the minds of many members of the School of Night. The barrier of ancient religious beliefs, that held men in a thrall of superstitious awe, was something that these scientists had to break in order to liberate themselves for the work they had set their hands to. That Marlowe was involved in this there can be no doubt. And it is significant that Hariot, who was one of those closest to him in this circle, was also evidently deeply concerned with the question of the absolute truth of theological tenets, and went so far as to question them at their source, in the Bible itself. Anthony à Wood asserts that Hariot 'made a philosophical theology wherein he cast off the Old Testament'. A distorted reflection of this may be seen in the statement made by the informer Baines, whose task was to scent out evidence of Marlowe's atheistical beliefs, that Marlowe had said 'that Moyses was but a Juggler, and that one Heriots can do more than he'. It is possible that the brilliant Hariot, only four years older than Marlowe, influenced him in his ideas in the first place, as is suggested by the fact that Marlowe is recorded as quoting Hariot as an admired authority, —'one Heriots can do more than he'—the great prophet Moses. When we look at the fantastic range of his studies and the originality of the ideas expressed in his writings, the bulk of which are extant only in his careless manuscripts discovered under a bundle of old stable accounts, one can understand that to Marlowe the mind of Hariot was more wonderful than the questionable reports of the miracles of Moses.[9]

Owing to his neglect of publishing his works, Hariot's true greatness has remained obscured. His treatise on algebra, *Artis Analyticae Praxis ad Æquationes Algebraicas resolvendas*, was posthumously published in 1631, but Dr. Pell is quoted by Aubrey as having maintained that if Hariot had 'published all he knew in algebra, he would have left little of the chief mysteries of that art unhandled.'

It was this genius whom Ralegh engaged, shortly after Hariot had graduated from Oxford in 1580, as tutor in mathematics and astronomy for his 'school' especially with a view to training his sea-captains. In 1585 he sent Hariot as surveyor on the first colonizing expedition to Virginia with Captain *John White* under the leadership of Sir Richard Grenville bearing letters patent from the Queen laying claim to the new land. The settlement failed and a year later the colonists, at their own request, were shipped back to England. But John White, who remained with the colony during this year and brought back an artistic record of the natives of Virginia in the many fine drawings and paintings he made of the Indians, was re-engaged by the dauntless Ralegh to lead a second expedition which he fitted out. This sailed in April 1587, with John White as Governor, bearing 150 householders and their families to constitute the colony. After a hazardous crossing, they eventually landed at Roanoke on 20 July, but met with so many difficulties that on 27 August White once more set sail for England to obtain help and further instructions. However, he left his daughter behind with the colony, and she had the distinction of becoming the mother of Virginia Dare, the first English child born in North America.

As an attempt at colonization both these ventures failed, but the experience gained added greatly to the knowledge of the new countries discovered. Hariot wrote his account of the 'New Found Land of Virginia' and dedicated it to Ralegh. The first edition, a small but tasteful quarto, published in 1588, bore no illustrations, but a second imprint, brought out in 1590 at Frankfurt-on-Main by Theodore de Bry, was in a handsome folio volume embellished with beautiful engravings by de Bry. These were based on watercolour drawings by John White depicting Indian chieftains in ceremonial attire, tribal customs, villages, and other aspects of Indian life, including their manner of burial, all meticulously observed and drawn in detail. The treatment of these engravings by de Bry, who was an artist in his own right, represents a new departure in excellence of book illustration, which aroused considerable interest in the book trade at the time.

De Bry followed this with a companion volume illustrated with engravings based on the drawings of *Jacques Le Moyne*, a French Huguenot painter in the service of Ralegh, who had sailed to Florida in 1564–1565 on Laudonnière's ill-fated expedition. His task had been to map the sea-coast and harbours, indicate the position of towns, plot the course and depth of rivers for navigation, and portray dwellings of natives and anything else of interest worth observation. On 20 September 1565 the Spaniards had attacked and captured the French Fort Caroline, killing most of the defenders. Le Moyne was one of the few lucky enough to escape. The survivors set sail for France in their ship, the *Levrière*, but were swept off course and landed at Swansea Bay. Le Moyne settled in London, probably because of Huguenot persecution in France, married and became the servant of Ralegh. John White also remained in Ralegh's service and settled on his estates in Ireland in 1590.

It is of interest that at Scadbury, the ancestral home of Sir Thomas Walsing-

A group of John White's paintings of Indians in Ralegh's Virginia colony at Roanoke Island. It is possible that the entire set originally hung at Thomas Walsingham's Scadbury Manor (see p. 258).

These entrancing watercolours of White's have an almost journalistic quality about them which Theodor de Bry was quick to recognize. They were eye-witness pictorial accounts and de Bry reinterpreted them in line engravings for his spectacular 1590 folio. How superior they were to the crude woodcuts which had illustrated the earlier French and Spanish books describing the exploration and settlement of America. No wonder they produced a sensation in their time.

143

An Indian campfire ceremony painted by John White. It is a 10¼ × 14 inch watercolour in muted tones of a group of Indian men and women, some holding ceremonial rattles, sitting around a log campfire into which they will cast some of their cherished tobacco powder.

TOBACCO AS DESCRIBED IN THE 'QUARTO HARIOT'

'There is an herbe which is sowed a part by it selfe & is called by the inhabitants *uppówoc:* In the West Indies it hath divers names, according to the severall places and countries where it groweth and is used; the Spaniardes generally call it *Tobacco.* The leaves thereof being dried and brought into powder: they use to take the fume or smoke thereof by sucking it through pipes made of claie into their stomacke and heade; from whence it purgeth superfluous fleame & other grosse humors, openeth all the pores & passages of the body by which meanes the use thereof, not only preserveth the body from obstructions; but also if any be, so that they have not beene of too long continuance, in short time breaketh them; whereby their bodies are notably preserved in health, & know not many greevous diseases wherewithall wee in England are oftentimes afflicted.

'This *uppówoc* is of so precious estimation amongst them that they thinke their gods are marvellously delighted therwith: whereupon sometime they make hallowed fires & cast some of the powder therein for a sacrifice: being in a storme upon the waters, to pacifie their gods, they cast some up into the aire and into the water: so a weare for fish being newly set up, they cast some therein and into the aire likewise: but all done with strange gestures, stamping, sometime dauncing, clapping of hands, holding up of hands, & staring up into the heavens, uttering therewithal and chattering strange words and noises.

'We ourselves during the time we were there used to suck it after their maner, as also since our returne, & have found manie rare & wonderful experiments of the vertues thereof; of which the relation would require a volume by it selfe: the use of it by so manie of late, men and women of great calling as else, and some learned Phisitions also, is sufficient witness.'

Written by Thomas Hariot in his A BRIEFE & TRUE REPORT OF THE NEW-FOUND LAND OF VIRGINIA. *Imprinted at London* 1588.

144

ham at Chistlehurst in Kent (where Marlowe was living in 1593), '17 large Indian pictures' are mentioned as having formerly hung over what was known as the 'White Staircase'. Possibly these were the original paintings by John White of Indian scenes from his voyages, commissioned or purchased by Walsingham, who was a patron of the arts. These paintings were among the effects listed at the time of the demolition of the Tudor manor house at Scadbury in 1727, and subsequently disappeared without trace. It is a curious fact that at the British Museum in London there is today an album of exactly seventeen watercolour mounts of Indian scenes by John White. They are very handsome paintings, beautifully executed in somewhat subdued colours, and still in perfect condition, showing scenes of American Indian life depicted with an eye for careful observation. The pictures are obviously intended as a series since they are mounted on large matching vertical panels, which when framed would have made a very fine addition to any house. Are these the same '17 large Indian pictures' listed as having hung on the 'White Staircase' at Scadbury until the time of its demolition in the early 18th century? It is a tantalizing thought. (For further tracing of the history of the John White paintings in the British Museum and their possible link with Scadbury see p. 258.)

It is not known definitely whether Thomas Walsingham was also a member of the School of Night, but his patronage of its two most distinguished poets, Marlowe and Chapman, suggests this as likely. He was also closely associated with one of the leaders of the School of Night, Henry Brooke, Baron Cobham, in an official capacity in connection with the defence of Kent. If in his magnificent moated manor of Scadbury he also had a large collection of paintings by John White of the American Indians, doubtless representing a most interesting subject for an Elizabethan connoisseur, the connection would be confirmed.

When John White returned from Virginia, he brought back a full-blooded Indian to show his countrymen what the natives of these parts were like. They landed at Southampton on November 8th, and shortly afterwards the Indian was baptized in Bideford parish church. Whether he was brought to London to be shown, perhaps at Court, is not known. Ralegh would doubtless have been delighted to receive the visitor, and he showed later on his own expeditions that he had a wonderful insight into the native mind, perhaps gleaned by careful observation of this Indian's behaviour and conversation. Marlowe, with his insatiable thirst for knowledge of all kinds, whether philosophical or anthropological, would have been equally interested, and perhaps may have had a chance to meet this redskin before the unfortunate soul died, succumbing probably to the rigours of the English climate, within a year of his arrival.

It seems inconceivable that Marlowe would not have shared his interests with his patron, Walsingham, who was also his friend, and Marlowe's own avid interest in travel, geography and astronomy, in particular, is evidenced in his writings. Kyd, in his letter to Sir John Puckering concerning Marlowe, named Hariot, the navigator of the Virginian voyage, and the famous astronomer, as

GEORGE CAREY, LORD CHAM-
BERLAIN, BARON HUNSDON
(1564–1603), *from a miniature by
Nicholas Hillyarde, owned by the
Duke of Buccleuch.*
(*Courtesy of British Museum*)

one of Marlowe's closest associates. White shared the hazards of this voyage with Hariot, and contributed the fine illustrations to Hariot's book, hence most probably knew Marlowe well. As the artist of the expedition he would have been of particular interest to Walsingham, so that the link would seem to be fairly conclusive.

Kyd specifically mentions three men, all members of the School of Night, as being often in Marlowe's company: 'such as he conversd withall, that is, as I am geven to understand, with Harriott, Warner, Royden.' Since Warner is mentioned in the same association with Hariot, it is probable that this was *Walter Warner,* the mathematician, philosopher and alchemist, who was patronized by Northumberland; although, since the third man in this trio is the poet *Matthew Royden,* the alternative cannot be ruled out that this may be *William Warner,* the author of *Albion's England,* a long episodic poem on the history of England, who was patronized by Sir George Carey, later Lord Hunsdon and Lord Chamberlain, also a nobleman of the School of Night.

Sir George Carey was the intimate friend of Henry Brooke, eighth Baron Cobham, whose father had been granted the former King's Lodging or converted priory of St. Augustine by Queen Elizabeth, where she was entertained during her royal progress at Canterbury in 1573.* Marlowe knew it well, and probably Brooke and Carey also, for his friend Matthew Roydon apparently was on intimate terms with George Carey.

Brooke has already been mentioned as one of the 'infamous triplicity' and

---

* *In* 1589 *Cobham's sister, Elizabeth Brooke, was married to Cecil, who in turn was very intimate with Sir Thomas Walsingham, and later more particularly with his wife, Lady Audrey Walsingham. She is reputed to have become Cecil's mistress and was closely associated with him in political intrigue during the reign of James I.*

146

now his friend Carey is singled out as another of the leaders of the School of Night. In George Chapman's dedication to Matthew Royden of his poem *The Shadow of Night*, published in 1594 after Marlowe had given him strong encouragement to put his work into print, he specially eulogizes three of the noblemen of the School of Night:

'When I remember my good Mat. how joyfully oftentimes you have reported unto me, that most ingenious Darby, deepe searching Northumberland, and skill-embracing heir of Hunsdon had most profitably entertained learning in themselves, to the vital warmth of freezing science, and to the admirable lustre of their true nobility, whose high-deserving virtues may cause me hereafter to strike fire out of darkness which the brightest Day shall envy for beauty.'

The 'heir of Hunsdon', Sir George Carey, who was patron of Marlowe's friend William Warner (if William is the man) and later patron of Shakespeare's company, had married the admired Lady Elizabeth Spenser, cousin of Edmund Spenser the poet, with whom Royden was also specially friendly. This intimacy between Royden and Spenser, on the one hand (both being under the patronage of Sir Philip Sidney), and Royden and Marlowe on the other, gives reason to suspect a somewhat closer connection between Marlowe and Spenser than has previously been allowed by most of his biographers. Of Royden, unfortunately, little is known except that he took an M.A. at Oxford, and made a reputation amongst his contemporaries as a writer worthy of comparison, according to Francis Meres, with the greatest poets of Italy. But very little of his poetry was published. His particular friends were Marlowe, Spenser, Chapman, and Lodge, all co-members of the School of Night with him. He commemorated his warm friendship with Sir Philip Sidney in his *Elegie, or Friend's Passion for his Astrophyll*, written in mourning for Sidney.

Sir Philip Sidney's own intense interest in scientific research is attested by his leadership of a parallel group known as the 'Areopagus', of which his cousin Fulke Greville was co-patron. Although primarily a literary society, Zouch in his *Life of Sidney* writes: 'In this fellowship philosophical and metaphysical subjects were discussed, and the doors of the apartments in which they met were kept shut.' The two 'schools' of Ralegh and Sidney, though separate in identity, had several members in common, notably Edmund Spenser, who was one of Ralegh's closest friends.

Sir Philip Sidney was allied by marriage both to the Walsinghams, by his own marriage with Frances, the daughter of Sir Francis Walsingham, and to Ralegh through his younger brother Robert's marriage to Ralegh's cousin, Barbara Gamage. It was through this lady's inheritance of large estates that the Sidneys and Walsinghams became bound to Ralegh's enterprise to found a colony in the New World, an ambition Ralegh nourished all his life.[10]

The great interest which these men shared, one might term it a passion, to discover new knowledge, received its impetus from the widening horizon of their world, the discovery of a new continent beyond the ocean. They knew the world was bigger than their ancestors had dreamed it to be. What else might lie beyond? And if beyond the limits of supposed earthly confines, what beyond the limits of other human knowledge? Even Northumberland, whose main studies were strictly scientific and experimental research, nevertheless evidenced his deep interest in world exploration. After his incompatible marriage with Essex's sister, Lady Dorothy Devereux, he retired himself more frequently to a 'bachelor' residence he kept at Barking, which became the rendezvous of those 'Sons of Neptune', Drake, Ralegh, and other sea-dogs.

Northumberland's steward, *Lawrence Keymis*, was one whose life also became bound up in these great enterprises. Keymis, an Oxford don with a genius for mathematics and geography, had joined Northumberland's household and became a faithful friend and partner of Ralegh in exploration. In 1599 he accompanied Ralegh on the expedition to Guiana, travelling 500 miles up the Orinoco into the heart of the jungle with him. Later Ralegh put him in charge of further exploration mainly in the hope of finding gold. He discovered the Pitch Lake of Trinidad, for which Ralegh found an immediate practical use in tarring the bottoms of his ships, and maintained that he had also located a gold mine in the heart of Guiana. He brought back glowing accounts of the wealth of the country and urged the advantages of taking possession of this rich land for the Queen—a matter to which Ralegh would have needed no pressing if he had had the forces to accomplish it. Later he shared imprisonment in the Tower with Ralegh, and accompanied him, twenty-two years after their first exploration, on this last and fatal expedition to Guiana. Here Ralegh's son was killed in ambush by the Spaniards, and Keymis, when unkindly upbraided by Ralegh for failing to press on against terrific odds to their goal, shot himself in grief and desperation. Ralegh, smitten by this double tragedy, wrote home, 'my brains are broken'.

Another explorer in spirit, if not in fact, was *Richard Hakluyt*, generally called 'the navigator' although he seems never to have made a sea journey further than the English Channel. He made his name in writing books on exploration, and was in a sense the exponent of the ideas of this circle, which comprised the driving force of British 16th-century exploration.

Hakluyt, though of Dutch origin, was an ardent English patriot, the family having settled in Herefordshire as long ago as the reign of Edward II, and his writings are inspired by the desire to see England at the forefront in the discovery of new lands. He was educated at Christchurch College, Oxford, taking his B.A. in 1574 and M.A. in 1577, and proceeding to holy orders. But he was already dedicated to the service of geography and history—particularly the former, which he studied avidly, reading, as he tells us, 'whatever printed or written discoveries and voyages I found extant, either in Greek, Latin, Italian, Spanish, Portugal, French or English languages'. He lectured on the subject, and in 1582 published his *Divers Voyages touching the Discovery of America*, which he dedicated to Sir Philip Sidney.

He continued his studies in Paris, whither he attended Sir Edward Stafford as chaplain, and where he was inspired to commence his greatest work, *The*

Title page of the first volume of Hakluyt's Principal Navigations.

Principal Navigations, Voiages, and Discoveries of the English Nation made by Sea or over Land to the most remote and farthest distant quarters of the earth, because of the bad repute in which Englishmen were held.

'During my five years abroad with him,' he writes, 'I both heard in speech, and read in books other nations miraculously extolled for their discoveries and notable enterprises by sea, but the English of all others, for their sluggish security and continual neglect of the like attempts.'

This persuaded him to take upon himself the 'burden' and 'huge toil' of writing an account that would 'recommend to the world the industrious labours and painful travels of our countrymen'. This he was well equipped to do, for 'in continuance of time, and by reason principally of my insight in this study, I grew familiarly acquainted with the chiefest captains at sea, the greatest merchants and the best mariners of our nation'. This great work, which has been called 'the prose epic of the modern English nation', was first published in 1589, and was followed by an enlarged edition ten years later. He dedicated it to Sir Francis Walsingham, and in the dedication gives a charming account of his conversion to geography when still a youth:

'To the Right Honourable Sir Francis Walsingham, Knight. Right Honourable, I do remember that being a youth, and one of her Majesty's scholars at

149

Westminster, that fruitful nursery, it was my hap to visit the chamber of Mr. Richard Hakluyt, my cousin, a gentleman of the Middle Temple, well known unto you, at a time when I found lying open upon his board certain books of cosmography, with an universal map. He seeing me somewhat curious in the view thereof, began to instruct my ignorance, by shewing me the division of the earth into three parts after the old account, and then according to the latter and better distribution, into more; he pointed with his wand to all the known seas, gulfs, bays, straits, capes, rivers, empires, kingdoms, dukedoms, and territories of each part, with declaration also of their special commodities and particular wants, which, by the benefit of traffic and intercourse of merchants, are plentifully supplied. From the map he brought me to the Bible, and turning to the 107 Psalm, directed me to the 23 and 24 verses, where I read, that they which go down to the sea in ships, and occupy by the great waters, they see the works of the Lord, and his wonders in the deep, etc. Which words of the prophet together with my cousin's discourse (things of high and rare delight to my young nature) took in me so deep an impression, that I constantly resolved ... I would by God's assistance prosecute that knowledge and kind of literature, the doors whereof (after a sort) were so happily opened before me.'

Hakluyt was responsible for the translation of Hariot's report on *The New Found Land of Virginia*, dedicated to Ralegh. He later became prebendary and then archdeacon of Westminster, and lies buried in Westminster Abbey. All his life he continued his geographical studies and left sufficient manuscript notes to constitute another volume. He became a principal promoter and investor in the South Virginian Company in King James' reign in support of Ralegh's indefatigable colonizing ventures.[11]

Others of this band who were in Northumberland's patronage and close friendship were the eminent philosopher *Nicholas Hill,** an Oxford M.A., the exponent of the Atomic Theory, who was a frequent visitor to the Martin Tower during Northumberland's and Ralegh's joint imprisonment in the Tower; and *Nathaniel Torporley*, also an Oxford M.A., who became rector of Salwarpe in Worcestershire, but contrived to live mainly at Sion College in London (not to be confused with Northumberland's residence at Sion House) and was liberally maintained with a pension from the earl's purse. Torporley was a noted astronomer and mathematician, and also a student of astrology, which taken in its serious aspect can be ranked as a science. Astrology got him into trouble, for he was later implicated in the Gunpowder Plot on a charge of having cast the king's nativity. He was also a lifelong friend of Hariot. The latter's will (discovered by Henry Stevens in 1900) appoints Torporley as the literary and scientific editor of his manuscripts, which he bequeathed to the Earl of North-

* *Hill's philosophical treatise*, Philosophia Epicures, Democritiana, Theophrastica, proposita simpliciter non edocta, *was published in two editions, Paris* 1601 *and Geneva* 1619. *Torporley's Latin work on astronomy*, Diclides Coelometriceæ, sea Valuæ Astronomicæ universalea, omnia artis titius memera Psephophoretica in sat medicis Finibus Duarum Tabularum methodo Nova, generaliet facillima continentes, *bears a preface on astrology.*

umberland. Torporley began the huge task of preparing his friend's manuscripts for publication, but left the work uncompleted at his own death in 1632.[12]

Another of Northumberland's scholarly protégés was *Thomas Allen*, the antiquary, philosopher and mathematician. His eminence as a scholar obtained him the entrée to noblemen's houses both in England and abroad, and he kept up a vast correspondence with other contemporary scholars, including William Camden, the historian, Sir Thomas Bodley, Sir Robert Cotton, Sir Henry Spelman, and John Selden. He was the close friend of Torporley and Walter Warner, and also of Dr. John Dee, whose evil reputation for necromancy he equalled. He kept so many instruments and glasses in his chamber that ignorant people believed him to be a sorcerer. One of his servants claimed that he had 'met the spirits coming up the stairs like bees'. Fuller states that Allen 'succeeded to the skill and scandal of Friar Bacon'.

Allen was amongst the associates of Ralegh against whom charges of atheism were brought in the proceedings at Cerne Abbas in March 1594. A commission then sat to examine the accusations levelled at Sir Walter Ralegh and his 'damnable crew' who met at his house at Sherborne in Dorset, close by Cerne Abbas. Ralegh had retired himself here after his disfavour at Court on account of his clandestine marriage, without the Queen's consent, to Elizabeth Throck-morton. At this charming country lodge the members of the School of Night used often to meet until local gossip as to their doings reached such proportions that legal proceedings were instigated. Perhaps the scandal of Marlowe's death the previous year led up to this, for by 1594 the School of Night were evidently under general attack.

Thomas Allen, who then held the post of Lieutenant of Portsmouth Castle, was especially hounded by slander. Eleanor Grace Clark writes:

'The persecution of Allen . . . began in the early days of his service to Ralegh; for ignorance, bigotry, malice, and envy all combined under the pro-tection of a specious political orthodoxy to turn the fair fame of these renais-sance scientists into the foul legend of criminal atheism.'[13]

Allen was, in fact, a staunch Catholic, and the accusations against him could not be substantiated beyond hearsay gossip, which credited him with having torn leaves out of the Bible in order to dry his tobacco on them. Allen's servant had made matters worse with lewd jokes about the number of concubines that Moses was supposed to have kept. The general tenor of the accusations brought against Christopher Marlowe by Baines and Kyd the previous year had been much on this same level of scandalmongering based on the hearsay of ribald jokes.

Marlowe's friend Hariot was also involved in the charges brought. The depositions of witnesses duly noted accused him of various heresies, including the allegation that he had denied the resurrection of the body.[14] The proceed-ings took on a more serious and dignified tone with the hearing of the evidence of the Rev. Ralph Ironside concerning a disputation about the nature of the soul which Sir Walter Ralegh had instigated during an after-supper conversa-tion at the house of Sir George Trenchard at Wolverton, in which the Rev.

Ironside had taken part. His half-brother, Carew Ralegh, had introduced the subject on a bantering note, but Ralegh brought it to serious discussion, saying that he had 'had taulke with diuines, yet heithervnto in this pointe (to witt what the reasonable soule of man is) have I not by anye beene resolved. They tell vs it is *primus motor*, the first mover in a man &c.'.

However, the Rev. Ironside, vicar of the country parish of Winterbottom, was not the man to resolve him either, for all he could do was to quote Aristotelian philosophy to him, which Ralegh rejected as too 'obscure and intricate', and tactfully closed the argument by suggesting that 'grace might be sayed; for that, quoth he, is better then this disputacion'.[15] As it turned out, it was a wise conclusion. For once Raleigh's head had curbed his reckless tongue.

No evidence has come to light to show that the Cerne Abbas enquiry was ever taken up further, and it seems that the proceedings were dropped. Hariot however, wrote to Kepler deploring that the times they lived in made it impossible to express their views freely. Aubrey reported accurately when he wrote of Sir Walter Ralegh that 'he was scandalized with atheism; he was a bold man, and would venture at discourse which was unpleasant to the churchmen'.[16] The nature of the soul, which none of the theologians could resolve for him satisfactorily, was a question that continued to intrigue him, and he eventually worked out his own answer which he wrote down in his *Treatise on the Soul*. This work is such a complete refutation of the accusations of atheism made against him that it is worth summarizing:

Ralegh's *Treatise on the Soul*

In his first proposition he argues the divinity of Christ and the divine origin and nature of the soul, which derives not from the material world but from God direct. 'There is no example in nature that a thing incorporate cometh of that which is corporal.' Therefore, he argues, the physical body only is made by procreation, whereas the soul of man is given by God direct, being breathed into the body of man by God at birth, as in the case of Adam. (Thus Ralegh was in advance of modern principles of morality which forbid abortion in the belief that this involves killing a human soul; Ralegh's mystique would argue that this is mere killing of 'animal' life, for the soul is first infused directly by God with the breath of life at birth.) Ralegh's differentiation between animal life, which is sans soul, and man, who is granted a soul, is based on scriptural evidence. (Job: He hath taught us rather than the beasts.) 'The soul, endued with reason, is found in all mankind', he declares further, and lays claim to the equal rights of women in this respect, a matter sometimes doubted by his contemporaries, who accorded women only an inferior kind of soul:

> 'Cyril affirmeth, "That the souls of women are very womanish; hard and slow to understand hard things." But by his leave, some women, even in this, have been able to match the greatest men.'

Thereafter he discusses the substance of the soul, stating that philosophers have 'debased the soul too much', some trying to make out that it consists of watery

152

substance, fire and other elements etc. For Ralegh it is divine, non-corporeal, and not of any substance of this world.

Next he discusses the seat of the soul: whether in the head as Galen maintains, at the base of the head (Xenocrates), or the bottom of the brain (Herophylus), or in the chest (Empedocles); Moscion, Augustin, and Hilarius agree 'that the whole is in the whole in every part'. For Ralegh 'The soul, as it is considered whole, with all the faculties, is in the whole . . . for it giveth life and motion to the whole, and is in it, not as a mariner in a ship, but being present everywhere'. Yet even so it must have a *seat* either in the brain or the heart. Ralegh chooses the heart, and quotes Christ's promise: Blessed are the clean in heart, for they shall see God.

Lastly he discusses whether the soul is immortal or subject to death, as the Sadducees believed, or whether it sleeps till the judgment day, as the Nazarites claimed. But Ralegh maintains that it is immortal, and never dies. Torment grieves the soul, but does not consume it, it being immortal. Though the soul may 'die' in sin, yet it is never dead. Christ stated: The body they can kill, the soul they cannot kill. And with Christ, Ralegh also declares: The soul 'liveth and abideth for ever after the body is dissolved'. His conviction is expressed in his own clear statement:

'The mind in searching causes is never quiet till it come to God, and the will never satisfied with any good till it come to the immortal goodness.'[17]

Ralegh's *Treatise* is the work of a noble mind more deeply and truly religious than the vast majority of people in any age, who in the past were mostly superstitious, and in later times heedless. But Ralegh, not content merely to accept what is decreed, works out his own salvation, and emerges as a figure to which all the mud that was slung at him would not cling.

★   ★   ★

Outside this group of true scientists, and yet connected with it through his friendship with Thomas Allen, was *Dr. John Dee*, a man who merits some comment because to a remarkable degree he represents within himself the paradox of his age.

Dr. Dee was getting on in years when Ralegh invited him to Sherborne to demonstrate some of his experiments in alchemy to the members of his circle. Throughout four reigns Dee had followed a successful, though rather turbulent career as a scholar and scientist, being most eminent in mathematics and astrology, with which he combined experiments in alchemy and occultism. It was Dee's misfortune that, despite his vast learning, his great library of priceless books and costly manuscripts, and his scholarly and learned mind in other matters, he became for a great part of his life the willing dupe of a charlatan named Kelly, who presented himself to Dee as a 'seer' who could interpret the messages of the spirits which Dee believed he could invoke by manipulation of his crystal globe, or 'shew stone'. (His beautiful globe of polished crystal of the smoky quartz variety is now in the British Museum.)

In partnership with Edward Kelly, Dee embarked on a series of fantastic adventures in foreign Courts (which may well be reflected in Marlowe's *Dr. Faustus*). The Emperor of Russia at one time offered Dee a pension of £2,000 a year with due honour as one of the chief men of his kingdom if he would become his adviser, but Dee's faith in his occult powers must have wavered, for the offer was declined. The 'Actions with Spirits', as he calls them, date from about 1581, and are recorded in Dee's writings on the subject, which display his extraordinary credulity at the hands of the preposterous Kelly (whose black cap concealed the fact that his ears had been cut off as a punishment for former misdemeanours, a secret which Dee never seems to have discovered). By contrast with this dabbling in demonology Dee wrote prolifically on mathematics, geometry, navigation, astronomy and philosophy. He was responsible for introducing into England the first astronomer's staff and ring of brass, constructed by Gemma Frisius, and also brought two great globes by Gerard Mercator which he presented to Trinity College, Cambridge, where he had been elected a Fellow at its foundation by Henry VIII. His greatest achievement was the reformation of the English calendar undertaken for Elizabeth, but not implemented until over a century and a half later.

Dr. Dee's reputation as a sorcerer, combined with his undoubted learning and wisdom, apparently kept his contemporaries in awe and protected him from further attacks after he had survived the imprisonment and accusations of heresy which threatened him early in his career. Under Queen Elizabeth he was never molested, but indeed honoured. She herself twice visited him at his house in Mortlake, and several times called him to the Court for consultation on matters appertaining to her health and safety. One such occasion was when

EDMUND SPENSER, *the 'New Poete'* (1552?-1599), *author of* The Faerie Queen. *He was the friend of Sidney, Ralegh, Gabriel Harvey and Matthew Roydon.*

a waxen image, believed to be of the Queen, with a pin stuck into its breast was found at Lincoln's Inn Fields; and the first time was in 1577 when a comet appeared, and the alarmed courtiers persuaded the Queen to call for Dr. Dee to expound its significance, which he did for three days while the Queen listened attentively. The young Marlowe revealed a more enlightened mind when he made his love-possessed queen, Dido, in his first dramatic work, cry out:

> *Only Æneas' frown*
> *Is that which terrifies poor Dido's heart:*
> *Not bloody spears, appearing in the air,*
> *Presage the downfall of my empery,*
> *Nor blazing comets threaten Dido's death;*
> *It is Æneas' frown that ends my days.*
> *If he forsake me not, I never die;*
> *For in his looks I see eternity,*
> *And he'll make me immortal with a kiss.**

The fact that there were poets like Marlowe, Chapman, Drayton, Watson, Peele, Lodge, Spenser and Campion in this circle of intellectual thinkers and scientists was typical of the Elizabethan age, to which the modern concept of specialization was something as yet foreign.

Sidney's group, the 'Areopagus', although also involved in philosophical and metaphysical discussions, was founded in the first place as a literary club during the time of Spenser's employment under the Earl of Leicester at Leicester House in the Strand, where meetings of the group were first held in 1578–9. Here Spenser had met Sidney, who was Leicester's nephew, and a firm friendship between them soon ripened. Sidney's main interest, if one may thus term it in one so versatile, was literature, as Ralegh's overriding passion was world exploration and colonization, and Northumberland's scientific and philosophical research. Sidney's bosom friends, *Sir Edward Dyer* and *Sir Fulke Greville*, were both poets and writers keenly interested in literary form, and the three constituted an important literary influence at the Court.

The 'Areopagus' was founded largely at the instigation of *Gabriel Harvey*, a self-opinionated and energetic literary critic who exerted a considerable influence over the young *Edmund Spenser* when they were both at Pembroke Hall, Cambridge, together, Harvey as a Fellow, and Spenser a poor struggling sizar whose poetic genius Harvey nurtured, or thought he did, with good intent. He proved a good friend to Spenser, assisting him materially in his preferment to

---

* *Compare this with Shakespeare's dramatic use of flaming skies and supernatural happenings in the night of the dreadful storm that presages Caesar's murder in Rome, upon which Cicero comments sarcastically:*

> *Indeed, it is a strange-disposed time;*
> *But men may construe things after their fashion.*
> *Clean from the purpose of the things themselves.*
>
> JULIUS CAESAR, Act I, Sc. iii.

Leicester's household, but his advice on poetics, fortunately, Spenser eventually discarded. But at this time Harvey's ideas about the application of classical rules of quantity to English metre had been taken seriously by Sidney and his circle, and Spenser also was much engaged in experimentation on these lines. The opinions of the 'learned Gabriell', as Nashe mockingly called him, carried weight in this circle, and it is one of the ironies of fate that Harvey's own posteritous reputation derives mainly from the vituperative paper war he had with Nashe, in which Nashe definitely had the edge on Harvey, and which has survived where so much else perished, despite the fact that the authorities had decreed that these combustible writings be consigned to the flames. Perhaps it is poetic justice to the man who took it upon himself to defame others.

Harvey was an unfortunate fellow, whose critical faculties were over-developed. It was said at Cambridge that he could scarcely find it in his heart to praise anyone. He adopted a puritanical moralising attitude towards his younger contemporaries which made him unpopular, and he probably developed a soft spot for the 'gentle Spenser' in the first place because the young man listened to all his advice and tried seriously to apply it. As a literary critic he was a classical purist who wished to impose literary strictures on the developing poetic forms which his gifted contemporaries were forging. He was mistaken in this, yet as a critic he recognised true genius when he saw it, as in Spenser, and he held a high opinion of Marlowe's literary achievements, if not of his person. Harvey's eccentricities, 'the affected accent of his speech', his 'Louelockes & his great ruffes and pantoffles', exposed him to Nashe's opprobrious ridicule,[18] but his intellectual brilliance cannot be doubted, and there is evidence of his scientific interests in his writings. He was a very early Copernican, and praises Copernicus, Rheticus and the anti-Aristotelian Petrus Ramus in his *Musarum lacrimae*, 1578. At Cambridge he became known for his 'strange opinions', and his support for the more advanced views in the Cambridge controversies in the philosopical as well as the mathematical field. His lectures on rhetoric in the public schools drew overflowing audiences. In his writings his great erudition is paraded at every opportunity with inordinate length and verboseness, but his style has a peculiarly pungent quality derived from his fantastic vocabulary and range, which makes it at times both unreadable and fascinating.

No doubt Harvey would have met Marlowe on an equal footing in the School of Night at some time in London, and possibly also through his brother Richard's connections with Thomas Walsingham as rector of Chislehurst parish church. Perhaps Marlowe's derogatory comment on Richard's preaching had reached Gabriel's ears, and added to his distaste for Marlowe, for aspersions against members of his family always touched a sensitive spot in Gabriel, sure sign of an inferiority complex. Later he was to dip his pen in vitriol at Marlowe's death and leave a bitter reflection on the great poet's 'Tamburlaine contempt'.

Harvey was a man who loved to patronize, and as Marlowe would obviously have none of this, perhaps even rejected advice when proffered, Harvey was

MICHAEL DRAYTON (1563–1631) *the Warwickshire poet and sonneteer, best known for his two sonnet cycles,* Idea, the Shepherd's Garland *and* Ideas Mirrour, *was one of the most prolific of the Elizabethan poets. Spenser much admired his work, and he was greatly esteemed as a man by his contemporaries. Francis Meres quotes the opinion of 'schollers, souldiers, poets, and all sorts of people' that Drayton was 'a man of virtuous disposition, honest conversation, and well-governed carriage'. He also wrote many plays, mainly in collaboration with others (Chettle, Dekker, Middleton, Munday and Webster) but his greatest work is the long narrative poem* Poly-Olbion, *describing 'all the Tracts, Rivers, Mountains, Forests, &c.' of Great Britain, the counterpart in a sense of William Warner's* Albion's England. *Warner (who was probably Marlowe's friend referred to by Kyd) was also Drayton's closest friend. Drayton's reputation as a poet in his own day was very high, and he adopted the literary name of Rowland for himself. He wrote an Epitaph on Marlowe:*

(*Courtesy of Dulwich College*)

Neat* Marlowe, bathed in the Thespian springs,
Had in him those brave translunary things
That the first poets had; his raptures were
All ayre and fire, which made his verses cleere;
For that fine madness still he did retaine,
Which rightly should possesse a poet's braine.

EPISTLES OF POETS AND POESY, 1635.

* *Neat – unsophisticated, natural, close to nature.*

nettled. Marlowe, in his eyes, was more conceited than he was himself, too arrogant by half! He did not hesitate to sum him up accordingly:

> *He that not feared God, nor dreaded Diu'll,*
> *Nor ought admired but his wondrous selfe*

Not so Spenser. Their early relationship as benevolent tutor and poor pupil had established a footing which Gabriel savoured to the full. His vanity was flattered when Spenser achieved such gratifying success, imagining he had a hand in it (as indeed he had, to do him justice), and he bathed happily in his pupil's reflected glory. Harvey assiduously nurtured their friendship with voluminous letter writing. He went so far as to publish a little book of his correspondence with his 'singular good frend' Edmund Spenser, whereupon Nashe caustically remarked: 'Immortall Spenser, no frailtie hath thy fame, but the imputation of this Idiots friendship.'

Spenser, however, was not the man to forget a kindness, and besides he was away from London and the Court for a good deal of the time. He genuinely

157

valued Harvey, and in his letters and poems Spenser affectionately nicknamed his sharp-countenanced friend 'Hobbinal', the name by which Peele also refers to him in his *Honour of the Garter*.

During Marlowe's London years Spenser was mainly resident in Ireland where he was completing *The Faerie Queene*, but in 1589–90 he was in London once more to see the first three books of his work to the press, to which Ralegh had urged him. The two men had returned from Ireland together, Spenser coming at Ralegh's invitation as his protégé to be introduced at Court, for Ralegh was sure that the Queen would be delighted with his work. If Spenser was the 'new poet', Marlowe was equally the 'new dramatist', and it would seem entirely natural that the two should now meet, and that Ralegh would have seen to it that they were introduced. As has been noted, Royden was also a mutual friend, and it seems unlikely that in such a close circle Spenser would not have made contact with Marlowe. Certain lines in *Tamburlaine* which re-echo passages in *The Faerie Queen* suggest an intimate knowledge of each other's works, though who borrowed from whom remains a mystery. *The Faerie Queene* was the first of the two works to appear in print by a short head, but *Tamburlaine* was already on the stage, and in any case manuscripts passed regularly from hand to hand, many a writer gaining a high reputation based on his manuscript works alone. The noverint or scribe also had to be kept busy for a livelihood.

Of the poets in this 'school' *George Peele*, who was a particular friend of Marlowe's, seems at first impression an unlikely candidate for membership of so eminent and serious-minded a group. He was a gay spark, whose merry pranks (doubtless embellished and exaggerated) form the basis of the anonymous tract *The Merry, Conceited Jestes of George Peele, Sometime a Student in Oxford* (registered at the Stationers' in 1605), and in Dekker's *A Knight's Conjuring*, 1607, he is similarly represented as the boon companion of Kit Marlowe and Robert Greene. (Perhaps it was this kind of practical joking, sometimes no doubt unkind to the unfortunate victim, to which Kyd was referring in his letter to Puckering.)

But any conception of the Elizabethans that does not allow for their tremendous versatility and zest for life, in which they ran the gamut of extremes of behaviour, can only distort for us the picture of these men. Their Queen was herself the epitome of her age in this: she could deliver an extempore Latin oration; converse in several European languages at will, having a magnificent command of English; she could play and sing and dance like an angel; and she also swore and spat like a trooper when she was displeased. Peele was very much an Elizabethan. He was also a brilliant scholar, taking a B.A. and M.A. at Oxford, where he quickly gained a reputation as a poet with his translation of Euripides' *Iphigenia* and his *Tale of Troy*. Being some six years older than Marlowe, he was already an established playwright when the other came to London, but was much influenced by Marlowe's work. Peele's *The Battle of Alcazar* is written very much in the manner of *Tamburlaine*, and his *Edward I* may have been inspired by Marlowe's *Edward II*. There is also some evidence to show

158

Euphues golden Legacie, found after his death in his Cell at Silexedra.

BEQVEATHED TO PHILAVTVS

Sonnes, nourſed vp with their Father in England,

Fetcht from the Canaries by T.L.Gent,

LONDON,
Printed by Abel Ieffes for T.G.
and *Iohn Burbie*. 1592,

George Peele's signature from Anglorum Feriae *(1595). British Museum MS Add. 1432, fol. 1.*

THOMAS LODGE (1558?–1625) *was the second son of Sir Thomas Lodge, Lord Mayor of London. He studied law, and later medicine, and indulged in a sporadic literary career. Shakespeare took his plot for* As You Like It *from Lodge's charming romance* Rosalynde, *and drew upon other works of Lodge as sources for* The Tempest *and* King Lear. *Lodge was keenly interested in exploration and made a voyage to the Canaries in 1588, and in 1591 he sailed on Thomas Cavendish's last ill-fated voyage to South America as far as the Straits of Magellan.*

(*Courtesy of British Museum*)

that he collaborated with Marlowe and Greene in *Henry VI*, Part i. (This is discussed in a later chapter.)

Peele gained the patronage of the Earl of Northumberland, who was raised to Knight of the Garter at Windsor in 1593. It was to commemorate this occasion that Peele wrote his 'poem gratulatorie' entitled *The Honour of the Garter*, in 1593, shortly after Marlowe's death. In it he apostrophizes the 'Thrice noble Earle',

> *The Muses loue, Patrone, and fauoret,*
> *That artizans and schollers doost embrace,*

and mentions the poets of 'heroicall spirits' in his patronage, particularly praising the Earl's 'admirable mathematique skill':

> *Familiar with the starres and Zodiack,*
> *(To whom the heauen lyes open as her booke)*
> *By whose directions vndeceiuable,*
> *(Leauing our Schoolemens vulgar troden pathes)*
> *And following the auncient reuerend steps*

Of Trismegistus *and* Pythagoras,
Through vncouth waies and vnaccessible
Doost passe into the spacious pleasant fieldes
Of diuine science and Phylosophie.

The poets he mentions are evidently those whom the Earl particularly admired:

Liberall Sidney, *famous for the loue*
He bare to learning and to Chiualrie.
. . . .

(Harvey)   *Great* Hobbinall *on whom our shepheards gaze*
And Harrington *well letter'd and discreet*
That hath so purely naturalized
Strange words, and made them all free-denyzons.

Sir John Harrington, whom the Queen called 'that saucy poet, my godson', was certainly an entertaining and spicy writer, but scarcely discreet! He was banished the court 'till he had grown sober' upon the publication of his satires on court personalities written under the pseudonym of Misacmos. He was the translator of Ariosto's *Orlando Furioso*, which he prefaced with 'An Apologie for Poetrie'. Then follows:

(Lodge)   . . . Rosamonds *trumpeter*
Sweet as the Nightingall.

This must be *Thomas Lodge*, who was most famous for his romance *Rosalynde* from which the plot of Shakespeare's *As You Like It* was later taken. Next he mentions:

Campion, *accompanied with our English* Fraunce,
A peerlesse sweet Translator of our time.

And lastly, 'Fellowes to these Apolloes fauorets', two who had recently died, and were mourned:

Watson, *worthy many Epitaphes*
For his sweet Poesie, for Amintas *teares*
And ioyes so well set downe. And after thee
Why hie thee not, vnhappy in thine end,
Marley, *the Muses darling, for thy verse,*
Fitte to write passions for the soules below.

Northumberland's liberal patronage to learning is attested by the entries in the Sion House Rolls which list numerous payments on behalf of the Earl to writers, geographers, physicians and colleges and schools. At this time also £3 was paid to 'one George Peele, a poett, as my Lord's liberalities', perhaps in connection with the above dedication.[19] But with George it is evident that money 'runs headlong to the boor', for he was often driven to 'extreme shifts' to make ends meet, and perhaps this is why he appeared on occasion as an actor with the Lord Admiral's and the Queen's Men. Like Marlowe he was a brilliant fellow

GEORGE CHAPMAN (155?–1634), *an engraving by William Hole which was used as frontispiece for Chapman's widely acclaimed translation of the Works of Homer (1616).*

of fairly humble origins, being the son of a London salter and clerk of Christ's Hospital where the family had lodgings, from which they were evicted in 1597, possibly on account of George's 'gaieties'. The exact circumstances and date of Peele's death are not known. He fades out of the picture some four years after Marlowe, leaving as his best memorial the many lovely lyrics which were deservedly popular with his contemporaries.

George Chapman was also one of Marlowe's closest friends in this group, and one more different from George Peele it would be hard to imagine. Wood describes him as 'a person of most reverend aspect, religious and temperate—qualities rarely meeting in a poet'. He attended both Oxford and Cambridge, where he 'was observed to be most excellent in the Latin and Greek tongues'. His intellectual stature is to be seen in the depth of moral reflection found in his works. It was Marlowe who first encouraged him to publish his poem *The Shadow of Night* and perhaps introduced him to Thomas Walsingham, who became his patron and lifelong friend after Marlowe's death. Chapman's plays and poems contain great passages, though his language tends to suffer from obscurity as dark as the 'Night' he constantly courts. His greatest work was undoubtedly his splendid translation of the Twelve Books of Homer, which remains one of the truly monumental achievements of the Elizabethan age.

Another poet suspected of being a member of this school, the mutual friend of Chapman and Marlowe, was the lawyer *John Marston*. He was a member of the Middle Temple, but forsook law for literature, writing satires at first, and later turning to drama. His plays are enlivened by caustic wit and ribaldry and a certain sardonic humour. His single reference to Kit is a testimony that sheds a gentle light; he called him 'kinde Kit Marlowe'.

Of singular interest, and not so far remarked, is the fact that Marlowe's former patron, *Ferdinando Stanley*, Lord Strange, who in September 1593 succeeded to the title of Lord Derby, was also associated in the School of Night. Chapman, in his dedication to Matthew Royden, gave us the clue: 'how

161

joyfully ofttimes you reported unto me, that most ingenious Derby, deep-searching Northumberland, and skill-embracing heir of Hunsdon had most profitably entertained learning &c.' Hunsdon (George Carey) was Ferdinando Stanley's brother-in-law, and the two are here associated in this circle of thinkers with the Earl of Northumberland.

Ferdinando Stanley was a Catholic nobleman noted for his patronage of men of letters. He also patronized Michael Lok, the world explorer, whose map of the world (1582) was widely used. Stanley's particular interest was the drama, and he kept a company of players of his own (in addition to that kept by his father as Lord Derby) known as Lord Strange's Men. Kyd, and on his testimony Marlowe also, wrote for them. Their repertoire in 1591–2 included Marlowe's *Jew of Malta*, Kyd's *Spanish Tragedy* and Greene's *Friar Bacon and Friar Bungay* and his *Orlando Furioso*. Edward Alleyn joined them for a time, and they became the strongest acting troupe then in existence. Ferdinando Stanley was himself an excellent poet and reputed one of the 'courtly makers' of plays. Among the poets and playwrights he patronized were Nashe, Spenser, Greene, Kyd, and presumably also Marlowe.

Not only as a patron of literature but as a man Stanley was evidently much beloved. His sudden and tragic death from poison, barely seven months after his accession to the title as Lord Derby, caused great consternation amongst all those close to him. The story of this dreadful event is quite remarkable.

Although a Catholic, Lord Derby does not appear to have been a fanatic in religion, and certainly his association in the School of Night would argue a broad and tolerant view. Evidently, however, the Catholic faction thought to use him in a plot against the Queen. The contemporary historian William Camden (who later purchased property at Chislehurst and became a close neighbour of Thomas Walsingham) wrote:

> 'Richard Hasket being secretly sent by the English fugitives persuaded Ferdinand, Earl of Derby (whose father Henry was lately deceased) to take upon him the title of the Crowne, fetching his pedigree from his great grand-mother Mary, daughter of Henry the seventh and made him large promises of men and money from the Spaniard threatening the Earl with assured destruction unless he would do it and conceal the matter.
>
> 'But the Earl, fearing lest some trappe were layed for him, accused the man, who by his own confession acknowledged the crime. . . . Yet those menaces sayled not of performance: for the Earle, after foure moneths, dyed miserably of a horrid kinde of death.'[20]

Hasket had been delivered to justice by the Earl, and was executed at the summer assizes at St. Albans. It was believed that the Roman Catholics in revenge poisoned Lord Derby, although some of the persons around the Earl believed that his sufferings had been caused by witchcraft. The symptoms strongly indicate poison, for he was 'seized and tormented by vomiting matter of a dark rusty colour' which was 'so violent and corroding that it stained the

FERDINANDO STANLEY, LORD STRANGE, LATER EARL OF DERBY (1559?–1594) *was a renowned patron of the drama, and himself a writer of plays and poetry. Some of his rarely published verses appeared in* Belvedere, Garden of the Muses, *ed. John Bodenham, 1600. Nashe, Greene, Kyd, and Marlowe were among those he patronized, although Kyd throws aspersions on Marlowe's association with him. He kept a company of players of his own called Lord Strange's Men, who were considered the leading acting ensemble in their time. At Stanley's death they were not taken over by his brother, the next Earl of Derby, but passed to Lord Hunsdon, and from him to his son George Carey, who succeeded him as Lord Hunsdon in 1596. It was for this company that Marlowe wrote* The Jew of Malta, *and in which Shakespeare's name was first listed in December 1594, and with which he remained throughout his career.*

silver and irons in the chimney of his room'. When he died, though his body was 'wrapped in sear cloth, and covered with lead', yet it so corrupted and putrefied, that for a long time after, none could endure to come near the place it was laid in till his burial.

His death was greatly lamented. He had been a generous master, good to his tenants, a munificent patron, a loving and indulgent husband and tender and affectionate parent, a loyal friend. Many poems were written in his honour, of which Spenser's elegy laments his death most movingly, designating Ferdinando under the name of Amyntas, and his wife, the Dowager Duchess of Derby, as Amaryllis:

> *Amyntas quite is gone,*
> *And lies full low,*
> *Having his Amaryllis*
> *Left to mourn:*
> *Help, oh ye shepherds!*
> *Help ye all in this,*
> *Help Amaryllis this her loss to mourn:*
> *Her loss is yours, your loss Amyntas is.*
>
> *Amyntas, flower of shepherds pride forlorn,*
> *He whilest he lived was the noblest Swain*
> *That ever pipéd in an oaten quill:*
> *Both did he other which could pipe maintain,*
> *And eke could pipe himself with passing skill.*

A long pastoral ballad in thirty-five stanzas by Sir John Hawkins, entitled *A Sonnet*, extolls Ferdinando Stanley as a 'shepherd' (i.e. a poet) whose only thoughts were for his 'sheep', and refers affectionately to him as this boy 'which yet was but a boy, did grow a man and men loved him'. Thus eulogized died one of the great noblemen of the School of Night, who must undoubtedly have known Kit Marlowe and was probably for a time his patron.

*   *   *

There came also to London, before Marlowe's time, one who exerted such a lasting influence on the thinkers of this group that he must be included. This was *Giordano Bruno* the Nolan, one-time Dominican monk, now a wandering scholar, teacher, and writer, 'Graduate of No Academy, called the Nuisance' as he whimsically styles himself on the title page of a play he wrote (*Il Candalaio* —*The Torch-bearers*).

Bruno was an uncomfortable genius whose piercing vision opened up a new concept of the universe far beyond that of contemporary scientific thought: a universe stretching out to infinity and governed by an all-pervading deity. He was a formidable heretic. Wherever he went he sowed trouble for himself and enlightenment for others, while his own fiery nature drew him ever onward in the path of martyrdom, into the flames of the stake at Rome where they finally imprisoned him for eight years before burning him.

On 28th March, 1583, Sir Henry Cobham, ambassador in Paris, wrote to Sir Francis Walsingham:

> 'Dr. Jordano Bruno Nolano, a professor in philosophy, intendeth to pass into England, whose religion I cannot commend.'[21]

There were many distinguished Italian émigrés in England at this time. Among them was Albericus Gentilis, who had great influence with the Queen and held strongly the liberal view that force should not be used as an instrument of religious conversion, which was shared by Sir Francis Walsingham. Among Gentilis's friends were Sir Philip Sidney, Sir Francis Walsingham's cousin-german Sir Thomas Walsingham, the Earl of Leicester, Lord Burghley, and John Florio, another distinguished Italian émigré. The Italians were much in favour at Court at this time, and their number among the foreign refugees was steadily rising, although as yet the smallest of the alien communities.

Bruno landed in England with royal letters of recommendation from Henry III to the French ambassador in London, *Michel de Castelnau, Marquis de Mauvissière*, who was a friend of John Florio and also of Sir Walter Ralegh. Mauvissière was a great humanist, the ofttimes spokesman for Protestants, although himself a devout Catholic. He was an outstanding man who did great credit to his office as ambassador, and in coming under his roof Bruno at once found himself in touch with a circle of brilliant intellectuals and the foreign émigrés who revolved in it. Of the latter, the most important was *John Florio*, the translator of Montaigne's *Essays* and compiler of the first Italian-English dictionary, who was a well-known figure in London literary society. A particular friend of Florio's was *Sir Edward Dyer*, co-founder of the literary *Areopagus* club with Sir Philip Sidney, although his own sole contribution to published litera-

JOHN FLORIO (1553?–1625) *was a distinguished Italian Protestant émigré with literary interests.* He gained fame as the translator of Montaigne's Essays, *and he was in the pay and patronage of the Earl of Southampton and the Earl of Pembroke.* He befriended Giordano Bruno in London and introduced him to Ralegh's circle. Florio features in Bruno's Dialogues under the name of Eliotropio. *(Florio's coat of arms bore this flower, and his motto 'chi si contenta gode' is echoed by this character.)*

(Courtesy of British Museum)

ture was his whimsical work *The Prayse of Nothing*. Florio was also on terms of intimacy with his publisher *Edward Blount*, who specialised in works of Italian origin and became the friend of Marlowe and his patron Thomas Walsingham. This argues that Blount was in all probability also a member of the School of Night.

Bruno's fame had gone before him, and he at once became the centre of eager discussions among Ralegh and his associates. At their invitation he began to expound his ideas to the glittering assembly of scholarly aristocrats, with their poets and protégés of science, who welcomed him into their midst and in turn stimulated him to his finest achievement. His single year in London saw the publication of his two greatest works, his *Heroici Furori* and *De Immenso et Innumerabilibus*.

On a personal level, however, Bruno's reaction to the English environment was a curious one. He was not, apparently, used to the kind of reception he received, and the ostentation of the English courtiers amused and amazed him, evoking his sarcastic personal comment, which he published with typical tactlessness in his *Dialogues*, describing his meetings with some of the distinguished learned members of the English society into which he was admitted.

In sharp contrast to his outbursts of poetic rhapsody over the English Muses, and his equally vehement admiration for the great Queen Elizabeth, comes his fierce castigation of persons whose pompous and self-opinionated ignorance he despised. Bruno's pen, when used against an adversary, was a deadly weapon. This portrait of one of the Philistine Englishmen he encountered is as brilliantly executed as a Goya painting. Describing his nameless victim, he tells us that he 'has an emphasis on his face such as the Father of the Gods wore when he sat at the celestial council to fulminate an awful sentence against impious Lycaeon. . . . [He] admired the gold chain round his neck and then glanced at the Nolan's breast where the loss of a button were more likely to be found. . . . Then he sat bolt upright, took his elbows off the table, shook himself a little, gave a short snort, adjusted his velvet cap, twirled his moustache, made his scented face assume a proper expression, arched his eyebrows, distended his nostrils, cast a glance backward, set himself in order, struck an attitude—left hand to left side, as if he were opening a fencing match—held three fingers of his right hand and began with a few preliminary flourhishes.'[22]

On the other hand, when Bruno admired an Englishman of true nobility, such as Sir Philip Sidney, the Earl of Leicester or Sir Francis Walsingham, his praise was lavish and wholehearted. Dedicating his two chief works on ethics, the *Spaccio* and *Heroici Furori*, to Sir Philip Sidney, he wrote: 'Philosophy displays her form unveiled to so clear an eye as yours. The way of heroism is pointed out to a heroic and generous spirit.'

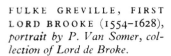

FULKE GREVILLE, FIRST LORD BROOKE (1554–1628), *portrait by P. Van Somer, collection of Lord de Broke.*

166

In the presence of such as Sidney, Greville, Ralegh and Mauvissière and their circle, Bruno deigned to display his extraordinary powers of inspirational thought. These Englishmen must have been amazed by the Italian's visionary eloquence, and many of them were deeply influenced by their discussions with him. These sessions sometimes took the form of intellectual supper-parties on the lines of Plato's *Symposium*, and an account of one of them in Bruno's lively and inimitable style has been left to us in his *La Cene de le Ceneri* or *The Ash Wednesday Supper*, which Bruno describes as having taken place at the home of *Sir Fulke Greville*, where, he states, 'we met in a chamber . . . to discuss moral, metaphysical, mathematical and natural speculation'.

The *Second Dialogue* gives an account of this evening:

THEOPHILO:

So Fulke Greville said: By your leave, Mr. Nolano, do explain why you maintain that the earth moves! The latter replied that he could furnish no proof as long as he was not sure of the other's powers of comprehension: as long as he did not know whether he would be understood he must take care to act like someone who is defending his opinion before a statue, or holding a discussion with a dead man. Would he (Greville) therefore first of all have the goodness to explain to him why he took the opposite view; then he (Nolano) would, according to the powers of comprehension and insight displayed, put forward his own counter-arguments. He added that it would be incumbent on him to prove the weakness of the opposing opinion; to show that he, starting from the same point of departure, would arrive at the contrary view, and it would therefore please him greatly to find people who were esteemed to be sufficiently mature for such an undertaking, and he would always be ready to give his reasons and explanations to such people. This reply pleased Lord Greville, and he said: May I be allowed to invite you to my house next Wednesday, Ash Wednesday, when there will be many distinguished gentlemen present? After supper we shall be able to discuss many things.

'With the greatest of pleasure,' said Nolano, 'I accept your kind invitation. I would be loathe to miss a good opportunity of extending my knowledge and learning. May I, however, make the proviso that you do not assemble a collection of uneducated, uncultured people who are not conversant with such and similar learned questions.' He had indeed good reason for fearing this, for already in literary circles in England he had come across far too many learned men who displayed in such discussions more the manners of ox-drivers than of gentlemen. Sir Fulke Greville replied that he need have no fear: the gathering to which he was invited would consist solely of cultured and deeply learned gentlemen. So it was arranged. But when the day came—O, ye Muses, help me to relate what happened.

PRUDENTIO:

Apostrophe, pathos, invocatio, poetarum more!

FRULLA:

I beg you, Mr. Prudentio, do be quiet!

PRUDENTIO:

Lubentissime.

THEOPHILO:

Nolano had waited until lunchtime, and since he had received no news by then, assumed that the good man had forgotten his promise, that something must have detained him. So he went for a stroll and visited some of his Italian friends and did not return home until sunset.

PRUDENTIO:

Already flaming Phoebus had turned his back on our peninsula in order that he might light the antipodes with his burning head.

FRULLA:

By your leave, Prudentio, do tell the story yourself, for your manner of delivery appeals to me greatly!

PRUDENTIO:

Yes, if I only knew the story.

FRULLA:

Then in the name of the Devil hold your tongue!

THEOPHILO:

Late in the evening he met before his door Mr. Florio and Mr. Guin,[23] who had long searched for him everywhere. When they saw him they said: 'Ah! By your leave, we have been looking for you the whole afternoon. A great many lords, gentlemen and doctors are waiting for you: one of them, who has the same Christian name as yourself, wants to hold a discourse with you.'

'Please forgive me,' said Nolano. 'I was under the impression that we were to hold the meeting during the day; now, however, I find that the discussion is to take place by candle-light.' Mr. Guin apologised for the delay which was on account of some noblemen who would have liked to be present, but who could only have come to supper and not to breakfast. 'Very well,' said Nolano, 'let us pray God to accompany us on our long, late journey in the dark night through such unsafe streets.'

Although we could have gone directly, we thought we might shorten our journey by turning off through side-streets to the Thames in the hope of finding a boat to convey us to the palace. Thus, we came to the bridge by the palace of Lord Buckhurst, where we wasted as much time shouting 'Oars'—that is, boatman, gondolier—as we would have taken to go by land, and taking our time about it at that. Finally, from afar, two boatmen answered and, as though they thought we were going to hang them, approached suspiciously. At length, after many questions and answers as to whither, whence and why, how, when and where, they lay alongside the lowest step. And lo, one of them, who looked exactly like the ancient boatman of the underworld, reached out his hand to Nolano, while the other—who seemed to be

168

his son, although to judge by his appearance he was at least 65 years old—took his other hand, and although there was no Hercules, no Aeneas or King of Sarza, no Rodomont among us

> *Gemuit sub pondere cymba*
> *Sutilis et multam accepit limosa paludem.**

There follows a lengthy digression in which Bruno and his companions, after a fruitless journey by water which brings them no nearer their destination, lose their way in London's muddy and ill-lit streets, until they eventually arrive at Sir Fulke Greville's house, and knock on the door. At last—

> 'We enter and find many sorts of people and many servants in the hall. They neither made way nor inclined the head nor gave any sign of reverence, but disdainfully did us so much favour as to point the way upstairs.'[24]

This unceremonious reception elucidates a further long digression in which Bruno catalogues the various classes of English society from the lowest desperados and ruffians, through servants and artisans, to noblemen with their protégés and various sub-classes of hangers-on, which takes the form of a virulently derogatory commentary on English manners. Though low-born himself, Bruno hated the 'stinking mob', particularly the arrogant English.

Bruno's account of this evening gives us a vivid glimpse (if, alas, only a glimpse, and a singularly unflattering one at that, for he views English table manners with distaste and is horrified at the custom of passing the cup of wine from lip to lip with occasional hairs from the previous imbiber's beard adhering to it!) of the School of Night at one of its convivial and intellectually stimulating social gatherings, as seen through the cynical eyes of this disturbingly outspoken Italian renegade monk. *The Ash Wednesday Supper* is, perhaps, the most extraordinary contemporary commentary made on this extraordinary age. The picture is coloured by Bruno's unabashed arrogance of mind, and one cannot help feeling that this curious literary offering must have made somewhat uncomfortable reading for the Englishmen who recognised themselves represented in the stark light of the Italian's uninhibited criticism. He spices his account with his peculiar brand of wry impish humour, which perhaps earned him forgiveness for his trespasses of etiquette, although it is quite apparent that he cares not one jot on whose toes he treads. He demands it as his right to criticise and expose with brisk indiscrimination, and while accusing others of lack of manners is blandly oblivious of the fact that he invites the accusation of making the most outrageous breaches himself. While his main aim is to use his canvas to paint his grand conception of the infinite universe for men to see and understand (providing their powers of comprehension permitted it) he is also, apparently, intent on entertaining his audience.

As a reflection of the times in the mirror of one of the most brilliantly original minds of that age, *The Ash Wednesday Supper* is worth our amused and atten-

---

*'The stitched boat groaned beneath his weight and took in much muddy marsh water.'
AENEID, Book VI

tive scrutiny. In it Bruno himself is doubly designated under the names of Nolano and Theophilo, the story-teller, who, with his two stooges, Prudentio and Frulla, takes the centre of the stage and holds our attention riveted with a mixture of clowning, caustic comment and poetry; and while leading us along every devious avenue of thought or fancy that occurs to him, he lures us on willy-nilly to the theme his soul loves, his fantastic vision of the Infinite Universe. It is when he finally reaches this that his exposition crystallises into a brilliant scientific argument which holds one spellbound, even as he must have done the members of the School of Night. The exposition of this is contained in *The Third Dialogue*, which commences with Elpino stating the orthodox view and Theophilo countering it:

ELPINO:

The opinion of diverse heavens hath then been caused by diverse motions of the stars and by the appearance of the sky filled with stars revolving around the earth . . . they appear to revolve round the earth, even as a wheel on which are nailed innumerable mirrors revolveth around his own axis. Thus it is considered obvious from the evidence of our own eyes that these luminaries have no motion of their own.

THEOPHILO:

Such is the common opinion. But once the motion is understood of our own mundane star which is no fixed orb, but impelled by her own intrinsic principle, soul, and nature, taketh her course around the sun through the vastness of universal space, and spinneth around her own centre, then this opinion will be dispelled. Then will be opened the gate of understanding of the true principles of nature, and we shall be enabled to advance with great strides along the path of truth which hath been hidden by the veil of sordid and bestial illusions and hath remained secret until today, through the injury of time and the vicissitudes of things, ever since there succeeded to the daylight of the ancient sages the murky night of the foolhardy sophists.

> *Nought standeth still, but all things swirl and whirl*
> *As far as in heaven and beneath is seen.*
> *All things move, now up, now down,*
> *Whether on a long or short course,*
> *Whether heavy or light;*
> *Perchance thou too goest the same path*
> *And to a like goal.*
> *For all things move till overtaken,*
> *As the wave swirleth through the water,*
> *So that the same part*
> *Moveth now from above downward,*
> *And now from below upward,*
> *And the same hurly-burly*
> *Imparteth to all the same successive fate.*[25]

170

Compare Bruno's stunning exposition above of the 'sacred vigour' and restless movement of the universe with Marlowe's conception of an immanent all-pervading and restless Deity in *Tamburlaine the Great*:

> *Open thou shining veil of Cynthia*
> *And make a passage from th' empyreal heaven*
> *That he that sits on high and never sleeps*
> *Nor in one place is circumscriptible,*
> *But everywhere fills every continent*
> *With strange infusion of his sacred vigour,*
> *May in his endless power and purity,*
> *Behold . . .*

TAMBURLAINE, *Part II, Act. II, Sc. ii.*

Bruno's influence on the School of Night was marked. At his trial he was questioned concerning the Ash Wednesday Supper and it is quite evident that this report is based on a real happening, although Bruno there stated that it had taken place at the house of Mauvissière and not at Fulke Greville's. Probably there were similar events at both, or several houses in London. Hariot would almost certainly have been among those who met Bruno during his year in England, and it is evident that he was deeply engrossed with the ideas propagated. Ethel Seaton discovered the words 'Nolanus de immenso mundi' written on a manuscript of Hariot's, and extant letters prove that he had been corresponding on the subject. Kepler, who also corresponded with Hariot, in a letter to his friend Wacker shows that he accepted Bruno's view 'that there are innumerable other worlds similar to ours', but he rejected his idea of an infinite universe. Sir William Lower, writing from Traven'ti in South Wales to his 'espesial good frind' Thomas Hariot (21 June, 1610), comments on Kepler's views:

> 'Wee Traventine Philosophers were considering of Kepler's reasons by which he indeavours to overthrow Nolanus and Gilberts opinions concerninge the immensitie of the spheere of the starres, and that opinion particularlie of Nolanus by which he affirmeth that the eye being placed in anaie parte of the universe, the apparence would be still all one unto us here.'[26]

Thomas Watson was also a disciple of Bruno's with regard to his work on mnemonics, the science of artificial memory, on which Bruno lectured in Paris to the great impression of King Henry III. Watson himself published a little book on the subject which he says, however, is not to be compared 'with the mystical and deeply learned Sigillus of the Nolan'.

Bruno's work on mnemonics was considered important in his day, but this was a mere trifle compared to the lasting value of the ideas developed in his cosmology, which were far in advance of his time. Because of their revolutionary impact on those whom Bruno influenced, including Marlowe, it is of importance to state briefly what these ideas represented.

In the 16th century the Aristotelian concept of the universe as an airy edifice of concentric spheres surrounding a central motionless earth still dominated European thought. According to their belief, the earth was wrapped around with three spheres, each of decreasing density: Water—Air—Fire. Outside this was the sublunary or mundane sphere. Then came seven more, each the abode of a particular planet. Outside this was the sphere of the fixed stars. Then, last of all, the sphere of 'primum mobile' or motion imparted by Divine Power. To make this concept workable various modifications and devices were added, making up the complicated theory of Ptolemy. Copernicus had caused a furore when he substituted the sun as the centre of this concept in place of the earth, but apart from this he had really made no revolutionary changes.

It was Bruno who was the revolutionary. He both anticipated Galileo and Kepler, and transcended them. His philosophy was based on his vision of an infinite universe with an infinity of worlds. He was neither astronomer nor mathematician, but a philosopher. By means of his inspired reasoning he developed a group of astonishing theories, both revolutionary and coherent: the theory of 'innate necessity' to which all motion and all changes of state are attributable; the theory of relativity, that all things and all states are relative to each other and to the *point of view*, recognising that the human eye can see only in part—a most significant development; the atomic theory, that the world is made of 'minima' and 'monads' which combine in different forms; and he vigorously combated Aristotle's argument of the *void*, which to Bruno was anathema. In his *De Immenso et Innumerabilibus* he argues:

'The order and power of light and darkness are not equal: light is diffused and penetrates to deepest darkness, but darkness does not reach to the purest regions of light. Thus light comprehends darkness, overcomes and conquers it throughout infinity.'*[27]

From this he develops the fatal heresy resolving the individual will in a universal pantheism:

'Hence it is clear that every spirit and soul has a certain continuity with the spirit of the universe, so that it has its being and existence not only there where it perceives and lives, but it is also by its essence and substance diffused throughout immensity as was realised by many Platonists and Pythagoreans.'[28]

He asks, 'Does not this simple spirit insinuate itself (into all things) pervading completely and everywhere throughout the infinity of Space?' This is the grand theme which runs through all Bruno's thought.

'The one infinite is perfect, in simplicity of itself, absolutely, nor can ought be greater or better. This is the one Whole, God, universal Nature, occupying all space, of whom nought but infinity can give the perfect image or semblance.'[29]

Here we have the very seed of the Arrian heresy which questioned the divinity of Christ on the grounds that a mere man, subject to earthly passions

* *Today we know that the light from stars billions of light-years distant eventually reaches us.*

and sufferings, however noble in himself, could not be equated with the majesty of God. It was a transcript of the Arrian heresy, found in the possession of his friend Kyd, but belonging to Marlowe, which later brought Marlowe into trouble.

As we have seen, there are echoes of Bruno's cosmology in Marlowe's writings, as also in Spenser's and Ralegh's.[30] At his trial Bruno defended the heresy of Arrius on the grounds that it was 'misunderstood', and it is evident that both Hariot and Marlowe were influenced by the same opinion; even Ralegh is in essence a Deist.

George Chapman seems particularly to have shared the Nolan's personal antipathy to the mob, which is expressed by Chapman in his dedication to Royden of *The Shadow of Night* in words remarkably similar to those used by Bruno in his more moving dedication to Mauvissière of his great work *On the Infinite Universe and Worlds*:

'I hate the mob, I loathe the vulgar herd and in the multitude I find no joy. It is Unity that doth enchant me. By her power I am free though thrall, happy in sorrow, rich in poverty, and quick even in death . . . They carry their chains with them; their spirit containeth her own hell that bringeth them low.'

Aware that he is held to be 'an unquiet spirit that would undermine the edifice of good discipline to establish the frame of perversity', he prays that

'the harvest of my labours may appear to the world useful and glorious, and the understanding of those in darkness be illumined. For assuredly, I do not feign; and if I err I do so unwittingly . . . Thus I present to you my contemplation concerning the infinite universe and innumerable worlds.'[31]

When he wrote this he did not know the penalty he would have to pay in the end. Yet here it seems he is prophetically preparing himself for it. And when it came it was 'this overwhelming vision' which upheld him. 'Its awful majesty alone enabled him to support the eight suffering years that culminated in his death.'[32]

> *Forth from the womb*
> *Of darkness, free and passionate, I dart.*
> *I dread no barrier of banished spheres;*
> *I cleave the sky, and other suns behold;*
> *Celestial worlds innumerable I see;*
> *One left, another company appears;*
> *My ọpinions fail not, and my heart is bold,*
> *To journey on through all infinity.*[33]

Giordano Bruno has been treated at some length here because he is the exemplar of all that the School of Night stood for in its fearless investigation and questioning of current beliefs, its scientific attitude towards material and spiritual phenomena.

Bruno

'set forth the essential element in the faith of the new age; the attitude that will accept no preconceived idea concerning any part of the infinite universe. Thereby he opened up a new approach to the interpretation of Nature, and with it a new ethic and a new philosophy.'[34]

As the extreme example, Bruno suffered the extreme penalty, in which, but for the hand of fate, Marlowe might have joined in martyrdom with him. The members of the School of Night here listed and described all played a part in this great pioneering movement of thought, in which art and literature went hand in hand with the sciences; even as a scientist Bruno calls upon the Muses to aid him in setting forth his philosophical ideas and breaks into poetry during his discourses. His *Heroic Raptures*, indeed, comprise a group of songs to the cithern, the lyre, the mandolin, viol, Spanish timbrel, lute, Irish harp, viol and bow, and rebeck. It may be said that it was poetry that made him a philosopher. Is it any wonder that he left his mark on the poets and thinkers of the English School of Night, who had stimulated him to his own finest achievement, and which was in itself a gathering of a singular and remarkable kind. As Eleanor Grace Clark has remarked:

'The story of the interrelation and artistic output of this little band of supermen has never been told.'[35]

STATUE OF GIORDANO BRUNO (1548–1600) *erected as a memorial to his martyrdom in the cause of human knowledge.*

'Escaped from the narrow murky prison
Where for so many years error held me straitly,
Here I leave the chain that bound me,
And the shadow of my fiercely malicious foe
Who can force me no longer to the gloomy dusk of night
For he who hath overcome the great Python
With whose blood he hath dyed the waters of the sea,
Hath put to flight the Fury that pursued me.
To thee I turn, I soar, O my sustaining Voice;
I render thanks to thee, my sun, my divine light,
For thou hast summoned me from that horrible torture,
Thou hast led me to a goodlier tabernacle;
Thou hast brought healing to my bruised heart.'

DE IMMENSO ET INNUMERABILIBUS 1584[36]

174

(Courtesy of the British Museum)

A page from Hariot's Mathematical Papers (Add. MS. 6788, f. 533).

Hariot's huge notebooks demonstrate his widespread scientific and intellectual interests. They are filled with miscellaneous calculations and notes on various subjects. Also included therein are tracts on harmony, infinite series, extracts from the gospel of St. Matthew and a treatise on algebra, in French, and occasional letters. Hariot corresponded with many of the outstanding scientific figures of his day, notably with Kepler, who attested great admiration for his English compeer. Hariot was important as an astronomer as well as mathematician. Anthony à Wood has aptly described him as 'The Universal Philosopher'.

The page of mathematical jottings shown here comes from the interesting seventh volume of Hariot's notebooks. This volume contains copious notes on ship construction and a section of detailed tables to find the declination of the sun at any time of the year, pages of mathematical calculations, and diagrams, some elaborately drawn and with movable parts. Included in this volume alone are pages on mechanics, hydrostatics, specific gravity and magnetism. A letter from Nathaniel Torporley is in the same notebook.

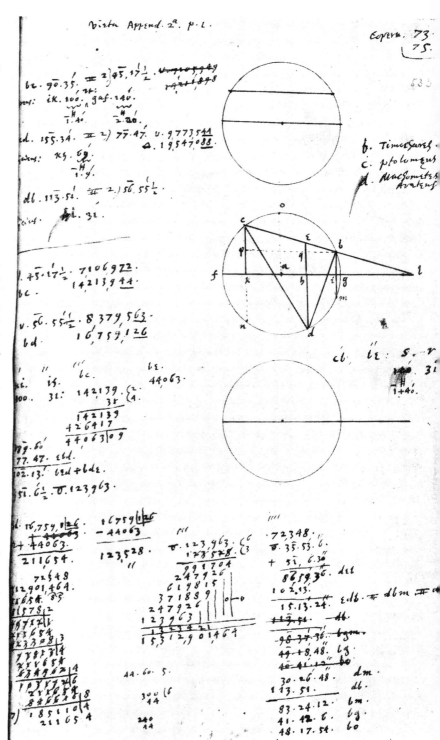

175

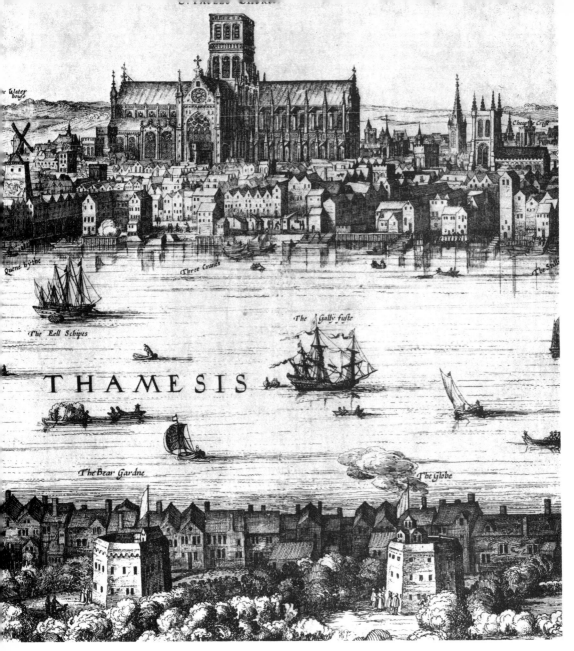

VIEW OF OLD ST. PAUL'S FROM BANKSIDE, *showing the Playhouses in the fore-ground. St. Paul's was notorious as the central meeting place of Londoners, who used its aisles freely as a thoroughfare or short cut for convenience, plastered its pillars with advertise-ments, and gossiped and conducted business there. Before it flowed the Thames, the great highway for those who chose to travel by water whenever possible to avoid the narrow, dirty streets. Boatmen plied their boats continually up-stream and down-stream and their cries of 'Eastward ho!' and 'Westward ho!' could be heard from shore to shore. To have a lusty voice was apparently a waterman's first necessity, as a contemporary writer has noted: 'He keeps such a bawling at Westminster, that if the lawyer's were not acquainted with it, an order would be taken with him. When he is upon the water, he is fare-company: when he comes ashore he mutinies, and contrary to all other trades is most surly to gentlemen, when they tender payment. The play-houses only keep him sober; and, as it doth many other gallants, make him an afternoon's man.'*[1]

From VISSCHER'S VIEW OF LONDON, 1616.

176

The Famous

TRAGEDY

OF

THE RICH IEVV

OF *MALTA*.

AS IT WAS PLAYD

BEFORE THE KING AND
QVEENE, IN HIS MAJESTIES
Theatre at *White-Hall*, by her Majesties
Servants at the *Cock-pit*.

Written by CHRISTOPHER MARLO.

LONDON;
Printed by *I. B.* for *Nicholas Vavafour*, and are to be sold
at his Shop in the Inner-Temple, neere the
Church. 1633.

Title page *to the only surviving edition of* The Jew of Malta, *written by Marlowe probably in* 1589. *This late edition, forty years after Marlowe's death, undoubtedly gives a somewhat mutilated version of Marlowe's play, and has presented scholars with the task of attempting to sort out Heywood's additions from the main body of Marlowe's original work. However, we may assume that these additions were restricted to minor alterations and editing rather than the introduction of whole new scenes as has been suggested by some scholars, since Heywood in his prologue pays tribute to both the author, Marlowe, and the actor, Alleyn, who first played the title role of the Jew.*

> 'We know not how our play may pass this stage,
> But by the best of Poets in that age
> The Malta Jew had being, and was made;
> And He, then by the best of Actors play'd.'

The Jew *achieved immense and long continued popularity on the Elizabethan and Jacobean stage, above all other works of Marlowe. Jews were banished from Elizabeth's England and Marlowe's model was necessarily a foreign Jew, through whose exotic person he felt free to attack the 'religious caterpillars' of the Church. This play would seem to belong to a genre of macabre farce which has since died out, and in many respects is unique in the annals of even the great variety and hotchpotch of Elizabethan drama.*

Marlowe and the Stationers of St. Paul's

As a writer Marlowe would soon have made the acquaintance of the booksellers, printers and publishers of St. Paul's Churchyard, where many of them had their stalls or shops, each with its sign hanging out, close by the walls. This was a favourite resort of Christopher Marlowe's during his London years, and it is evident from contemporary allusions that his figure browsing among the books at the stalls was a familiar sight. On the authority of Marlowe's friend and fellow playwright, Thomas Kyd, we learn that Marlowe was on more than mere nodding acquaintance with 'some stationers of Paules churchyard'[2], that these were of his intimate company, with whom he was often to be seen conversing, and that they would be well aware of his views on such matters as religion.

177

PAUL'S CHURCHYARD (from a drawing by F. Watkins)

St. Paul's churchyard was the centre for London's writers and publishers. In many ways this was the cultural hub of the city, a favourite meeting-place, and often the site of controversial discussions. Surrounding the churchyard various London printer-publishers had their stalls.

St. Paul's Cathedral originally had a spire as shown in this drawing but it fell in 1562 when struck by lightning and, as depicted in Visscher's view on page 176, was not replaced.

Amongst these stationers was certainly *Edward Blount*, a gentleman publisher who was a man of genuine literary taste and refinement, as may be evidenced by his later close connection with the publication of the greatest literary work of the Elizabethan age, the First Folio of Shakespeare, for which recent researches have established his main responsibility.

Edward Blount was both Marlowe's admirer and friend, and also enjoyed the friendship of Marlowe's patron, Thomas Walsingham, to whom he later dedicated the first posthumous publication of Marlowe's poem *Hero and Leander*. This dedication especially argues his friendship for the dead poet since in it he is concerned to do what he can to restore the author's besmirched reputation. It is his answer to the venomous Puritan pamphleteers who heaped scandal on Marlowe's name after his murder and the accusations of his atheism had been made public. Blount's action was that of a sincere friend, not merely a business acquaintance.

'To the Right Worshipfull, Sir Thomas Walsingham, Knight.':

'Sir, wee think not our selues discharged of the dutie wee owe to our friend, when we haue brought the breathlesse bodie to the earth: for albeit the eye there taketh his euer farwell of that beloued obiect, yet the impression of the man, that hath beene deare vnto us, liuing an after life in our memory, there putteth vs in mind of farther obsequies due vnto the deceased. And namely of the performance of whatsoeuer we may iudge shal make to his liuing credit, and to the effecting of his determinations preuented by the stroke of death. By these meditations (as by an intellectual will) I suppose my selfe executor to the vnhappily deceased author of this Poem, vpon whom knowing that in his life time you bestowed many kind fauors, entertaining the parts of reckoning and woorth which you found in him, with good countenance and liberall affection: I cannot but see so far into the will of him dead, that whatsoeuer issue of his brain should chance to come abroad, that the first breath it should take might be the gentle aire of your liking: for since his selfe had been accustomed thervnto, it would prooue more agreeable & thriuing to his right children, than any other foster countenance whatsoeuer.'[3]

A second interesting documentary piece of evidence testifying to Blount's friendship with Marlowe is the amusing and curiously cryptic letter of dedication written to him by Thomas Thorpe, another publisher of the Churchyard, in his edition of Marlowe's *First Book of Lucan*, which he brought out in 1600:

To his Kind, and True Friend:
Edward Blunt.

Blount: *I purpose to be blunt with you, and out of my dullnesse to encounter you with a* Dedication *in the memory of that pure elementall wit*, Chr. Marlow; *whose ghoast or* Genius *is to be seene walke the Churchyard in (at the least) three or foure sheets. Me thinks you should presently looke wilde now, and grow humourously frantique upon the tast of it.*
   Well, least you should, let mee tell you.
This spirit was sometimes a familiar of your own, Lucans first booke translated; *which in regard of your old right in it) I have rais'd in the circle of your Patronage. But stay now,* Edward *(if I mistake not) you are to accommodate your self with some fewe instructions, touching the property of a Patron, that you are not yet possest of; and to study them for your better grace as our Gallants do fashions.*
   First, you must be proud and thinke you have merit inough in you, though you are ne're so emptie; then when I bring you the booke take physicke, and keepe state, assigne me a time by your man to come againe, and afore the day, be sure to have chang'd your lodging; in the meane time, sleepe little, and sweat with the invention of some pittiful dry jest or two which you may happen to utter, with some little (or not at al) marking of your friends when you have found a place for them to come in at: or if by chance something has dropt from you worth the taking up weary all that come to you with the often repetition of it; censure scornefully inough, and somewhat like a travailer; commend nothing least you discredit your (that which you would seem to have) judgement. These things if you can mould your self to them Ned *I make no question but they will not become you. One speciall vertue in our Patrons of these daies I have promist my selfe you shall fit excellently, which is to give nothing; Yet, thy love I will challenge as my peculiar Object both in this, and (I hope) manie more succeeding offices: Farewell, I affect not the world should measure my thoughts to thee by a scale of this Nature: Leave to thinke good of me when I fall from thee.*
   Thine in all rites of perfect friendship,

THOM. THORPE

What strange news or momentous manuscript 'touching the property of a patron' Thorpe was to bring him is a matter of conjecture. The reference to '*Lucans first booke translated*; which (in regard of your old right) I have rais'd in the circle of your Patronage' has been interpreted by most scholars to mean that Blount once held the rights for this, as he did for *Hero and Leander*, and there seems to be sufficient indirect evidence to make this an acceptable explanation. However, the letter is full of the favourite Elizabethan form of cryptography, excruciating punning by double meanings. And until we have the right clues Thorpe's letter will remain an almost incomprehensible puzzle, and perhaps one of the most intriguing of all the many intriguing and challenging pieces of documentary evidence touching Marlowe, because potentially the most revealing concerning the relationship between Blount and Walsingham and Marlowe, and possibly also George Chapman. But the complete answer to this must await further scholarship and research.

Edward Blount has been cited by Eleanor Grace Clark as a co-member with Marlowe of the School of Night, and, as we have seen, the members of this, from Sir Walter Ralegh and Northumberland downwards, were generally suspected the heinous 'crime' of atheism. If this is so Blount must have been well aware how wide of the real truth the slanderous accusations against Marlowe fell, and this would have been an added incentive for him to try to reinstate his dead friend's honour.

Printers at Work *from a woodcut by Jost Amman*.

Controversy in Literary London

Apart from his associates in the School of Night, Marlowe's circle of acquaintances also included gentlemen from among London's literary aspirants, the so-called 'University Wits', and of these his closest friends seem to have been Thomas Nashe and Robert Greene. Others of this group of poets and dramatists intimate with Marlowe, such as Matthew Roydon, George Chapman, George Peele, Michael Drayton, John Marston and Thomas Lodge, were almost certainly members with him of Ralegh's circle, but there is no evidence connecting either Nashe or Greene with this 'school', unless their patronage by Lord Strange as dramatists writing for his players constitutes any link. Nashe, in particular, seems to have been friendly with his patron. Their writings, however, belie any connection with, and rather evidence their complete dissociation from, the 'atheists' of the School of Night. They were nevertheless closely associated with Marlowe in their literary pursuits, particularly as dramatists, and also as friends. Nashe especially maintained a close personal relationship to Marlowe, and their friendship throws an interesting sidelight on Kit's character.

Witty *Tom Nashe*, some two years younger than Marlowe, was one of the brightest stars of the 'University Wits'. His father was a minister at Lowestoft, descended of a Herefordshire family who 'boasted longer pedigrees than patrimonies',[1] and he accordingly entered young Tom at St. John's College, Cambridge, as a poor sizar at the age of fifteen. There he took a B.A. in 1584, but proceeded no further, although he boasted to Gabriel Harvey that 'it is well known I might have been Fellow if I had would.'[2] Whether there was any truth in the rumour that his studies were cut short as a result of a scandal concerning a play of which he was part-author is not definitely established, but in Covell's *Polimanteia* there is a hint that the university had been 'unkind' to Nashe in 'weaning him before his time'. Be that as it may, he was certainly a young man of original personality, with a ready wit and an inherent scorn of pretentious learnedness and insincerity.

On leaving the university 'before his time' he seems to have consoled himself by making a brief tour of France and Italy before settling in London to a literary career.[3] He tried his hand at play-writing, but soon found his natural bent in satire. Under the nom-de-guerre of 'Pasquil' he entered the lists of satirical pamphleteers against the Martin Marprelate faction (the Puritan pamphleteers who were flooding the London reading market with their strident tracts) and achieved resounding success, creating greater havoc among their ranks with his 'merry wit' than many a more sober critic.

In the final stages of the Marprelate battle of the pamphlets, a new protagonist made his entry waving an olive branch in an attempt to becalm the heated controversy. He was Richard Harvey, the younger brother of Gabriel Harvey. Richard had been a student of divinity at Cambridge contemporaneously with

Caricature of Thomas Nashe *in irons from* The Trimming of Thomas Nashe, 1596 (*author unknown, although formerly attributed to G. Harvey*).

Marlowe, took the cloth, and as his first living acquired the rectorship of Chislehurst, at Thomas Walsingham's own parish church of St. Nicholas, in 1586.[1] Marlowe had evidently heard him preach, for he is reported to have remarked that Harvey was but 'an asse, good for nothing but to preach in the Iron Age'.[5] This Harvey now took up his pen and, while ostensibly making a plea for peace, openly attacked those literary pen-men who had, he contended, prolonged and embittered the issues, specifically naming Lyly, Greene and Nashe. Nashe, not to be outdone, retaliated by satirising poor Harvey's ineffective efforts in astrology in a pamphlet which he called 'A Wonderful Strange and miraculous Astrological Prognostication for this year of our Lord God 1591, by Adam Foule-weather, Student in Asse-tronomy'.

Such was the rather ribald manner of the Elizabethan literary world. If we imagine Christopher Fry and Wolf Mankowicz having a slanging match with certain reverend gentlemen (under thinly-disguised pseudonyms) we can have some idea of what the vogue for pamphleteering meant, and how this sort of thing was lapped up by the reading public.

Robert Greene had enthusiastically applauded Nashe's satirical efforts, naming him in his death-bed diatribe, 'Young Juvenal, that biting satirist' whose business it was to 'inveigh against vain men'. Greene died in the autumn of 1592 in circumstances of miserable poverty and sickness. His death became fuel for the renewal of the Puritan controversy on an even more heated level of virulent personal attack, this time through the entry of *Gabriel Harvey*. This censorious Cambridge don and literary critic had never forgotten the insults his brother Richard had received at Nashe's hands, which Greene had abetted with his own slighting remarks in *A Quip for an Upstart Courtier* concerning Harvey's father and another brother, the physician John Harvey. Both this much-loved brother as well as his father, an eminently respected citizen of Saffron Walden, had recently died, and Gabriel as head of the family felt that their honour was at stake. Stung by personal grief at this double loss, he launched an attack on the dead Greene in an attempt to tear his posthumous reputation to shreds and so be revenged. Harvey's *Foure Letters*, the third in particular, contain vitriolic invective against Greene, in which he noses out every sordid detail of his last hours from the woman in whose house Greene had died. He gleefully published his findings for all the world to read. It was a ghoulish action that redounded to his discredit.

Nashe had previously been singled out by Harvey for complimentary mention in his literary criticisms. Indeed, he had placed Nashe among those who were 'the dear lovers and professed sons of the Muses'. Despite this, however, and despite the fact that Nashe had disclaimed being Greene's bosom friend (his 'inwardest companion') as Harvey had alleged, and therefore had not owed the dead man this duty, he leapt into the breach to defend poor Greene's maligned character. He gave Harvey his answer thus:

'Why should art answer for the infirmities of manners? He had his faults, and thou thy follies—Debt and deadly sin who is not subject to?—with any notorious crime I never knew him tainted—He made no account of winning credit by his works, as thou dost, that dost no good works, but thinks to be famoused by a strong faith of thy own worthiness: his only care was to have a spel in his purse to conjure up a good cup of wine with at all times.' [As for] 'the lowsie circumstances of his poverty before his death, and sending that miserable writ to his wife, it cannot be but thou lyest, learned Gabriell—I and one of my fellows, *WILL MONOX* (hast thou never heard of him and his great dagger) were in company with him a month before he died, at that fatal banquet of Rhenish wine and pickled herrings (if thou wilt needs have it so), and then the inventory of his apparel came to more than three shillings (though thou sayest the contrary). I know a broker in spruce leather jerkin with a great number of gold Rings on his fingers, and a bunch of keys at his girdle, shall give thirty shillings for the doublet alone, if you can help him to it. Hark in your ear, he had a very fair cloak with sleeves, of a grave goose turd green; it would serve you as fine as may be; No more words, if you be wise, play the good husband and listen after it, you may buy it ten shillings better cheap than it cost him.'

And with a final dig at Harvey's origins (the son of a rope maker, this being the vulnerable spot Greene had first aggravated) and his preening over his friends at the Court, he adds:

'By S. Silver, it is good to be circumspect in casting for the world, there's a great many ropes go to ten shillings. If you want a greasy pair of silk stockings

Caricature of Gabriel Harvey *from Thomas Nashe's* Have With You to Saffron Walden (1596).

183

also, to show yourself in at the Court, they are there to be had amongst his movables.'[6]

With this sampling of Nashe's caustic wit we get a picture of life in literary London and its colourful characters. Who Will Monox was, with his great dagger, we shall probably never know. He never appears again. Elizabethan society, aristocratic and literary, mingled freely with its underworld. Nashe frankly admits as much and is evidently trying to frighten Harvey. From this extraordinary and often highly amusing public correspondence, it is Nashe who emerges as a man of, at least, some principles. He stoutly defended Greene's reputation, but he would have no truck with his friend's last, controversial and bitter legacy to literature, his famous *Groatsworth of Wit*, which Nashe called a 'scald, trivial lying pamphlet'.

By the end of 1593 Nashe began to repent 'his fantasticall satirisme in whose veine', he said, 'I misspent my spirit', and to wish to be 'at peace with all men'.[7] He made amends to Harvey, in print. But Harvey declared himself unmoved by 'the tears of the crocodile'[8] and only renewed the battle with increased venom, which drew retaliatory salvoes from Nashe. This mud-slinging match finally reached such a pitch that the Archbishop of Canterbury saw fit to step in and ordered that 'All Nashe's bookes and Doctor Harvyes bookes be taken . . . and that none of theire bookes be ever printed hereafter'.[9]

Contemporary sympathy seems to have been mainly on Nashe's side. Middleton posthumously excused Nashe by writing:

> *Thou hadst a strife with that Tergemini,*
> *Thou hurt'st them not, till they had injured thee.*[10]

Of his more serious labours Nashe's romance *The Unfortunate Traveller* was probably his most important contribution to literature; as the first English novel it presages Defoe in its powers of realistic description. Nashe also wrote for the stage, mainly in collaboration with Greene. Among his friends he numbered the three greatest Elizabethan actors: William Kempe (to whom he dedicated an early work); Tarleton, the great comic actor; and Edward Alleyn, the great tragedian.

Nashe's relations with Marlowe give evidence of a side of the latter's character to which his biographers have paid scant attention. When Marlowe, fresh from the university, succeeded at once in making a terrific hit with *Tamburlaine the Great*, a play of such patent originality that it set a new fashion and established blank verse as the medium for the drama of that day, the effect was a shattering one for his rival contemporaries. With superb self-confidence (some no doubt termed it self-conceit) Kit had introduced his drama in the prologue:

> *From jigging veins of rhyming mother wits*
> *And such conceits as clownage keeps in pay,*
> *We'll lead you to the stately tent of war,*
> *Where you shall hear the Scythian Tamburlaine*

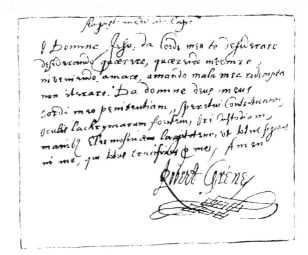

Caricature of Robert Greene, *the poet and dramatist, from* Greene in Concept.

Nashe and Greene, both eager to criticise this conceited playwright, were
riled. Nashe answered with a reply evidently intended to take Marlowe down a
peg or two. Perhaps he also felt that his former Cambridge friend was flaunting
his M.A. degree, and that this status, which Nashe had not achieved, had given
him too big an opinion of himself. He wrote:

> 'Idiot art-masters that intrude themselves to our ears as the alcumists of
> eloquence, who (mounted on the stage of arrogance) think to outbrave better
> pens with the swelling bombast of a bragging blank verse.'[11]

And he goes on to sneer at 'the spacious volubility of a drumming decasyllibon'.
Marlowe never retaliated, and so far as we know never resented these literary
jibes but evidently forgave Nashe for these attacks, for they stayed firm friends.
After Marlowe's death Nashe edited an early play *The Tragedy of Dido, Queen of
Carthage*, and published it as the joint work of Marlowe and himself (although
modern critics have doubted that Nashe had any part in actually writing it) and
prefaced it with a Latin elegy to Marlowe's memory. Three copies of this
quarto edition of 1594 are in existence but none of them contains the elegy which
was first mentioned by Thomas Tanner in his *Bibliotheca Britannico-Hibernica*,
1748 (p. 512) as '*Tho. Nash in Carmine elegiaco tragœdiæ Didonis præfixo in
obitum Christoph. Marlovii*'. A copy of the edition bearing Nashe's elegy inserted
immediately after the title page was seen in the book shop of T. Osborne in 1754
by Thomas Warton, so he assured Malone. But it has since disappeared without
trace; a most unfortunate loss. Elsewhere Nashe wrote affectionately of 'poor
deceased Kit Marlowe'[12] and seems to have held him in high esteem. Nashe is
indeed the sort of person whose spicy company Kit would have enjoyed.
Dekker tells us that in Nashe's soul 'the raptures of that fierie and inconfinable
Italian spirit were bounteously and boundlessly infused'.[13] Despite his satirical
pen Nashe was well liked for his sparkle and easy wit; he must have been an
amusing conversationalist. Like Greene he died in poverty in 1601, bewailing
the fact that he had often prostituted his pen 'in hope of gain' to penning
unedifying toys for gentlemen—probably sonnets and lewd ballads, of which
one exceptionally licentious example survives in manuscript.[14]

So much for Nashe, an amusing, brilliant, and somewhat 'fair weather' friend of Marlowe, whose witty commentaries on the contemporary scene have left us an enlightening record of his times. His delicious parody of Marlowe's *Hero and Leander* compensates us for the loss of his elegy on Kit (which time and good fortune may perhaps yet discover again) and is a fitting memorial to his friend's posthumous fame, testifying to the tremendous popularity his work attained.

A *Parody on* HERO AND LEANDER *by* Thomas Nashe
From Nashes Lenten Stuffe . . . (1599)

Let me see, hath any bodie in Yarmouth heard of Leander and Hero, of whome diuine *Musaeus* sung, and a diuiner Muse than him, *Kit Marlow*? Twoo faithfull louers they were, as euerie apprentise in Paules churchyard will tell you for your loue, and sel you for your mony: the one dwelt at Abidos in Asia, which was Leander; the other, which was Hero, his Mistris or Delia, at Sestos in Europe, and she was a pretty pinckany and Venus priest; and but an arme of the sea diuided them; it diuided them and it diuided them not, for ouer that arme of the sea could be made a long arme. In their parents the most diuison rested, and their townes that like Yarmouth and Leystoffe were stil at wrig wrag, and suckt from their mothers teates serpentine hatred one against each other. Which droue Leander when he durst not deale aboue boord, or be seene aboorde any ship, to saile to his Lady deare, to play the didopper and ducking water spaniel to swim to her, not that in the day, but by owle-light.

What will not blinde night doe for blinde Cupid? And what will not blinde Cupid doe in the night, which is his blindmans holiday? By the sea side on the other side stoode Heroes tower, such an other tower as one of our Irish castles, that is not so wide as a belfree, and a Cobler cannot iert out his elbowes in; a cage or pigeonhouse, romthsome enough to comprehend her and the toothlesse trotte, her nurse, who was her onely chatmate and chambermaide; consultiuely by her parents being so encloistered from resort, that she might liue chast vestall Priest to Venus, the queene of vnchastitie. Shee would none of that, she thanked them, for shee was better prouided, and that which they thought serued their turn best of sequestring her from company, serued her turne best to embrace the company she desired. Fate is a spaniel that you cannot beate from you; the more you thinke to crosse it, the more you blesse it and further it.

Neither her father nor mother vowed chastitie when she was begote, therefore she thought they begat her not to live chaste, & either she must proue her selfe a bastard, or shew herselfe like them. Of Leander you may write vpon, and it is written vpon, she likte well, and for all he was a naked man, and cleane dispoyled to the skinne, when hee sprawled through the brackish suddes to scale her tower, all the strength of it could not hold him out. O, ware a naked man; Cythereas Nunnes haue no power to resiste him: and some such qualitie is ascribed to the lion. Were hee neuer so naked when he came to her, bicause he shuld not skare her, she found a meanes to couer him in her bed, and, for he might not take cold after his swimming, she lay close by him, to keepe him warme. This scuffling or bopeepe in the darke they had a while without weame or bracke, and the olde nurse (as there bee three things seldome in their right kinde till they bee old, a bawd, a witch, and a midwife) executed the huckstring office of her yeres very charily & circumspectly til their sliding starres reuolted from them; and then, for seauen dayes togither, the winde and the Hellespont contended which shuld howle lowder; the waues dashed vp to the cloudes, and the clouds on the other side spit and driueld vpon them as fast.

Hero wept as trickling as the heauens, to thinke that heauen should so diuorce them. Leander stormed worse than the stormes, that by them hee should be so restrained from his Cinthya. At Sestos was his soule, and hee coulde not abide to tarry in Abidos. Rayne, snowe, haile, or blowe it howe it could, into the pitchie Helespont he leapt, when the moone and all her torch-bearers were afraide to peepe out their heads; but he was peppered for it, hee hadde as good haue tooke meate, drinke, and leisure, for the churlish frampold waues gaue him his belly full of fish-broth, ere out of their laundry or washe-house they woulde graunt him his coquet or *transire*, and not onely that, but they sealde him his *quietus est* for curuetting any more to the mayden tower, and tossed his dead carcasse, well bathed or parboyled, to the sandy threshold of his leman or orenge, for a disiune or morning breakfast.

Roberto Greene and the Actor-Manager of the Rose

Of *Robert Greene*, with his red beard, and his 'goose turd green' cloak, his love of carousel and a profligate life, history has left us a fascinating if incomplete portrait of a gifted wastrel who was in a sense one of the evil genii in Marlowe's life, for it was he who first publicly, and in print, accused Marlowe of atheism. He did this not once, but repeatedly, and never so damagingly as when he lay dying in 1592.

Greene, although blessed with a good education (being a Cambridge B.A. and an M.A. of both Oxford and Cambridge, as he liked to boast) and a man of the world, for he had travelled in Italy, Spain, France, Denmark and Poland, was on his own admission a restless, unfortunate and discontented soul, who turned to minor vices for consolation, deserting his wife and leaving to the world a bastard son, whimsically named Fortunatus. But whatever his life, and probably he exaggerated and dramatized his own profligacies, his literary works have a fresh-ness and delicacy which belie this. He was a prolific writer of plays, romances, pamphlets amd poems, which gained him fame but insufficient monetary success. The generous patronage he needed seemed to elude him, possibly because of his own unfortunate personality. This may have been the root which nourished his envy of Marlowe.

Greene, much more than Nashe, was Marlowe's persistent reviler. It was envy that prompted him after the instantaneous success of *Tamburlaine* to castigate the author for 'blaspheming' and 'daring God out of heauen with that Atheist *Tamburlan*' in whose mouth he set 'such impious instances of intoller-able poetrie', and in his *Menaphon* he sneeringly called Marlowe 'a cobbler's eldest son'.[1] There is no doubt that he knew Marlowe well personally, and probably had many an intellectual argument with him, for he upbraided him for studying Machiavellian policies. He claims that he was influenced at some time by Marlowe's 'atheism', and in repudiating it makes it sound as diabolically compromising as possible (a view not borne out by Marlowe's writings or by those of other members of the School of Night who were similarly accused). Greene himself never quite struggled free from the fear of hell hereafter, and was really shocked by Marlowe's fearless criticisms of orthodox religion. The sensual sins of this world dragged him down; he could never inhabit the rarer air of Marlowe's questioning spirit, and his final reaction was violent. His degrading end discovers him a terror-stricken penitent, ready to purchase his salvation with a last desperate stab at converting others who, he feels, might be in need of it, and lashing out in hate at the 'painted puppets' who had failed to support him in his extremity. Greene knew that he was dying when he penned his *Groatsworth of Wit, bought with a Million of Repentance*

8 If thou be poore, be also patient, and strine not to grow rich by indirect meanes; for goods so gotten shal vanish like smoke.

9 If thou bee a Father, Maister, or Teacher, ioyne good example with good counsaile; else little auaile precepts, where life is different.

10 If thou be a Sonne or Seruant, despise not reproofe; for though correction bee bitter at the first, it bringeth pleasure in the end.

Had I regarded the first of these rules, or beene obedient to the last; I had not now at my last ende, bene left thus desolate. But now, though to my selfe I giue Consilium post facta; yet to others they may serue for timely precepts. And therefore (while life giues leaue) I will send warning to my olde consorts, which haue liued as loosely as my selfe; albeit weaknesse will scarse suffer me to write, yet to my fellow Schollers about this Cittie, will I direct these few insuing lines.

To those Gentlemen his Quondam acquaintance,
that spend their wits in making plaies, R.G.
wisheth a better exercise, and wisdome
to preuent his extremities.

IF wofull experience may moue you (Gentlemen) to beware, or vnheard of wretchednes intreate you to take heed: I doubt not but you wil looke backe with sorrow on your time past, and indeuour with repentance to spend that which is to come. Wonder not, (for with thee wil I first begin) thou famous gracer of Tragedians, that Greene, who hath said with thee (like the foole in his heart) There is no God, shoulde now giue glorie

glorie vnto his greatnes: for penetrating is his power, his hand lyes heauie vpon me, hee hath spoken vnto mee with a voice of thunder, and I haue felt he is a God that can punish enemies. Why should thy excellent wit, his gift, bee so blinded, that thou shouldst giue no glorie to the giuer? Is it pestilent Machiuilian pollicy that thou hast studied? O peeuish follie! What are his rules but meere confused mockeries, able to extirpate in small time the generation of mankind. For if Sic volo, sic iubeo, hold in those that are able to commaund: and if it be lawfull Fas & nefas to do any thing that is beneficiall; onely Tyrants should possesse the earth, and they striuing to exceed in tyrannie, should each to other be a slaughter man; till the mightiest outliuing all, one stroke were left for Death, that in one age mans life should end. The brocher of this Diabolicall Atheisme is dead, and in his life had neuer the felicitie hee aymed at: but as he began in craft, liued in feare, and ended in despaire. Quàm inscrutabilia sunt Dei iudicia? This murderer of many brethren, had his conscience seared like Caine: this betrayer of him that gaue his life for him, inherited the portion of Iudas: this Apostata perished as ill as Iulian: and wilt thou my friend be his disciple? Looke but to me, by him perswaded to that libertie, and thou shalt finde it an infernall bondage. I knowe the least of my demerits merit this miserable death, but wilfull striuing against knowne truth, exceedeth all the terrors of my soule. Defer not (with me) till this last point of extremitie; for litle knowst thou how in the end thou shalt be visited.

With thee I ioyne yong Iuuenall, that byting Satyrist, that lastly with mee together writ a Comedie.
F   Sweet

---

and addressed himself 'To those Gentlemen his Quondam acquaintance, that spend their wits in making plaies,' piously adding, 'R.G. wisheth a better exercise, and wisdome to preuent his extremities'.

No doubt he was genuine, for he was suffering cruelly. He continues:

'If wofull experience may moue you (Gentlemen) to beware, or unheard of wretchednes intreate you to take heed: I doubt not but you wil looke backe with sorrow on your time past, and indevour with repentance to spend that which is to come.'

In what follows he obviously addresses himself to Marlowe:

'Wonder not, (for with thee wil I first begin) thou famous gracer of Tragedians, that Greene, who hath said with thee (like the foole in his heart) There is no God, shoulde now give glorie unto his greatnes: for penetrating is his power, his hand lyes heavie upon me, hee hath spoken unto mee with a voice of thunder, and I have felt he is a God that can punish enemies. Why should thy excellent wit, his gift, bee so blinded, that thou shouldst give no glorie to the giver: Is it pestilent Machiavilian pollicy that thou hast studied? O peeuish follie! What are his rules but meere confused mockeries, able to extirpate in small time the generation of mankind.' (And here he appears to be recalling arguments he has had with Kit.) 'For if *Sic volo, sic iubeo*, hold in those that are able to commaund: and if it be lawfull *Fas & nefas* to do any thing that is beneficiall; onely Tyrants should possesse

Sweet boy, might I aduise thee, be aduisde, and get not many enemies by bitter wordes : inueigh against vaine men, for thou canst do it, no man better, no man so well : thou hast a libertie to reproue all, and name none; for one being spoken to, all are offended; none being blamed no man is iniured. Stop shallow water still running, it will rage, or tread on a worme and it will turne : then blame not Schollers vexed with sharpe lines, if they reproue thy too much liberty of reproofe.

And thou no lesse deseruing than the other two, in some things rarer, in nothing inferiour ; driuen (as my selfe) to extreme shifts, a litle haue I to say to thee: and were it not an idolatrous oth, I would sweare by sweet S. George, thou art vnworthy better hap, sith thou dependest on so meane a stay. Base minded men all three of you, if by my miserie you be not warnd: for vnto none of you (like mee) sought those burres to cleaue : those Puppets (I meane) that spake from our mouths, those Anticks garnisht in our colours. Is it not strange, that I, to whom they all haue beene beholding: is it not like that you, to whome they all haue beene beholding, shall (were yee in that case as I am now) bee both at once of them forsaken ? Yes trust them not : for there is an vpstart Crow, beautified with our feathers, that with his Tygers hart wrapt in a Players hyde, supposes he is as well able to bombast out a blanke verse as the best of you : and beeing an absolute Iohannes fac totum, is in his owne conceit the onely Shake-scene in a countrey. O that I might intreat your rare wits to be imploied in more profitable courses : & let those Apes imitate your past excellence, and neuer more acquaint them with your admired inuentions. I knowe the best husband of you

you all will neuer proue an Vsurer, and the kindest of them all will neuer proue a kind nurse : yet whilest you may, seeke you better Maisters; for it is pittie men of such rare wits, should be subiect to the pleasure of such rude groomes.

In this I might insert two more, that both haue writ against these buckram Gentlemen : but lette their owne workes serue to witnesse against their owne wickednesse, if they perseuere to maintaine any more such peasants. For other new-commers, I leaue them to the mercie of these painted monsters, who (I doubt not) will driue the best minded to despise them : for the rest, it skils not though they make a ieast at them.

But now returne I againe to you three, knowing my miserie is to you no newes : and let mee hartily intreat you to be warned by my harms. Delight not (as I haue done) in irreligious oathes ; for from the blasphemers house, a curse shall not depart. Despise drunkennes, which wasteth the wit, and maketh men all equall vnto beasts. Flie lust, as the deathsman of the soule, and defile not the Temple of the holy Ghost. Abhorre those Epicures, whose loose life hath made religion lothsome to your eares : and when they sooth you with tearmes of Maistership, remember Robert Greene, whome they haue often so flattered, perishes now for want of comfort. Remember Gentlemen, your liues are like so many lighted Tapers, that are with care deliuered to all of you to maintaine : these with winde-puft wrath may be extinguisht, which drunkennes put out, which negligence let fall : for mans time is not of it selfe so short, but it is more shortned by sinne. The fire of my light is now at the last snuffe, and for want of wherewith to su-

staine it, there is no substance left for life to feede on. Trust not then (I beseech ye) to such weake staies : for they are as changeable in minde, as in many attyres. Wel, my hand is tyrde, and I am forst to leaue where I would begin : for a whole booke cannot containe their wrongs, which I am forst to knit vp in some fewe lines of wordes.

Desirous that you should liue,
though himselfe be dying:
Robert Greene.

Now to all men I bid farewel in like sort, with this conceited Fable of that olde Comedian Aesope.

the earth, and they striving to exceed in tyrannie, should each to other be a slaughter man; till the mightiest outliving all, one stroke were left for Death, that in one age mans life should end.'

In this Greene shows some knowledge of Machiavelli's opportunist policies, and one can imagine Marlowe, to whose mind the essentially scientific approach of Machiavelli's analysis of power politics would appeal, countering with arguments upholding and explaining the Italian's subtle statecraft. What Machiavelli had done in his book *The Prince* (which Harvey mentions as avidly read by the Cambridge students even before Marlowe's time there)[2] was to hold up a mirror to the policies of great princes, and to advise a course which, he believed, in this imperfect world might yet bring peace and unification under a strong ruler to the warring States of Italy. Machiavelli was himself one of the leading Italian Renaissance dramatists, the friend of Leonardo da Vinci and Michelangelo, as well as a politician. With the dispassionate eye of the dramatist who observes and notes the conditions of men, he wrote his incisively brilliant little book, dedicated to Lorenzo the Magnificent, laying bare the very bones of the political motivation of popelings and princes. Thereby he made known to the uninitiated what should not be known, and drew odium upon himself. His books, posthumously published, were ordered to be burnt by the edicts of popes and governments. Like most banned works *The Prince* managed to survive. Elizabeth herself was doubtless familiar with it.

As a result, Machiavelli was fair game. Anyone in fear of his soul, or the inquisitorial authorities of Church and State, grasped for a cudgel to beat Machiavelli and his latter-day disciples who were all lumped together as 'atheists', and immediately he felt safe. Machiavelli became a kind of popular whipping boy, and Marlowe, who defended him, seems to have cared so little for the foolish opinions of the 'gross multitude' that he even added to the legend by taking a perverse and impish delight in identifying himself (evidently with his tongue in his cheek) with the more criticized aspects of Machiavelli's political thought. (See his prologue to *The Jew of Malta*). Machiavelli was being currently misrepresented as a monster, the archetype of all evil. Thomas Heywood's poisonous little tract *Machiavel, as he lately appeared to his deare sons* (published 1641) is an example. In it the great Italian thinker is accused of being the origi- nator of every kind of scurrility and wickedness. To read this, and then to com- pare Heywood's loathsome, muck-raking diatribe with the writings of Machiavelli himself, can only make us have a greater admiration for Marlowe, who attempted courageously and foolhardily to argue with his prejudiced and fearful contem- poraries. Such a comparison between Heywood and Marlowe shows us once again the vast gap there was between Marlowe as a thinker and his contempo- raries. No such work could ever possibly have come from Marlowe's pen. The modern reader shuts it with a snap of disgust.

Marlowe, however, did not realise or did not care how far he was flying in the face of deep-seated conservative prejudice when he engaged in philosophical discussions with those he took for his friends. Nor did he grasp the fact that Greene was the last person to whom he should have opened his mind. What came now from the dying Greene's pen as he wrote in a torment of bodily anguish and mental terror of hell fire was hotly scented bait for the mediævally- minded men who were soon to hunt Kit to his doom. For them Marlowe's nick- name 'Machevil' had only sinister and dangerous connotations, which had been further bedevilled by the evil reputation of Machiavelli's 'climbing follower', Pietro Aretino.

Machiavelli (1469–1527) had been the first writer to apply scientific method to politics, and by his observation of human nature and the forces which activate it had tried to formulate useful universal laws. While his analysis of political society and human behaviour in action must have deeply interested Marlowe, who had had ample opportunity to observe men's use, or abuse, of religion as a cloak for political ends when engaged in government service,[3] yet at the same time Marlowe was himself not an out-and-out Machiavellian disciple, for his drama of St. Bartholomew's Eve, *The Massacre at Paris*, is an exposition of Machiavellian policy defeated and here represented as evil. It is the heroic Navarre, who declares that ' God will still defend the right', who wins the throne in the end. But it is the Machiavellian character of the Guise which Marlowe fills out as the central figure of the play, and it was evidently men of this type who had a fascination for Marlowe at this time. Marlowe was ever one to sweep away false illusions, and it was this aspect of Machiavelli's thinking which appealed to him.

Machiavelli was a cynic who believed men were inherently evil (as indeed the Bible taught) and did good only rarely, when in a state of God-given grace, or when forced to do so through control of law. He maintained that such control was necessary, and opposed those teachings of Christianity which stressed humbleness and passivity, for he felt this was against the best interest of the State. He believed, like the Romans, that a man should be strong both in body and mind and he felt the need for men of action who would see clearly enough to act ruthlessly if need be for a good end. He postulated that men, being by nature lazy, are more willing to conform than to pioneer, and therefore must be led.

Despite this frequent accusation Machiavelli was not by any means an atheist. He felt that both Church and State must co-operate to create the proper habits of thought, customs, and community life, and thus maintain order in society. He urged the importance of religious sentiment and taught that where fear of God is lacking a state becomes degenerate and will go to ruin unless a strong prince can take over to compensate for the lost influences of religion; but, paramountly, observance of religious tenets makes for a kingdom's greatness. Machiavelli believed in control by force, as necessitated by circumstances which in themselves justified the action taken. He may therefore be accused of advocating an amoral opportunism. He dared to disregard certain Christian precepts and defined 'good' as that which corresponded to the interests of the majority; but he apparently never fully realised the consequences of this statement.

Machiavelli attracted an infamous disciple, Pietro Aretino, born twenty-three years later, who exemplified the misuse of *The Prince's* precepts for unscrupulous personal ends. The weakest principle in Machiavelli's argument was his partial subordination of morals to political expediency, and this was seized upon by Aretino and distorted to its most devilish extreme. He was a handsome man who wrote scurrilous poetry and had learned that to hold power one must instil fear. Through his shrewdness he managed to become the adviser and confidante of princes and men of influence; he then used his pen to blackmail them for purposes of further self-aggrandisement. Nothing was sacred to him and no crime beneath him if it served his ends. The son of a shoemaker, he became one of the most feared and powerful men in Italy, but at his death was generally reviled and considered the Antichrist of his epoch. In the passage that follows Greene is undoubtedly referring to this Aretino, and in likening Marlowe to such a man he is drawing a dastardly parallel:

'The brocher of this Diabolicall Atheisme is dead, and in his life had never the felicitie hee aymed at: but as he began in craft, liued in feare, and ended in despaire *Quam inscrutabilia sunt Dei iudicia?* This murderer of many brethren, had his conscience seared like Caine: this betrayer of him that gave his life for him, inherited the portion of *Iudas*: this Apostata perished as ill as *Iulian*: and wilt thou my friend be his disciple? Looke but to me, by him persuaded to that libertie, and thou shalt find it an infernall bondage. I knowe the least of my demerits merit this miserable death, but wilfull striuing against knowne truth, exceedeth all the terrors of my soule. Defer not (with me) till this last point of extremitie; for little knowst thou how in the end thou shalt be uisited.'

In his pious ecstasy Greene becomes prophetic, little realising that he himself was playing Judas to Marlowe in this last farewell to the man he calls 'my friend'. So he leaves Marlowe for the moment and turns to Nashe. In admonishing his younger friend he becomes for a while endearingly paternal:

'With thee I ioyne yong *Iuuenall*, that byting Satyrist, that lastly with mee together writ a Comedie. Sweet boy, might I aduise thee, be aduisde, and get not many enemies by bitter wordes: inueigh against ueine men, for thou canst do it, no man better, no man so well: thou hast a libertie to reprooue all, and none; for one being spoken to, all are offended; none being blamed no man is iniured. Stop shallow water still running, it will rage, or tread on a worme and it will turne: then blame not Schollers vexed with sharpe lines, if they reproue thy too much liberty of reproofe.'

As it turned out Nashe took no heed of this advice, for Greene's death was the prelude to Nashe's bitterest battle of his career with Harvey, and it was in Greene's defence. Lastly Greene turns to one who is generally accepted as being George Peele.

'And thou no lesse deseruing than the other two, in some things rarer, in nothing inferiour; driuen (as my selfe) to extreme shifts, a little haue I to say to thee: and were it not an idolatrous oth, I would sweare by sweet S. George, thou art unworthy better hap, sith thou dependest on so meane a stay. Base minded men all three of you, if by my miserie you be not warnd: for unto none of you (like mee) sought those burres to cleaue: those Puppets (I meane) that spake from our mouths, those Anticks garnisht in our colours.'

Here he is launched full pelt onto what rankles with him most, his desertion in his hour of need by the players whose mouths he has fed with words and stomachs with food, while he now lies starving and unable to buy even the medicines he needs. The relationship between players and playwrights in those days was an extraordinary one to our mind, giving Greene's resentment full justification. The dramatist sold his play outright to the actors' company for a sum of a few pounds, the transaction often being agreed on in some tavern where players and author met to read over and approve the new play script. Once sold, it became the property of the players' company together with its publication rights, although in very exceptional cases some rights of publication adhered to the author. If the play was a success it constituted a sound investment that continued to make money for the company that owned it. Sometimes plays changed hands from one company to another, and the history of these transactions can be traced through records of the money passed from hand to hand.

Greene had all this in mind. His own plight was not unique; unless dramatists allied themselves to the actors, as did Heywood and Shakespeare, they not infrequently ended their days in poverty. Men like Burbage and Alleyn, on the other hand, became propertied gentlemen, Alleyn acquiring such wealth that he founded a scholastic institution that flourishes to this day. It is evident that it was the actors who were on the lucrative side of this bargain; the actor-managers in particular seem to have been hard-driving business men who saw to it that the bargain was to their advantage. Alleyn reveals a particularly astute business mind (he personally owned several of Marlowe's plays), and his steady accumulation of wealth testifies to this. It is evidently such an actor-manager, who was also well-known as the 'shake-scene' of his day, and a hard bargain-driver in his dealings with the playwrights, to whom Greene is referring in the virulent attack that follows:

'Is it not strange, that I, to whom they all haue beene beholding: is it not like that you, to whom they all haue beene beholding, shall (were yee in that case as I am now) bee both at once of them forsaken? Yes trust them not: for there is an upstart Crow, beautified with our feathers, that with his *Tygers hart wrapt in a Players hyde*, supposes he is as well able to bombast out a blanke verse as the best of you: and beeing an absolute *Iohannes fac totum*, is in his owne conceit the onely Shake-scene in a countrey. O that I might intreat your rare wits to be imploied in more profitable courses: & let those Apes imitate your past excellence, and neuer more acquaint them with your admired inuentions. I knowe the best husband of you all will neuer proue an Usurer, and the kindest of them all will neuer proue a kind nurse: yet whilest you may, seeke you better Maisters; for it is pittie men of such rare wits, should be subiect to the pleasure of such rude groomes.'

With further fulminations against 'these painted monsters', followed by a rehearsal of the vices he would have his three friends abjure, he begs them 'to remember *Robert Greene* . . . [who] perishes now for want of comfort'.

There is some evidence of Alleyn having acted as broker to his playwrights when they were in financial difficulties, and it seems that Greene had either appealed for a loan and been refused, or felt that he had been cheated out of some payment which was his due, or both. His bitterness is the more because he senses he has been refused aid only because he is dying and therefore of no further use to the actors or the actor-manager to whom he turned for help. He is no longer a good security; the relationship is one of business, not of charity. Greene knows that the players have done well out of him in the past ('I, to whom they all haue beene beholding') for some of his plays were money-spinners, (*Friar Bacon and Friar Bungay* in particular). The injustice of the unequal bargain to which he has subscribed appears glaring to him now that he is finished and dying for want of sustenance, with the helping hand refused.

It has been so generally accepted that the hard-hearted 'Shake-scene' referred to is identifiable with William Shakespeare, who, it is assumed, *must* therefore at this time have been a rising actor-playwright in London, and that Greene is fulminating in anger because Shakespeare has plagiarised a line from a play in which Greene had a hand, that it is no longer the 'done thing' to question it. There are, however, several serious difficulties in the way of such an acceptance, apart from the fact that there are unsavoury connotations for Shakespeare involved in the dubious light cast on his alleged activities by the *Groatsworth* reference. All the existing evidence points to the conclusion that Shakespeare was at this time not connected with any players' company in London; it is far more probable that he did not make his appearance in London until the following year, 1593, with the publication of *Venus and Adonis*, than that he was elusively acting and plagiarising other men's works. Yet, despite these inherent contradictions and inconsistencies, the theory of Shakespeare's identity with 'Shake-scene' has been espoused with an eagerness that the available evidence does not warrant. Professor Halliday puts his finger on it:

> 'The first official notice of Shakespeare as a player occurs in the Chamber Accounts for performances at Court on 26th, 27th December, 1594, for which he was one of the payees on 15th March, 1595: "William Kempe, William Shakespeare, & Richard Burbage seruantes to the Lord Chamberleyne." If he were with Strange's before this, as he may have been, it is odd that he should not have been mentioned in the cast of *The Deadly Sins*, in the Licence of 1593, or by Alleyn in his correspondence, for after all Strange's had acted one of his plays, and perhaps more, while Greene's oblique attack and Chettle's apology of 1592 testify to his importance.'[4]

Immediately we are faced with an insoluble contradiction in the evidence. *First*, Shakespeare was *not* mentioned documentarily in any of the records in which we would look to find his name if he were in fact at this time (1591–2) connected with Strange's Men. *Secondly*, there is the inferred contradiction of his fame as an actor and a playwright, assumed by Greene's reference to 'Shake-scene'. (Chettle's apology may be discountenanced as *evidence* as it merely replies to Greene's accusations, and whether or not Chettle is referring to Shakespeare is entirely dependent upon whom Greene means by the term 'Shake-scene'.) *Thirdly*, there is the assumption that one of his plays had been acted by Strange's Men in 1592. This refers to the play entered by Hens-

194

owe as *harey the vj** at its first performance on March 3, 1591–2, identifiable with Shakespeare's *Henry VI, Part 1*, which, as Dr. Allison Gaw has impressively argued in his book *The Origin and Development of 1 Henry VI* (University of Southern California Studies, 1926, Series 1, No. 1), was originally in its 1592 version the collaborative work of Marlowe and several other hands, one of which may be identified as that of Robert Greene.

The difficulties regarding the Shakespeare/Shake-scene identification are so glaring as to make it remarkable that all objective discussion of this question should have been so complacently shelved; while the work of such an exceptionally gifted researcher as Dr. Gaw has been allowed to pass almost completely unnoticed, although in his book every facet of the argument has been brilliantly followed through, and in the process has revealed an aspect of Marlowe as a working dramatist collaborating with his friends which is of the utmost importance in placing Marlowe in his proper context. These friends were probably Greene and Peele, and one whom we shall endeavour to show to have been none other than the actor-manager Edward Alleyn, whose early career was so closely interwoven with Marlowe's.

Dr. Gaw has clearly demonstrated that the argument on which the popularly accepted 'Shake-scene-alias-Shakespeare' theory is based is confused. It is not borne out by other evidence concerning Shakespeare at this time, and runs 'in circulo', assumptions being based on *a priori* assumptions which, in the context of what we know of the Elizabethan theatre world, are not tenable.

To summarize the argument:

Greene's reference in his *Groatsworth of Wit* to 'an upstart Crow, beautified with our feathers, that with his *Tygers hart wrapt in a Players hyde*' is obviously a parody of the line 'Oh Tygers hart wrapt in a womans hide' which appears in *The True Tragedy of Richard Duke of York*, a play originally owned by the Pembroke Players (for whom Marlowe wrote *Edward II*) and which, on the basis of verse tests and parallel passages in Marlowe's other works, has been shown by Dr. Tucker Brooke to be definitely Marlowe's work. Thirty-four years later it was included in Shakespeare's revised version as *Henry VI, Part 3*, no less than two-thirds of the lines being taken over from Marlowe's original play practically unaltered. Shakespeare himself had never made any claim to the work as his, and the responsibility for its inclusion in the Folio rests entirely with the survivors of Strange's Men who assembled the plays for posthumous publication. The question of the date of the revision by Shakespeare, which is relevant to this argument, has been placed by Dr. Gaw, on excellently presented evidence, as subsequent to 1592. I would suggest as subsequent to 1593 (and probably considerably after that date), since there would be no reason to call in another playwright to revise Marlowe's play while he was yet alive. *The True Tragedy* in its original form was published no less than three times: once in 1595, when, according to the title page, it had been 'sundrie times acted by the

---

* *The Elizabethan numerals vj mean vi, the j being commonly employed as an 'i' when it is a terminal number.*

Right Honourable Earle of Pembroke his Servants' (for whom Marlowe probably wrote it); again in 1600; and lastly in 1619, in a single quarto edition which bears some slight alterations in the text. The revised version by Shakespeare only appeared in the First Folio in 1623. Prior to the Folio there is therefore no evidence of his revision, and to suggest that he had revised the play as early as 1592 is contrary to all existing evidence and against reasonable supposition.

In that case the line quoted had no connection with Shakespeare, since it was taken from a well-known play ('sundrie times acted &c.') by Marlowe, and the reason for Greene's parody is not far to seek. He is not accusing 'Shake-scene' of plagiarism, which was a matter so generally indulged in by Elizabethan writers as to merit little comment. Besides there was no evidence whatsoever that Shakespeare was ever guilty of plagiarising from any of Greene's plays. What Greene is seeking is invective to epitomize 'Shake-scene's' pitiless treatment of himself, a man dying in poverty, and therefore he chooses a line from a scene in a play well-known to theatregoers at the time which would have all the overtones of emotion he wished to communicate. Dr. Gaw summarises the argument thus:

> 'The "tiger's heart" line from *The True Tragedy* was parodied by Greene, evidently as well-known, just before Sept. 3, 1592. It is usually taken for granted that Greene, in quoting it, is referring to Shakespeare's "plagiarism" of it in *3 Henry VI*. But the whole theory of such an accusation is, as Dr. Brooke has well shown, baseless. (See Dr. Tucker Brooke, *The Authorship of 2 and 3 Henry VI*, pp. 164–71). Further, the line is almost always referred to by critics as simply "a line that occurs in *The True Tragedy*" or "in *3 Henry VI*". But this is an understatement, born of our habit of considering plays from the standpoint of the study rather than the theatre. It is really the opening line of the climactic accusation in perhaps the most powerful speech of invective that had, up to that time, ever been heard upon the English stage—a speech for which Shakespeare, in revision, could do little more than slightly mend the metre. In it the captured York, surrounded by his triumphant foes and confronting the bitterest of them, Queen Margaret, scathingly answers her heartless mockery, his passion mounting step by step until, holding out to her the napkin soaked with the blood of his little son, Rutland, he comes to the crowning instance of her unwomanliness.
>
> > *Oh Tygers hart wrapt in a womans hide!*
> > *Hovv couldst thou draine the life bloud of the childe,*
> > *To bid the father wipe his eies withall,*
> > *And yet be seene to beare a womans face?*
>
> And in the next four lines his self-control breaks, and the rest of the fifty-four lines is given in tears. The speech on the stage must have been memorable, and the quoted line, the chilled steel point to the anger as it bores down in the recollection, unforgettable.'[5]

196

As Ivor Brown has also remarked:

'The passage must have been powerfully delivered in the theatre and left its mark on the memory of the audiences, otherwise there would have been no point in pulling out the first line quoted, altering one word, and so talking of "Shake-scene's" possession of a "Tygers hart wrapt in a Players hyde". Nor would there have been any point in the taunt if Shakespeare had not been known as an actor.'[6]

That Shakespeare was *not known* as an actor in 1592 seems clear from the evidence quoted by Halliday, or rather the complete lack of it, which is the same thing, for it is not for us to invent evidence where it does not exist, and invented evidence is rather what the *Groatsworth* reference has been allowed to become. In the absence of evidence of Shakespeare's employment with any of the leading actors' companies at this time, it is improper to twist the interpretation to make it fit Shakespeare as 'Shake-scene' (which it does as ill as a raven's croak would fit a lark). We must look elsewhere for our man, and realise that 'Shake-scene' is referred to by Greene not as a play on the name Shakespeare, but as synonymous with a great actor's rant—to 'shake a stage' with passion. In order to fully meet all the requirements of Greene's 'Shake-scene' this man must be:

1. a well-known actor
2. someone connected with Greene, Marlowe, Nashe and Peele in their business relationship with the actors
3. a hard bargain-driver and known to be so in 1592
4. a *Johannes Factotum* in his own conceit, who turned his hand on occasion to playwriting.

All these conditions are fulfilled by Edward Alleyn, who in that year, 1592, had, I suggest, collaborated with Greene, Peele and Marlowe in the hasty writing of *harey the vj* which, as Dr. Gaw has demonstrated, was produced on March 3, 1591–2 as a new play especially written for the reopening of the Rose theatre in the early months of 1592, then newly refurbished with the novel addition of a 'turret', the first of its type, under the management of the enterprising Henslowe, assisted by Edward Alleyn. At this time Alleyn was at the head of Strange's Men, shortly after to go into permanent partnership with Henslowe and become his son-in-law.

That the play entitled by Henslowe *harey the vj* is substantially the same as *1 Henry VI*, which had later undergone some revision by Shakespeare and was first published in the First Folio in 1623, is generally accepted by all scholars. The revision by Shakespeare is not in question, but considerable argument about the origin and authorship of *1 Henry VI* has so far failed to resolve whether it is mainly Marlowe's or mainly Shakespeare's work. That the play is the composite work of *several* hands has long been accepted. Neither Marlowe nor Shakespeare ever wrote anything quite as bad as whole sections of *1 Henry VI* demonstrably are. The problem has been one of detailed textual analysis in an endeavour to identify the several hands involved. Dr. Allison Gaw's conclusions, which it is only possible briefly to summarise here, seem to me to be the most logical, the more so as they are firmly based on Dr. Tucker Brooke's ascription of the two apocryphal plays: *The True Tragedy of Richard Duke of York* and *The First Part of the Contention of the Two Famous Houses of York and Lancaster*, to Marlowe.*

In his analysis of the text Dr. Gaw has detected four writers, designated by him as A (the main author), B (second in importance) and C and D. He assigns the major work of A in plotting the synopsis and handling the scenes dealing with the conflicting relationships of Winchester, York, Gloucester and Somerset to Marlowe, who carried on here at a somewhat higher level with the development of the characters he had already conceived in his two plays, *The True Tragedy* and *The First Part of the Contention*. That Marlowe, who usually preferred to work on his own, in this case was forced to accept help because of the great haste in which the play was required by Alleyn for the reopening of the Rose theatre, is established by Dr. Gaw from both internal and external evidence. Marlowe's long association with Alleyn is well known, and it is inconceivable that Alleyn should on this important occasion have called in Shakespeare, a then totally unknown writer, for there is no evidence, as Professor Halliday has pointed out, of his presence in London or with Strange's Men at this time.

The starting point then, is with Marlowe as author A. The second collaborator B, who deals with the main Talbot story, has been confidently accepted by both Fleay and Greg as being Robert Greene, although Dr. Gaw feels less certain of this ascription. He is a careful and unbiased investigator and the reasons for his caution here are to be found in the fact that 'even the central thread of the play, the Talbot story, is certainly by more than one writer, as if the original author had discovered that he could not complete his section within the necessary time and had found it necessary to obtain assistance in the latter part'.[7] However, he is forced to admit that there are many points of similarity with Greene's work which support Fleay's and Greg's ascription to Greene. I would suggest that there has been some interference in B's scenes by the fourth writer C, which has clouded the issue, and as I hope to show there are good reasons for suspecting this to have been the case. The third collaborator D, who was evidently called in at a later stage than B, because the others found

---

* See Dr. F. C. Tucker Brooke's The Authorship of 2 and 3 Henry VI *in* Transactions of the Connecticut Academy of Arts and Sciences, 1912. *Dr. Boas comments on this work:* 'The literary quality of The Contention *and* The True Tragedy, *in Brooke's view, points to Marlowe as being their author. They exhibit* "a brilliant synthesis of plot and emotion", *and* "the whole tangled story is resolutely pitched in a single key". *Moreover, the respective relations of Henry VI, Queen Margaret, Suffolk, and Prince Edward in these two plays are closely akin to those of Edward II, Queen Isabel, Mortimer, and Prince Edward in* Edward II. *The versification, with its predominant number of end stopped lines, and its absence of double endings, is characteristic of Marlowe. But the most concrete support for Marlowe's claim is found by Brooke in the remarkable number of passages in* The Contention *and* The True Tragedy *which have parallels in Marlowe's accepted plays or which are repeated in the quartos themselves. Such parallelism and repetition are both characteristic of Marlowe's technique. Brooke gives a list of twenty-eight parallels with plays in the recognized Marlovian canon, fourteen of which are with* Edward II *and nine with* The Massacre at Paris. *He gives also fifteen examples of repetitions within* The Contention *and* The True Tragedy.*

Dr. F. S. Boas, CHRISTOPHER MARLOWE, Appendix, Chap. XI, p. 194 (1940).

198

JOHANNES DE WITT, a student from Leyden, visited London in about 1596 and wrote his *Observationes Londonienses* to which he attached a sketch and description of the Swan Theatre, which had been built at the western end of Bankside in 1595. His original sketch was lost but a copy made by his friend Arend van Buchel has survived. England was famous for its great theatrical tradition in Elizabethan times, the splendour of the shows being a subject of remark by foreigners. The Swan was the largest of the theatres, according to De Witt seating 3,000. It was a circular building with an apron stage projecting into the 'arena' where the 'groundlings' stood. There are three rows of seats in each of the three galleries round the circular building. There was no 'inner stage' and, as Hotson has shown, this was an erroneous belief. The Elizabethans staged their theatre 'in the round'. They costumed their plays magnificently and used delicately constructed and beautifully painted, free-standing 'mansions' for their sets. De Witt said that this theatre was 'built of a concrete of flints (which are very numerous in Britain) and is supported by wooden columns so painted that they would deceive the most acute observer into thinking that they were marble. As it appears to resemble a Roman building, I have drawn it above.' (Trans. from the Latin.)

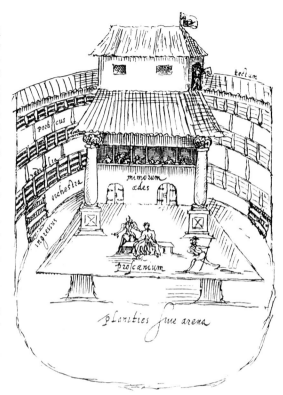

He did not omit to show the 'turret' from which the flag flies and a man appears sounding a trumpet. This was also blown to call people to the performance at the start. Play-going was an enormously popular pastime, in which women indulged as much as men, often going unattended, or in company with other women. The audiences entered into the excitement and the emotions of the drama unabashed and uninhibited, loudly weeping or laughing as they were moved.

It was the theatre of Marlowe and Shakespeare to which the Scottish chronicler Robert Johnston was referring when he wrote: 'For variety and magnificence of plays, England in our age surpassed all nations.'

themselves unable to complete the play in time without further assistance, has been more certainly identified as Peele.

Lastly, collaborator C, whom Dr. Gaw coyly refuses to identify, remarking merely that 'the exact identity of the author is of little consequence' (he was no literary genius), might well have been Edward Alleyn, who was hovering around the playwrights, eager to expedite the completion of the play for performance (it bears all the marks of a rush job) and decided to take a hand in it himself. It is significant that C is the one who evidently had a personal interest in the featuring of the newly-built superstructure, the 'turret', to its best theatrical advantage. Dr. Gaw writes: 'the facts suggest that after Act IV had been assigned to D, a fourth writer discovered another method of utilizing the turret, and was therefore asked to work it out and to write the following scene, and that he made the most of his scanty material . . . Apparently his first interest was in the second turret scene.'[8] Such a writer's presence on the scene, and interest and abilities, would well accord with Alleyn's.

It is in the discovery of the featuring of the turret as something remarkable and novel at the time that the most fascinating aspect of Dr. Gaw's research emerges. In establishing this Dr. Gaw argues from the text of the play itself:

'observe that *1 Henry VI*, the first new play presented in the rebuilt house (*the Rose*) . . . seems especially and uniquely to "feature" the turret, as the New York Hippodrome might "feature" a new artificial lake.'[9]

In the following passage he reconstructs for us the scene and its dramatic featuring of the turret, as it must have been played at the Rose under Alleyn's direction. Alleyn, suggests Dr. Gaw, recalling one of the greatest theatrical successes of his career, *Tamburlaine the Great Part II*, may have reminded Marlowe of the scene in which he had 'hung a living man in chains and directed volleys of musketry against him'. A similar sensational dramatic effect is evidently being attempted in this scene, which was based on material found in Holinshed (one of the divers sources used for *1 Henry VI*, as it was used by Marlowe as his source for *Edward II*) in which a cannon is to be directed against certain of the protagonists placed *in the turret*:

'In the scene as written, I, iv, the Master Gunner and the Boy first place the piece of ordnance on the extreme front of the stage and explain its purpose, thus creating dramatic tension. Salisbury, Talbot, Gargrave and Glansdale then appear, probably on the turret platform on which the trumpeter stands in the De Witt sketch. For the benefit of the audience Salisbury immediately identifies Talbot, inquires concerning his release from captivity, and calls attention to their (theatrically) novel position: *Discourse I prethee on this Turrets* (not Tower) *top*. Through eighteen lines Talbot complies, the tension of the audience increasing in the presence of the loaded cannon, and the unsuspecting victims. On Talbot's line, *Ready they were to shoot me to the heart*, the Boy enters below with the lighted fuse. The actors above probably here enter the turret itself and appear at the window, looking through this narrow *secret Grate*. They are then facing generally east from the westerly located stage. They briefly consult as to the best method of attack on the city. From the stage level the fatal shot is fired, being probably aimed somewhat high. The hero is spared, but Salisbury and Gargrave fall below the level of the turret window. Talbot describes in detail their wounds and their actions, which are invisible to the audience; refers, in his promise of revenge, to the one-eyed sun, then prominent in the Southern heavens; and likens himself to Nero, who from a similar height had *Play(ed) on the Lute, beholding the Townes burne*. At the entering Messenger's tale of French success Salisbury, who while hidden has roughly changed his make-up, *lifteth himself up to the window again and groanes*; and Talbot, for the benefit of the pit below, identifies the now blood-bespattered face fleetingly seen at the aperture: *Heare, heare, how dying Salisbury doth groane*, and with a climactic threat closes the scene.'[10]

Further pursuing his dramaturgical and literary detection Dr. Gaw continues:

A section of Visscher's View of London (1616) showing London Bridge with the Tower of London in the distance. The site of the Rose Theatre would have been to the left of the bottom corner of this print at the north side of Maiden Lane at the corner of Rose Alley and was not far from the river. An actor standing in the Rose's turret would easily have been able to see and indicate the bridge with the Tower of London beyond.

'Now it certainly seems to be too striking to be a mere coincidence that as the actors stood in the turret of the Rose theatre in the Bankside suburb and looked out of the east window of the turret over the pit and over the theatre wall toward the eastern section of the city, the two most prominent structures before them were the Tower of London and London Bridge, the former the citadel of London, *there* and the latter *here* just as described in the scene . . . |so that| the audience, with the sudden thrill of pleasure that always comes in the theatre when more is meant than meets the ear, recognised that their own London was being made to serve as the imagined Orleans of the play. Here again would be an opportunity for an added element of novelty in the use of the turret; and it is certainly worthy of note that *the Rose is the only theatre of London before* 1599 *that fits the indicated topography.*'*[11]

It was evident that Henslowe and Alleyn wanted a new play that would be an immediate success and bring a quick return of the money expended on the improvements to the theatre which Greg says 'must have been extensive and

* *Compare this with Professor Leslie Hotson's researches regarding the topographical references abounding in* Twelfth Night *revealed in his book* The First Night of Twelfth Night (1954). *Shakespeare follows Marlowe in using the same technique in audience communication.*

affected in no small measure the general structure'. That *harey the vj* fulfilled these hopes is testified by the box-office receipts which had averaged 22s. 11d. for the 11 previous performances given, but leapt to 78s. 5d. with the first performance of *harey the vj*. It is interesting to compare this with the financial success of Marlowe's *Massacre at Paris* the following year at the Rose, which again gave Henslowe his box-office record for the season with takings of £3 14s. for the first performance (see p. 225).

The continued popularity of *harey the vj* is further evidenced by the number of performances given: 14 for *harey the vj* as compared with 13 for Kyd's *Spanish Tragedy*, 11 for Peele's 'Muly Mollocco' (*The Battle of Alcazar*) and 10 for *The Jew of Malta*. Nashe's topical reference to a popular play in which Talbot is portrayed as the hero can only mean the original *harey the vj*.

> 'How much would it have joyed brave Talbot (the terror of the French) to think that after he had lain two hundred years in his tomb, he should triumph again on the stage, and have his bones new embalmed with the tears of ten thousand spectators at least (at several times), who in the tragedian that represents his person imagine they behold him fresh bleeding.'[12]

For those who would still like to claim *harey the vj* as Shakespeare's play in origin rather than by derivation in much later revision, as has been postulated, the difficulties are, to my mind, insuperable. First, there is a complete lack of evidence connecting him with Strange's Men at this time (*vide* Halliday) and if Shakespeare had been with another acting company it is inconceivable that he should have sold a play, destined to prove a lucrative investment for the company owning it, to Strange's rather than to his own men. Further, if the successful *harey the vj* were Shakespeare's, why did he not follow it up with another success soon after? Unlike Marlowe, who had a second string to his activities in his government service and was under Walsingham's patronage, Shakespeare would have had need of continued financial support from his plays, and the incentive to establish himself, but there is a complete suspension of that prolific playwriting activity for which he is noted, quite inexplicable were this assumption correct. All the evidence points to the intrinsic correctness of Dr. Gaw's ascription of the play to Marlowe in hasty collaboration with the three other hands suggested, and negates the supposition that Shakespeare had anything to do with the play until long after, in revising it.

The confusion derives from Shakespeare's revision, analysed by Dr. Gaw to show that his obvious intention was to marry it with Marlowe's two earlier plays on the Wars of the Roses, *The True Tragedy* and the *First Part of the Contention*, making them into a coherent trilogy by the addition of the Garden scene (ii, iv) setting the theme for the Wars of the Roses. This scene at the end introducing the betrothal of King Henry to Margaret of Anjou, together with the interpolation of Suffolk's wooing of Margaret on behalf of the king and Henry's rejection of Armagnac's daughter, is obviously designed to dovetail the play chronologically with the opening of *2 Henry VI* and the arrival of Margaret as Henry's queen in England. These scenes hardly affect the structure of the play which,

RICHARD BURBAGE (*c.* 1568–1619) *was the actor who became Alleyn's greatest rival as a tragedian. He had the theatre in his blood. His father, James Burbage, was also an actor, and had pioneered London's first playhouse, the Theatre, which he built in 1576 in the Liberty of Holywell, just east of Finsbury Fields. It was a large circular structure, unroofed and uncomfortable, but the theatre-hungry Londoners flocked to it 'thick and threefold' to pay their 1d. admission. Later Richard Burbage became the leading actor in Shakespeare's company.*

(Courtesy of Dulwich College)

Dr. Gaw argues, stands substantially as it was in 1592. In fact Shakespeare's later revision weakened it structurally as a play, for this new ending (replacing the original stronger dramatic finish with the conclusion of the peace) is artistically bad and only excusable within the context of the trilogy. That the play was originally intended to stand on its own is evident from the fact that the other two plays, which later formed part of the trilogy, were *at that time* the property of Pembroke's Men, for whom Marlowe had probably written them at a date not long before his *Edward II*. That the revision of *harey the vj* would not have taken place before such time as the Earl of Pembroke's Men sold the other two plays to Strange's is self-evident. Further supporting Marlowe's authorship of the original play, Dr. Gaw convincingly argues that in the context of Marlowe's known works, and the ascription by Dr. Tucker Brooke and others of *The True Tragedy* and the *First Part of the Contention* to Marlowe, the 'chain of probabilities exactly fits all the known facts concerning the plays in question, once *harey the vj* takes its place in the list'.[13]

Textually, it has long been recognised, *1 Henry VI* represents an extraordinary mixture. It bears all the marks of hasty collaboration as, for instance, the 'number of irreconcilable inconsistencies in the play, betraying work delivered before it had been matured'.[14] The various authors evidently resorted to different chroniclers for their source material. As Dr. Gaw points out, 'in its drawing from four distinct sources—Halle, Holinshed, Fabian, and the source of the Talbot epitaph—and in treating these historical materials with unusual dramatic licence, *1 Henry VI* presents a fundamental heterogeneity unparalleled in any English historical play in the Shakespearean canon. And finally, these facts will be found to be completely in harmony with the conclusions as to the authorship of the play . . . presented.'[15] Its hasty composition for the opening of the Rose theatre, as suggested, answers all the problems of the play's internal structure and supplies the external reasons.

An Elizabethan production of Titus Andronicus *of approximately* 1594, *from the drawing attributed to Peacham.*   *In the 'Harley Papers' owned by the Marquis of Bath at Longleat.*

The reader wishing to further examine and test the validity of these claims can do no better than to read Dr. Gaw's lucid presentation of them in his fascinating book *The Origin and Development of 1 Henry VI*, in which he has made a conclusive case for the attribution of this play to Marlowe, enlivening the scene of his activity for us with this glimpse of Kit as a working dramatist.

In the light of the scene thus reconstructed for us, the Rose with its 'new look' rises into our view as a very important little theatre, having a marked effect on the development of the Elizabethan theatrical tradition, for in that case it was *via* the Rose that the turret was first introduced into the Elizabethan theatre.

This little turret evidently loomed large in the mind of Alleyn when he was commissioning the new play. Henslowe would probably have taken the advice of the theatrically experienced Alleyn in having such a superstructure built, possibly a promise from Alleyn going with it that he would find some sensational use for it in a new play. His close connections with Marlowe are too well established to need arguing, except to underline Alleyn's business acumen in acquiring Marlowe's most successful plays to date, *Tamburlaine* and *The Jew of Malta*, as his personal property and not that of the players' company. The person to whom Alleyn would naturally turn for a play that he would feel confident would provide a 'hit' for the new Rose was obviously Marlowe. Marlowe would as naturally turn for his material to a further development of the historical theme he had successfully begun around Henry VI, featuring the 'Proud Cardinall of Winchester' whose 'Tragicall end' is shown in *The Contention*, and the aspiring Duke of York, the advertising power of whose name, as Dr. Gaw points out, 'was so great that it gave the title to the *True Tragedy*, although the Duke himself dies before the play is one quarter finished'.[16]

In the production of *harey the vj* for the Rose, Alleyn's part was evidently that of director rather than actor, for the heroic role of Talbot was played by the younger Richard Burbage, just then emerging as a leading tragedian. Alleyn was therefore more free to concern himself vitally with the successful production of the play and the completion of the script in time, in which he would have been especially interested to see that opportunities for featuring the turret in some sensational way were given.

As has been seen, this the script did in two separate scenes: the first in which the ordnance is shot off at leading characters in the turret; and the second, written, as Dr. Gaw suggests, by a fourth writer C, who especially concerned himself with devising a further use for the new addition. C's hand commences in III, ii of *1 Henry VI*, in which scene La Pucelle (Saint Joan) enters with four of her soldiers, disguised as country folk, intending thereby to gain entry into the gates of Rouen.[17] Once inside the city they plan to give a signal to the rest of their followers as to how they may enter,

> *By thrusting out a torch from yonder tower;*
> *Which once discerned shows that her meaning is——*

Next comes the stage direction: *Enter La Pucelle, on the top, thrusting out a torch burning.* Triumphantly she cries,

> *Behold, this is the happy wedding torch*
> *That joineth Rouen unto her countrymen,*
> *But burning fatal to the Talbotites.*
> BASTARD:
> *See, noble Charles, the beacon of our friend;*
> *The burning torch in yonder turret stands.*
> CHARLES:
> *Now shine it like a comet of revenge,*
> *A prophet to the fall of all our foes!*
> ALENCON:
> *Defer no time, delays have dangerous ends;*
> *Enter, and cry 'The Dauphin' presently,*
> *And then do execution on the watch.*

It is not great writing, but effective theatre. C's love of the rather outdated use of alliteration is noticeable. It is not fanciful to surmise that this would not be beyond the capacity of Edward Alleyn as author. He was not only an exceptionally astute business man, and a great actor with a flair for what was theatrically 'right' for contemporary taste; he was also a literate man with an interest in learning, as evidenced by his founding of the school at Dulwich.

In putting Alleyn forward as the 'Shake-scene' of the *Groatsworth of Wit* it is highly relevant that Greene's dedication to 'those Gentlemen his Quondam acquaintance' prefaces an allegorical story in which a character makes his appearance who introduces himself as a *Player*, a bombastic fellow well pleased with himself, who informs the reader that he also turns his hand to playwriting on occasion. He might well be the personification of Alleyn the actor-manager,

205

who employed Robert Greene, just as this 'King of the Fairies' employs *Roberto*, the hero of the story who becomes in time 'famous for an Arch-plaimaking Poet'. Evidently this is meant as an autobiographical allegory, and *Roberto* is none other than Robert Greene.[18] In this context, the *Player* must be Alleyn, for Robert Greene was never in his life employed by Shakespeare!

The story is worth a brief glance. Greene's tale, *A Groatsworth of Wit bought with a million of repentance*, concerns a pious old usurer, Gorinius, who on his death-bed bequeathes all his considerable worldly wealth to his favourite son, Lucanio, 'as himself, brought up to be Golds bondsman'. His other son 'was a Scholler, and married to a proper Gentlewoman and therefore least regarded'. Greene, it will be noted, was also respectably married to a lady who would fit the description of 'a proper Gentlewoman' and in the story *Roberto* deserts her for courtezans, just as in real life Greene resorted to their company. Gorinius' only bequest to his second son 'Roberto, thy wel red brother [is] an old groat, (being ye stocke I first began with) wherewith I wish him to buy a groats-worth of wit: for he in my life hath reprooud my manner of life, and therefore at my death shall not be contaminated with corrupt gaine'.

Whether the portrait of old Gorinius is also that of Greene's father, who was a respectable citizen of Norwich, is an intriguing question. He continues:

> 'Yet was not the father altogether unletered, for he had good experience in a Noverint, and by the uniuersall tearmes therein contained, had driuen many a yoong Gentleman to seeke unknowen countries; wise he was, for he boare office in his parish and sat formally in his foxfurd gowne, as if he had been a very upright dealing Burges: he was religious too, neuer without a booke at his belt, and a bolt in his mouthe, readye to shoote through his sinfull neighbor. And Latin hee had somewhere learned, which though it were but little, yet it was profitable, for he had this Philosophye written in a ring, *Tu tibi cura*, which precept he curiously obserued, being in selfe loue so religious as he held it no poynt of charitie to part with anything, of which hee liuing might make use.'

An interesting psychological study of Greene might one day be compiled. Was the origin of his unhappy nature to be sought in his childhood friction with a father who carped at and disapproved of the feckless Robert, whose 'only care was to have a spel in his purse to conjure up a good cup of wine with at all times'? If there is an authentic ring in the portrait of old Gorinius (howsoever exaggerated) there is little doubt that father and son would inevitably have fallen out.

With his groat, *Roberto* sets off into the world and has various adventures, during which he falls into the clutches of the cunning courtezan *Lamilia*, and is outwitted by her. Down on his luck, he weeps and sings a song against the evil ways of courtezans. He is overheard by a man on the other side of the hedge, who pops up and introduces himself. 'I am a Player,' he tells *Roberto*.

'A Player, quoth Roberto, I took you rather for a Gentleman of great liuing, if by outward habit men should be censured . . . (Player): Why I am as famous for Dephrigus, and the King of the Fairies, as euer was any of my time. The twelue labors of Hercules haue I terribly thundred on the Stage . . . Nay more (quoth the Player) I can serue to make a prettie speech, for I was a countrey Author, passing at a Morrall for twas I that pende the Morrall of Mans Witte, the Dialogue of Diues, and for seuen yeares space was absolute interpreter to the puppets. But now my Almanacke is out of date:

> *The people make no estimation*
> *Of Morrals teaching education.*

Was not this prettie for a plaine rime extempore? if ye will ye shall haue more . . . Nay, tis enough, said Roberto, but how meane you to use mee? Why sir, in making Plaies, said the other, for which you shall be well paid, if you will take the paines.'

In the autobiographical context of the *Groatsworth* such an employer of play-making poets could only have been Alleyn, then at the head of Strange's Men which was currently the strongest acting contingent in existence, and for whom Greene had chiefly written. Incidentally, in their repertoire of 1591–2 were two plays of Greene's which had proved failures: his *Orlando Furioso* (only played once in the entire season) and *A Looking Glass for London* (only played four times in a season of 134 performances), possibly an added source of bitterness between Greene and his employer. If Alleyn is 'Shake-scene' (alias the Player-manager of the *Groatsworth* story), here is evidence that Robert Greene knew, and more, was employed by an actor-manager who also turned his hand to playmaking. An absolute *Iohannes Factotum* evidently. Probably Alleyn, whose acting career by that time must at least have covered a seven-years period (for he had risen to fame early in life), did some writing for the players when they were on tour and away from the London dramatists. Perhaps in his early days he suited his style to the simple country tastes with morality type plays. It is necessary to remember that the Elizabethan drama had undergone an exceptionally rapid development within a matter of a few years, largely due to Marlowe's influence.

The certainty with which scholars have connected the composite name 'Shake-scene' with Shakespeare bears no relation to the facts and practice of Elizabethan times. Will Kempe, the actor, in his pamphlet *Nine Days Wonder* (1599), addresses his colleagues thus:

'My notable Shake-rags, the effect of my suit is discerned in the title of my supplication, but for better understanding for that I know you to be a sort of witless bettleheads that can understand nothing but that is knocked into your scalp; so farewell and crosse me no more with thy rabble of bold rhymes lest at my return I set a crosse on thy forehead that all men know that for a fool.'

Are we to assume that this, published at a time when Shakespeare *was* known, is also to be taken by his contemporaries to be a reference to William Shakespeare? It should be quite evident that both 'Shake-scene' and these 'Shake-rags' are generally intended for an actor or actors, and that in common Elizabethan parlance the term was so well known as to have left no doubt as to what was meant, otherwise we may be sure that neither Kempe nor Greene would have used it in this connection. At the time when Greene wrote I suggest that there was no William Shakespeare known with whom there could have been confusion, and *even if there had been* the term stands on its own popular interpretation as meaning clearly an actor, a great ranting actor, who shakes a stage with his passion. Since at this time we can find no trace of Shakespeare as an actor on the lists of the players' companies, the association falls to the ground.

It has been shown that the circumstances of the writing of *harey the vj* must have been such as to breed tension and possibly hasty tempers. Greene was probably already a sick man. With Alleyn breathing down his neck to finish the play in time, who knows what fractious scenes might not have taken place? Perhaps Alleyn was interfering too much (in Greene's opinion) in the matter of the first turret scene in B's section of the play. Perhaps a blazing row developed between the red-bearded Roberto and Alleyn. Alleyn may have acted harshly, not realising how sick a man Greene really was, dismissing him perhaps and taking over part of the writing himself as a result. That B's contribution to the play, the Talbot story, bears the marks of *more than one hand* is a conclusion to which Dr. Gaw has been forced. Certainly the writing in the first turret scene (I, iv, reconstructed on p. 200) is sufficiently curious to merit quotation; and in it again actors' 'business' is strikingly to the fore, as well as some good strong sensationalist histrionic rant.

> TALBOT:
> *Then broke I from the officers that led me,*
> *And with my nails digg'd stones out of the ground*
> *To hurl at the beholders of my shame;*
> *My grisly countenance made others fly;*
> *None durst come near for fear of sudden death.*

Is this the actor who played Tamburlaine turning his hand to bombasting out a blank verse? Later the graphically gruesome description of Salisbury's injuries and death is almost comical. After the stage direction *Here they shoot and Salisbury and Gargrave fall down*, with cries of *O Lord, have mercy on us wretched sinners!* and *O Lord, have mercy on me, woeful man!* we have Talbot's comments:

> *What chance is this that suddenly hath cross'd us?*
> *Speak, Salisbury; at least, if thou canst speak.*
> *How far'st thou, mirror of all martial men?*
> *One of thy eyes and thy cheek's side struck off!*
> *Accursed tower!* (designating the turret again) *accursed fatal hand*
> *That hath contriv'd this woeful tragedy!*

208

Joan Alleyn (*née Woodward*), *stepdaughter of Philip Henslowe. Her marriage to Edward Alleyn 'led to the Henslowe-Alleyn theatrical enterprises'.*

(Courtesy Dulwich College)

Here it would seem that we have C's favourite trick of alliteration again, and there is very obviously present a strong if rather crude sense of theatrical effect. This kind of writing would typify Alleyn's attitude and approach to the problem. Whoever C was, he would have to be someone close to the scene of action, and present to take a hand in the writing at what was probably short notice. Alleyn's practical and theatrical mind is noticeable in the devices resorted to for featuring the turret in both the scenes quoted, and there seems to be no reason to doubt his ability to turn his hand to 'bombast out a blanke verse' since we have Greene's evidence that he knew an actor who could do just that. His imputation is obviously a somewhat sarcastic one!

In thus seeking to identify the fourth collaborator in *harey the vj*, who can bombast out a blank verse passably well for the purpose in hand, all the evidence considered points to no one so much as Alleyn, who of all those concerned with this composite play must have had a clear working knowledge of *how* he was going to use the turret. Every reference in Greene's *Groatsworth of Wit* to 'Shake-scene' would likewise seem singularly applicable to Alleyn. With Greene's collaboration in the play *harey the vj* fairly well established, the links between writers B and C, as Greene and Alleyn, make an unbroken chain of identification with 'Shake-scene'.

It should also be noted that Nashe, in his *Epistle* to Greene's *Arcadia* (1587), refers to actors as a 'company of taffaty fools with their feathers', and again to the players as 'decked with poet's feathers like Aesop's Crow'; thus the 'upstart Crow, beautified with our feathers' is quite obviously and incontrovertibly an actor first and foremost. 'Our feathers' may perhaps be taken as a reference to their joint works; certainly the implication is that 'Shake-scene' is someone who has *already* made capital out of the dramatist and his friends, otherwise there would be no point in the bitterness with which Greene writes.

With Alleyn in the picture we need look no further for 'Shake-scene' whose shadow has haunted Shakespeare for so long. Greene was probably dead and in his grave several months before Shakespeare made his appearance in London, and therefore did not know that he would be innocently guilty of confusing scholars 400 years later with his reference to 'Shake-scene', the leader of a company of 'Shake-rags', the 'Puppets', 'Apes', and 'painted monsters' against whom Greene railed in impotent anger at his pitiful death.

Dr. Gaw has summed up his findings thus:

'If the present investigation has done nothing else it should at least have made clear the indisputable fact that there is not one atom of evidence connecting Shakespeare with *harey the vj* or with *1 Henry VI* prior to a date later than February 1, 1593, and that he is thus totally dissociated from all authorial connection with the early success of *harey the vj*. Further . . . it is highly improbable that by June 23, 1592, he had already revised the *True Tragedy* into *3 Henry VI*: and if he had, it is certain that Strange's Men did not then own that play or they would indubitably have used it as a "trailer" for the popular *harey the vj* .'[19]

With regard to the *Groatsworth* reference he has this to say:

'The mythical character of Greene's supposed allegation in the *Groatsworth of Wit* that Shakespeare plagiarized from him in *1* or *3 Henry VI* has been demonstrated. Such an interpretation of the Tygers hart passage is certainly chronologically impossible as to *1 Henry VI*, and almost certainly so as to *Part 3* also, while on other grounds as well the theory is logically and factually fallacious.'[20]

Actor Will Kempe *dancing a 'Morris'. Perhaps his clothes could be called 'shake-rags'.*

From the title page of his NINE DAYS' WONDER, 1600, *'an account of his dance from London to Norwich in 1599'.*

210

In that case it is necessary to look elsewhere for 'Shake-scene', and his identification with Alleyn should recommend itself as being singularly apt, and free from all those inherent contradictions which have so beset the Shakespeare theory. It has, in fact, the ring of truth.

Dr. Gaw did not go so far as to suggest the identity of 'Shake-scene', but his researches in revealing the origin of *1 Henry VI* and its close connections with the rebirth of the Rose theatre have illuminated a page in the history of the Elizabethan drama that ranks with the most brilliant research done on this period.

We can now see also that Marlowe, working in close collaboration with Alleyn, a man with an inborn sense of theatre, had a first-hand knowledge of *how* the play would be produced. We have more recently learned to study Shakespeare in his context as a working dramatist and actor close to the scene of the performance of his dramas—the 'wooden O'. We can no longer doubt that this was the way Marlowe, the shoemaker's son, also worked. Marlowe's dramas were the undoubted box-office 'hits' of their day because they were tailor-made to the tastes and requirements of the Elizabethan theatre and its audiences, hence their striking success. At the same time his superb language had a refining influence on the crude Elizabethan drama, lifting it to an unprecedented height of artistic excellence. Along with his poetic gift and sensitivity Marlowe also had that inborn sense of theatre which made him the leading dramatist of his day, the first and chief creative genius of the Elizabethan drama. Chapman boasted that he did not trouble to see his own plays in performance, and the result is that today they are almost unactable. It is inconceivable that this would have been Marlowe's attitude; and although the tradition that he also acted at the Curtain for a time seems to be unsupported (but for a ballad in J. P. Collier's forged hand), it is the sort of thing that one might have expected of him.

With *harey the vj* so successfully launched, Kit probably collected his payment and dashed off on some other activity, a government assignment perhaps, or back to Canterbury to see his parents with money in his purse, or perhaps for a spell of relaxation at his patron's home at Scadbury in Kent.

The play had been a roughly-finished affair, in which, as Dr. Gaw remarks, with only rare exceptions, we miss Marlowe's 'characteristic élan' in the writing. The conditions imposed had not been conducive to inspiration from his Muse. But with the audiences it was a resounding success, and for us it shows once more that Marlowe was developing with giant strides towards ever greater sureness as a dramatist. Although he did not write it all, he had plotted the play, and once more scored a 'hit', which, with but slight revision, has held its place in Shakespeare's *First Folio* unblushingly these many years.

*   *   *

Meanwhile, Greene's attack, as he intended it should, had created a ripple through the literary waters of London, discussed with sly delight, no doubt,

Signature of Edward Alleyn *on a letter to his wife dated 'from Chellmsford 2 of Maye* 1593'
'thyn ever & no bodies els by god of heaven Edwards Alleyn'
Underneath appear the words 'mousin & mouse', Elizabethan endearments by which Alleyn called his wife. In another letter of the same year from Bristol, he writes: 'mouse you send me no newes of any things you should send of yo' domesticall matters such things as hapens att home as how yo' distilled watter proves or this or that or any thing what you will.'

(*Courtesy of Dulwich College, MS. I, 9.*)

by men who gossiped as they travelled by boat along the Thames, or talked in the ten-penny alehouses. It was obvious to them, if not to us, whom Greene was 'knocking'. We have the evidence of Henry Chettle, who had published Greene's *Groatsworth of Wit*, that his 'letter written to diuers play-makers, is offensiuely by one or two of them taken, and because on the dead they cannot be auenged, they wilfully forge in their conceites a liuing Author: and after tossing it to and fro, no remedy, but it must light on me'. Chettle also some-times wrote plays.

Accordingly, Chettle finds it expedient to clear himself in a letter of apology prefacing his *Kind-Harts Dreame*, published in December, 1592. Again we have only the context to guide us, for Chettle mentions no names; but he is obviously replying to those *Gentlemen* of Greene's *Quondam acquaintance*, with the addition of 'Shake-scene'. Here the identification of the latter as Edward Alleyn again holds exceedingly well.

Of the two who took offence one must be Nashe, who denounced Greene's book as a 'scald, trivial, lying pamphlet'. He had presumably been to see Chettle about it, probably at the same time lodging a complaint on behalf of his friend Marlowe. Kit had never previously taken offence at either Nashe's or Greene's earlier pin-pricks against him, but this blatant accusation of 'Machiavellian atheism' was decidedly dangerous. If he didn't see it, his friends did. Alleyn evidently also made a point of seeing Chettle personally about the imputations against his 'uprightness of dealing' with his play-making poets, and the sarcastic aspersions concerning his own ability to 'bombast out a blank verse'. The intriguing question of the authorship of several anonymous plays of no great literary merit which have survived is perhaps here relevant. No one suggests that these are from the pen of Shakespeare, nor even from the lesser dramatists whose works are known to us. But someone must have written them, perhaps that someone was Alleyn.

But let Chettle speak for himself first:

'How I haue all the time of my conuersing in printing hindred the bitter inueying against schollers, it hath been very well knowne, and how in that I dealt I can sufficiently prooue. With neither of them that take offence was I acquainted, and with one of them I care not if I neuer be:

'The other, whome at that time I did not so much spare, as since I wish I had, for that as I haue moderated the heate of liuing writers and might haue vsde my owne discretion (especially in such a case) the Author beeing dead, that I did not, I am as sory, as if the original fault had beene my fault, because my selfe haue seene his demeanor no lesse ciuill than he exelent in the qualitie he professes:

'Besides, diuers of worship haue reported, his vprightnes of dealing, which argues his honesty, and his facetious grace in writting, that aprooues his Art.

'For the first, whose learning I reuerence, and at the perusing of *Greenes* Booke, stroke out what then in conscience I thought he in some displeasure writ: or had it beene true, yet to publish it, was intollerable: him I would wish to vse me no worse than I deserue.

'I had onely in the copy this share, it was il written, as sometimes *Greenes* hand was none of the best, licensed it must be, ere it could bee printed which it could neuer be if it might not be read. To be briefe, I writ it ouer, and as neare as I could, followed the copy, onely in that latter I put something out, but in the whole booke not a worde in, for I protest it was all *Greenes*, not mine nor Maister Nashes, as some vniustly haue affirmed.'

Chettle's reference to 'the first, whose learning I reuerence' is evidently Marlowe, who had been more severely taxed by Greene than either Nashe or Peele, and with a deadly charge. Chettle, recognising the danger, had 'stroke out' some of this; and lest any should impute him with those same 'monstrous opinions' which later led to Marlowe's arrest, he makes a point of publicly dissociating himself from a man so dangerously accused. He was not acquainted with him and cared not if he never knew him. It was the first hint of impending disaster. The taint of 'atheism' was around him. The Chettles and the Heywoods scuttled to safety. Even his friend Nashe was eventually to desert him. But now, perturbed at first on Kit's behalf, Nashe had requested Chettle to let it be known that he had nothing to do with Greene's accusations. He further publicly announced, 'I never abused Marloe, Greene, Chettle in my life, nor anie of my friends that vsde me like a frend.'[21] Yet after Marlowe's death and the tragic events of 1593, we find Nashe hysterically avowing his hatred of atheists, fearful that after Marlowe, who had been his close friend in his lifetime, the deadly finger of accusation might be pointed at him; for certes, the times were not yet safe for a man to think or speak as he thought.

*   *   *

Two Portraits

In 1953 the 'Marlowe' portrait was discovered at Corpus Christi College, Cambridge, and has been accepted as a presumptive portrait of Christopher Marlowe. The 'Grafton' portrait, which was discovered in 1907 by Thomas Kay and presented by him to the John Rylands Library in Manchester, is now also fairly generally accepted as being a presumptive portrait of Shakespeare if one may judge by the freedom with which it has been used in connection with publications of a serious and scholarly nature about him. Evidence to support this assumption is, however, quite unsubstantiated. All that can be stated definitely is that it is an attested genuine Elizabethan portrait of a young man who, according to the inscription, was aged twenty-four in 1588, and is therefore the exact contemporary of Shakespeare and Marlowe, since they were both born in the same year, 1564, within two months of each other.

As in the case of the Corpus Christi portrait, the sitter in the 'Grafton' portrait is left tantalisingly unnamed. What is immediately apparent is that there is a striking resemblance between the young men in these two portraits, one aged twenty-one in 1585, and the other, three years later, aged twenty-four in 1588, which suggests the question: Are these two sitters *one and the same person*—not Shakespeare, but Marlowe?

It should be noted that the 'Grafton' portrait is completely unretouched, and had at one time been subjected, by the lady who owned it, to a violent 'cleaning' by means of scrubbing with soda water! This has removed the varnish and some of the pigment, especially in the area of the sitter's left eyebrow where considerable paint has been scrubbed away. This over-vigorous cleaning has also resulted in a curious area on the left side of the hair which has previously caused much puzzlement. At one time it was thought to be a flower; Charlotte Stopes considered it an ornament. However, careful scrutiny of the portrait reveals it to be part of an ear, painted on a larger scale than the portrait itself. This is undoubtedly due to a previous underpainting which, when the portrait was too well scrubbed, became inadvertently revealed. The 'Marlowe' portrait, on the other hand, has been skilfully restored so that today it looks remarkably fresh and 'new'. The retouching was fairly extensive, including restoration of the carnation tints in the face and overpainting repairs. For purposes of comparison, the unretouched 'Marlowe' portrait has therefore been here juxtaposed with the 'Grafton Shakespeare' portrait.

A fundamental resemblance between the two sitters is immediately apparent, despite the contrasting styles in which the portraits are painted, each being from the hand of an artist of a different school employing opposing techniques. The 'Marlowe' portrait is evidently by an artist of the Spanish school, which indulged in the use of dramatic chiaroscuro, or heavy shadowing. The 'Grafton' portrait, on the other hand, is by an artist of the English school of Nicholas

Hillyarde, who considered that shadowing was a blemish which 'smudged' the painting. Delicacy of line and fine chiselling of the features were aimed at, and artists of this school sometimes have a tendency to idealise the face by representing it as more slender than in fact for the sake of refinement.

The mood evoked by the 'Grafton' portrait is distinctly romantic and English, somewhat withdrawn and dreamy. It has a poetic quality much favoured by English portrait artists of this time. This delicate charm is apparent in all of Hillyarde's exquisite miniatures, and it is his influence which pervades this portrait. By contrast, the chief quality of the 'Marlowe' portrait is its vivacity and robustness. Here is no romanticised ideal, but a direct statement of character and personality enhanced by dramatic light and shade; the subject looks, not dreamy, but 'alive' and eager even in repose. If the 'Grafton' shows us the poet, the 'Marlowe' shows us more the dramatist, intensely observant of humanity, the thinker, yet there is also hidden fire in his look. This difference in mood and quality of the two portraits may be attributed to the projections of the artists, each striving after the expression of a different artistic ideal, each seeing his subject with different eyes—the English temperament as opposed to the Latin. This difference in treatment and technique of the two schools, as well as in interpretation, would go far to explain such apparent superficial dissimilarity as exists in the two portraits.

But when we turn to examine the facial structure of the two sitters it is the extraordinary similarities which are immediately apparent. They are particularly striking in the high spacious foreheads, with their identical growth of hair line; the wide spacing of the eyebrows and the similar sweep above the eye (the eyebrow in the 'Grafton' being partly obliterated, but the same line is there); the bony structure of the nose, with its identically rounded end, and similar shape of the nostrils; the shape of the mouth and the upper lip with a similar small moustache, and what appears to be the same style of close beard outlining the jaw-line like an extended growth of sideboards (although this may conceivably be a shadow; but it is apparent in both portraits).

The dress worn is also remarkably similar in style and cut, both sitters having on a slashed velvet doublet (black in the 'Marlowe' portrait, red in the 'Grafton') with the collar of the shirt showing under the sheer lawn in both portraits. The lawn is completely plain in the earlier portrait and has faint line markings in the later one. However, the two collars are of similar pointed shape, with the sides joining just above the top button of the doublet so that a fair amount of the sitter's neck is in evidence. Charlotte Stopes in her letter to *The Times Literary Supplement* (Nov. 4, 1915), discussing the 'Grafton' portrait, remarks that a simple collar of this type is unusual in a period when ruffs or lace collars were customarily worn.

Photographs of these two portraits have been submitted for comparison to the scrutiny of several professional portrait artists; the unanimous verdict given is that the two are almost certainly different representations of the same sitter. The similarity of the features is considered to be striking, and such variations

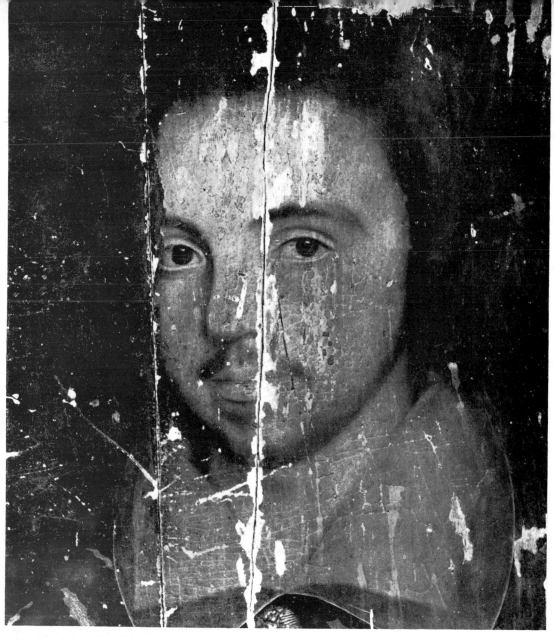

Above: The 'Marlowe' portrait (*close up*) *as it looked when first found in* 1953, *before any retouching or restoration had been done.*

At right: The 'Grafton' portrait (*which has never been retouched*) *shows a young man who is exactly contemporaneous with the sitter in the* 'Marlowe Portrait', *now three years older in* 1588. *He bears a striking resemblance to the subject of the Corpus Christi portrait. The possibility of their identity is considered in the subsequent chapter.*

The unretouched 'Marlowe' *portrait has a smudge on the tip of the nose obscuring its rounded shape. In the cleaned and retouched portrait it can clearly be seen that the shape is identical to that of the sitter in the* 'Grafton' *portrait.*

Æ·SVÆ·24   ·1·5·8·8·

217

as appear to exist can legitimately be attributed to the widely different techniques of the two artists, one painting in the 'dry manner' of the English and Netherlands schools (without clearly defined shadows) and the other in the manner of the Spanish school (with dramatic lighting and heavy chiaroscuro).

The only apparent difference between the sitters for the two portraits is in the eyes: in the 'Grafton' these are a slate grey, whereas in the retouched 'Marlowe' portrait they are quite dark, definitely brown. There is no colour photograph to record the colour of the eyes of the unretouched 'Marlowe' portrait, and from what can be recalled the colours generally were quite obscured. Hence their darkness may in some degree be attributed to the retouching which, skilful as it is, was a difficult task. Grey eyes often have a changeable character, and when the pupils are enlarged can give the impression of being dark. It is possible that a Spanish artist, accustomed to the dark eyes of his countrymen, would have interpreted them so, for, as has already been noted, the artist sees with his own eyes and interprets accordingly. The 'Grafton' portrait has had pigment removed by scrubbing, and the colours lightened accordingly, any discrepancy being increased thereby.*

It should be noted that for the purposes of a comparison of this nature a colour photograph or transparency is not reliable, and the original portraits at the John Rylands Library in Manchester and at Corpus Christi have been consulted. The resemblances between the originals of the 'Grafton' and the Corpus Christi 'Marlowe' portrait are too striking to admit of doubts as to the correctness of this attribution. However, the identification of any portrait must in the last resort rely on expert opinion (and this is here stated for what it is worth) and the individual eye.

Of all the young men aged twenty-four in England in 1588, it would certainly be a most remarkable coincidence if this should have been William Shakespeare, and on the face of the evidence concerning him it is highly unlikely. At that time Shakespeare was quite unknown, and there is moreover nothing to connect him with Grafton Regis.[1] Marlowe, on the other hand, was an M.A., and a famous playwright, had undoubtedly acquired wealthy patronage, was entered into the circle of the noblemen involved in the School of Night in London, and was also a tried and tested servant of Her Majesty's secret service. If the edict of the Statute of Apparel is to be argued, this would also rule out Shakespeare, although not Marlowe, who definitely had exemption in 1588.

1588 was the year of the Great Armada when Walsingham's agents were more than usually busy keeping him informed of every slightest move of the Spaniards. The secret service he had painstakingly built up over the years did him sterling service now in providing him with fantastically detailed information about every facet of the armada preparations, until May of that year when his sources

---

* *The artist responsible for the restoration of the 'Marlowe' portrait at Messrs. W. Holder & Sons of Brook Street, London, W.1—the late Mr. Vallence, snr.—was unfortunately deceased when this enquiry was made and precise information was not available as to the extent of the retouching to the eyes or their original colour. The likeness is considered to have been perfectly preserved, although it should be noted that the portrait was in very poor condition, and colours especially were practically obscured.*

suddenly failed him. It seems probable that Marlowe, a secret agent who was so intimately connected with the Walsinghams, would have been employed actively at this time of greatest danger. Possibly he was even militarily engaged. In the second armada threat which occurred ten years later, in 1598, Marlowe's patron, Thomas Walsingham, was given charge of the defence of Kent and sent with 1,080 men under himself and Sir Thomas Leveson to guard the chain defending the Medway, which had previously been prepared in readiness for the 1588 armada. Perhaps he may also have been called up in connection with the defence of Kent in the first armada, and Marlowe, as a man of Kent, might have been with him. 1588 was a memorable year, and possibly this second portrait was painted as some kind of commemoration of dangers overpassed.

One would imagine that Kit was a young man who liked to have himself painted, and if the first portrait was now given away to Dr. Copcott and hanging at Corpus Christi, perhaps this one was commissioned by his patron. It is a fascinating speculation, and would suit well with all that we can glean of Marlowe's character, to find that he had sat for his portrait no less than twice during his short life, and that he had left us two such very fine examples from contemporary artists of different schools, who were unfortunately as careless of identifying themselves as their sitter.

The story of the discovery of the 'Grafton' portrait and its past history is in itself an extraordinarily fascinating one.

The 'Grafton' Portrait

The announcement of the discovery by Thomas Kay of the 'Grafton' portrait appeared in the *Manchester Guardian* of February 18, 1907, together with a photograph of the portrait purporting to be that of Shakespeare. It had been found in the possession of the Misses Ludgate of the Bridgewater Arms at Winston-on-Tees to whom it had recently descended. The Ludgates had for some 200 years been tenant farmers at an old farmhouse belonging to the Dukes of Grafton, in the village of Grafton Regis in Northamptonshire. They, in turn, were an offshoot of the older established family of the Smiths, whose tenancy of farms at Grafton can be traced back to the 16th century.

Grafton Regis lies a few miles from Northampton beyond Old Stratford on the London road, which winds on northwards to Northampton passing on the right the site of the burnt-down dwelling-place of the Smiths, yeomen farmers of Grafton Regis, where the portrait formerly hung. The district is particularly rich in historical associations with the Plantagenets and the Wars of the Roses.

When King Edward IV was hunting in Whittlebury Forest nearby he visited Grafton House, where he met the Lady Elizabeth Gray (formerly Woodville), then the widow of Sir John Gray of Groby who had been slain on the Lancastrian side in the battle of St. Albans. She pleaded with the king for return of her late husband's confiscated lands, doing this so successfully that he fell in love with the beautiful widow and married her privately at Grafton House on May Day in 1464.

Upon the death of Edward IV, Richard, Duke of York, later to become King Richard III, passed this way to Northampton to meet Earl Rivers and Lord Richard Gray, and the district around Grafton became the scene of the struggle for the throne. Rivers was seized in an ambuscade near Stony Stratford, a few miles further along the London road, with others of the Woodville party. Later, King Richard stayed at Grafton while levying his troops for his advance in Northamptonshire.

In Henry VIII's reign Grafton Regis became a favourite hunting lodge of the king, who often stayed here, and also used it for important state occasions. In 1529, when he was preparing his divorce from Katherine of Aragon, he met the cardinals Campeggio and Wolsey at Grafton House. In 1531 he also received the ambassadors from Hungary at Grafton. The surviving accounts recording payments to keepers of hounds, foresters, servants, and for produce for the king's table show that Grafton was a place of royal entertainment in Tudor times. Queen Elizabeth also stayed at Grafton House in 1568, but used it less frequently than her royal father. Charles I mortgaged the manor to Sir Francis Crane, and it was during the Civil War that the ancient manor of the Woodvilles suffered destruction. The subsequent history of the portrait is possibly connected with this incident.

When Thomas Kay purchased the portrait from the Misses Ludgate, believing it to be an authentic likeness of Shakespeare, he conducted careful research into its history, and published this in his book *The Grafton Portrait of Shakespeare*, 1914. In it he gives this pedigree obtained from Mr. Solomon Wilcox, the parish clerk of Grafton Regis, then in his eighty-first year, who had known the Smiths, former owners of the portrait:

'He states that for many generations the Smiths lived at the "Manor Farm" on the site of which the village school now stands, and that they moved into a house which was destroyed by fire in 1908. This house stood by the roadside and was tenanted for many generations by another branch of the family, and was the home of Selina Smith before her marriage to Harry Ludgate. It was from this house that the picture was sent to Winston-on-Tees and received there by Mrs. Ludgate, to whom it had been left by her father John Smith, who had it from his great uncle Joseph Smith, one of the later tenants of the "Manor Farm".'[2]

The significance of the 'Manor Farm' apparently lay in that this old house (now demolished and replaced by the village school) was the nearest building to the manor house of Grafton Regis. During the Civil War Grafton House was held as a Royalist stronghold. On December 21, 1643, the Parliamentarians attacked and besieged the Royalist garrison at Grafton Regis, who finally surrendered. The Roundhead soldiers then entered the house and looted freely before firing the manor, most of which was destroyed. The suggestion is that the portrait was possibly carried to the Smiths' farmhouse at this time, either as loot or as part of the possessions of Lady Crane, which she and her servants were attempting to save. Thomas Kay writes:

> 'The principal yeoman of Grafton Regis was Anthony Smith whose farmstead was the nearest building for receiving the storage of valuables from the plundered and burning house. The picture may have been left with him then, either because the plunderer was unable to carry it, or because someone from the house had managed to save it.'[3]

In the opinion of Kay 'the picture known as the "Grafton Shakespeare" undoubtedly formed part of these spoils'. The house of this tenant farmer, Anthony Smith, would have been especially suitable for hiding property from the looters, not only for its nearness, but also because it possessed a secret chamber in which Stephen Blunt, a nephew of the Smiths, was hidden for some time. This room was situated behind the parlour chimney within the inner wall above the dairy. There is a tradition that the portrait had for a long time for some reason been kept in this secret chamber, before it was brought out and hung in the living-room and subsequently in the best bedroom of the house.

Thomas Kay argues as follows:

> 'The lost identity of the picture may be readily understood when it is considered that after the restoration of King Charles II he would have been a bold man and a foolish one who would allow it to be known that plunder taken from Grafton House was in his possession. For this reason it is extremely unlikely that the Duke of Grafton ever saw it, hidden away as it was in the secret chamber of a farmhouse.'[4]

Whether this was the reason for the portrait being hidden away in the secret chamber or its appearance in the Smiths' home at Grafton Regis or not, the claims of the Smiths to descent from Anthony Smith, the tenant of the 'Manor Farm' adjacent to Grafton House, at the time of the destruction of the royal manor during the Civil War, are certainly borne out by the Grafton parish registers. Tradition says that the Smiths had for some 300 years occupied the house in which Corbett Smith died, and Kay found this generally accepted as true. Payments of farm rents by the Smiths bear this out, although the farms on this estate in fact have no names in these records, but it may be assumed that it was the 'Manor Farm' which the Smiths held in continuous succession.

The obscurity in which the 'Grafton' portrait was apparently kept for a long time seems like a curious reflection of the obscurity in which the 'Marlowe' portrait is also believed to have languished.

One must be grateful to Thomas Kay for having rescued this fine portrait and for his painstaking researches in establishing its Grafton pedigree. But it is unfortunate that the excessive eagerness with which even the most spurious and uncorroborated evidence concerning anything relating to Shakespeare tends to be embraced, has here misled the public into an unquestioning acceptance of the portrait as a likeness of William Shakespeare. This it definitely is not, or, to be as gentle as possible with those who are loath to give up their sentimental prejudices in all matters Shakespearean, at the very best it is highly *unlikely* to be for the various reasons stated.

The alternative suggestion that this is a second presumptive portrait of Christopher Marlowe should recommend itself to scholars, and may perhaps be seen as one more instance of the way in which evidence concerning Marlowe is slowly accumulating and widening to fill out for us the picture of this truly fascinating Elizabethan.

★   ★   ★

LAMPORT HALL in Northampton, only about three miles from Grafton Regis, was the scene of another important discovery in connection with Marlowe. In the lumber room (right) at Lamport Hall, home of the Isham family, two unique copies of Marlowe's *Hero and Leander* (the only surviving copies of the hitherto unknown 1598 edition published by Paul Linley) were discovered. In 1867 Sir Charles Edmonds, antiquarian and friend of the current owner of Lamport Hall, was asked by the latter to look through a pile of volumes that had been stored in the attic lumber room to see if there was anything worth keeping, so that the rest of the volumes might be cleared away. Edmonds found a great number of nearly valueless books, but among them he was overwhelmed to discover priceless treasures: in addition to the two *Hero and Leander* copies was a volume in which were bound together: 1. A unique 1599 edition of *Venus and Adonis*; 2. A first edition of the 1599 *Passionate Pilgrim*, a volume published by William Jaggard containing poems of various authors (including

Lumber room at Lamport Hall *where* Hero and Leander *and other rare early editions of Marlowe's works were found.* 'There in a back lumber room, covered with dust and exposed to the depredations of mice, which had already digested the contents of some of the books, and amid hundreds of old volumes of various dates and sizes, the far greater part of which are of very trifling value, I discovered a little collection of volumes . . . the very sight of which would be sufficient to warm the heart of the most cold-blooded bibliomaniac.'

Description by Charles Edmonds of his 1867 discovery.

Marlowe's *Passionate Shepherd*, some Shakespeare verses, and one poem now ascribed to Barnfield). The author of the entire *Passionate Pilgrim* collection is designated on the title page as 'W.S.'; Jaggard was not always too scrupulous in his ascription of authorship. 3. The third part of the bound volume contained the *Epigrammes of Sir John Davies and Certaine of Ovid's Elegies: translated by Christopher Marlowe.* It was a most significant haul for Marlowe and for Shakespeare.[5]

The portion of the house where the lumber room is situated was rebuilt in 1842, at which time many books were moved from the Elizabethan part of the house, presumably these volumes among them. It is interesting to speculate as to why it was here and nowhere else that the single copy of the 1599 *Venus and Adonis* and the only two copies of the 1598 *Hero and Leander* were found. The latter are of special interest as being the only edition bearing the dedication to Lady Audrey Walsingham signed by George Chapman, Marlowe's friend who was patronized by the Walsinghams and completed Marlowe's unfinished poem.

A likely theory is that these three little volumes were part of the collection made by the young John Isham, a student at Cambridge in the late 16th century,

223

who was reputed to be an avid purchaser of books both for himself and to read to his father, Thomas ('The Blind Squire'). He was in close contact with the stationers and authors, and frequently bought books when first published, and was therefore an early connoisseur of first editions. His purchase may have been the instrument which protected these valuable books from the ravages of the outside world. In 1599 there was a great burning of books at Stationers Hall under the orders of Archbishop Whitgift; Marlowe's *Ovid* and Davies' *Epigrammes* were among those consigned to the flames, although the two more valuable books were not. These latter needed to survive another kind of threat, however: that of disregard of first editions. Even Oxford University's library at that time disposed of many valuable first editions in order to replace them with the then more desired *latest* edition.

Marlowe's Manuscript: A Comparison of Calligraphy

TWO VERSIONS OF A SCENE FROM 'THE MASSACRE AT PARIS'

It has been suspected that much of Marlowe's work has come down to us only in mutilated versions. *The Massacre at Paris* as printed in the octavo edition brought out by Edward White in particular seems to be but half the play. On the stage it runs for little over one hour and the sketchiness of much of the writing seems to indicate that this is one of those 'surreptitious copies' either taken down in shorthand during the performance, or possibly reconstructed with an actor's collaboration in supplying memorized lines, and then sold illegally to a printer. The fact that the edition bears no date makes it suspicious. The discovery of a folio manuscript page which, in comparison with the printed text, shows a speech of the Guise over twice as long would seem to bear this out. Both versions are given below:

OCTAVO VERSION:
> *Enter a Soldier.*

SOLDIER:

Sir, to you sir, that dares make the duke a cuckold, and use a counterfeit key to his privy-chamber-door; and although you take out nothing but your own, yet you put in that which displeaseth him, and so forestall his market, and set up your standing where you should not; and whereas he is your landlord, you will take upon you to be his, and till the ground that he himself should occupy, which is his own free land; if it be not too free—there's the question; and though I come not to take possession (as I would I might!) yet I mean to keep you out; which I will, if this gear hold.

> *Enter Mugeroun.*

What, are ye come so soon? Have at ye, sir!

> *He shoots at him and kills him.*

> *Enter the Guise*

GUISE: Hold thee, tall soldier, take thee this, and fly.   *Exit Soldier.*
Lie there, the king's delight, and Guise's scorn!
Revenge it, Henry, as thou list or dare;
I did it only in despite of thee.

> *Take him away.*

224

MS. VERSION (transcript from manuscript overleaf)
Enter A Souldier wth a muskett

SOULDIER:
Now ser to you y^t [that] dares make a duke a Cuckolde and vse a Counterfeyt Key to
his privye Chamber thoughe you take out none but yor owne treasure yett you putt
in y^t [that] displeases him. And fill up his rome y^t [that] he shold occupie. Herein
ser you forestalle the markett and sett vpe yor standinge where you shold not: But
you will saye you leave him rome enoughe besides: Thats no answere hes to have the
choyce of his owne freeland. Yf it be not to free theres the questione, now ser where
he is your Landlorde you take vpon you to be his, and will needs enter by defaulte,
whatt thoughe you were once in possession yett Comminge vpon you once vnawares
he frayde you out againe. Therefore your entrye is mere Intrusione this is againste the
Lawe ser: And thoughe I Come not to keep possessione as I wold I mighte, yet I Come
to keepe you out ser. you are wellcome ser have at you.
Enter minion   *He Kills him*

MINION: Trayterouse guise ah thou has murthered me.
                        Enter guise
GUISE: Hold thee tale soldier take the this and flye   *Exit*

                        Thus fall Imperfett exhalatione
                        W^{ch} our great sonn of fraunce Cold not effecte
                        a fyery meteor in the firmament
                        Lye there the kinges delygint and guises scorne
                        revenge it henry yf thou liste or darst
                        I did it onely in dispyght of thee
                        fondlie hast thow in Censd the guises sowle
                        Y^t [that] of it self was hote enoughe to worke
GUISE: thy Iust degestione wth extreamest shame
                        the armye I have gathered now shall ayme
                        more at thie end then exterpatione
                        and when thou thinkst I have forgotten this
                        and y^t [that] thou most reposest one my faythe
                        then will I wake thee from thie folishe dreame
                        and lett thee see thie self my prysoner.   *Exeunt*

Entry in Henslowe's Diary,
January 26, 1592/3.

*R(eceived) at the tragedy of
the gvyes* 30² . . . *iij^{li} xiij^s
The Guise, as he calls* The
Massacre at Paris, *was here
marked by him as a new
(ne) play. It was acted by
Lord Strange's Players at
the Rose during their season
of January/February* 1592/
3. *The takings of* £3 14s. *at
the box office were the highest
on record for this season.*

Enter A souldier w a muskett

Now ser to you yt dares make a Duke a Cuckolde
and vse a counterfeyt key to his privye Chamber

Souldier thoughe you take out none but yor owne treasure
yett you putt in yt displeases him / And fill vp his rome
he shold occupie. Herein ser you forestalle the markett
and sett vpp yor standinge where you shold not. But you
saye you leaue him rome enoughe besides: hate no answer
hes to haue the Choyce of his owne freeland/ yf it be
not to free whope the andthrone / now ser where he is
your landlord . you take vpon you to be his and will need
Enter by defaulte/ what though you were once in possess
yett domininge vpon yor once vnackuoes he forayds you
out againe. A wherefore your entrye is more Intrusion
this is againste the lawe ser: And thoughe I doue not
to keep possession as I wold I mighte. yet I doue lo
keepe you out ser. you are wellcome ser haue at you

Enter minion
minion Traytorouse guise ah thou hast murthered me **He Kills him**

Enter guise

Guise Nowe the take souldier to be the this and flye EC
the fatal Imperfett occulations
wth our greater forme of frances dold not offerte
a fiery meteor in the fermament
he the the knight delyght and guises fronne
revenge it henry yf thou lyfe or darst
I did in onely in dispyght of the

: fondlie hast thou incente the guises foule
yt of it self was hote enoughe to worke
thy Iust degestion w thwameyst shame

Guise the armye I haue gathered now shall ayme
more at the and the occupahorie
and when thou thinkst I haue forgotten this
and yt thou most reposest one in faithe
then will I wake thee from the foll he dreame
and lett thee see the self my presence Exent

Opposite: recto (above) and verso (below) of the 'Collier Leaf' now in the Folger Shakespeare Library, Washington, D.C. It is believed to be a draft in Marlowe's handwriting of a scene in The Massacre at Paris *beginning 'Enter a Souldier with a Muskett' as originally written by Marlowe, and considerably extending the brief version which has been given in the printed text.*

The 'Collier Leaf' is so-called because in 1825 it was acquired by J. P. Collier, the 19th-century Shakespearean scholar. He had bought it from a London bookseller named Rodd. Collier later turned to the practice of blatant forgery, and as a result many genuine Elizabethan manuscripts in his possession were for a time held suspect.

It was later purchased by the Folger Library, who believed in its authenticity. Joseph Quincy Adams, custodian of the Folger manuscripts until his death in 1946, wrote a detailed paper expressing the opinion that the 'Leaf' represents a draft in Marlowe's own hand. His arguments were based on careful examination of the leaf and of its handwriting and on an analysis of the internal evidence in the text itself. His interpretation of the physical aspects of the leaf were corroborated by Seymour de Ricci, specialist in 16th-century manuscripts, who stated it to be unquestionably a manuscript of this period. Adams' analysis of the internal evidence was seconded by Frank Boas, who in 1940 wrote:[1]

'I agree with Adams that the strongest internal evidence of the genuineness of the leaf lies in two passages which at first sight are questionable. The word "digestion" in line 10 of Guise's speech here means dissolution by heat, and carries on the metaphor of "incens'd" and "hot" in the two previous lines. This is a verbal use natural to Marlowe, but one which is very unlikely to have occurred to a forger. And when Guise declares, 11–12, that his aim now will be more at affecting King Henry's end than at "exterpatione" of the Huguenots, he is continuing the contrast of the two motives that drive him in different ways' (see two versions on previous pages).

Adams puts forth the suggestion that the 'Leaf' is probably one of the 'foul sheets' or a first draft of this episode, from which Marlowe then made his 'fair copy' and that being separated from the rest of the play it became 'shuffled' with loose papers which have strangely survived. It seems more probable, however, that this was already a 'fair copy' or transcript, perhaps for the actors, since there are no crossings out and perhaps Marlowe mislaid it, as he had the heretical treatise which later brought him to disaster. It is fluently written in an English secretary hand similar to that of Marlowe's signature, and is obviously the penmanship of a man who does a lot of writing. Most educated Elizabethans were able to write in either the old secretary hand or the new italic, and alternated these at will, as the manuscript also shows.

Had either Adams or Boas been able to compare the leaf with the signature of Marlowe their beliefs would have been further confirmed. In the opinion of Dr. William Urry, who has inspected both, there is no doubt that the leaf and the signature are in the same hand, that of Christopher Marlowe.

The greene Willow

Alas by what meane may I make you to know
The vnkindnesse for kindnesse that to me doth grow
That one who most kind loue on me should bestow
Most vnkinde vnkindnesse to me she doth show
  ffor all the greene wyllow is my garland

To haue loue and hold loue where loue is so spod
Oh delicate foode to the louer soo fed
ffrom loue won to loue lost when louers be led
Oh desperate dolor the louer is dead
  ffor all the greene willow is his garland

*A brief glance at the patent forgeries in J. P. Collier's 'Elizabethan' hand (British Museum)
should convince anyone still in doubt that the 'Leaf' is not from Collier's pen. The question
is whether it is from Marlowe's hand or from some other Elizabethan scribe who was
making a copy of part of the play for the actors. A comparison of the individual letter
formations with those in Marlowe's signature tends to support Adams' theory of identity.
More particularly the pen pressure and flow of the hands in the Marlowe signature and
The Massacre folio leaf are similar. A signature would be more carefully written as part
of a legal document than this draft of a play script, and there is a difference of some six or
seven years between the date of the signature and the writing of the play (see pp. 230-1).*

While Marlowe was still at the university, during one of his visits home to
Canterbury, he was called in to witness the will of a neighbour, Mistress
Katherine Benchkin of St. Michael's parish in Canterbury. Thanks to this good
lady we have the only signature of Christopher Marlowe in existence. This
was in November, 1585, when Christopher was twenty-one and a Bachelor of
Art, and no doubt cut quite a figure in his home town. It was a Marlowe family
gathering around the old lady, for those who witnessed her will with Marlowe
were his father, his brother-in-law John Moore, also a shoemaker, who had
married Kit's sister, Joan, in 1582—a precocious lass, for she was only thirteen
at the time; and Thomas Arthur, the fourth witness, was probably an uncle on
his mother's side, the Dover Arthurs. The will was discovered in 1939 by Mr.
Frank W. Tyler of Canterbury and is now in the archives of the Maidstone
Public Record Office.

(Courtesy of Kent Record Office, Maidstone)

Signature of Christopher Marlowe *discovered on the will of Mistress Katherine Benchkin.*
The signatories read:

John Marley
Thomas Arthur
Christofer Marley
John Moore

John Marley is Christopher's father; Thomas Arthur probably an uncle on his mother's side;
and John Moore his brother-in-law, husband of his sister Joan and also a Canterbury shoe-
maker. The will was witnessed in November 1585.

The discovery of a genuine
signature of Marlowe's on a
Canterbury will has made it
possible to compare a sample of
his handwriting with that in
the folio leaf of The Massacre
at Paris. *These photographs*
represent the first publication of
such a comparison, and the
striking similarity in 'style' of
hand and in pen pressure used
corroborate the belief that the
leaf is in Marlowe's autograph
(see enlargement overleaf).

229

See p. 226 for the full manuscript.

In the left-hand column are tracings of the enlargement of Marlowe's signature shown at top of page. In the right-hand column are tracings of these letters as found in a photograph of the Massacre at Paris *leaf enlarged to approximately the same size. A portion of the latter is shown on facing page and gives evidence of the similarity in character of the two calligraphic samples.*

The letters of The Massacre *tracings are from the following words:*

C from *Cuckolde, line 2*
h   ,,   *him, line 5*
r   ,,   *landlorde, line 11*
i   ,,   *degestione, 7th line from bottom*
s   ,,   *hast, 9th line from bottom*
t   ,,   *degestione, 7th line from bottom*
o   ,,   *you, line 12*
f   ,,   *forgotten, line 6*
e   ,,   *take, line 11*
r   ,,   *intrusione, line 14*
M   ,,   *Muskett, line 1*
a   ,,   *take, line 11*
r   ,,   *from, next to last line*
l   ,,   *landlorde, line 11 (second l)*
e   ,,   *once, line 13*
y   ,,   *entrye, line 14*

COMPARISON OF MARLOWE'S SIGNATURE WITH THE 'MASSACRE AT PARIS' LEAF

As shown in the chart above, all of the letters in Marlowe's name match extremely well with the playscript leaf, with the exception of the 'r' and to some extent the 'i' and the capital 'C', and the change here is one of simplification of letter forms in the later document, a necessity for a man who has much writing to do and especially to be looked for in a fluently written manuscript. There is also a seven years' interval of time between the 1585 signature and 1592, the approximate time when the *Massacre* was written. What seems striking, however, is that the character of both hands appears the same and the method of letter formation with the strokes of the quill changes very little. The instances of parallel letters in the two documents may be further multiplied by the reader's examination of the two samples of penmanship. One can also compare combinations of letters such as 'is', 'ist', 'st', 'to', 'of', 'fe', 'er', 'ar', and find strong similarities between the two samples, provided the letters are not used

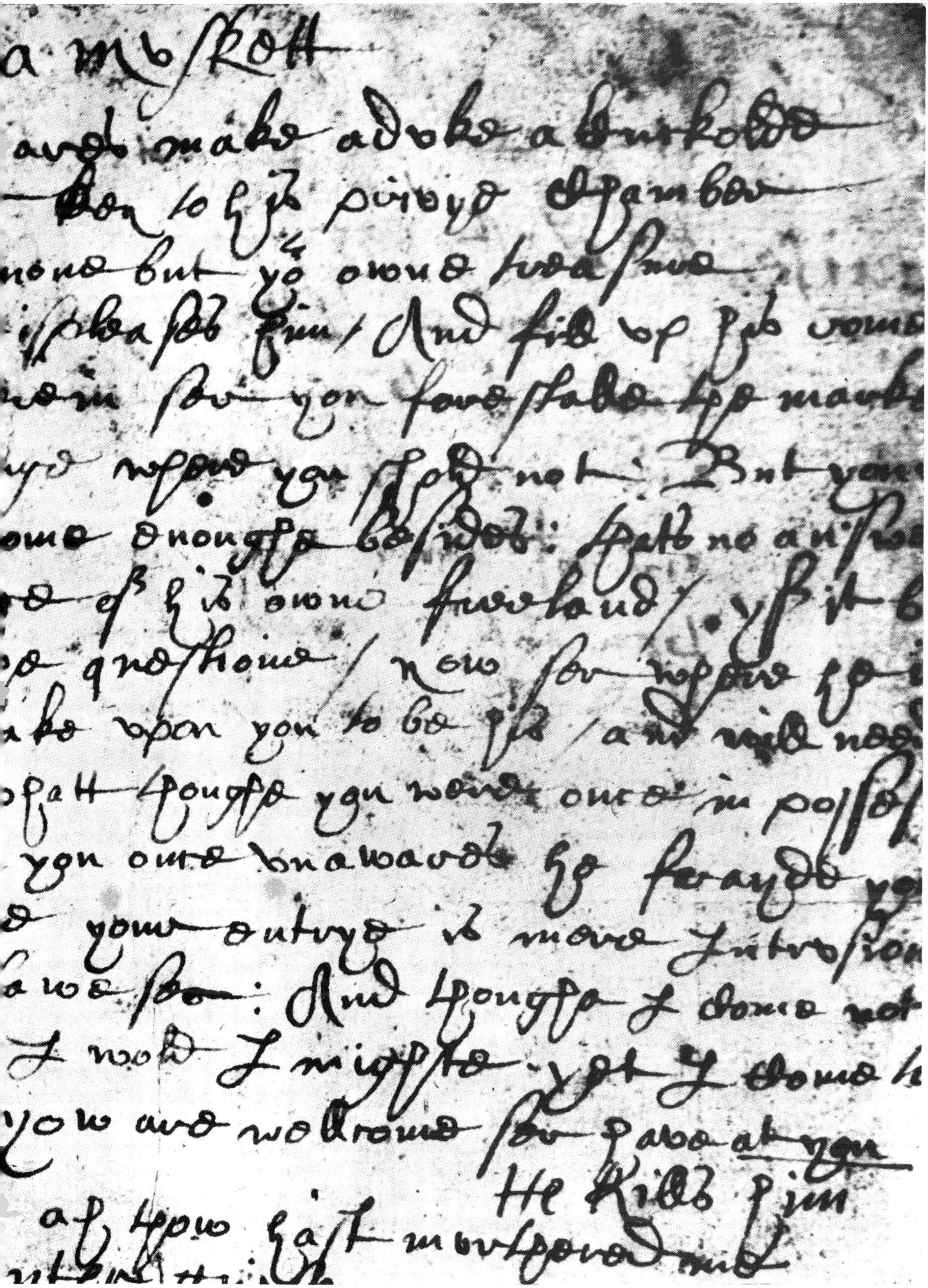

a mr Skott

and make adoke a burkolde
— ben to his piruyo agembe
none but yo owne tra fno
ifpeafed him, And fil op hib come
now for you fore ftabe hro maube
up nopow you hod not But yow
ome onougho befides: fhabe no anfwe
re of his owne fuveloud / yf it b
po another, now for wofow ye
ibe opon you to be hi / and will neg
fatt hougfo ygu woure out in poffe
you ome onawarot hy forayfo ye
o your outoyo is moure Jutoufou
a we for: And hougfo I come not
I wot I miglfo yet y come h
you and woltome for pave abyou
                He kilb him
at pow hajt mortgorod mi

at the beginning or end of a word where letter structure often includes flourishes or other change. Significantly, the pen pressure used in both the Marlowe signature and the MS. is the same, as also the general flow of the writing.

Dr. S. A. Tannenbaum, in his chapter on the identification of the holographs of Chettle and Heywood in *The Book of Sir Thomas More* (1927), writes:

'It is a matter of universal experience that the handwriting of a person who writes much . . . undergoes considerable change as he grows older; sometimes only a few years or even only a change in circumstances suffice to bring about recognizable and significant changes in a penman's calligraphy, as well as in his spelling, punctuation, habits as to capitalization, employment of abbreviations and flourishes, etc. But notwithstanding these changes, there always remain enough of his essential characteristics to enable the careful investigator to establish his identity.'[2]

Writing tools *employed in the late sixteenth century: ink pots with quill pen; scrivener's knife for making erasures lies across bottom of manuscript. The pen shown here is a goose quill. Its popularity among writers is thought to be responsible for the goose becoming the symbol of folly. During this period quill pens were sometimes made from the feathers of swans, peacocks, or crows.*
From a sketch by Aida C. Valenciano

Marlowe now turned to history for material for his dramas, and probably about the same time as he wrote *The Massacre at Paris* he found inspiration in Holinshed's *Chronicles* for what is generally considered his most mature work, *Edward II*, which stands as the prototype of Shakespearean historical drama. In addition to Holinshed, he may also have used as a source the Latin chronicles of Thomas Walsingham, the monk of St. Albans, who gives more detailed documentation on Piers Gaveston's relationship with King Edward, than is found in Holinshed.

EDWARD II

by CHRISTOPHER MARLOWE

From the production at the Theatre Royal, Stratford, London, by Joan Littlewood, 1956.

Photographs by John Spinner.

GAVESTON:

I must have wanton poets, pleasant wits,
Musicians, that with touching of a string
May draw the pliant king which way I please:
Music and poetry is his delight;
Therefore I'll have Italian masks by night,
Sweet speeches, comedies, and pleasing shows;
And in the day, when he shall walk abroad,
Like sylvan nymphs my pages shall be clad;
My men, like satyrs grazing on the lawns,
Shall with their goat-feet dance an antic hay;

Sometime a lovely boy in Dian's shape,
With hair that gilds the water as it glides,
Crownets of pearl about his naked arms,
And in his sportful hands an olive-tree,
To hide those parts which men delight to see,
Shall bathe him in a spring; and there, hard by,
One like Actæon, peeping through a grove,
Shall by the angry goddess be transform'd,
And running in the likeness of an hart,
By yelping hounds pull'd down, shall seem to die:
Such things as these best please his majesty.

233

EDWARD:

But what are kings, when regiment is gone,
But perfect shadows in a sunshine day?
My nobles rule; I bear the name of king;
I wear the crown; but am controll'd by them,
By Mortimer, and my unconstant queen,
Who spots my nuptial bed with infamy;
Whilst I am lodg'd within this cave of care,

. . . .

But what the heavens appoint I must obey.
Here, take my crown; the life of Edward too:
Two kings in England cannot reign at once.
But stay a while: let me be king till night,
That I may gaze upon this glittering crown;
So shall my eyes receive their last content,
My head, the latest honour due to it,
And jointly both yield up their wished right.
Continue ever, thou celestial sun;
Let never silent night possess this clime;
Stand still, you watches of the element;
All times and seasons, rest you at a stay,
That Edward may be still fair England's king!

KING EDWARD:

These looks of thine can harbour naught but death;
I see my tragedy written in thy brows.
Yet stay awhile; forbear thy bloody hand,
And let me see the stroke before it comes,
That even then when I shall lose my life,
My mind may be more steadfast on my God.

LIGHTBORN:

What means your highness to mistrust me thus? . . .
You're overwatch'd, my lord: lie down and rest.

KING EDWARD:

But that grief keeps me waking, I should sleep;
For not these ten days have these eyes' lids clos'd.
Now, as I speak, they fall; and yet with fear
Open again. O, wherefore sitt'st thou here?

LIGHTBORN:

If you mistrust me, I'll be gone, my lord.

KING EDWARD:

No, no; for, if thou mean'st to murder me,
Thou wilt return again; and therefore stay.

LIGHTBORN:

He sleeps.

KING EDWARD (waking):

O, let me not die yet! O, stay a while.

LIGHTBORN:

How now, my lord!

KING EDWARD:

Something still buzzeth in mine ears,
And tells me, if I sleep, I never wake:
This fear is that which makes me tremble thus:
And therefore tell me, wherefore art thou come?

LIGHTBORN:

To rid thee of thy life.—Matrevis, come!

234

Kyd and The Book of Sir Thomas More

In the spring of 1593 the citizens of London were in angry mood. Discontent against the alien refugees, the Flemings and French Huguenot settlers, was growing and riots threatened. On May 11 the Council of the Star Chamber met to deliberate counter-measures to stem this unrest: present were the Lord Archbishop, Whitgift; Her Majesty's Chancellor and Keeper of the Great Seal, Sir John Puckering; the Lord Treasurer, Burghley, and his son, Sir Robert Cecil; the Earl of Derby; Lord Buckhurst; and Sir John Fortescue. From this august assembly a letter was despatched to Sir Richard Martin and the aldermen of the city authorizing the taking of extraordinary measures against anyone responsible for inciting the people to riots:

'There have bin of late divers lewd and mutinous libells set up within the citie of London, among the which there is some set uppon the wal of the Dutch Churchyard that doth exceed the rest in lewdness, and for the discouerie of the author and publisher thereof hir Maiesties pleasure is that some extraordinarie paines and care be taken by you commissioners appointed by the Lord Mayor for th' examining such persons as maie be in this case anie way suspected. Theis shalbe therefore to require and aucthorize you to make search and apprehend euerie person so to be suspected, and for that purpoze to enter into al houses and places where anie such maie be remayning. And, uppon their apprehancion, to make like search in anie the chambers, studies, chestes, or other like places for al manner of writings or papers that may geue you light for discouerie of the libellers. And after you shall haue examined the persons, if you shal finde them dulie to be suspected, and they shal refuze to confesse the truth, you shal by aucthoritie hereof put them to the Torture in Bridewel, and by the extremitie thereof, to be used at such times as often as you shal think fit, draw them to discouer their knowledge concerning the said libells.' [1]

Little did my Lord of Derby, whose son, Ferdinando Stanley, Lord Strange, was the patron of Kyd, or Sir Robert Cecil, who had been at Cambridge with Marlowe, realise that this order was to bring both playwrights to their tragic ends.

Thomas Kyd was one of a group of London writers who had collaborated as joint authors of the play *Sir Thomas More*, written in the early months of 1593 to make capital out of the current dissatisfaction with the influx of 'Strangers', who came to England to seek the great Protestant Queen's protection, and whose success in business had engendered jealousy as well as hatred amongst the native population. In the historical figure of Sir Thomas More, Sheriff of London at a time of parallel riots against foreign settlers, an apt subject for dramatisation had presented itself, and this was eagerly seized upon by the penurious playwrights, who no doubt felt they had found material for a certain 'hit' in the playhouses. But their hopes were due for disappointment. The play failed to pass the censor. Sir Edmund Tillney, Master of the Revels, quickly perceiving the inherent danger in such a theme, which if enacted on the public stage would inflame the smouldering anti-alien sentiments of Londoners, decisively refused a licence. His remarks scribbled in the margin of the MSS. leave no doubt as to the slant he wished the play to be given:

'Leave out ye insurrection wholy & ye cause thereoff & begin w^t Sr Tho: More att ye mayors sessions w^t a reportt afterwards off his good servic don being Shriue off London vppon a mutiny agaynst ye Lumbards. Only by a shortt reportt & nott otherwise att your own perrilles. E. Tillney.'[2]

The warning note was sounded. Reluctantly they took heed and decided to scrap the offending insurrection scene and, in order to salvage the play, completely rewrite this part. It was at this point that a new playwright, not hitherto involved in the collaboration on the play, was apparently called in to help. The identity of this new playwright who stepped in to make his contribution to *The Booke of Sir Thomas More* has been suggested as William Shakespeare.

The playscript or 'Booke' of this composite play clearly shows the various handwritings of the collaborators employed in its making, and presents a fascinating study of such a collaborative venture which has survived in manuscript. It may be compared with *harey the vj*, alias *1 Henry VI* discussed in a previous chapter, in which Marlowe was involved, and for which the identification of authorship has represented a much more difficult task of detective work since only the printed page and not the manuscript is available. In the case of *Sir Thomas More* the number of collaborators is even greater, no less than six different handwritings being shown; although it is suggested they did not all work on it at one and the same time, the play possibly having changed hands from one company of players to another, with consequent rewriting, and finally underwent extensive revision in order to conform with the requirements of the censor. The hands identified in the MS. are those of Anthony Munday, Thomas Heywood, Henry Chettle, Thomas Dekker, Thomas Kyd, and the new playwright who was responsible for writing the revised insurrection scene, designated by the investigating researchers as hand D. This completely rewritten scene comprises three folio pages in the manuscript, which have been the subject of enormous research and controversy. The case for Shakespeare has been put by a formidable galaxy of scholars headed by Edward Maund Thompson, and answered by the equally redoubtable Dr. S. A. Tannenbaum. Whether the author was Shakespeare, or some other contemporary playwright whose autograph has not survived for comparison, is an interesting poser.[3]

Was this, perhaps, the point at which William Shakespeare entered to make his modest debut with this contribution to *The Booke of Sir Thomas More*? If so it seems certain that he never met or knew Christopher Marlowe, as has generally been assumed, though no evidence whatsoever can be shown to support such an assumption. All that can be stated, on the basis of any existing

236

evidence, is that Shakespeare obviously admired Marlowe's work, revised it after his death, absorbed it, and learnt from the 'famous gracer of Tragedians'.

In London meanwhile, the air was unhealthy with discontent and impending riots and the dreaded plague brooding over all. Strange's Men were the only company remaining in the city, for the theatres were closed. Instead of touring the country, they had chosen the more dangerous course of waiting in the plague-ridden metropolis in the hope that the death-rate would soon fall to the point where the Rose theatre might be reopened, as had happened the previous December. They would then be in a position to take a good box office from the theatre-starved populace ready to turn to giddy pleasure in relief after the dreadful terror-haunted days past. It was a gamble with death. The Elizabethans, it has often been remarked, lived dangerously.

Kyd worked on to finish the playscript, his ears by now inured to the tale of the tolling death-bell, with a sponge drenched in white vinegar, a posy of rue or mint, or a clove-bestuck orange on his writing-table to keep the shadow of the 'grand disease' at bay. Marginal notes in the manuscript indicate that the play was already being cast, presumably in the hope of putting it on as soon as a licence could be obtained for the revised version.

As Kyd put the final touches to the manuscript he was unaware that the net cast by the Star Chamber order to search the 'chambers, studies, chestes, or other like places for al manner of writings or papers that may geue you light for discouerie of the libellers' was fast closing in on him. Someone had evidently suggested that a likely place to search for the authorship of those certain lewd verses that had been pinned up on the wall of the Dutch Churchyard between eleven and twelve o'clock on the night of May 5th would be amongst the papers and writings of the playwrights concerned in the play *Sir Thomas More*, which had recently been rejected by the censor precisely because it voiced similar opinions to those crudely expressed in the verses, which went so far as to threaten openly:

> *You strangers that inhabit in this land,*
> *Note this same writing, do it understand;*
> *Conceive it well for safeguard of your lives,*
> *Your goods, your children and your dearest wives.*[1]

And more to this tune. Kyd, as has been noted, seems at this stage to have taken main responsibility for the composite play *Sir Thomas More* in completing it for Lord Strange's Men, and must have been first on the list to be questioned. His room was entered and searched.

No libellous verses were found, and in all probability the Mayor's officers were on the wrong scent here, for it is unlikely that Kyd and his friends were interested in openly inciting the people to rioting. But, unfortunately for Kyd, his friend Marlowe was a member of the School of Night. He was also careless with his papers. Amongst Kyd's writings he had left a manuscript copy of a treatise on the heretical beliefs of an anonymous heretical thinker designated under the name of Arrian. (This had been published in 1549 as the basis of a work of refutation by John Proctor under the title *The Fal of the Late Arrian*, and dedicated to the Catholic princess Mary Tudor, before she came to the throne.) Probably this was the 'Atheist Lecture' Marlowe is reputed to have read to Sir Walter Ralegh,[5] presumably as a dissertation for a discussion on religion by the members of the group. Their avid search for knowledge took them far beyond the permitted bounds of their time when any questioning of the accepted religious dogma was labelled atheism.

It was this paper that the eye of the commissioner lighted upon. What was this? Heresy? Atheism? A find indeed! In vain poor Kyd attempted to explain, protesting that the papers belonged not to him but to Marlowe, and that they had apparently been 'shuffled with some of myne (unknown to me) by some occasion of or wrytinge in one chamber twoe yeares synce'. His story was not believed. He was arrested and marched off to Bridewell under the authority of the order of the Star Chamber, and there put to the torture.

Despite his sufferings Kyd stuck to his original story, which was in part no doubt the truth, although the transcript of the document is in the beautiful italic of a noverint's hand, and Kyd, who was also a professional noverint or copyist of manuscripts, may have copied this for Marlowe. However, if this was so he did not confess it. Knowing that the worse fate of death on the stake awaited the heretic or confessed atheist, he did his best to minimise his relationship with the 'atheist' Marlowe, as is evident from his later correspondence to Sir John Puckering, Keeper of the Tower.

Meanwhile the other playwrights, hearing with alarm of Kyd's arrest, would doubtless have good reason to keep their close counsel and know as little as possible about the fatal play of *Sir Thomas More*, which had brought the secret police onto Kyd's tracks. Perhaps its curious survival in manuscript to this day owes something to its being tucked away out of sight at this point. Dr. S. A. Tannenbaum writes:

'There is not a particle of evidence extant to show that the play was ever put on the stage. From the fact that the revised portions bear no trace of Tyllney's pen, not even opposite highly objectionable utterances, it is reasonably certain

The Rack *consisted of a large oak frame raised some three feet from the ground. The prisoner was placed on his back with his wrists and ankles fixed by cords to two rollers at the end of the frame. By means of levers worked in opposite directions, the body of the prisoner was pulled up level with the frame and thus left suspended by ankles and wrists. If desired information was still not forthcoming, levers were worked farther.*
From L. A. Parry: HISTORY OF TORTURE IN ENGLAND (*London* 1913).

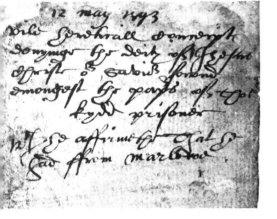

vile hereticall Conceiptes
Denyinge the Deity of Jhesus
Christ our Savior fownd
emongest the papers of Thos
kydd prisoner
Which he affirmeth that he had ffrom
Marlowe.

(Courtesy of the British Museum, Harl. MS., 6848 f.188 9)

that the revised manuscript was not re-submitted to him, even though the producer had gone so far as to plan the casting of the play. When we ask ourselves what the reason was for the play's not being completed, not being re-submitted to the Master of the Revels, and its not being acted, the obvious answer is: Thomas Kyd's arrest on a charge of being involved in the publication of seditious libels which threatened to involve the capital in rebellion. . . . With that the play was doomed.'[6]

And, alas, so were Kyd and Marlowe on a deadlier charge. For although Kyd pleaded innocence, and seems to have maintained his plea throughout his tortures, he had succeeded in incriminating Marlowe. The papers found in Kyd's room were labelled: 'vile hereticall Conceiptes Denyinge the Deity of Jhesus Christ our Savior fownd emongest the papers of Thos kydd prisoner', and, in another hand, ominously indicative of a pause, perhaps while the prisoner was undergoing his trial by torture, is added 'which he affirmeth that he had ffrom Marlowe'. Marlowe was now a marked man, and a government informer, Richard Baines, was given charge of Marlowe's case and set out to prepare a dossier on the poet's alleged atheism.

THE PLAGUE

In 1593 Simon Kellwaye published his *Defensative Against the Plague* in which he advises a frightened populace how to cope with this dread disease which was responsible for the deaths of 10,675 persons within the year. The table of contents (reproduced below) gives an idea of the variety of aspects with which he dealt. In Chapter Three (at right) he gives general instructions for avoiding infection, and advises that one 'frequent not any places or persons infected'. The worried Elizabethan owner of the book has underscored these instructions and has appended an apt marginal note: 'fuge locū' (flee the place).

Marlowe's sentiments were evidently the same, for he promptly left London and sought the clearer air of contagion-free Scadbury.

(*Photographs courtesy of the British Museum*)

O   Eyes

The causes and cures

and vertue of the same, with strength of ŷ hart. For as Auicen sayth: They that are manly, and confidently beare out their sicknesse without any showe of feare, they are those which for the most part escape. Likewise to haue a good appetite to sleepe in repose, without disturbance of the body, it is a good signe. The Botches, and Carbuncles to retaine a good colour, and without great paine to be brought to ripenesse and suppo∣nation, to haue a moderate heate mayntained through all the body: The vrines, in digestion, colour, substance, ŧ contents, to be good: To haue easie breathing, swet warme, ŧ vniuersall through all the body, appearing on a decretory or criticall day. All these signes appearing in the infected person, giue great hope of his recouery. These bee the signes and tokens by which you may gather a sure and vnfained iudgement of that which shall befall him that is attainted with the Plague.

CHAP. IIII.

A Rule and instruction to preserue such as be in health, from the infection.

WHen as (by the will of GOD) the contagion of the Plague is getten into any place, Citie, or Countrey; we ought to haue an especiall regard of the generall good, and by all meanes to study for their preseruation who are in health, least they fall into such inconuenience. First of all, therefore it behoueth euery man to haue speciall care that he frequent not any places or persons infected, neither that hee suffer such to breath vpon him: but as Galen hath learnedly aduised, in his Booke *De Differentijs Frebrium*, Chap.2. Estrange himselfe as farre as him lyeth, from their societie. The first and chiefest remedie then, is to chaunge the place, flie farre and returne late: Hipocrates, likewise in his Booke *De Natura humana*, saith; that wee ought to for∣sake the place, whereas a generall sicknesse rangeth, accor∣ding to the common Prouerbe, *Cito, longe, tarde.* And if ne∣cessitie constraineth vs to frequent the infected, (either to be as∣sistant to our friends, or otherwise:) euery man ought to see

locū

means

Scadbury

THE ENTRANCE TO SCADBURY, *home of Thomas Walsingham at Chislehurst in Kent. Here Marlowe escaped from plague-ridden London to live with his patron in May 1593.*

This magnificent avenue, down which the gallant retinue of Queen Elizabeth also passed in 1597, leads straight to the site of the moated 14th-century fortified manor house of Scadbury, part stone, part half-timbered Tudor apartments, which constituted the Walsinghams' country seat.

Even today rustic seclusion envelops Scadbury, though barely twelve miles from the centre of London on the Kentish border. The original estate comprised over one thousand acres.

Poetic Interlude

Far away from the stench of London's plague-infected streets in the quiet of his patron's home at Scadbury, surrounded by Kentish woodlands and meadows, and the apple orchards in bloom in May, Christopher Marlowe was composing a poem. Wrapt in the inspiration of his Muse, he was creating a work of exquisite delicacy and unabashed sensuality based on the story of the star-crossed lovers of the Hellespont, Hero and Leander. This Greek love story had gained great popularity during the 16th century, having already been translated from the Greek of Musæus into French, Italian and Latin, but it was evidently the Latin version of F. Paulinus of 1587 that Marlowe used as his source.

Once more he was the scholar-poet of his Cambridge days drawing his inspiration from a classical source, and memories of Ovid are strong in him. But this time it is not a mere translation that he is attempting, but an original transmutation of his material into which he breathes the undying fragrance of his genius that speaks to us with 'silver-charming tongue'. He sits, not beside the Cam, but by the still, wide, lily-padded moat of Scadbury, where the lush growth of tangled flowering weeds mirrored in the waters invokes the image of Ophelia leaning too far and tumbling in to find her watery grave. Nature to this day seems to love Scadbury, and in its fertile soil scatters her choicest flowers and fruits unasked to grow in careless abundance. No poet seeking a tranquil spot in which to work could have wanted more delightful surroundings than these. As he mused on love, and wrote, it seems impossible that he himself had never felt something of the emotions his words convey:

> He touch'd her hand; in touching it she trembled:
> Love deeply grounded, hardly is dissembled.
> These lovers parled by the touch of hands:
> True love is mute, and oft amazed stands.
> Thus while dumb signs their yielding hearts entangled,
> The air with sparks of living fire was spangled;

In his poem Marlowe paints a charming portrait of his heroine, Hero,

> so wondrous fair,
> So young, so gentle, and so debonair,

the votaress of Venus whom Cupid smites with love so 'deeply grounded' that though she strives to keep her chastity it is 'all in vain':

> Cupid beats down her prayers with his wings;
> Her vows above the empty air he flings:
> All deep enrag'd, his sinewy bow he bent,
> And shot a shaft that burning from him went;
> Wherewith she strooken, look'd so dolefully,

R

243

> As made Love sigh to see his tyranny;
> And, as she wept, her tears to pearl he turn'd,
> And wound them on his arm, and for her mourn'd.
> Then towards the palace of the Destinies,
> Laden with languishment and grief, he flies.

But his request that Hero and Leander 'might enjoy each other, and be blest' is sternly refused, and so the stage is set for the tragedy. And here Marlowe digresses to tell the classic story of the reason why the path of true love never runs smooth, which concerns Mercury's affair with a pretty shepherdess, whose womanly wiles call forth an amusing comment from Marlowe showing that he had more discernment of the nature of women than he is sometimes credited with:

> Still vow'd he love: she, wanting no excuse
> To feed him with delays, as women use,
> Or thirsting after immortality,
> (All women are ambitious naturally,)
> Impos'd upon her lover such a task,
> As he ought not perform, nor yet she ask;
> A draught of flowing nectar she requested,
> Wherewith the king of gods and men is feasted.
> He, ready to accomplish what she will'd,
> Stole some from Hebe (Hebe Jove's cup fill'd),
> And gave it to his simple rustic lover.

The inevitable consequences of this are, of course, visited on Hero and Leander, Romeo and Juliet, and all true lovers since. Marlowe next returns to Leander, who is meanwhile pining at home, a perfect pattern of the love-lorn young Elizabethan gentleman:

> Home when he came, he seem'd not to be there,
> But, like exiled air thrust from his sphere,
> Set in a foreign place;

And all his efforts to hide the cause of his disconsolation only serve to betray him to the eyes of his father, who guessed where he had been,

> And for the same mildly rebuk'd his son,
> Thinking to quench the sparkles new-begun,
> But love resisted once, grows passionate,
> And nothing more than counsel lovers hate;

Professor Boas has pointed out that this episode with the father is entirely original to Marlowe. It is not too fanciful to see in him a hint of old Polonius, and Boas' comment is a tantalising one: 'If we are to speculate about what might have been, we may perhaps regret that Marlowe did not make a play out of the tragic story, and provide what might have been a companion piece to *Romeo and Juliet*, as *Edward II* is to *Richard II*.'[1]

244

Scadbury, the moat.

Leander, unable to endure their separation longer, now plunges in to swim the Hellespont and keep his tryst with Hero at the tower of which she had told him:

> *Upon a rock, and underneath a hill,*
> *Far from the town, (where all is whist and still,*
> *Save that the sea, playing on yellow sand,*
> *Sends forth a rattling murmur to the land,*
> *Whose sound allures the golden Morpheus*
> *In silence of the night to visit us,)*
> *My turret stands:*

This 'solitary tower' is Leander's goal, at which he arrives eventually, wet and exhausted from his swim, and knocks and calls; 'at which celestial noise the longing heart of Hero' sends her flying to the door.

> *She stay'd not for her robes, but straight arose,*
> *And, drunk with gladness, to the door she goes;*
> *Where seeing a naked man, she screech'd for fear,*
> *(Such sights as this to tender maids are rare,)*
> *And ran into the dark herself to hide.*

By this Marlowe has captured the hearts of his readers as surely as ever did Leander his Hero's.

> *Even as a bird, which in our hands we wring,*
> *Forth plungeth, and oft flutters with her wing,*
> *She trembling strove: this strife of hers, like that*
> *Which made the world, another world begat*
> *Of unknown joy. Treason was in her thought,*
> *And cunningly to yield herself she sought.*
> *Seeming not won, yet won she was at length:*
> *In such wars women use but half their strength.*
> *Leander now, like Theban Hercules,*
> *Enter'd the orchard of th' Hesperides:*
> *Whose fruit none rightly can describe, but he*
> *That pulls or shakes it from the golden tree.*
> *Wherein Leander, on her quivering breast,*
> *Breathless spoke something, and sigh'd out the rest;*
> *Which so prevail'd, as he, with small ado,*
> *Enclos'd her in his arms, and kiss'd her too:*
> *And every kiss to her was as a charm,*
> *And to Leander as a fresh alarm:*
> *So that the truce was broke, and she, alas,*
> *Poor silly maiden, at his mercy was.*
> *Love is not full of pity, as men say,*
> *But deaf and cruel where he means to prey.*

SCADBURY'S MOAT *is of an unusual width, giving the effect of a beautiful lake entirely surrounding the island on which the manor house was situated. The beauty of these waters could not but have stirred the poetic imagination of Marlowe, and the felicity of his last unfinished work,* Hero and Leander, *perhaps owes something to the idyllic surroundings in which he composed it. He left only the first two sestiads completed, but these stand apart as one of the most perfect poetic achievements of the entire Elizabethan age. With their posthumous publication Marlowe's reputation amongst his contemporaries immediately rose to even greater heights than before.*

And now she wished this night were never done,
And sigh'd to think upon th' approaching sun;
For much it griev'd her that the bright day-light
Should know the pleasure of this blessed night,
And them, like Mars and Erycine, display
Both in each other's arms chain'd as they lay.
Again, she knew not how to frame her look,
Or speak to him, who in a moment took
That which so long, so charily she kept;
And fain by stealth away she would have crept,
Leaving Leander in the bed alone.
But as her naked feet were whipping out,
He on the sudden cling'd her so about,
That, mermaid-like, unto the floor she slid;
One half appear'd, the other half was hid.
Thus near the bed she blushing stood upright,
And from her countenance behold ye might
A kind of twilight break, which through the hair,
As from an orient cloud, glimps'd here and there;
And round about the chamber this false morn
Brought forth the day before the day was born.

HERO AND LEANDER

247

THE AVENUE *leading to Scadbury Manor, down which Marlowe and Walsingham must often have ridden and walked together.*

Thomas Walsingham

Thomas Walsingham IV, Marlowe's patron, was the scion of a noble Norfolk family who trace their descent from Geoffrey Walsingham, lord of Little Walsingham in Norfolk in the reign of Henry III. The estates of Scadbury in Chislehurst, Kent, were purchased in the 14th century by the great-great-grandfather of Thomas Walsingham IV, Thomas I, who cemented this Kentish link further by marrying Margaret, the daughter of Adam Bamme of Gillingham, Kent, the Lord Mayor of London in 1391. During two centuries the family prospered, especially so during the lifetime of Thomas's grandfather, Sir Edmund Walsingham, who became Lieutenant of the Tower under Henry VIII, and received monastic lands from the King.

In the will of Thomas's father, Sir Thomas Walsingham III, we get a glimpse of the magnitude of the estates which young Thomas was to inherit upon the death of his elder brother, Edmund II, who first became lord of the manor in 1584 upon his father's death:

> 'my mannor at Scadburie &c. in Chislehurst, Pauliscray, Footescray, St. Marye Cray, Northcray, Eltham, Motingham, Lee, Orpington, Bromley, & Bexley . . .'[1]

All these passed to Edmund, who held the estates for only five years until his own demise in 1589, still a bachelor at the age of thirty-two. For his younger son, Thomas, the next surviving male heir, he made provision for an annuity of £24 'out of my mannor & p'sonage of Croydon in Surrey for 7 years, and after that my saide sonne Thomas shall have an annuyte of £50 from the Demeasnes of the mannor of Burwell in Cambridge, & the mannor of Rypleye, and from the lands called Apletons att Apletons Lands in Kent . . .'

We also hear mention of a London house in the bequests to his wife: 'To my wife, Dame Dorothie, my plate, ringes, cheynes, &c. and my right interest, &c. in my howse in London, and my lynnen, napery &c. there and in my howse at Footescray.' Where exactly this London house was situated is not known, but these bequests give us some idea of the luxury and style of domestic comfort of the Walsingham home at a time when the new refinements of the Renaissance age were apparent everywhere in English life. In contemporary records the Walsingham manor at Scadbury is placed on a par with the other great Elizabethan houses of Kent, such as Knole and Penshurst.

Thomas was aged just twenty-six years when he became the lord of these great possessions upon his brother's death in November, 1589. Many of the Walsingham children's baptisms are recorded in the parish register of St. Nicholas, the little church rebuilt by Thomas Walsingham II, but Thomas's birth *c.* 1563 must have taken place in London or elsewhere, as his baptism is not recorded here. The pedigree lists his birth as 1568,* the youngest of the four sons of Thomas Walsingham III and his wife, Dorothy Guldeford, the

---

* This must be an error, see *pp.* 280-2.

daughter of Sir John Guldeford, Knt., of Hempsted in Benenden, Kent, whose ancestors had owned Hempsted since 1387. Dorothy's great-uncles had been with Sir Edmund Walsingham at the Field of Cloth of Gold attending Henry VIII, one being Sir Edward Guldeford, Marshal of Calais, Lord Warden of the Cinque Ports and Master of the Ordnance, the other Sir Henry Guldeford, Comptroller of the Household to Henry VIII. No doubt it was through this close association in their joint service of the King that the match between Sir Edmund Walsingham's heir, Thomas, and Dorothy Guldeford had been made. Young Thomas was therefore nobly descended on both sides from ancient families of Norfolk and Kent.

Most of Marlowe's biographers have assumed when referring to his patron Thomas Walsingham that there was also a Lady Walsingham presiding at Scadbury during the poet's lifetime. There is, however, no evidence to support this. No record of the wedding of Thomas Walsingham and Audrey Shelton has so far been traced, and all the existing evidence would seem to point to a much later date for the marriage. At the time of Marlowe's recorded sojourn at Scadbury in 1593 Thomas was probably still a bachelor, for we hear no mention of a Lady Audrey Walsingham in any official documents of this time, or in reportage of Court gossip in which she later figured so prominently.

Lady Audrey Walsingham's name does not appear in any Court references until 1599, but from then on regular mention of her in association with Sir Thomas Walsingham in the giving and receiving of New Year's gifts to and from Queen Elizabeth is recorded. In the New Year's Gifts List of 1599–1600 Sir Thomas Walsingham is linked with 'the Lady Walsingham, Junior' in giving the Queen 'parte of a petty cote of clay-color satten, embrothered all over with branches of silver. Delivered to the Robes'.[2] In return Lady Walsingham received twenty-seven and a half ounces of gilt plate, and Sir Thomas likewise.

We know that Queen Elizabeth visited Scadbury on what appears to have been a purely private matter, as this was not during one of her royal progresses, in 1597. The Court then being at Greenwich, the ride to Scadbury would not have taken her long, but we know that she not merely visited but also slept there, for rooms in Scadbury Manor thereafter retained the names the 'Queen Elizabeth' room and the 'Maids of Honour' chamber. Cecil, writing from the Court, informed the Earl of Essex at this time: 'I being at Greenwich and the Queen at Mr. Walsingham's.'[3] But he was not to remain Mr. Walsingham for much longer; it is believed that it was during this visit that the Queen knighted her host 'Sir Thomas', and further showed her pleasure by planting trees in commemoration of her visit, both fitting ceremonies with which to honour a young man who might, perhaps, be contemplating matrimony with a certain young lady of an ancient Norfolk family well known to the Queen: a marriage for which he would undoubtedly be anxious to receive the Queen's blessing. Young gentlemen of Elizabeth's Court who failed to obtain her approval for their matrimonial ventures not infrequently found themselves spending their honeymoons in the Tower. In this same year, 1597, the demise of the manors of Dartford, and Cobham, Combe and Chislehurst were granted to Walsingham for a lease of twenty-one years. There seems to have been no doubt that he was in high favour with the Queen.

In 1598 Marlowe's poem *Hero and Leander*, composed, we believe, at Scadbury, was posthumously published in two editions: first appeared his unfinished fragment dedicated by his publisher friend, Edward Blount, to Sir Thomas Walsingham; and shortly after followed the version completed by George Chapman and dedicated to Lady Audrey Walsingham. This double dedication, together with the nature of the poem, perhaps the most luscious piece of love poetry which the Elizabethan age produced, and dealing with the wooing of two virgin lovers of classical Greece, suggests that here we have a form of epithalamium to the marriage of Audrey and Thomas. George Chapman's dedication to Lady Walsingham seems to hint at their recent union:

'This poor Dedication, in figure of the other unity betwixt Sir Thomas and yourself, hath rejoined you with him, my honoured best friend, whose continuance of ancient kindness to my still-obscured estate, though it cannot increase my love to him, which hath ever been entirely circular, yet shall it encourage my deserts to their utmost requital, and make my hearty gratitude speak.'

This dedication by Chapman, addressed 'To My Best Esteemed and Worthely Honoured Lady, the Lady Walsingham, one of the Ladies of her Majesties Bed-chamber', significantly represents the first record of her name as Lady Walsingham. The inference from the dates of these references to her is that she only became Lady Walsingham in that year, 1598.

George Chapman, Marlowe's friend and fellow member of the School of Night, seems to have followed him in Walsingham's patronage and friendship, and, as Eleanor Grace Clark has remarked, although no direct evidence of Thomas Walsingham's connection with Ralegh's circle has been discovered, his warm patronage of the two outstanding poets of this group, Marlowe and Chapman, forms a significant link. In *Hero and Leander*, superbly begun by Marlowe, and finished, not so unworthily as some critics have suggested, by George Chapman, we have a curious and unique example of the linking of the work of two famous poets under one patron. And the occasion when Thomas Walsingham was so honoured by both his poets was, we suggest, upon his marriage, which probably took place in 1598.

In 1599 the first recorded appearance of Lady Audrey Walsingham at Court is made, and the following year, 1600, saw the birth of Audrey and Thomas's only son, also named Thomas. The charming dedication to little Thomas, then aged eight years, of Chapman's play *The Conspiracy of Charles Duke of Byron* (1608), which links father, son and mother, gives us a final glimpse of the Walsinghams as patrons of the Arts:

This BLASTED OAK TREE *probably lent its shade to Queen Elizabeth when she visited Scadbury in* 1597. *This was apparently a private visit, as it was not made during one of her royal progresses. While she was here she planted a tree 'in the beautiful avenue leading from St. Paul's Cray common to the site of the old house'. She also planted some fig trees from Marseilles near the* 14th-*century brick archway giving entrance to the draw-bridge over the moat. This archway still stands. (See picture opposite.)*

To My Honourable and Constant Friend SIR THOMAS WALSINGHAM, KNIGHT, and to my Much Loved from his Birth, the Right Toward and Worthy Gentleman his Son, THOMAS WALSINGHAM, ESQUIRE.

Sir,—Though I know you ever stood little affected to these unprofitable rites of Dedication (which disposition in you hath made me hitherto dispense with your right in my other impressions), yet, lest the world may repute it a neglect in me of so ancient and worthy a friend, having heard your approbation of these in their presentment, I could not but prescribe them with your name; and that my affection may extend to your posterity, I have entitled to it, herein, your hope and comfort in your generous son; whom I doubt not that most reverenced mother of manly sciences, to whose instruction your virtuous care commits him, will so profitably initiate in her learned labours, that they will make him flourish in his riper life, over the idle lives of our ignorant gentlemen, and enable him to supply the honourable places of your name; extending your years and his right noble mother's, in the true comforts of his virtues, to the sight of much and most happy progeny; which most affectionately wishing, and dividing these poor dismembered poems betwixt you, I desire to live still in your graceful loves, and ever

The most assured at your commandments,

GEORGE CHAPMAN

THE DRAWBRIDGE TO SCADBURY *has long since disappeared, demolished with the splendid old manor house early in the 18th century, we must assume. But this ruined wooden bridge shows where it stood, positioned in direct line with the 14th-century brick archway giving access to the outer court and moat. A partial reconstruction of Scadbury was undertaken by Mr. Hugh Marsham-Townshend, father of the present owner, in the 1920's in an attempt to restore something of Scadbury's ancient glory. It was at this time also that the moat was drained and restored to its former beauty.*

253

THE RUINS AT SCADBURY.
The visitor here is overcome with a sense of intrusion. It is a place of haunted memories.

> '*For whilst I live, here lives my soul's sole hope,*
> *And when I die, here shall my spirit walk.*

THE JEW OF MALTA.

SCADBURY'S HALL

The exterior shown here is a modern reconstruction covering the original timbers of Scadbury's Great Hall which have been re-erected on this site after their recovery in 1921 by Major Hugh Marsham-Townshend, father of the present owner of Scadbury. Prior to this the site had been completely cleared except for the foundations, and these timbers had apparently been incorporated into an 18th-century farmhouse, at Foot's Cray which was compulsorily demolished in 1921 when the road was widened. Major Marsham-Townshend's attention was drawn to the splendid timbers of massive proportions which were being torn down from the farmhouse then under demolition, and he at once thought to compare them with the measurements of the foundations of the Great Hall at Scadbury and was amazed to find that they tallied exactly. This suggested that they were none other than the beams and roof timbers of the old Hall at Scadbury, and he thereupon purchased them and re-erected them over their original foundations. As the lower walls of the Hall on which the timbers had rested had disappeared, and to resurrect them would have involved tremendous extra expenditure, he decided to commence the reconstruction directly at ground level, using only the timbers he had salvaged and roofing them over. This gives a truncated version of the original Great Hall, with its roof resting almost on the ground. Nevertheless, by this means something of the fine timbered structure within has been preserved. The original exterior was probably part brick, part half-timbered. Webb, in his *History of Chislehurst* (1899), writes:

'It is said that in the old house at Scadbury two rooms retained to the last, in the eighteenth century, names commemorative of Queen Elizabeth's visit. One was called "the Queen's Apartment", another that of "the Maids of Honour".'

In the foreground above is the moat and part of the original wall of the manor house, showing a well adjoining the kitchens.

254

Interior of the Great Hall. *The roof timbers dating from the 14th century showing the king-post and musicians' gallery of what was once the Great Hall of Scadbury, now only a sad ruin. These timbers were removed at the time of the demolition of Scadbury Manor at the beginning of the 18th century, incorporated into a large farmhouse built about this time at Foot's Cray some two or three miles away, and brought back to their original site for re-erection by Major Hugh Marsham-Townshend in 1921. This reconstruction is now fast falling into disrepair and ruin again.*

Contents of Scadbury Manor

In 1727, upon the demolition of Scadbury Manor, an inventory of its household goods and furnishings was made by the Hon. Sir Edward Betenson, a collateral descendant of the Walsinghams. There is a complete listing of the rooms and of those contents which would be of value. The majority of these are not of a perdurable nature and seem likely to have been installed not long before 1727, but the following items are of interest in attempting to reconstruct visually the manor house of Thomas Walsingham IV.[1]

Among the contents of the house are a great number of pictures, maps and drawings, some in black and some in gold frames.

The portraits include:

> Lady Walsingham (one wonders whether this was Lady Audrey Walsingham. The picture has so far not been traced)
> Lord Cecil (probably Sir Robert Cecil, as he was exceedingly intimate with the Walsinghams and particularly with Audrey Walsingham in King James's reign)
> Lord Cecil's son
> Earl of Leicester
> Mary, Queen of Scots

There are maps of:

> The World, Europe, Scotland, Barbados, Kent, Ireland, France, Germany, Holland, Flanders and Milan.

Other pictures include:

> Assorted pictures of Roman aqueduct, two of the Church of St. Peter, and another of Rome
> The Dome of Milan, A Dutch fighting piece, A fountain, Lions in France, 5 little landscapes, 17 large Indian pictures*, A Dutch Fair, Triumphal arch of and landscape of London, The Nine Muses, Sense of Tasting, Sense of Seeing, Hieroglyph of a Woman, Our Saviour's Head, Of the Heathen Gods, A fish piece, The Assembly.

Rooms and parts of the house listed:

> The Great Gates
> The Great Hall
> The Great Brown Parlour
> A passage next to this with two closets
> Another brown parlour and an adjoining Privy Garden
> A Brown Dressing Room
> Brown Chamber
> Queen Elizabeth Room over the Great Parlour. (This is undoubtedly the room where she stayed on her visit to Scadbury in 1597. Another room was said to have been named the 'Chamber of the Maids of Honour' but is not listed as such here.)
> Another passage
> A Nursery
> Sir Edmund Walsingham's Chamber
> The Old Nursery
> A chamber next to it
> The Linen Room
> The Plod Room (probably a work room of some kind)
> Brown Chamber going to the Plod Room
> The Andrew Room (an 'Andrew' was a gentleman's valet)
> A little brown parlour
> Harvard's Hall
> A passage

---

* These are described as hanging on the White Staircase. Staircases of that period are hardly likely to have been white in colour, dark brown woods being universally used, as indication of the other rooms listed suggests. It is not too fanciful to suggest that the White Staircase was so named because the seventeen large Indian pictures by John White made a striking exhibit there.

A pantry leading to dressing-room

Dressing Room (*probably for dressing the meat*)

Servants' Hall

Another pantry

A kitchen and two little rooms adjoining.
The kitchen was well-equipped with copper, pewter, tinware, and woodware.

Three cellars. In the innermost cellar were gallon casks, and in the third cellar a hogshead (2 hands) ana 6 large vessels.

One can still see the various levels of cellars in the foundation ruins still remaining at Scadbury today.

Brew House with cider and cheese press

The History of the John White Paintings

The beautiful John White watercolours of Indians and Indian life may today be seen and enjoyed in the print room of the British Museum (Add MS 5270). This album of watercolours of Virginia Indians contains eighteen paintings mounted on seventeen panels—sixteen with a single vertical painting and one panel bearing two small horizontal paintings of related subject-matter: 'The broiling of their fish over the flame of fire' and 'The seething of their meate in pots of earth'. It seems logical that these watercolours were originally mounted in a series as seventeen framed pictures, and there is reason to suspect that these may be the '17 large Indian pictures' which hung on the White Staircase, as listed in the 1727 inventory of Scadbury Manor.

The British Museum records purchase of these paintings for the sum of 200 guineas from Henry Stevens, who had bought them at auction. Before parting with them he had expressed his enthusiasm by commenting that 'beautiful as de Bry's work is, it seems tame to me in the presence of the original drawings'. (De Bry had made engravings from the drawings in order to reproduce them for publication—see pp. 143–4.) The paintings which Stevens had purchased had been put up for auction by Lord Charlemont, who had bought them at the suggestion of Edmund Malone. In perusing Thomas Payne's 1788 catalogue Malone had noted the mention of a folio of seventy-five coloured drawings and realized that they were far beyond the listed value of fourteen guineas. Within this large album Malone recognized what he believed to be John White's Indian watercolours and described them in a letter to Lord Charlemont as 'finely executed drawings . . . many whole length figures of savage persons discovered on Sir Walter Ralegh's voyage'. Where Payne got them we do not know; there is an unexplained interim of sixty-one years (with perhaps an intervening owner or two) if these are the Scadbury pictures, and there seems reason to concede that they probably are. When Scadbury was demolished in 1727, they were evidently disposed of with the other household effects as listed in the inventory. It seems likely that these are the same paintings (by that time incorporated into a larger collection of pictures) that were advertised for sale by the well-known book and art dealer, Thomas Payne, in 1788.

258

Lady Audrey Walsingham *may possibly be the subject of this exquisite miniature by Isaac Oliver of a lady of King James's Court dressed in masque costume. Audrey Walsingham took a prominent part in all the Court masques so popular under James I. She was always a great favourite with the King, and was nominated his 'Valentine' in 1616 although she was by then forty-eight years old. She and Sir Thomas jointly held the office of Chief Keeper of the Queen's Wardrobe from the time of King James's accession, and Audrey herself received many additional favours, including a pension of £200 for life from the Queen.*

The unnamed beauty in the portrait is wearing a dress in the style of Inigo Jones's elegant designs for costumes worn in Ben Jonson's masques as performed at the Court of James I. Audrey Walsingham is known to have taken part in both his Masque of Blackness *in 1604 and his* Masque of Beauty *in 1607.*

Lady Walsingham

Lady Audrey Walsingham was born Audrey or Etheldred Shelton, the daughter of Sir Ralph Shelton and his first wife, Mary Wodehouse. Sir Ralph was High Sheriff of Norfolk in 1571 and came of an illustrious family with an ancient history tracing their descent from the Norfolk and Suffolk Sheltons who had huge grants of land from the Crown from before the time of the Conquest as well as subsequently in all parts of the country.

Audrey's ancestor in the reign of Henry V had possession of both the Suffolk and Norfolk estates as well as Skelton Castle in Yorkshire and Armathwaite Castle in Cumberland. Her grandfather, Sir John Shelton, had married Anne Boleyn, an aunt of the unfortunate queen, mother of Queen Elizabeth, and it was to them that Elizabeth fled for protection when she was persecuted by her half sister, Mary Tudor. Sir John Shelton could afford her this as he had rallied at Kenninghall to advance Queen Mary to the throne and was in the good graces of both sides. Later when Elizabeth came to the throne she showed her gratitude by inviting members of the family to live with her at the Court. Audrey's aunt, Mary, sister of her father Sir Ralph Shelton, was a Maid of Honour and later Mistress of the Robes to Queen Elizabeth. Another uncle, a brother of Sir Ralph also named Sir John Shelton, fought at Cadiz with Ralegh and Essex, and the

Ruins of Scadbury. *These steps led down to what were the kitchens of the Walsingham's home. Food brought up from here was served in the Great Hall.*

family could boast a proud record of soldiering, including service at Crécy and Agincourt. Thomas Walsingham could scarcely have chosen to marry into a family more acceptable in the Queen's eyes.

Audrey was the youngest of the six children born to Sir Ralph Shelton and Mary Wodehouse. Her birth is recorded on the family tomb in St. Mary's Church in Shelton, Norfolk, as June 10, 1568. She was therefore five years younger than Thomas Walsingham. Shortly after her birth, and possibly as a result of it, her mother died. Perhaps Audrey herself was a delicate or ailing child, and this may have been the reason for her absence from Court until relatively late in life.

As has been noted, the first mention of her as a lady of the bed-chamber is in 1598 in the dedication to her of *Hero and Leander*. This being the conjectural date of her marriage, she would then have been thirty years old, and Thomas thirty-five. The fact that this was relatively late in life for a first marriage does not necessarily argue against this date for the event: Sir Walter Ralegh was forty when he married Elizabeth Throckmorton; Lady Arabella Stuart was thirty-nine, and still accounted a beauty, when she made a romantic love-match with one of the noblest and most eligible bachelors of the Court who was twelve years her junior.

Audrey's and Thomas's case would by no means have been unique in Elizabethan marriage records. As has been suggested, a delicate constitution, the legacy of her mother's childbed death, may have kept her secluded from the Court, or there may have been other reasons at which one can only guess. The fact that she herself only bore one child suggests that she may not have been very robust; although, as is not unusual with delicate people, she managed to

260

live to a ripe old age, and was evidently a fascinating woman who, like Arabella Stuart, retained her youthful looks and charm so as to belie her years.

The theory of Audrey's and Thomas's marriage in 1598, hymned by the exquisite invention of their two poets in *Hero and Leander*, is too attractive to dismiss without contrary evidence, and is borne out by events both preceding and succeeding the year 1598.

One of these is the first documentary mention of Lady Walsingham, Junior, in the Court records of 1599. In that year she suddenly emerges and takes the scene with a very pretty gesture to the Queen in which she presents Her Majesty with a 'Robe of Rainbowes' in an entertainment presumably spontaneously arranged to divert the Queen while the heavens poured rain outside during the visit of the Court to Harefield, the country seat of the Countess of Derby. Audrey Walsingham is represented as 'a guileless lady' who presents her 'humble petition' before Her Majesty, relating in six suitably guileless verses 'how St. Swythin in heaven, being dissatisfied with the conduct of Iris in providing such rainy weather during Her Majesty's visit, took her rainbow robes from her, and had commissioned her Ladyship to present them to the Virgin Monarch'. The verses, which may have been her own composition, began:

> *Beauties rose and Virtues looke,*
> *Angells mind and Angells looke*
> *To all Saints and Angells deare,*
> *Clearest Majestie on Earth*
> *Heaven did smile at your faire birth.*[1]

In this, our first glimpse of her, we see Audrey in her favourite role of Court actress, which she was to fill so assiduously and, one imagines, with genuine aptitude and grace in the lavish masques so popular at the Court of King James.

An old well *belonging to the original house.*

An impressive giant of a beech tree *stands in this typical woodland grove at Scadbury where oak and beech grow in profusion. In general, the beech is not an exceptionally long-lived tree, specimens over 250 years old being rare. However, at Burnham Woods huge beeches have been reported to have reached an age of as much as 500–600 years. The reason for this seems to lie in the way they were treated early in life. According to the authorities at Kew's Royal Botanic Gardens, at Burnham the beeches were always pollarded for charcoal, and the absence of heavy limbs in middle life may have been responsible for their living to a greater age than is normal.*

This beech at Scadbury seems also to have been pollarded, since there are marks on its trunk where lower branches have been removed. Because of this, coupled with its tremendous height and girth of well over eighteen feet, it is quite possible that it was a mature tree even in Marlowe's time. It is a curious fact that the initials 'C M' are carved vertically but fairly clearly in the bark, although moss has encrusted the incisions. Farther up the trunk and to the rear several 'W's can be discerned.

262

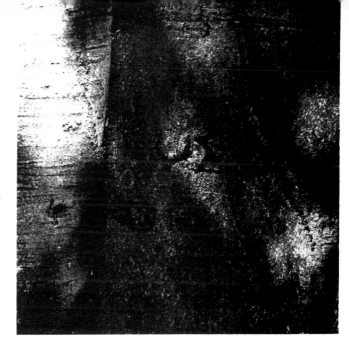

Close-up of left side of trunk of beech tree (picture opposite) showing deeply-carved initials 'C M'.

Queen Elizabeth seems to have been taken with her, for the Walsinghams continued in high favour and Thomas received a house, called Walsingham House, at Whitehall near to the Court, as a gift from the Queen. It adjoined Wallingford House.[2]

It was, however, in King James's reign that Audrey Walsingham came into her full prominence, not only socially but also in politics, and then, alas, not always in the most favourable light. She allied herself with the Secretary of State, Sir Robert Cecil,* the able and ambitious successor of his father Lord Burghley and Sir Francis Walsingham. Audrey Walsingham is spoken of as his favourite, but some suspected that she was his political tool as well as his mistress. She was one of those who made the journey to Scotland to welcome the new queen, Anne, and accompanied her on the long progress back to London. Upon King James's accession she and Sir Thomas became joint holders of the office of Chief Keeper of the Queen's Wardrobe, and Audrey in particular gained many favours besides. In 1609 she was accorded precedence over all the ladies in her rank. In later life a certain amount of unpleasant Court scandal attached itself to her name, particularly through the discreditable friendship she formed with the Countess of Somerset, wife of the King's favourite Robert Carr, who together had connived at the murder of Sir Thomas Overbury during his imprisonment in the Tower, and thus brought themselves to public trial and disgrace.

What intrigues and entertainments Lady Audrey Walsingham inaugurated at Scadbury while she was mistress here may perhaps one day be fully investigated. The full story of the Court beauty and gracer of masques who married Marlowe's patron, and died 'leaving to the world only her ill name',[3] would make fascinating reading.

* *The 1727 inventory of Scadbury Manor lists a portrait of Cecil, presumably this would be Sir Robert Cecil.*

A piece of ornamental masonry, perhaps fallen from the ruins of the manor house gateway, lies half buried in lush undergrowth. It looks as though it might be a gravestone, but on closer investigation this has turned out not to be correct.

The beauty of this wild garden is now protected as a nature reserve, having been purchased as a conservation area for wild life by the Bromley Council who administer it. The public have access to this land which formerly was part of the Scadbury Estate.

Woodland scene *in the heart of Scadbury much as it would have been in Walsingham's time.*

> *'Where woods and forests go in goodly green,*
> *I'll be Adonis, thou shalt be Love's Queen.'*

THE JEW OF MALTA, Act IV.

Foundations of Scadbury (below). *The original house rose up directly above this brick wall, forming a quadrangle of buildings overlooking the moat on its four sides. The basic structure of Scadbury shows it to have been similar to Ightham Mote (opposite).*

SCADBURY VISUALIZED IN IGHTHAM MOTE ▶

Thomas Walsingham's Scadbury Manor is today in ruins, but we are fortunate in having a likeness of it supplied to us by its almost exact counterpart, the well-preserved Tudor manor house Ightham Mote. In the following pictures of Ightham, Scadbury can be glimpsed as it must have been during Marlowe's sojourn there.

266

The West Front of Ightham Mote, *showing the stone bridge over the mote replacing the original drawbridge. This fortified manor dates back in part to the 14th century as did Scadbury. To the older stone buildings shown here were added fine Tudor half-timbered apartments to complete the quadrangle. In size and construction it is remarkably similar to the original Scadbury manor, and the following photographs present a nobleman's house substantially as Thomas Walsingham's home would have appeared in Marlowe's day.*

Ightham Mote is now beautifully preserved and restored to its original aspect under its present owner, Mr. C. H. Robinson, who purchased the Mote in 1953 when plans for its demolition were already imminent. His prompt action saved one of the loveliest examples of English domestic architecture from oblivion. The name, Ightham Mote, refers not to the waters surrounding the house, but is presumed to be a derivation from 'moot', a council meeting of Saxon times, testifying to the antiquity of the site.

267

The back or North Front *showing the juncture of Tudor half-timbered work with the original 14th-century stone construction similar to Scadbury.*

Although the moat at Ightham Mote *is not nearly so wide as that at Scadbury, the house has much the same aspect of being set amid waters because of the beautiful lake which faces it on the south side.*

Façade of the Tudor chapel *with its belfry dating from* 1521 *which adjoins the north side of the quadrangle. The cobbled inner courtyard is enveloped in an atmosphere of unruffled peace. Time seems to have stood still here.*

Opposite. The Tudor Chapel *built in* 1521 *by Sir Richard Clement, contains some priceless 'linen roll' panelling and fine Jacobean stalls and pulpit. Its painted 'barrel' ceiling and Elizabethan stained glass are also noteworthy.*

270

Interior of a room, *showing a Tudor window and wooden floor set into the original* 14th-*century stone construction. In Tudor times much domestic comfort and refinement were added.*

The Great Hall *at Ightham Mote has much the same dimensions as that at Scadbury would have had. It measures 30 feet by 20 feet and the oak roof timbers are 37½ feet from the floor at their highest point. The timbering is similar in construction. The panelling was added in 1872.*

273

13th-century window *in the crypt at Ightham Mote displays the fortress aspect of this ancient house.*

A last look backward across the stone causeway *towards Ightham's great gates.*

Chislehurst Parish Church of St. Nicholas. *Thomas Walsingham II who died in 1467 was responsible for the rebuilding of this charming Parish Church of Chislehurst much as it stands today, on the foundations of an earlier 12th-century church. The shingled broach spire and flint walls mark it as typically Kentish. The Walsinghams lie buried here in the family vault.*

Chislehurst. *This village signpost, erected in 1958 by the inhabitants of Chislehurst in honour of the four hundredth anniversary of the accession of Queen Elizabeth I to the throne on November 17, 1558, recalls the visit of the great Queen to Chislehurst in 1597 when she stayed at Scadbury as the guest of Thomas Walsingham and conferred on him his knighthood. The representation of Scadbury Manor in the background was based on the Tudor apartments at Ightham Mote.*

277

The Walsingham tomb *in the Scadbury Chapel of St. Nicholas' Church, Chislehurst. This ancient table tomb, with carved front panels of the 'Decorated' period, is the family tomb of the Walsinghams. It stands against the north wall of the church, above the vault in which members of the Walsingham family have been laid to rest ever since Thomas Walsingham II built this church, until the departure of the family from Chislehurst after the Civil War.*

The commemorative Renaissance tablets above the tomb were placed there in 1581 by Thomas Walsingham III, who had the left-hand tablet inscribed to the memory of his father, Sir Edmund Walsingham, Lieutenant of the Tower of London. The second tablet bears the Latin inscription to his son, Sir Thomas Walsingham IV, the patron of Christopher Marlowe.

This is the tomb that was opened on May 1, 1956, after five years of negotiations between the Church authorities, and the present owner of Scadbury, Major Marsham-Townshend, and the American researcher, Mr. Calvin Hoffman, in a search for manuscripts or relics of Christopher Marlowe (the authorship of the works of Shakespeare has been attributed to Marlowe by Hoffman). An altar tomb of this type occasionally does contain a body 'lapped in lead', but in this case the burials were all in the vault below, and the tomb itself was found to contain only sand brought over from Normandy to serve as a damp course. Permission to enter the actual vault, which can only be granted by the Home Office, had been refused, and the investigations were therefore inconclusive.

The Walsingham Coat of Arms *hangs on the wall of Scadbury Chapel to the right of the tomb. Sir Edmund Walsingham's sword and helm with its tiger crest had hung above the tomb for 370 years before they were stolen in 1952.*

SACRED TO POSTERITY

To the memory and honour of Thomas Walsingham, Knight, sixth of the men of his family, who in continuous succession have been illustrious in that order. A man most wise in conducting the affairs of his country, most zealous for peace, most friendly to his neighbours, most generous to the poor, most famous for his liberal hospitality to all, who, when he had completed his 69th year, on the 11th of the Ides of August, A.D. 1630, was released by a peaceful death, abundantly mourned and lamented by his kindred and by all men, the mortal remains of his body were entrusted to the keeping of this marble tomb until it shall rise again immortal through Christ's will. Thomas Walsingham, his heir and only son, erected this in piety. 1581.

(The inscription on the tomb of Thomas Walsingham, Marlowe's patron, translated from the Latin (right-hand tablet below). The date refers to the original placing of the tablets).

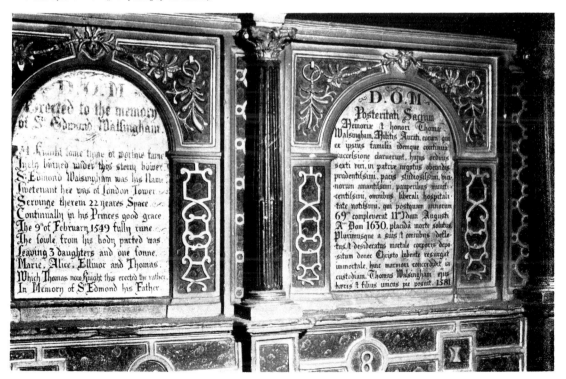

ARMS.—Gu. beneath, a cross couped chequy ar. and az.
CREST.—In a mural coronet gu. a tiger's head or, ducally gorged ia.

WALSINGHAM OF SCADBURY, KENT.

GEOFFREY WALSINGHAM,
Lord of Little Walsingham, co. Norfolk.

SIR RICHARD WALSINGHAM, Knt.,
Lord of Little Walsingham, flourished in times temp. Hen. III. and Edw. I.

SIR RICHARD WALSINGHAM, Knt.,
temp. Edw. I., ob. 1336. = CHRISTIANA, living in the 13th year of Edw. II., when she released lands to William Achetorto at Sutwerdbre.

THOMAS WALSINGHAM,
living temp. Edw. II., ob. 1333.

SIR RICHARD WALSINGHAM, Knt.,
temp. Edw. III., ob. 1365. = MARGARET, daughter and co-heiress of Thomas, and sister to Sir Adam Nortoh of Egmere, near Little Walsingham, co. Norfolk.

RICHARD WALSINGHAM, Esq.,
living 1390. = ELIZABETH, daughter of Sir Thomas Pallingray. | OSMOND WALSINGHAM,
living temp. Rich. II. | THOMAS WALSINGHAM,
ob. 1409.

THOMAS WALSINGHAM, Esq.,
M.P. for Lynn Borough, 1413. = KATHARINE, sister to Sir William Bellhouse, Knt. | ALAN WALSINGHAM,
temp. Hen. IV. and Hen. V., living 1412, citizen of London, and cordwainer. | OSMOND WALSINGHAM.

THOMAS WALSINGHAM (I.),
citizen of London, purchased the Manor of Scadbury, 1424; ob. March 13, 1457; will proved May 7, 1457; buried at St. Katherine's by the Tower. = MARGARET, daughter and heiress of Adam Bamme of Gillingham, Kent, Mayor of London, 1391, ob. 1445. | KATHERINE,
m. Sir Richard Butteler, Knt., of Essex.

'ND WALSINGHAM, | SIR THOMAS WALSINGHAM (IV.) = | AUDREY (or ETHELDRED), | ANN, | BA
q., of Scadbury, | Knt. of Scadbury, | n. 1568 daughter of Sir Ralph | m. Sir Thomas | m. A
1557, to whom | n. 1568; M.P. for | Shelton, Knt., of Norfolk, | Randolph, | Esq.,
Elizabeth demised | Rochester; had demise of | Lady of Honour to | Ambassador to | S
anor of Chislehurst; | Manor of Chislehurst, 1597, | Queen Elizabeth and | Scotland, Russia, | ob
.p. 1589, ætat 32; | purchased 1611; ob. 1630; | Queen Anne (of Denmark), | and France,
at Chislehurst; will | buried in Scadbury Chapel; | ob. 1624; buried with | Chancellor of
ed Nov. 22, 1589. | will proved Aug. 25, 1630; | her husband; | Exchequer at time
| Inq. P.M. Oct. 21, 1630. | called Adrian in Parish | of death in 1590.
| (cf. error on tomb | Registers.
| Aged 62 not 69 at death.)

THY, | ELIZABETH, | ELIZABETH, daughter of | = SIR THOMAS WALSINGHAM (V.) = | ELIZABETH, d
• Boken- | m. John Scryvenor | Sir Peter Manwood, Knt., | n. 1600 Knt., of Scadbury, | Richard Bourne
1., Lord | of Sylton, | of Hackington, Kent, | M.P. for Rochester, | worth, ob. 1676
Manor | Sussex. | ob. 1632; buried at | Vice-Admiral of Kent | Feb. 6,
aethan; | | Chislehurst. | during Commonwealth; | 2nd w
l with | | 1st wife. | sold estate in Kent;
band at | | | ob. 1669; buried
ethan, | | | at Chislehurst; will
olk. | | | proved Feb. 4,
| | | 1677.
| | | (Thomas Sir... aged 69 at his death to

THE PEDIGREE OF THE WALSINGHAMS, prepared, as reproduced opposite, from E. A. Webb's *History of Chislehurst*, 1899, shows the birth date of Thomas Walsingham IV as 1568. If this is correct he was sixty-two years of age at his death in 1630, and not sixty-nine as the inscription on his tomb states. That the inscription on the tomb is manifestly in error is corroborated by the entries in the Chislehurst parish registers of St. Nicholas. Several of the Walsingham children have their baptisms recorded in the baptismal register of this church, although not all, and they do not include Thomas, who was evidently born elsewhere, probably at the Walsinghams' London house.[1] If Thomas had been aged sixty-nine in 1630 as stated, his birth year would have been 1561 instead of 1568, but the baptisms recorded of Walsingham children for that year at St. Nicholas make this impossible. The entries in the book are as follows:

> '1559–60 Jan. 8 Walsingham Katherin
> 1561   Oct. 18 Walsingham Francis'

There was therefore hardly the possibility of the birth of another child to the Walsinghams in 1561. The correctness of the entry for the baptism of a son named Francis Walsingham, and not Thomas, is not in doubt. It is known that the Walsingham child named Francis had died in infancy, as indicated in the pedigree, in which both Francis and James, who also died in infancy, are listed together, although the exact date of Francis's death was not then known. I have since traced the record of this little boy's burial in the burial register of St. Michael, Cornhill in London, in which the following entry appears:

> '1563 Sep. 13 Francis Walsyngham'

This, then, is evidently the burial of little Francis Walsingham, aged not quite two years.

In 1568 there were seventeen christenings recorded at St. Nicholas Church, Chislehurst, but no Walsingham children figure among them. We must therefore conclude that Thomas was not born at Scadbury. Unfortunately not all the parish registers of this period have survived. In Elizabeth's reign all old parish registers of baptisms, burials and marriages were ordered to be transcribed on to parchment. It is interesting to note that the rector of Chislehurst who made these transcriptions was none other than Marlowe's contemporary at Cambridge, that 'Asse' as he called him, Richard Harvey, the brother of Gabriel. He did his job with commendable thoroughness, inserting explanatory notes here and there such as (for 1562 and 1563):

> 'I cannot fynde any Christening registered in the olde notes and papers.'

In the marriage register, at the end of the year 1586, appears this note:

> 'De praeteritis nil polliceor, de futuris iam certus sum, i.e. de meo tempore.' (Of what is past I promise nothing, of the future I am now certain, i.e. of my own time.)[2]

Regarding the baptisms under the entry for November 24, 1585, is appended:

> 'Hactemus ex veteribus et mihi incognitis exemplaribus haec desumpi sequuntur anni in quibus qui scribsit ista Rector ecclesiae sua manu commisit

fideli Registro.' (Thus far I have taken these records from copies that are old and unknown to myself; some years follow in which he who transcribed these records, himself being Rector of the Church, committed them to the trustworthy Register with his own hand.)

Richard Harvey was appointed Rector of Chislehurst in 1586. Apparently the old book was in a parlous state, for immediately after the transcription of the baptismal entry for James Walsingham, January 12, 1564–5, appears the memorandum: 'Hic erat sane vitium scriptorio quem in tritis chartis secuti sumus' (Here no doubt was a mistake of the writer whom we have followed in these much-worn papers). The previous baptismal entry for a Walsingham child had been Mary Walsingham, September 29, 1564; hence it was scarcely possible for James, even if he had been premature, to make his appearance after only five months, unless there had been reason for delaying the christening of Mary for several months, but this would have been unusual. It is reassuring, therefore, to find confirmation of both the birth and infant death of Francis Walsingham in the records of 1561 and 1563. Only six of the thirteen children born to Thomas Walsingham III and Dorothy Guldeford were in fact christened at Chislehurst.

E. A. Webb, who published both the Walsingham pedigree and the tomb inscription for Thomas Walsingham IV in its original Latin with his own translation, did not notice the discrepancy between the two, and in discussing this Thomas Walsingham he calculates his age from the erroneous tomb inscription, thus making him seven years older. He specifically states that Thomas Walsingham was aged twenty-eight when he inherited the Scadbury estates upon his brother Edmund's death in 1589. (In fact he was twenty-six.) On the other hand, Webb remarks on several other minor errors in the tomb inscription, although he missed this important one. For instance: 'The date of his [Thomas Walsingham's] death was really 11th August, *not* 11th of the Ides of August. By aid of a candle it can be seen that the 11 has been painted over by a 4; but this too would be wrong, because the 4th of the Ides of August would be the 10th.'[3] Webb further remarks that in the tomb inscription Sir Thomas Walsingham is referred to as 'the sixth man of the family who in continuous succession had been illustrious in that order' (i.e. of knighthood). But Sir Thomas was only the third knight since the arrival of the family at Scadbury, 'unless he counted Sir Francis, when the number would still be two short of that on the tablet'.

There are therefore no less than three errors in the inscription and a further error in the Pedigree. The Inquisition Post Mortem on Edmund Walsingham, dated May 2, 1590 (which Webb does not appear to have consulted), clears up the problem. In a clear hand it states that at his brother's death on November 16, 1589, Thomas was aged '26 years and more'.[4] He was probably some six to twelve months older than Marlowe, having been born in 1563, one of the years for which the Rev. Harvey notes that he 'cannot fynde any Christenings registered'. When not too busy scribbling pamphlets, or kissing the wives of his parishioners, Harvey liked to keep the books straight.[5]

The Arrest

O lente, lente currite, noctis equi!
The stars move still, time runs, the clock will strike.

DR. FAUSTUS

In the seclusion of Scadbury, Marlowe worked on the tragedy of *Hero and Leander* oblivious of the fateful thread which the 'adamantine Destinies' were also spinning for him. As he completed the second sestiad of his long poem he probably read it aloud to Thomas Walsingham, whose critical judgment would, one feels, have been desired and no doubt given with a full measure of praise for this enchanting new offering. Marlowe was twenty-nine years old and at the height of his powers. *Hero and Leander* in its exquisitely delineated characterisation of the two young lovers reveals his as the master-hand of narrative love poetry beside which *Venus and Adonis* stands as a cruder first effort.

Walsingham seems to have been a young man of some aesthetic discrimination, blessed with good taste as well as wealth, as may be judged by his patronage of so brilliant a poet as Marlowe, and after him of the intellectual Chapman. Since Marlowe was now living at Scadbury it seems evident that their friendship was a close one, and not the mere formal relationship of poet to patron. One may imagine the two young men delighting in each other's company in this Kentish springtime, walking and talking together, riding together, laughing and perhaps making music, and certainly listening to it, for a patron who had befriended Tom Watson could not fail to have been a lover of music. The plague and troubles of the city seemed far away. But catastrophe broke, with the suddenness of a thunderstorm on a fair summer's day.

On May 18th, or 19th, or 20th, we cannot be sure, a messenger from Her Majesty's Court arrived at Scadbury. He galloped down the long avenue and presented himself at the drawbridge as Master Henry Maunder, messenger of Her Majesty's Chamber, bearing a warrant for the arrest of Christopher Marlowe. The order expressly states that he was:

'to repair to the house of Mr Tho: Walsingham in Kent, or to anie other place where he shall vnderstand Christofer Marlow to be remayning, and by vertue hereof to apprehend, and bring him to the Court in his Companie. And in case of need to require ayd.'

Kit was in trouble—he did not yet dream how far. Evidently he accompanied Henry Maunder back to London. Possibly Maunder, as a Court messenger, would have been known to him or Walsingham. On May 20th Marlowe accordingly complied and entered his indemnity before the Star Chamber. The Privy Council note for that day reads:

'This day Christofer Marley of London, gent., being sent for by warrant from their L[ordshi]ps, hath entered his apparance accordinglie for his Indemnity therein; and is commaunded to giue his daily attendaunce on their L[ordshi]ps vntill hee shalbe lycensed to the Contrary.'

Warrant of arrest *to Henry Maunder for the apprehension of Christopher Marlowe* (*Privy Council entry dated May* 18, 1593):

> '*Warrant to Henry Mavnder one of the Messengers of her Ma^{ts} Chamber to repaire to the house of Mr Tho: Walsingham in Kent, or to anie other place where he shall vnderstand Christofer Marlow to be remayning, and by vertue hereof to apprehend and bring him to the Court in his Companie. And in case of need to require ayd.*'

This was the usual form of warrant and not, as Charles Norman has suggested, an indication that they 'know their man'—i.e. expected *Marlowe to offer violent resistance. The next entry, which is a warrant to John Slaughter, another Messenger of the Chamber, for the apprehension of Roger Stamford the elder and Robt. Stamford, his son, also concludes with the rider 'and in case of need to requier ayd of all publique officers', presumably because in this case there are two men involved. It was no more than the usual precaution taken in all cases of apprehension by the law.*

Marlowe's immediate release on bail is in the sharpest contrast to the vicious treatment meted out to poor Kyd, who lay bruised and bleeding in Bridewell. If Kyd heard of it, his aggrieved spirits must have received added fuel for resentment from this blatant favouritism. Its reason may be looked for in Marlowe's aristocratic and influential connections. Kyd's relationship with his 'Lord' or patron, who is presumed to have been Ferdinando, Lord Strange, as evidenced by his deferential references to him in his letters to Sir John Puckering, were those of servant and master; Marlowe's relationship with Walsingham was one of intimate friendship, and in the circle of the School of Night it has been

'*This day Christofer Marley of London, gent. being sent for by warrant from their L[ordshi]ps, hath entered his apparance accordinglie for his Indemnity herein; and is commaunded to giue his daily attendaunce on their L[ordshi]ps, vntill he shalbe lycensed to the Contrary.*'

seen that poets, scientists and noblemen met on an equal footing of intellectual brilliance, not of rank.

The twelve miles from Chislehurst to the city was not too great to enable Marlowe to present his 'daily attendaunce' as required, and the prevalence of the plague and subsequent events both suggest that he remained at Scadbury and in the closest contact with Walsingham during the nine remaining days of his life.

The scene now shifts to Deptford Strand, in the county of Kent, the little shipping port on the Thames where Drake's ship the *Golden Hind* rode at anchor. The distance from Scadbury is only seven miles across country, and could have been accomplished in half an hour's ride. There Marlowe had a rendezvous with three men, all of whom were closely connected with Thomas Walsingham, and at the hands of one of them he met his death.

The Star Chamber

The dread Star Chamber before which Marlowe had been summoned to appear was, at the end of the 16th century, a powerful court which owed little obedience either to law or precedent. Historically it is said to have been descended from the judicial side of the old King's Council, coming into use as a 'Court of Justice' during the reign of Henry VII and originally deriving its power from the royal person. It was designated 'Camera Stellata', or 'Star Chamber', because of its place of meeting, which was a hall whose roof was adorned with gilt stars, located in the outer quadrangle of Westminster Palace next to the river. Sessions were from nine to eleven o'clock on Wednesdays and Fridays and the day after the end of term. After each sitting the Lords dined together in the Inner Star Chamber at the public expense. There are records of sumptuous banquets with rare and expensive delicacies and extravagant quantities of flesh and fish. Burleigh became much concerned at their cost.

There were some thirty judges of the court, peers of the realm presided over by the Lord Chancellor, although they did not all serve at the same session. Marlowe was called before the following: Lord Archbishop of Canterbury (presiding), Lord Keeper, Lord Treasurer, Lord Derby, Lord Chamberlain, Lord Buckhurst, Sir John Wolley, and Sir John Fortescue.

Although the exact inter-relationship between the Privy Council and the Star Chamber is not completely clear, the basic function of the former was to act as a deliberative body of advisers to the Crown, whereas the Star Chamber was primarily a court of justice whose special function was the correction of slanders, libels, and riots. The Privy Council was the smaller body and most, if not all, of its members served on the Star Chamber. This latter, although supposedly a court of equity, was limited by no set statutes but exercised jurisdiction over those summoned at the discretion of the executive (the Lord Chancellor or Archbishop of Canterbury), other members being subservient to him. The court operated on the theory that once a man was arrested, regardless of the reason, any other wrongs that he had committed might be dealt with by them; this inquisitorial process was called 'scraping the conscience'. It even became an accepted procedure to arrest a defendant to answer a fictitious trespass in order to draw out unrelated subjects.

Although they stopped short of prescribing the death penalty, cruel and inhuman punishments were ordered by the august peers of the Star Chamber: cutting off of ears, amputation of hands and plunging the stumps into hot pitch, branding, whipping, 'peine forte et dure' (a method of torture by loading increasingly heavy weights on a supine man's chest until he either agreed to confess or his rib cage was crushed—needless to say, an effective way of extorting confessions). Then, too, there were fines—severe and exorbitant ones, far exceeding the amount of conceivable damages. (There is a record of a £5,000 fine being levied on a defendant for not accepting knighthood.) Although this is more applicable to James I's reign, the Crown often granted such fines, or a large portion of them, to private individuals, often to the accusers themselves regardless of the justice of their accusations.

Fear of the court was due also to its practice of hearing witnesses in secrecy. Originally regular records of the proceedings had been kept, but by the 1590's there was a complete laxity in this, and records of this period (if ever they were made) seem to be non-existent today. Nor were defendants allowed benefit of any kind of legal counsel.

Also to be contended with were the elaborate verbal quibbles and meaningless discussions of legal forms and distinctions *ad nauseam*, which became an involved intellectual gambit in the course of which justice and reason were often quite lost sight of. Such sessions are referred to in a humorous way in the fifth act of *Hamlet* in a discussion by the gravediggers in regard to the legal meaning of suicide:

> FIRST CLOWN:
> *Here lies the water: good; here stands the man: good; if the man go to this water, and drown himself, it is, will he, nill he, he goes; mark you that? but if the water comes to him, and drowns him, he drowns not himself: argal, he that is not guilty of his own death shortens not his own life.*
> SECOND CLOWN:
> *But is this the law?*
> FIRST CLOWN:
> *Ay, marry, is't; crowner's quest law.*

Furthermore sessions were generally conducted in a mysterious jargon of Latin, French, and English calculated to completely obfuscate the layman.

Unlucky the man, no matter how innocent, who was called before such a court. His chances of eluding their tentacles and escaping scot-free were extremely slim.

286

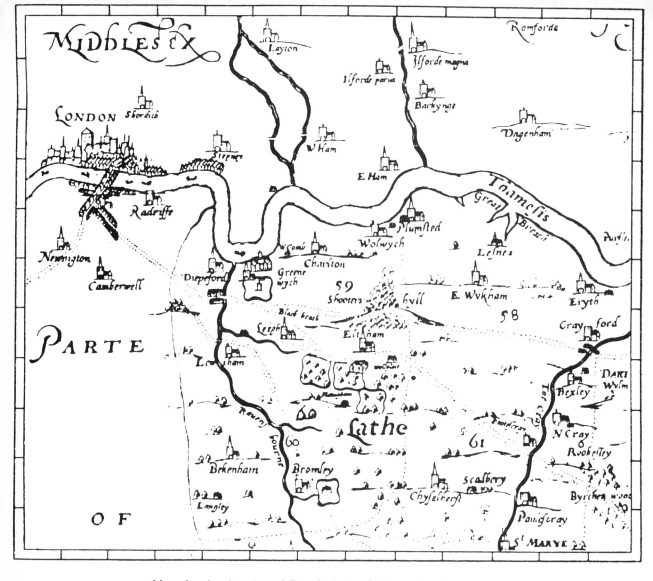

Map showing location of Deptford *in relation to Scadbury, from Symonson's* A New
Description of Kent (1596). *Just east of London on the south bank of the Thames, 'Diept-
ford' is shown, with 'Greenewych' in close proximity. 'Chyselherst' and 'Scadbery', near
the south-east corner of the map, are less than seven miles distant from Deptford.*

MAP OF DEPTFORD STRAND. 'Depetford Stronde' derives its name from a deep
ford in the river Ravensbourne, the mouth of which forms Deptford Creek. In the time
of Henry VIII the little town became important for its royal dockyard. In 1513, typically,
the remains of an old monastery were appropriated for conversion to use as a dockside
storehouse. Further grants were made by Elizabeth I, and ships of the Royal Navy were
built and repaired here and royal yachts fitted and laid up.

The wooden bridge over the Ravensbourne was replaced by stone in 1628, and by
1730 the town had grown so much that it was divided into two parishes, St. Nicholas
and St. Paul. It was at the Church of St. Nicholas (in the old parish) that Marlowe was
buried. Almshouses, built in Henry VIII's reign, then adjoined the churchyard.

Ships going to Flushing regularly docked at Deptford, and Poley might have arrived
here on the morning of May 30, 1593, to be met by Marlowe, Frizer and Skeres.

288

It is not known where Eleanor Bull's house stood, nor whether this was, in fact, a tavern. Probably she was the widow of Richard Bull, Gent., who was buried at St. Nicholas' Church in Deptford on April 19, 1590, as suggested by Hotson. The Bulls were a fairly well-established family in Deptford and the surrounding district of Kent, for the Acts of the Privy Council, April 23, 1548, record the granting of '4d. per diem', in consideration of their 'long and good service', to another Richard Bull, designated as a shipwright, and John Smith and Robert Holborn, with the proviso that they should continue to 'instruct others in their feats'. In 1550 the payment to Richard Bull was raised to 12d. a day. In 1572 Matthew Baker succeeded to Bull's annuity, who is referred to in the letters patent as 'a certain Richard Bull, dead'. The Probate Registry of Canterbury for 1573 contains the record of the will of Richard Bull, mariner, of Up-church, who is probably the man. Later Bulls are also recorded.

Of the jurors at the inquest on Marlowe's death, Henry Awger, George Halfepenny, Henry Dabyns (Dobbins) and William Curry (or Carrey) were all holders of tenements in Deptford, Curry also owning a 'wharfe and yarde'. Halfepenny also appears as a baker of Limehouse. Giles ffeld (or Field) was a Deptford grocer. James Batt is described as a 'husbandman' of Lewisham, and Thomas Batt, senior, a 'yeoman' of Bromley, Kent; Lewisham is only two miles from Deptford, and Bromley some two miles from Chislehurst and less than four miles from Lewisham. Robert Baldwyn has been traced as a 'yeoman' of East Greenwich (less than one mile from Deptford), and Lime-house, where George Halfepenny had his bakery, forms part of this district. Wolstan Randall, who was one of the two jurors designated as a 'gentleman', left a house and stable, on lease from the Lord Admiral in Deptford to his wife by his will of February 18, 1602/3. Of the other 'gentleman', Nicholas Draper, so far nothing has been discovered, but it would appear that the jury were all drawn from Deptford and its vicinity, and were mainly from the class of artificers and small-propertied men. Several of these left fairly substantial legacies in houses, chattels, or farm animals.[1]

To this great Ship which round the Globe has run, And matcht in Race the Chariot of the Sun . . .
Abraham Cowley

On April 4, 1581, Queen Elizabeth came to Deptford to knight Sir Francis Drake aboard his ship the Golden Hind *which lay at anchor at Deptford ever after, pre-served as a sacred relic and monument of the three-years voyage circumnavigating the globe. The famous ship attracted many sightseers to Deptford, and served into the next century as a favourite holiday supper and drinking room—a kind of floating tavern—until at last, much patched and repaired, it fell into complete decay.*

Woodcut from the title-page of The True and Perfecte Newes of the woorthy and valiant exploytes, per-formed and doone by that valiaunt Knight Syr Frauncis Drake (1587).

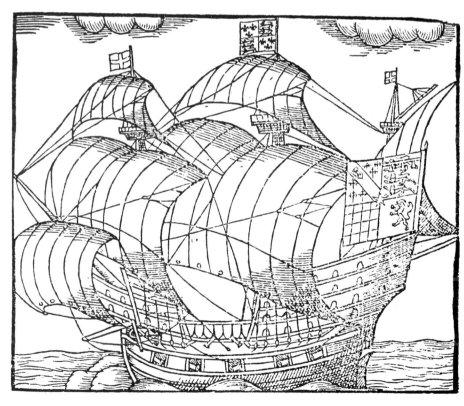

Deptford 1593

The Death of Christopher Marlowe, May 30th

I know, sir, what it is to kill a man;
It works remorse of conscience in me.
TAMBURLAINE THE GREAT, Part II, IV, i.

The story of the murder of England's foremost dramatist in that 'wonderfull yeare' 1593, as Gabriel Harvey afterwards called it, is told in the Inquisition on his death. This intriguing document was discovered in 1925 by the brilliant researches of Dr. Leslie Hotson, who tracked it down amid the rolls of the British Public Record Office, where it had escaped detection for 332 years. Its curious relation has shed a new and somewhat puzzling light on Marlowe's murder at Eleanor Bull's house in Deptford.

The Inquest took place under the presidency of the Queen's Coroner, William Danby, who superseded the local coroner in the case since Deptford lay 'within the verge' of the royal jurisdiction, which held sway for a circuit of twelve miles from the Court, then at the Queen's palace at Greenwich. Within twenty-four hours of Marlowe's death a jury had been assembled, speedy burial being the practice in those days for obvious reasons, especially in that time of plague.

The translation from the Latin of the original document here following is given according to Hotson's book, *The Death of Christopher Marlowe*, 1925.

'KENT/INQUISITION Indented taken at Detford Strand in the aforesaid County of Kent within the verge on the first day of June in the year of the reign of Elizabeth by the grace of God of England France & Ireland Queen defender of the faith &c thirty-fifth, in the presence of William Danby, Gentleman, Coroner of the household of our said lady the Queen, upon view of the body of Christopher Morley, there lying dead & slain, upon oath of Nicholas Draper, Gentleman, Wolstan Randall, gentleman, William Curry, Adrian Walker, John Barber, Robert Baldwyn, Giles ffeld, George Halfepenny, Henry Awger, James Batt, Henry Bendyn, Thomas Batt senior, John Baldwyn, Alexander Burrage, Edmund Goodcheepe, & Henry Dabyns . . .'

being the jury of sixteen good men and true drawn from Deptford and the district surrounding. They included a carpenter, a grocer, and two bakers. While most of them were holders of tenements in Deptford, others have been traced to Chatham, Bromley, East Greenwich and Limehouse, although the most distant of these, Chatham, probably represents a place of later removal. John Barber, who died there in 1608, shows by his will that he had properties at

Deptford which he left to his son. Evidently they were men who could have been speedily assembled for the urgent business in hand.

The three men who faced them in the witness box were:

> 'Ingram ffrysar, late of London, Gentleman
> Nicholas Skeres, late of London, Gentleman
> Robert Poley of London aforesaid, Gentleman'

Since all three are entered as 'Gentleman' there seems no warrant for the suggestion frequently put forward that any of the three were a disreputable crew drawn from London's low life of 'maisterles men & cut-purses'. It is not their status, but their honesty that is in question. The records of these three show that they were all clever, unscrupulous and unprincipled men who would have been ready to lie, to swindle, or to do a deed of shame if it would benefit themselves, their master, or their royal mistress Queen Elizabeth. Both Poley and Skeres were evidently in the Queen's service, the former as a secret agent of some importance, the second as a Court messenger, and probably also as a secret agent. Dr. Boas identifies him with the 'Skyrres' who was in company with the conspirators at a supper held in Poley's garden on August 2, 1586, just before the disclosure of the Babington Plot, in which the subtle Poley played such a decisive part.[1] Frizer, or ffrysar, was a trusted family retainer of the Walsinghams, formerly in the employ of Thomas Walsingham's father, and now the 'man' or personal servant of young Thomas, Marlowe's patron, in whose service he remained for the rest of his life.[2] He proved himself a subtle rogue, but more of that later.

As far as standing went, these three ranked as 'gentlemen', and doubtless they turned up at the Inquest wearing their most innocent expressions and as fine a suit of clothes as would become their station; which might have been very fine indeed, for as a contemporary writer remarked, 'Now there is such a confuse mingle-mangle of apparel in England, and such preposterous excess thereof . . . that it is very hard to know who is noble, who is worshipful, who is a gentleman, who is not.'[3]

However, to return to poor Christopher lying there 'dead and slain', whose 'aspiring mind' would never soar again to delight the world with its magnificent flights of fancy, silenced at last by the knife of Walsingham's servant, Ingram Frizer. How it happened, according to the version of Frizer, Skeres and Poley, the only three witnesses of his death, is reported in the Indenture of the Inquisition.

The scene of the tragedy is set in the house of Eleanor Bull, widow, at Deptford Strand. Where exactly in Deptford this was situated, or whether it was a tavern as has generally been suggested, is not known. If so, it seems a curious omission that it was not named as such. Perhaps she was just a lady who sold 'vittels', as Marlowe's father did later in his career, as a money-making sideline. The four men, Frizer, Poley, Skeres, and Marlowe, had evidently hired a room in her house, dined and supped there, talked and walked 'in quiet sort

Coroner's Inquisition *discovered by Leslie Hotson in Public Record Office in 1925.*

together' in the garden adjoining the house, being there for a space of some ten hours all told. It seems that it was a day's business of some kind that engrossed them, rather than mere pleasure in each other's company. But this the Inquisition does not vouchsafe to tell us, but confines the report (at somewhat greater length than is usual in Elizabethan indentures)[4] to the circumstances of the death struggle, which in themselves are curious enough to raise a host of questions and conjectures.

On the thirtieth day of May (which was a Wednesday that year)

'about the tenth hour before noon [the aforesaid gentlemen] met together in a room in the house of a certain Eleanor Bull, widow; & there passed the time together & dined & after dinner were in quiet sort together there & walked in

292

the garden belonging to the said house until the sixth hour after noon of the same day & then returned from the said garden to the room aforesaid & there together and in company supped; & after supper the said Ingram & Christopher Morley were in speech & uttered one to the other divers malicious words for the reason that they could not be at one nor agree about the payment of the sum of pence, that is, *le recknynge*, there; & the said Christopher Morley then lying upon a bed in the room where they supped, & moved with anger against the said Ingram ffrysar upon the words aforesaid spoken between them, and the said Ingram then & there sitting in the room aforesaid with his back towards the bed where the said Christopher Morley was then lying, sitting near the bed, that is, *nere the bed*, & with the front part of his body towards the table & the aforesaid Nicholas Skeres & Robert Poley sitting on either side of the said Ingram in such a manner that the same Ingram ffrysar in no wise could take flight: it so befell that the said Christopher Morley on a sudden & of his malice towards the said Ingram aforethought, then & there maliciously drew the dagger of the said Ingram which was at his back, and with the same dagger the said Christopher Morley then & there maliciously gave the aforesaid Ingram two wounds on his head of the length of two inches & of the depth of a quarter of an inch; whereupon the said Ingram, in fear of being slain, & sitting in the manner aforesaid between the said Nicholas Skeres & Robert Poley so that he could not in any wise get away, in his own defence & for the saving of his life, then & there struggled with the said Christopher Morley to get back from him his dagger aforesaid; in which affray the same Ingram could not get away from the said Christopher Morley; and so it befell in that affray that the said Ingram, in defence of his life, with the dagger aforesaid to the value of 12*d.* gave the said Christopher then & there a mortal wound over his right eye of the depth of two inches & of the width of one inch; of which mortal wound the aforesaid Christopher Morley then & there instantly died; And so the Jurors aforesaid say upon their oath that the said Ingram killed & slew Christopher Morley aforesaid on the thirtieth day of May in the thirtyfifth year named above at Detford Strand aforesaid within the verge in the room aforesaid within the verge in the manner and form aforesaid in the defence and saving of his own life, against the peace of our said lady the Queen, her now crown & dignity; And further the said Jurors say upon their oath that the said Ingram after the slaying aforesaid perpetrated & done by him in the manner & form aforesaid neither fled nor withdrew himself; But what goods or chattels, lands or tenements the said Ingram had at the time of the slaying aforesaid, done & perpetrated by him in the manner & form aforesaid, the said Jurors are totally ignorant. In witness of which thing the said Coroner as well as the Jurors aforesaid to this Inquisition have interchangeably set their seals. Given the day & year above named &c

                        '*by* WILLIAM DANBY
                            '*Coroner*'

John Whitgift, Archbishop of Canterbury. *Whitgift was head of both the Ecclesiastical judicial court and the Star Chamber, and as such the decisions made in the House of Convocation may have considerably influenced his feelings towards Marlowe in the Star Chamber.*

Whitgift's involvement in Marlowe's life was both benevolent (he was instrumental in conferring his M.A. degree) and malevolent; he would probably have ordered his torture and presided at his trial, had Marlowe lived to face it.

The jurors having done all that was required of them, Coroner William Danby set his seal to theirs. Apart from committing Frizer back to prison to await the Queen's official pardon for his breach of the peace, the legal business in the matter was closed.

Yet what a curiously unsatisfactory story it is. If Coroner Danby and Nicholas Draper, Gentleman, Wolstan Randall and company did not doubt Frizer's word, or the bland testimony of Poley and Skeres, by their leave, permit us to do so. There has not been a modern scholar, since the day Dr. Hotson's discovery made the story of the Inquisition available to us, who has not expressed his doubts as to the veracity of the testimonies given. Dr. Hotson himself suggests that the evidence makes it possible 'to suppose that Frizer, Poley and Skeres, after the slaying, and in order to save Frizer's life on a plea of self-defence concocted a lying account of Marlowe's behaviour to which they swore at the Inquest and with which they deceived the jury'.[5]

It scarcely seems credible or likely that Marlowe would have lost his temper over a little matter of the payment of the bill for their entertainment at Mistress Bull's house, or certainly not to the extent of seizing Frizer's dagger and bashing him over the head with it. Is this what one would expect of the poet who was the associate of Walsingham, Hariot, Ralegh, Chapman, Watson and Blount? Is it conceivable that such would be the violent reaction of a man who never seems to have been in need of money, and who at that time had just been living at his patron's sumptuous home at Scadbury? Scholars have tended to accept Kyd's letter as representing evidence of Marlowe's violent nature which appears to lend a spurious corroboration to the quarrel that led to his death; but, as will be seen when examining Kyd's statements, the chronology of events as well as the nature of Kyd's evidence make a different interpretation both possible and likely.

Apart from the question of Marlowe's extraordinary behaviour as reported by Frizer, the surrounding evidence of the case raises a host of queries. As Professor Bakeless puts it, 'Dr. Hotson's brilliant discovery of the documents relating to Marlowe's death, raises almost as many questions as it answers'.[6]

Briefly to enumerate these:

1. Why was it that Frizer, the surprised defendant, sustained only two minor scalp wounds, though assailed by Marlowe with every advantage from above and behind, but in return, despite being so placed that he 'in no wise could take flight', managed to deal a mortal blow that struck home to the depth of two inches to where the blade was one inch thick?

2. Why did Poley and Skeres, who were hemming Frizer in on either side, not come to his assistance since there apparently was time to have intervened, according to Frizer a considerable struggle having preceded the slaying?

3. What is the significance of the blow which dealt 'a mortal wound over his right eye' and where exactly would this have been placed? Dr. Tannenbaum has

produced medical evidence to show that a knife thrust of two inches in depth into the brain would not result in instantaneous death, or necessarily in death at all. Moreover a wound 'over the right eye' would be a practical impossibility if it is meant that the knife penetrated the forehead, since the bone structure of the forehead is of such thickness as to make penetration of such a dagger as would have been used well-nigh impossible even with an absolutely tremendous blow.*

Charles Norman comments: 'Frizer found it impossible, he said, to get away from Marlowe's sudden attack. But the table could have been pushed forward or overturned, or Poley and Skeres could have shoved the table aside, or rushed in, between the bed and the table, to separate the two men. What were they doing while the fight was in progress, for apparently it was not a matter of seconds? If this question was asked of them, the answer was not thought worth setting down.'[7]

Miss Eugenie de Kalb has suggested that Frizer's scalp wounds are 'such insignificant cuts (on the evidence) as might be self-inflicted to corroborate a put-up story'.[8] Dr. Tannenbaum agrees with this; his theory that the slaying of Marlowe was a political murder begins with the premise, arguable from the evidence, that Frizer murdered with intent, aided and abetted by Poley and Skeres, and that their story was a tissue of lies covering up the real facts.[9] Ancillary to his theory is the assumption that Frizer, Skeres and Poley, acting on orders, were protected. Evidence for this is supplied by the readiness with which their story was evidently accepted by the royal coroner, William Danby, who, it is suggested, was priorly suborned and guided the jury in their decision to acquit Frizer of murder, commuting the charge to the pardonable one of manslaughter in self-defence. That Frizer's account, although so obviously questionable to our minds, was accepted not only by William Danby and the jury but also with a remarkable readiness by the higher authority (possibly Elizabeth herself) who granted the Queen's pardon, is evident from the fact that the document giving Frizer his release actually rehearses the story of the Inquisition almost word for word, before ending with the happy conclusion:

'We therefore moved by piety have pardoned the same Ingram ffrisar the breach of our peace which pertains to us against the said Ingram for the death above mentioned & grant to him our firm peace Provided nevertheless that the right remain in our Court if anyone should wish to complain of him concerning the death above mentioned. In testimony &c Witness the Queen at Kewe on the 28th day of June.'[10]

Even Thomas Walsingham, Marlowe's friend and patron, did not it seems 'wish to complain' of his servant Ingram Frizer's action, but, on the contrary,

* In a re-examination of the Inquisition on Marlowe's death by Gavin Thurston, secretary of the Coroners' Society of England and Wales, shortly to be published, Mr. Thurston conclusively demonstrates the physical impossibility of piercing the forehead itself, and develops an alternative theory that the knife slipped into the eye-socket, thus causing instantaneous death.

condoned it, for we find evidence that on the very next day after his release from prison he was once more received into his master's employment, and that he remained with the Walsinghams until the end of his days. By strange contrast Kyd, who had been unjustly imprisoned and tortured, found upon his release that his former Lord's doors were closed to him, and he left masterless and without means of support. By further extraordinary good luck, or perhaps there was more than luck to it, Frizer became a free man within the incredibly short space of four weeks after the murder had been committed. Compare this with the dreary five months which Thomas Watson, who was not a servant but a gentleman of the Inns of Court, poet and friend of both Sir Francis and Thomas Walsingham, languished in Newgate jail awaiting his pardon from the Queen after the slaying of William Bradley on a similar plea of self-defence.

Such are the strange contrarieties which this history presents. Little wonder, then, that conjecture as to the real story behind the murder of Marlowe has run riot.

Basic to any attempt to resolve this mystery are the relationships and characters of the three witnesses. The most important of these is the murderer Ingram Frizer. A revealing case had been unearthed by Dr. Hotson which discovers Frizer in association with Nicholas Skeres as the instigators and perpetrators of a prize piece of 'connycatching' relating to transactions in which a poor dupe, named Drew Woodleffe, was successfully fleeced by Frizer and Skeres of a tidy sum of money.[11] This incident is just such a real-life example, historied and chronicled by the law, as those described with wicked humour by Robert Greene in *A Notable Discouery of Coosnage*, 1591.

> 'The Conny-catchers, apparalled like honest ciuill gentlemen, or good fellows, with a smooth face, as if butter would not melt in their mouthes, after dinner when the clients are come from Westminster hal and are at leasure to walke vp and downe Paules, Fleet-street, Holborne, the sttrond, and such common hanted places, where these cosning companions attend onely to spie out a praie: who as soone as they see a plaine cuntry felow well and cleanly apparelled, either in a coat of home spun russet, or of freeze, as the time requires, and a side pouch at his side, there is a connie, saith one. At that word out flies the Setter, and ouertaking the man, begins to salute him thus: Sir, God saue you, you are welcom to London, how doth all our good friends in the countrie, I hope they be all in health? The countrie man seeing a man so curteous he knoweth not, halfe in a browne studie at this strange salutation, perhaps makes him this aunswere . . .'

Drew Woodleffe, from Aylesbury in Buckinghamshire, was evidently such a country conny. It transpires that he became bound to Skeres for a sum of money he had loaned, and through various dubious transactions, in which the mythical sale of a number of guns, iron cannons etc. on Tower Hill were involved, which Woodleffe had been persuaded by Frizer to 'buy' so that he could resell them for him at a vast profit, Skeres and Frizer tricked the poor man into an ever increasing debt. Written bonds as well as ready cash were inveigled out of Woodleffe, until in the end he found himself bound over for the staggering sum of £200 to Frizer's 'gentleman of good worshipp', who turns out to be none other than his master, Sir Thomas Walsingham, as he was by then. The case came up in 1598, but the transactions referred to had taken place about five years before, i.e. in 1593. On June 29, 1593, only one month after Frizer was involved in the Marlowe murder case, 'Drew Woodleffe of Peterley, Bucks, gentleman' was bound to Thomas Walsingham of Chislehurst, Kent, Esquire, in the sum of £200 to be paid by July 25, 1593.[12] This extraordinary revelation of the relationship between Frizer and his master Thomas Walsingham throws a sharp and not too flattering light on Marlowe's wealthy patron. Thomas Walsingham was evidently not above taking a cut in a shady deal if it could be done discreetly. The case also gives us an insight into Elizabethan amorality. Such tricks were not so uncommon, nor apparently considered as reprehensible, in Elizabethan society as in ours. The Elizabethans rather prided themselves on their knavery, or 'one-upmanship' one might perhaps call it.

Ingram Frizer was indubitably a most skilful cozener. His value to his none too scrupulous master lay probably therein that he could do his dirty work for him if required, and could be trusted to get away with it. He had evidently learned in his younger days 'to court it like a gentleman', and knew the soundness of Spenser's advice to Baldock:

> *'Tis not a black coat and a little band,*
> *A velvet cap'd cloak, fac'd before with serge,*
> *And smelling to a nosegay all the day,*
> *Or holding of a napkin in your hand,*
> *Or saying a long grace at a table's end,*
> *Or making low legs to a nobleman,*
> *Or looking downward, with your eye-lids closed,*
> *And saying, 'Truly, an't may please your honour',*
> *Can get you any favour with great men:*
> *You must be proud, bold, pleasant, resolute,*
> *And now and then stab, as occasion serves.*

> EDWARD II

After his master's marriage Frizer is also revealed in cases involving several leases 'in reversion' which are skilfully manipulated so that benefits accrue to Lady Audrey Walsingham. These occur as late as September and December, 1603.[13] Frizer was granted a house at Eltham on Walsingham's estate, where it seems he comfortably ended his days after long service to the unabashed Machiavellian principles of his noble lord and lady.

Nicholas Skeres' connections with Frizer and Thomas Walsingham are thus also established in 1593, and the records give us several other interesting glimpses of the man. He is almost certainly the 'Skyrres' who was in Poley's company on August 2, 1586, during the time Poley was working on the Babington Plot. Dr.

An ecclesiastical assembly. *Here representatives of the clergy consulted on ecclesiastical matters and sent recommendations to parliament. The Archbishop of Canterbury was president of the convocation, and the presiding officer was designated the 'Prolocutor'. Such a body as this would have urged parliament to take sterner measures in suppressing the atheistical doctrines which they feared were becoming rampant in certain circles in London and might spread to the detriment of religion and the State.*

Boas places him as the younger son of Nicholas Skeres senior, a merchant-tailor and parishioner of All-hallows-the-Less, who by his will, proved September 9, 1566, left his two sons, Jerome and Nicholas, then still in their minority, one third of his estate. On January 6, 1581/2, a Jerome and a Nicholas Skeres (the latter by then of Furnival's Inn) were associated with Marlowe's friend Matthew Royden, apparently as Royden's securities, in a bond to a goldsmith for payment of £40 by the beginning of February.[14] Roydon, I believe, was also employed by the government in secret service (see p. 318), and hence it seems that the Nicholas Skeres associated with Royden, Poley and Marlowe was evidently also of this fraternity. A further record of a payment in 1589 to Nicholas Skeres for carrying important letters between the Court and the Earl of Essex confirms his employment in a capacity similar to Poley's.[15]

The fact that the issue has been clouded by the appearance of another 'Nicholas Skeeres', who turned up as one of a band of 'maisterles men & cut-purses, whose practice is to robbe Gentlemen's chambers and Artificers' shoppes in and about London' mentioned by William Fleetwood, recorder of London, in a report to Lord Burleigh on July 7, 1585 (just as there have been two Christofer Morleys at Cambridge, who have been identified and separated by Dr. Hotson), has led to the unwarranted assumption that Marlowe consorted with riff-raff. This view, granted the unscrupulous nature of Elizabethan society, cannot be upheld.

Robert Poley's standing as an important government agent is attested by the significant role he played in the unravelling of the Babington Plot, which led directly to the execution of Mary Queen of Scots. His part in this conspiracy was so devious that at one stage in the proceedings it became doubtful as to on whose side he really was. The implications landed him in the Tower for a space, but he was eventually cleared and upon his release in the autumn of 1588 was reinstated in his former government service. Miss Ethel Seaton has identified ciphers used by Poley in his correspondence with government officials, some relating to the period of his activities as a bearer of secret despatches to and from the Low Countries during 1590-1, and including Flemish names and addresses in Antwerp, which link up with other evidence of his activities.[16]

Poley continued over the years to act as a trusted government courier carrying confidential despatches to and from the Court, which involved him in constant journeys abroad, in particular to Holland and the Low Countries, also to Denmark. In the early months of 1592/3 he made journeys to Scotland to the Court of King James, and, as Dr. Boas has pointed out, this was about the time when, according to Kyd's statement in his letter (to be dealt with in the next chapter), Marlowe was intending to go there, and apparently Matthew Roydon also. Poley's warrants of payment on January 6 and March 23, 1592/3 state that his journeys to Scotland had been in connection with 'her heighness speciall and secret affayres of great importaunce', as indeed most of Poley's affairs were.[17]

The special significance of Poley's movements covering the period of Marlowe's murder was first noted by Eugenie de Kalb. According to the warrant for his payment for the 'carryinge of lettres in poste for her Majesties speciall and secrete afaires of great ymportaunce from the Courte at Croydon' dated June 8, 1593, we know that he departed for The Hague on May 8, and that he delivered the answers on June 8. The warrant specifically states that his employment (for which he received payment of 30s.) covered the entire period from May 8 until June 8, 'being in her majesties service all the aforesaid tyme'. Yet during this time he had returned to England on May 30, been present at Marlowe's murder, and further testified at the Inquest on June 1. Both Miss de Kalb and Dr. Boas feel that this 'unusual formula' seems to be intended as some kind of safeguard covering Poley's actions during this time to make certain that he should not in any way suffer as a consequence of his involvement in the killing at Deptford.[18] The implication is that someone high in government authority knew of his involvement in the murder and condoned it.

That Poley would not have scrupled to play any part assigned to him in this affair, providing he was assured that he would come out well as a result, is to be deduced from his own testimony concerning his principles. He had once gone on record as having said, 'I will sweare and forsweare my selfe rather then I will accuse my selffe to doe me any harme.'[19] This then was the slippery gentleman Robert Poley. Sir Robert Cecil has also given us his opinion of the man. Referring to an interview he had had with Poley in a letter to Sir Thomas Heneage, under whom Poley worked for many years, Cecil writes:

'I haue receauyd your lettre & I will shew it as occasion may serue. I haue spoken with Poly & find him no Foole. I do suspend all tyll our meeting which I wish may be shortly.'[20]

Poley's long career in government service shows him pretty constantly mixed up in the most secret and important affairs of the State. He had worked hand in glove with Sir Francis Walsingham in drawing out Babington. He had been in the confidence of such great personages as Mary Queen of Scots, Sir Christopher Blunt, and the Sidneys. We know of his close collaboration in espionage with Thomas Walsingham. He had even talked through the barred windows of the Bastille with Morgan. His life was spent in devious intrigue. Danby and his jury of bakers and grocers and country gentlemen would have been child's play in Poley's hands. Drew Woodleffe, we know, was an easy dupe for Skeres and Frizer.

As Dr. Tannenbaum has remarked, 'Here . . . was an excellent trio for a contrived murder.'[21] And the connecting link between all three men? Evidence shows that it was none other than the lord of Scadbury, Marlowe's patron, Thomas Walsingham.

Arguing from circumstantial evidence, Dr. Tannenbaum has boldly suggested that the murder was a plot involving the School of Night.

'The circumstances considered, it seems to me much more likely that on the fatal Wednesday, Marlowe was lured to Eleanor Bull's inn at Deptford Strand, was wined liberally till he fell into a drunken stupor; the time being ripe and Eleanor Bull safely out of the way in another part of the building, Ingram Frizer deliberately plunged his dagger into Marlowe's brain to a sufficient depth to cause his instant death.'[22]

Dr. Tannenbaum would pin the responsibility for engineering the murder fairly and squarely on Sir Walter Ralegh, but in order to do so he finds it necessary to represent him as an unscrupulous arch-Machiavellian ready to resort to murder for fear that Marlowe will blab under torture and implicate himself and others of the School of Night in the charges of atheism levelled against Marlowe, as Kyd had done before him. This, however, is not the picture of Ralegh which the full testimony of his life affords. Ralegh's true nobility of character and singularly fearless attitude of mind do not admit of such a ready assumption; indeed, they make such an assumption preposterous. Ralegh, we know, was as arrogant and careless of public opinion as was Marlowe. The Cerne Abbas enquiries, instigated the following year after Marlowe's death, resulted from careless talk of Ralegh's and his associates in much the same way as Marlowe's accusations grew, and even the warning of Kit's death had evidently not taught Sir Walter sufficiently to beware of disclosing his thoughts to those who might misconstrue them. That Ralegh, Northumberland, and many others of this circle would have been in sympathy with Kit in his troubles is self-evident, for they were constantly harried with similar accusations. That they would have stooped to having him murdered as some kind of sacrificial lamb is scarcely credible.

Nevertheless, there was obvious danger present in the latest damaging indictment prepared by Richard Baines (or Bames), the government informer set on Marlowe's track, and delivered to the Privy Council on the day before Marlowe's murder. The fact that in the copy of Richard Baines' Note detailing Marlowe's atheist opinions sent to the Queen the original title is scored through and altered is suggestive of a withholding of the delivery of the indictment, possibly for a day or so, since there is a discrepancy in the dates, for the heading reads: 'A Note deliuered on Whitson eve last of the most horrible blasphemes vtteryd by Cristofer Marley who within iii days after came to a soden & fearful end of his life.' However this may be explained, Baines had otherwise done his work with a fiendish thoroughness, and had appended a rider in the last paragraph of his indictment which must have made Marlowe quake had he read it:

'*These thinges, wth many other shall by good & honest witness be aproved to be his opinions and Comon Speeches and that this Marlow doth not only hould them himself but almost into euery Company he Cometh he perswades men to Atheism willing them not to be afeard of bugbeares and hobgoblins and vtterly scorning both god and his ministers as J Richard Baines will Justify & approue both by mine oth and the testimony of many honest men, and almost al men with whome he hath Conversed any time will testify the same, and as J think all men in Christianity ought to indevor that the mouth of so dangerous a member may be stopped, he saith likewise that he hath quoted a number of Contrarities oute of the Scripture wth he hath given to some great men who in Convenient time shalbe named. When these thinges shalbe Called in question the witnes shalbe produced.*'

'RICHARD BAMES'

The one person closest to Marlowe who would have been most concerned about his fate, was obviously Thomas Walsingham, at whose home Marlowe had been arrested. There is no doubt that as one high in the espionage service he would have had means to gain access to documents relating to Marlowe's case, had he so wished, and would have known about this latest damaging indictment. If Walsingham had discovered the fate that was in store for Marlowe, it is possible that others in the School of Night were apprised of it. Basing her arguments on this premise, and the close connections between Walsingham and the three men involved in the murder, Miss de Kalb suggests that it was Walsingham who was responsible for Marlowe's murder.[23]

Dr. Boas, soberly considering the evidence, rejects Dr. Tannenbaum's theory of Sir Walter Ralegh's complicity. Regarding the possibility of a political murder, he feels that this cannot be entirely ruled out, although it seems improbable that the Privy Council would have taken 'such a roundabout way of getting rid of an atheist playwright' since they had all the judicial means readily at their disposal for dealing with him as they had with Kyd. The difficulty, he feels, is 'to find an adequate motive for it or to trace a convincing origin for it in any special quarter'.[24]

However, he neglects to mention Walsingham's close connections with the three men involved as relevant to the murder, nor has any other scholar squarely faced the fact that the members of the School of Night were obviously those who were most in danger from Marlowe's further inquisition. Although this group included 'great men' it was not synonymous with the Privy Council and was openly at odds with the ecclesiastical authorities who were behind Marlowe's apprehension. It would have been in their interest if anyone acted swiftly and secretly to remove Marlowe from danger, howsoever it might be done.

Probably it would have occurred to Walsingham that there were more ways than one of achieving such a desirable end. His early apprenticeship in the subtle methods of espionage favoured by his cousin Sir Francis would not have been wasted. Thomas Walsingham's connections with the School of Night are, on the face of the evidence, sufficiently slender to exonerate him from any immediate danger in connection with accusations of Atheism as a result of Marlowe's apprehension; on the other hand, his intimate relationship with Marlowe and Chapman, the two outstanding poets of the School of Night, is not to be doubted. He was both their patron and their friend. He was also in a position to pull strings, possibly in high circles, certainly with Poley, Frizer and Skeres. There is no doubt that if he managed to save the situation in any way the members of the School of Night would have approved, providing it could be done with honour.

Now Dr. Boas has posed the pertinent question, 'If Frizer had been the actual instrument of such a design, could he have remained for years afterwards in the service of Thomas Walsingham, Marlowe's friend?'[25] One might also add, how could the noble Chapman, Marlowe's friend, have continued in such close friendship with Walsingham if he suspected that Marlowe had been slain at his patron's instigation?

There are only three possible alternatives as answer to this conundrum. The first is to assume that Frizer's story was absolutely true (which has been doubted by every scholar writing on the subject since Hotson's discovery). The second is to hold that Thomas Walsingham murdered Marlowe by the agency of his servant Ingram Frizer in an approved plot which safeguarded Poley, Frizer and Skeres alike, for the repercussions were singular in their complete absence only. In that case Walsingham may definitely be called *Omnium bipedum nequissimus*, of all two-legged creatures the basest. The third is seriously to consider the alternative that will immediately make all Shakespearean scholars quake and turn pale. Namely, the suggestion put forward by Mr. Calvin Hoffman that Walsingham, who was more personally and deeply concerned for Kit's safety in the first instance, and probably also for the repercussions that might eventually ensue for the members of the School of Night in the second, engineered not his murder but his escape by means of his 'death' and substituted another corpse.[26]

Intrigue, with this wealthy young Elizabethan gentleman, was evidently as much a passion as was art. There is no reason whatsoever to doubt his ability to have carried off such a ruse successfully, given the subtle knaves he had as his accomplices, nor his peculiar genius for conceiving such a daring plan. Meticulously scrupulous or conventionally ethical Walsingham was not. But even a superficial acquaintance with Elizabethan literature will convince the reader that the basest crime was held to be treachery to a friend. Friendship was rated the most sacred of all human bonds.

> *The name of friend is more than family,*
> *Or all the world besides.*
> THE MAID'S TRAGEDY, *Beaumont and Fletcher.*

> *A friend should bear his friend's infirmities.*
> JULIUS CAESAR, *Shakespeare.*

> *A villain and a traitor to his friend!*
> .   .   .   .
> *Give me a name, you whose infectious tongues*
> *Are tipp'd with gall and poison. As you would*
> *Think on a man that had your father slain,*
> *Murder'd your children, made your wives base strumpets,*
> *So call me, call me so; print in my face*
> *The most stigmatic title of a villain,*
> *For hatching treason to so true a friend.*
> A WOMAN KILLED WITH KINDNESS, *Thomas Heywood.*

Whatever else Walsingham was, it is extremely doubtful, indeed incredible, that he would have betrayed his friend to the murderous hand of his servant if there would have been any other way out. A possible alternative is surely that not Marlowe, as proposed by Dr. Tannenbaum, but some nameless sailor from Deptford dockside was 'lured' to Eleanor Bull's house, perhaps with plausible proposals of drinking and wenching; we do not know what kind of house it was. Having caught their 'conny' they would soon have got to work and either drugged him or made him dead drunk, and then exchanged his clothes with Marlowe's, who might have taken ship from Deptford for the Continent then and there.

An interesting confirmation of Elizabethan ethics in similar circumstances is found in Shakespeare's *Measure for Measure* which has so far escaped remark.

(It will be remembered that Angelo, the epitome of self-righteous man, ruling in the Duke's absence, has unjustly sentenced Claudio to death, and in proof of his speedy execution has demanded that his head be sent to him. The Duke, who has returned in the disguise of a friar, orders the Provost of the gaol to delay the execution and substitute the decapitated head of another prisoner.)

> PROVOST:
> *Alack! How may I do it, having the hour limited, and an express*
> *command, under penalty, to deliver his head in the view of Angelo?*
> *I may make my case as Claudio's, to cross in the smallest.*
> DUKE:
> *By the vow of mine order, I warrant you, if my instructions may be your*

> guide. *Let this Barnardine be this morning executed, and his head borne to Angelo.*
>
> PROVOST:
>
> *Angelo hath seen them both, and will discover the favour.*
>
> DUKE:
>
> *O, death's a great disguiser.*
>
> MEASURE FOR MEASURE, IV, ii.

In the next scene a happy chance resolves the problem for them:

> PROVOST:
>
> *Here in the prison, father,*
> *There died this morning of a cruel fever*
> *One Ragozine, a most notorious pirate,*
> *A man of Claudio's years; his beard and head*
> *Just of his colour . . .*
>
> DUKE:
>
> *O, 'tis an accident that heaven provides!*
> *Dispatch it presently; the hour draws on.*
>
> Op. cit. IV, iii.

Whether the plague, then rampant, might also have provided the heaven-sent accident in Marlowe's case is perhaps more doubtful, though not to be dismissed altogether. Gabriel Harvey's sonnet on Marlowe's death refers to the 'graund Dissease' that 'Sternely struck-home the peremptory stroke' as though he would imply that Marlowe had died of the plague. Yet it would have been curious indeed if he had not known the real story of Frizer's

Entry in the burial register *of St. Nicholas, Deptford:*
Christopher Marlowe slaine by ffrancis ffrezer; the · 1 · of Iune.

hand in the matter, since his brother was rector of Walsingham's own church and presumably prayers would have been said for the dead there at least. The mystery that clings around Marlowe's death still obscures the issue for us, as it did, apparently by deliberate fabrication, in the 'wonderfull yeare' 1593.

Dr. Hotson's great discovery, instead of resolving the mystery once and for all, has opened the way for further research. But while scholars cling with blind-shuttered prejudice to their determination that Marlowe, if he was not in fact the sacrificial lamb to the security of the School of Night, shall be their sacrificial lamb to the image of Shakespeare, any real progress in discovering the truth, whichever way it may lie, will be hindered. For it is evident from the attitude of the united front of Shakespearean scholars that Marlowe would only be of interest to them dead in 1593, not living in 1594. Hotson in his brilliant investigation into *The First Night of Twelfth Night*, which links Shakespeare so closely with the fascinating Don Virginio Orsino, Duke of Bracciano, has himself sounded the warning that must be heeded:

> 'We are all aware . . . of an ever-present danger: nothing is easier in any kind of investigation than to overlook a vital piece of evidence staring us in the face. For if that piece of evidence does not seem to corroborate or to fall in with our already-settled ideas, our minds either simply ignore it, or else wrest it by "interpretation" to make it mean what we think it ought to mean. Such behaviour is certainly human, but it blocks the road to knowledge.'[27]

The mystery of Marlowe's death remains a challenge awaiting the fortitude of unbiased scholarship.

Marlowe Vilified

> *'Tis better to be vile than vile esteemed,*
> *When not to be, receives reproach of being.*
> SONNET CXXI, *Shakespeare*

'Not inferiour to any of the former in Atheisme & impiety, and equall to all in manner of punishment was one of our own nation, of fresh and late memory, called *Marlin*, by profession a scholler, brought vp from his youth in the Vniuersitie of Cambridge, but by practise a playmaker, and a Poet of scurrilitie, who by giuing too large a swinge to his owne wit, and suffering his lust to haue the full raines, fell (not without iust desert) to that outrage and extremitie, that hee denied God and his sonne Christ, and not only in word blasphemed the trinitie, but also (as it is credibly reported) wrote bookes against it, affirming our Saviour to be but a deceiuer, and *Moses* to be but a coniurer and seducer of the people, and the holy Bible but vaine and idle stories, and all religion but a deuice of pollicie. But see what a hooke the Lord put in the nosthrils of this barking dogge: It so fell out, that in London streets as he purposed to stab one whome hee ought a grudge vnto with his dagger, the other party perceiuing so auoided the stroke, that withall catching hold of his wrest, he stabbed his owne dagger into his owne head, in such sort, that notwithstanding all the meanes of surgerie that could be wrought, hee shortly after died thereof. The manner of his death being so terrible (for hee euen cursed and blasphemed to his last gaspe, and togither with his breath an oth flew out of his mouth) that it was not only a manifest signe of Gods iudgement, but also an horrible and feare-full terrour to all that beheld him. But herein did the iustice of God most notably appeare, in that hee compelled his owne hand which had written those blasphemies to be the instrument to punish him, and that in his braine, which had deuised the same.'

Thomas Beard: THEATRE OF GODS IUDGEMENTS, 1597.

'As *Iodelle*, a French tragical poet beeing an Epicure, and an Atheist, made a pitifull end: so our tragicall poet *Marlow* for his Epicurisme and Atheisme had a tragicall death; you may read of this *Marlow* more at large in the *Theatre of Gods iudgments*, in the 25. chapter entreating of Epicures and Atheists.

'As the poet *Lycophron* was shot to death by a certain riual of his: so *Christopher Marlow* was stabd to death by a bawdy *Seruing man*, a riuall of his in his lewde loue.'

Francis Meres: PALLADIS TAMIA, 1598.

' Not inferiour to these was one Christopher Marlow by profession a play-maker, who, as it is reported, about 7. yeeres a-goe wrote a booke against the Trinitie: but see the effects of Gods iustice; it so hapned, that at Detford, a little village about three miles distant from London, as he meant to stab with his ponyard one named Ingram, that had inuited him thither to a feast, and was then playing at tables, he quickely perceyving it, auoyded the thrust, that withall drawing out his dagger for his defence, hee stabd this Marlow into the eye, in such sort, that his braines comming out at the daggers point, hee shortlie after dyed. Thus did God, the true executioner of diuine iustice, worke the ende of impious Atheists.'

William Vaughan: THE GOLDEN GROVE, 1600.

' We read of one *Marlin*, a *Cambridge* Scholler, who was a Poet, and a filthy Play-maker, this wretch accounted that meeke seruant of God *Moses* to be but a Coniurer, and our sweete Sauiour but a seducer and a deceiuer of the people. But harken yee braine-sicke and prophane Poets, and Players, that bewitch idle eares with foolish vanities: what fell vpon this prophane wretch, hauing a quarrell against one whom he met in a streete in London, and would haue stabd him: But the partie perceiuing his villany preuented him with catching his hand, and turning his owne dagger into his braines, and so blasphem-ing and cursing, he yeelded vp his stinking breath: marke this yee Players, that liue by making fooles laugh at sinne and wickednesse.'

Edmund Rudierde: THE THUNDERBOLT OF GODS WRATH AGAINST HARDE-HEARTED AND STIFFE-NECKED SINNERS, 1618.

'Sitting in a Baudy-house, hee writes Gods Iudgements. Hee ends at last in some obscure painted Cloth, to which himselfe made the Verses, and his life like a Canne too full spils vpon the bench. He leaues twenty shillings on the score, which my Hostesse looses.'

(*Portrait of a 'pot-poet' evidently based on Marlowe*)
John Earle: MICRO-COSMOGRAPHIE, 1628.

(Ben Jonson) 'killed Mr. Marlow, the poet, on Bunhill, comeing from the Green Curtain play-house.'

John Aubrey: BRIEF LIVES, written between 1669 and 1696.

'But see the end of this person, which was noted by all, especially the Precisians. For it so fell out, that he being deeply in love with a certain Woman, had for his rival a bawdy serving man, one rather fit to be a Pimp, than an ingenious *Amoretto* as *Marlo* conceived himself to be. Whereupon *Marlo* taking it to be a high affront, rush'd in upon, to stab, him, with his dagger. But the serving man being very quick, so avoided the stroke, that with all catching hold of *Marlo's* wrist, he stab'd his own dagger into his own head, in such sort, that notwithstanding all the means of surgery that could be wrought, he shortly after died of his wound.'

Anthony a Wood: ATHENAE OXONIENSES, 1691.

The aftermath of the happenings at Deptford were, in a sense, the real tragedy of Marlowe. Charles Norman has movingly summed it up for us:

'The Puritan tide of obloquy rose slowly, but it finally overwhelmed the memory of Marlowe. Their story of a divine visitation on the man and his works carried all before it. Within a century of his death even writers attempting a critical estimate of his achievements were under the spell of his calumniators. The wrath finally spent itself, but the righteousness stayed. Those who had known him and might have defended him were dead; his books had all but disappeared.

'The outburst of Puritan wrath against Marlowe is without parallel in literature. No vile epithet was too vile for his detractors to use, yet most of them wrote only from hearsay, or merely embroidered one another's accounts, hardly one able to contain his gloating . . .

'In the tragic end of the poet who blazed the trail that Shakespeare followed they saw only the terrible justice of heaven appropriately meted out, and added fuel to the fiery legend which has persisted to this day of Marlowe as the very archetype of Elizabethan roaring boy—hot-blooded, bellicose, wearing pride like a feather in his hat, and iniquitous before God and man. In truth, he sat for this portrait, distorted though it is; but there was something else, as we have seen.' *Charles Norman:* THE MUSES' DARLING, 1947.[1]

RICHARD BAINES' NOTE

A note Containing the opinion of on[e] Christopher Marly Concerning his Damnable Judgment of Religion, and scorn of gods word.

That the Jndians and many Authors of antiquity haue assuredly writen aboue 16 thousand yeares agone wher as Adam is proued to haue lived w'hin 6 thowsand yeares.

He affirmeth that Moyses was but a Jugler, & that one Heriots being Sir W Raleighs man can do more then he.

That Moyses made the Jewes to travell xl yeares in the wildernes, (w'h Jorney might haue bin Done in lesse then one yeare) ere they Came to the promised land to thintent that those who were privy to most of his subtilties might perish and so an everlasting superstition Remain in the hartes of the people.

That the first beginning of Religioun was only to keep men in awe.

That it was an easy matter for Moyses being brought vp in all the artes of the Egiptians to abuse the Jewes being a rude & grosse people.

That Christ was a bastard and his mother dishonest.

That he was the sonne of a Carpenter, and that if the Jewes among whome he was borne did Crucify him theie best knew him and whence he Came.

That Christ deserved better to Dy then Barrabas and that the Jewes made a good Choise, though Barrabas were both a thief and murtherer.

That if there be any god or any good Religion, then it is in the papistes because the service of god is performed w*th* more Cerimonies, as Elevation of the mass, organs, singing men, Shaven Crownes & cta. that all protestantes are Hypocriticall asses.

That if he were put to write a new Religion, he would vndertake both a more Exellent and Admirable methode and that all the new testament is filthily written.

That the woman of Samaria & her sister were whores & that Christ knew them dishonestly.

That St John the Evangelist was bedfellow to C[hrist] and leaned alwaies in his bosome, that he vsed him as the sinners of Sodoma.

That all they that loue not Tobacco & Boies were fooles.

That all the apostles were fishermen and base fellowes neyther of wit nor worth, that Paull only had wit but he was a timerous fellow in bidding men to be subiect to magistrates against his Conscience.

That he had as good Right to Coine as the Queene of England, and that he was acquainted w*th* one poole a prisoner in newgate who hath great Skill in mixture of mettals and hauing learned some thinges of him he ment through help of a Cunninge stamp maker to Coin ffrench Crownes pistolets and English shillinges.

That if Christ would haue instituted the sacrament w*th* more Ceremoniall Reverence it would haue bin had in more admiration, that it would haue bin much better being administred in a Tobacco pipe.

That the Angell Gabriell was Baud to the holy ghost, because he brought the salutation to Mary.

That on[e] Ric Cholmley hath Confessed that he was perswaded by Marloe's Reasons to become an Atheist.

These thinges, w*th* many other shall by good & honest witnes be aproued to be his opinions and Comon Speeches, and that this Marlow doth not only hould them himself, but almost into every Company he Cometh he perswades men to Atheism willing them not to be afeard of bugbeares and hobgoblins, and vtterly scorning both god and his ministers as J Richard Baines will Justify & approue both by mine oth and the testimony of many honest men, and almost al men with whome he hath Conversed any time will testify the same, and as J think all men in Cristianity ought to indevor that the mouth of so dangerous a member may be stopped, he saith likewise that he hath quoted a number of Contrarieties oute of the Scripture w*ch* he hath giuen to some great men who in Convenient time shalbe named. When these thinges shalbe Called in question the witnes shalbe produced.

RICHARD BAMES [Baines]

Even today Marlowe's biographers have not quite wrested themselves free from the ghost of his 'monstrous opinions' raised by Richard Baines. For the modern critic, however, it is in the final analysis neither the evidence of Baines' Note, which is refuted by the thought of the men with whom Marlowe discussed his religious criticisms seriously, as well as by his own writings, nor yet the fulminations of the 'Precisians' or Puritans with their hearsay gossip, but the word of his one-time friend Kyd that has tainted his reputation, lending a spurious veracity to the testimony of Frizer and his accomplices.

In the hectic atmosphere of Elizabethan witch-hunting and atheist name-calling that prevailed, backed by the deadly instruments of the law, it is not surprising to find men (and women) veering violently from the brink of free thought back into the worst kind of mediæval pseudo-religious clap-trap, in order to safeguard themselves from the taint of suspicion and its consequences in this life, or from the fears of hell hereafter in the next. Greene's death-bed 'Repentance' was an example of the latter; Kyd's abject appeal, in the letters he wrote after Marlowe's death, an example of the first. Fear had broken both these men.

Kyd's two extant letters, which have done so much damage to Marlowe's reputation in the critical assessment of scholars, are addressed to Sir John Puckering, Lord Keeper of the Privy Seal. Both were written after Marlowe's death and after Kyd's release from prison, although when exactly he regained his freedom is not known. The letters are not dated, and only the first is signed with Kyd's exquisite signature subscribed with elegant flourishes.

In considering the evidence of Kyd's letters, it is the chronology of the events which is all-important: Kyd's arrest and torture, Marlowe's arrest and bail, Marlowe's murder, Kyd's release and rejection by his lord, Kyd's two letters. In this brief history we have the kaleidoscopic picture of Kyd's disintegration as a man. By the time he took up his pen to write to the Lord Keeper his integrity was lost, his body and spirit broken by unjustly inflicted suffering, and his mind poisoned against the man who had been the unwitting cause of it all.

Kyd's frantic concern is only to exonerate himself from the taint of atheism. Upon his release from prison he had been given to understand that his services were no longer required by his former patron and employer. If Kyd had learned of Frizer's return to the bosom of the Walsinghams, how this must have rankled! One might murder an atheist with impunity it seems, and accordingly he sets out to murder the reputation of the atheist in question. It is the only revenge he can now have on him.

Kyd, tantalisingly omits to put a name to his 'Lord' in his letters, but scholars have generally identified him with Ferdinando Stanley, Lord Strange, for whose company of players Kyd was working on the playscript of *Sir Thomas More* just before his arrest.* Kyd's letter is significantly vague concerning the reason for

---

* *Dr. Boas writes, after putting forward Lord Strange as the most likely patron for Kyd's 'Lord', that 'the matter must remain in doubt'. However, he neglects to mention the connection with Kyd and the* Booke of Sir Thomas More *and Strange's Men, which, as incontestable documentary evidence, would seem to clinch the matter.*[2]

his dismissal, as though he had been given this news at second hand, presumably by Lord Strange's steward. The poor man is left wondering why he is not to be reinstated. Does his Lord suspect him of atheism, perhaps? The answer, if it came, was unequivocal. Perhaps the steward kindly suggests to the pathetically broken figure that a good word from Lord Keeper Puckering clearing him of all such imputations might regain him Lord Strange's favour; or, as is much more likely, perhaps he was left so much in the dark as to the reasons for his cold reception that his tormented mind puts its own construction on his Lord's displeasure. Kyd's comments on Lord Strange's sentiments concerning atheism figure so largely in his letter as to merit remark. Are they true? Or do they represent Kyd's feverish imaginings in his determination to win back his Lord's good will? This is a puzzle for the discerning scholar.

In his desperate masterless plight Kyd goes to see the Lord Keeper to 'entreate some speaches' from him, with no success; so he decides to put his request in writing:

'At my last being wth yor L.P. [Lordship] to entreate some speaches from yo^u in my favor to my Lorde, whoe (though I thinke he rest not doubtfull of myne inocence) hath yet in his discreeter iudgment feared to offende in his reteyning me, wthout yor honor^s former pryvitie. So is it now R. Ho: [Right Honourable] that the denyall of that favo^r to my thought resonable hath moved me to coniecture some suspicion, that yor L.P. holds me in, concerning *Atheisme*, a deadlie thing wch I was vnderserued chargd wthall, & therefore have I thought it requisite, aswell in duetie to yor L.P., & the Lawes, as also in the feare of god, & freedom of my conscience, therein to satisfie the world and yo^u:

'The first and most (thoughe insufficient surmize) that [once?] therein might be raisde of me, grewe thus. When I was first suspected for that Libell that concern'd the state, amongst those waste and idle papers (wch I carde not for) & wch vnaskt I did deliuer vp, were founde some fragments of a disputation toching that opinion, affirmd by Marlowe to be his, and shufled wth some of myne vnknown to me by some occasion of o^r wrytinge in one chamber twoe yeares synce.'

Charles Norman has noted that Kyd is careful not to state that these 'fragments of a disputation' are in Marlowe's handwriting, but only accuses him of ownership of the papers, since it is obvious that they are a transcript in a professional noverint's hand; he suggests that 'Perhaps Marlowe had paid him, as a professional penman, to copy them out for him—another humiliation.'[3] (See document on p. 239.) Marlowe's friend Nashe had once taunted Kyd, calling him 'a sort of shifting companions, that runne through every arte and thriue by none, to leaue the trade of *Noverint* whereto they were borne, and busie themselues with the indeuors of Art, that could scarcelie Latinize their necke-verse if they shoulde haue neede'[1]. Kyd had not had the benefit of a university education, but his answer to Nashe may be seen in his copious use of Latin quotations in his careful letter to Puckering. He had always been an outsider as far as the 'University Wits' were concerned, but Marlowe befriended him. Kyd had talent. *The Spanish Tragedy* was one of the first and greatest successes of the new drama, ranking with *Tamburlaine* in popularity and rivalling it as claimant for the honour of being first on the scene, although it is a possibility, not previously considered by scholars, that this may actually have been a work of collaboration between Marlowe and Kyd.

Kyd's unctuous denunciations of Marlowe doubtless stem in part from a rabid inferiority complex, nurtured by envy. In trying to see our way into the mind of Kyd as revealed by his poison-pen letters, and to sort out the truth of the slander concerning Marlowe, it is necessary once more to stand back from the scene and to see both Kyd in his abject misery and degradation, and Marlowe as we have hitherto known him, and set both into the context of the Elizabethan atmosphere of unhealthy superstition bolstered by the tyrannical cruelty of the methods of persecution then in use.

Marlowe, according to Baines' report (confirmed by Kyd's references to his 'table talk'), went around persuading men to 'Atheism' and 'willing them not to be afeard of bugbeares and hobgoblins'. This one can readily believe of him. Marlowe acted as the catalyst in the muddled mediæval minds of the men he met. To shock them out of their superstitions he evidently went too far and revealed too much of his own thought. Their fears no longer touched him; but like Bruno he could never resist the temptation to expose these ulcerous depths, employing the barb of irony when argument failed. Intellectually arrogant he doubtless was, but there is nowhere else in his life any sign of a petty vindictiveness, such as Kyd imputes to his character. On the contrary, Marlowe would seem to have been above rancour; even in the face of vicious personal attacks on him by Nashe and Greene he remained their friends. Yet, according to Kyd, he was given to such reprehensible behaviour as would have lost him the respect of friendship: 'he was intemperate & of a cruel hart', and he was guilty of 'rashnes in attempting soden pryvie iniuries to men'. The importance in considering Kyd's statements at some length is that these have been accepted, with certain reservations, as essentially the truth concerning Marlowe. It is Kyd's word that has coloured the assessment of Marlowe by scholars. From his apparent corroboration of the account of Marlowe's behaviour at Eleanor Bull's house a picture of Marlowe as 'intemperate & of a cruel hart' has become accepted as the true representation of the man; but, as we shall see, there exist both contradictions and a chronological bearing on the events to which scant attention has so far been paid.

Kyd was quite obviously intent upon regaining his own lost reputation by murdering Marlowe's. He was on the opposite end of the seesaw, and saw no reason why the dead body of his former friend should not weight this down to send him up to better fortunes than he had undeserved received. To this end, in bitterness of heart, he now prostituted his pen.

That Kyd would have gone out of his way to enquire into the circumstances of Marlowe's death is an obvious conclusion. Having learnt the story of his violent end in a murderous quarrel, he would naturally have seized upon this as a weapon to his own use, which he now deploys skilfully to ingratiate himself into the good graces of the Lord Keeper. Just as he contrasts his pious God-fearing self with the atheist Marlowe, he also contrasts his own gentle nature with that of the intemperate, cruel-hearted man who would have slain Frizer, if Frizer 'in defence of his life' had not peradventure slain him. The story of Marlowe's death was an added means to blacken Marlowe, and I suggest that Kyd did not hesitate to make use of it, for if Kyd was blasting Marlowe's reputation before his friend was dead, how much more readily would he have done so after he was murdered.

> 'That I shold loue or be familer frend wth one so irreligious, were very rare, when *Tullie* saith *Digni sunt amicitia quibus in ipsis inest causa cur diligantur* [Those are worthy of friendship in whom there resides a cause why they should be esteemed] wch neither was in him, for pson [person], quallities, or honestie, besides he was intemperate & of a cruel hart, the verie contraries to wch my greatest enemies will saie by me.'[5]

Lord Keeper Puckering, fully acquainted with the details of the Inquisition on Marlowe's death, would nod his head at this, or so Kyd hopes, and soften his heart towards the wronged Kyd. But lest the unseemliness of speaking ill of the dead should strike a jarring note, he takes the precaution of paying lip service to the sentiment condemning such profanity:

> 'It is not to be nombred amongst the best conditions of men, to taxe or to opbraide the deade *Quia mortui non mordent* [Because the dead do not bite], But thus muche haue I (wth yor Lp^s favo^r) dared in the greatest cause, which is to cleere my selfe of being thought an *Atheist*, which some will sweare he was.'

He returns to harp on this string again in his second letter, this time introducing yet more forcibly a hint of Marlowe's end, and slipping his tidbits of information concerning Marlowe's reprehensible nature quite irrelevantly into an accusation concerning Marlowe's atheist opinions. This appears as No. 4 of his list of criminal atheist denunciations against Marlowe:

> '4. That things esteemed to be donn by devine power might haue aswell been don by observation of men all wch he wold so sodenlie take slight occasion to slyp out as I & many others in regard of his other rashnes in attempting soden pryvie iniuries to men did ouerslypp though often reprehend him for it & for which god is my witnes aswell by my lordes comaundmt as in hatred of his life & thoughts I left & did refraine his companie.'

Whether Marlowe really was in bad odour with the lord in question, assuming that this was in fact Lord Strange, or whether the virtuous Kyd is taking

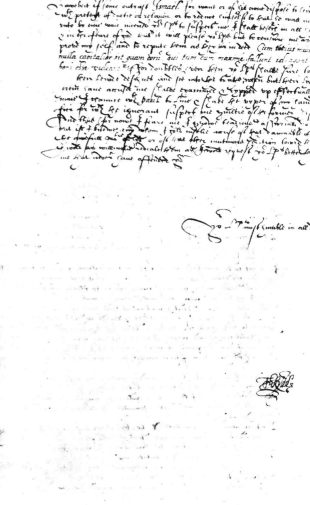

KYD'S LETTER TO SIR JOHN PUCKERING (*signed*)

At my last being wth yo' Lp. [Lordship] to entreate some speaches from yo" in my favor to my Lorde, whoe (though' I thinke he rest not doubtfull of myne inocence) hath yet in his discreeter iudgment feared to offende in his reteyning me, w^thout yo' honor^s former pryvitie. So is it nowe R. Ho: [Right Honourable] that the denyall of that favo' to my thought resonable hath n.ovde me to coniecture some suspicion, that yo' Lp. holds me in, concerning Atheisme, a deadlie thing wch I was vndeserved chargd w^thall, & therfore haue I thought it requisite, aswell in duetie to yo' Lp. & the Lawes, as also in the feare of god, & freedom of my conscience, therein to satisfie the world and yo":

The first and most (thoughe insufficient surmize) that [once?] therein might be raisde of me, grewe thus. When I was first suspected for that Libell that concern'd the state, amongst those waste and idle papers (wch I carde not for) & wch vnaskt I did deliuer vp, were founde some fragments of a disputation toching that opinion, affirmd by Marlowe to be his, and shufled

314

wth some of myne vnknown to me by some occasion of o' wrytinge in one chamber twoe years synce.

My first acquaintance wth this Marlowe, rose vpon his bearing name to serve my Lo: [Lord] although his Lp never knew his service but in writing for his plaiers, ffor never cold my L. endure his name, or sight, when he had heard of his conditions, nor wold in deed the forme of devyne praiers vsed duelie in his Lp^s house haue quadred wth such reprobates.

That I shold loue or be familer frend wth one so irreligious, were verie rare, when Tullie saith Digni sunt amicitia quibus in ipsis inest causa cur diligantur [Those are worthy of friendship in whom there resides a cause why they should be esteemed] wch neither was in him, for pson [person], quallities, or honestie, besides he was intemp[er]ate & of a cruel hart, the verie contraries to wch my greatest enemies will saie by me.
It is not to be nombred amongst the best conditions of men, to taxe or to opbraide the deade Quia mortui non mordent [Because the dead do not bite], But thus muche haue I (wth yo' Lp^s favo') dared in the greatest cause, which is to cleere my selfe of being thought an Atheist, which some will sweare he was.

ffor more assurance that I was not of that vile opinion, Lett it but please yor Lp to enquire of such as he conversd wth all, that is (as I am geven to vnderstand) wth Harriot, Warner, Royden, and some stationers in Paules churchyard, whom I in no sort can accuse nor will excuse by reson of his companie; of whose consent if I had been, no question but I also shold haue been of their consort, for ex minimo vestigio artifex agnoscit artificem. [The craftsman recognises craft by the slightest trace].

Of my religion & Life I haue alredie geven some instance to the Late comission^{ers} & of my reverend meaning to the state, although phaps [perhaps] my paines and vndeserved tortures felt by some, wold haue ingendred more impatience when Lesse by farr hath dryven so manye imo extra caulas [even outside the fold] wch it shall never do wth me.

But whatsoeuer I haue felt R. Ho: this is my request not for reward but in regard of my trewe inocence that it wold please yor Lp^s so to [? mark] the same & me, as I maie still reteyne the favo^{rs} of my Lord, whom I haue served almost theis vj yeres nowe, in credit vntill nowe, & nowe am vtterlie vndon without herein be somewhat donn for my recoverie. ffor I do knowe his Lp holdes yor hono^{rs} & the state in that dewe reverence, as he wold no waie move the Leste suspicion of his Loves and cares both towards hir sacred Matie [Majesty] yor Lp^s and the Lawes wherof when tyme shall serve I shall geue greater instance wch I haue observd.

As for the Libel Laide vnto my chardg I am resolued wth receyving of ye sacram^t [sacrament] to satisfie yor Lp^s & the world that I was neither agent nor consenting thervnto. Howbeit if some outcast Ismael for want or of his owne dispose to Lewdnes, haue with pretext of duetie or religion, or to reduce himself to that he was not borne vnto by enie waie incensd yor Lp^s to suspect me, I shall besech in all humillitie & in the feare of god that it will please yor Lp^s but to censure me as I shall prove my self, and to repute them as they ar in deed Cum totius iniustitae nulla capitalior sit quam eorum, qui tum cum maxime fallunt id agunt vt viri boni esse videant^{ur} [Since of all injustice none is more pernicious than that of those who, when they most deeply deceive, do it in sucn manner that they shall seem good men]. ffor doubtles even then yor Lp^s shalbe sure to breake open their Lewde designes and see into the truthe, when but their Lyues that herein haue accused me shal be examined & rypped vp effectually, soe maie I chaunce wth paul to Liue & shake the vyper of my hand into the fier for wch the ignorant suspect me guiltie of the former shipwrack. And thus (for nowe I feare me I growe teadious) assuring yor good Lp that if I knewe eny whom I cold iustlie accuse of that damnable offence to the awefull Matie of god or of that other mutinous sedition towrd the state I wold as willinglie reveale them as I wold request yor Lp^s better thoughtes of me that neuer haue offended yo^w

Yo^r LP^s most humble in all duties
T KYDDE

315

KYD'S SECOND LETTER (*unsigned*)

Pleaseth it yo' hono'able Lp [Lordship] toching marlowes monstruous opinions as I cannot but wth an agreved conscience think on him or them so can I but p[ar]iculariz fewe in the respect of them that kept him greater company, Howbeit in discharg of dutie both towardes god yo' Lp^s & the world thus much haue I thought good breiflie to discouer in all humblenes. ffirst it was his custom when I knew him first & as I heare saie he contynewd it in table talk or otherwise to iest at the devine scriptures gybe at prai^rs, & stryve in argument to frustrate & confute what hath byn spoke or wrytt by prophets & such holie men.

1. He would report St John to be o' savio' Christes Alexis I cover it wth reverence and trembling that is that Christ did loue him wth an extraordinary loue.

2. That for me to wryte a poem of St paules conversion as I was determined he said wold be as if I shold go wryte a book of fast & loose, esteeming Paul a Jugler.

3. That the prodigall Childes portion was but fower nobles, he held his purse so neere the bottom in all pictures, and that it either was a iest or els fowr nobles then was thought a great patrimony not thinking it a p[ar]able.

4. That things esteemed to be donn by devine powe' might haue aswell been don by observation of men all wth he wold so sodenlie take slight occasion to slyp out as I & many others in regard of his other rashnes in attempting soden pryvie iniuries to men did ouerslypp though often reprehend him for it & for which god is my witnes aswell by my lordes comaundmt as in hatred of his Life & thoughts I left & did refraine his companie.

He wold pswade wth men of quallitie to goe vnto the K[ing] of Scotts whether I heare Royden is gon and where if he had liud he told me when I sawe him last he meant to be.

the name of God in vain or is writing in the desperate belief that Lord Strange would only consider taking him back into service if he clears himself of all taint of atheism because he (like Kyd) is in fear of the like taint, is a matter that remains obscure. Ferdinando Stanley was a Catholic, yet proved himself no fanatic in this respect, for he lost his life in dreadful manner the following year for offering up to justice the Catholic traitor who came to him with treasonable offers against the Protestant Queen. Stanley showed himself in this to be both a man of principle and courage. Can we take Kyd's word, the testimony of a perjured man, capable of writing letters scurrilously slandering Marlowe, as the truth? His whining letters to Puckering do not give the impression of a courageous man. It is also evident that Baines' Note (see pp. 308–9) contains many accusations directly from Kyd's lips, for Kyd reiterates these allegations against Marlowe in his second letter to Puckering. His constant theme is his slight acquaintance of this Marlowe, with whom he claims he has had nothing more to do since 'wrytinge in one chamber twoe years synce'. He takes it upon himself likewise to dissociate his Lord from Marlowe's personal acquaintance, as also from condonance of his atheist opinions. One wonders what Lord Strange might have thought of this? Had the master asked the servant to speak for him? Is this really what Kyd's Lord had given him to understand he wished him to do, or was this merely Kyd's interpretation of the significance of his master's rebuff? As with the Inquest story, we are once more wandering in a maze of conjecture and contradictions. That Kyd never did regain his Lord's service is clear. He had to seek patronage elsewhere. He dedicated his last work to the Countess of Sussex—a translation of Garnier's *Cornelie*. She, poor desolate wench, was left to 'stand naked vpon euery poste', for the book did not sell.

Kyd was a shunned man. Not only his Lord had cast him off, but even his own family. Kyd thought that Lord Strange did so because he suspected him of atheism. Strange was himself a member of the circle accused of atheism. He was mentioned by Chapman to Royden in a eulogy in association with the Earl of Northumberland (that arch-atheist) and George Carey, the friend of Cobham. Is it not, therefore, more likely that he cast Kyd off because he suspected him of bringing perjured evidence against Marlowe? Had Kyd turned informer? Charles Norman asks the pertinent question,[6] prompted by the phrase in Kyd's letter,

'this is my request not for reward but in regard of my trewe inocence . . .'

Innocent of atheism one feels sure the poor man was, but not innocent of perjury. The opinions credited by Baines to Marlowe, and which form the basis of the indictment which brought him into mortal peril had he lived to face it, evidently represent in part, if not in whole, the accusations wrung from Kyd with every turn of the rack. They have the semblance of truth given an ugly twist of blasphemy, possibly as a direct result of insinuations by the informer Baines, who was no doubt present at Kyd's questioning and torture;

but Kyd's reaffirmation of them item by item in his second letter to Puckering (which he left unsigned possibly out of apprehension) testifies to the extent of his responsibility in bringing Marlowe to book. The letter was written after Marlowe was dead (and Kyd knew it) but it re-echoes so exactly Baines' Note, prepared while Marlowe was yet on bail, that there can be little doubt of the link between the two.

Kyd further accuses both Marlowe and Royden of what would appear to be treasonable intentions in the last piece of information he offers for Lord Keeper Puckering's ear:

'He wold perswade wth men of quallitie to goe vnto the K[ing] of *Scotts* whether I heare *Royden* is gon and where if he had liud he told me when I sawe him last he meant to be.'

As has been pointed out in the previous chapter, Robert Poley was employed in important government business carrying despatches to the Scottish Court in the early months of 1593. Royden's journey thither was very likely on a similar errand, for it seems probable that he was also a government agent as were Skeres and Marlowe. They all knew each other. The suggestion that Marlowe, who had such favourable patronage and such assured success in London, should be considering making off to Scotland on a treasonable matter is hard to accept. Here Kyd has surely overreached himself, and we see the black heart of the man. Marlowe had evidently treated him as a friend and had taken him, at least partially, into his confidence in matters which, as a secret agent, he should not have done. If Marlowe really intended to go to Scotland he was a long time about it, since Kyd avers he had not seen him for two years. An unlikely tale, whichever way one looks at it.

In fact Kyd was probably lying in two ways. Firstly in implying that Marlowe had intentions of going to Scotland as a traitor; and secondly in stating that he had not seen Kit for two years. The probability is that Marlowe, as also Royden and certainly Poley, was engaged, or about to be engaged, on secret missions in connection with the Scottish threat which was causing Elizabeth grave concern at the beginning of 1593. Camden writes that in 1593 the Queen

'had lately received certain intelligence that the Popish Noblemen in *Scotland* had by the cunning practices of the Priests conspired to call the *Spaniards* into *Scotland*, to change Religion there and to assayle *England* on that side . . . She foresaw also how easily the people of *Scotland* in the West parts, being for the most part poore and needy, might be corrupted with *Spanish* gold; how full of havens and harbours those coasts were . . . how easie the entrance was from thence into *England*, as it were by the back doore, moreover how doubtfull was the loyalty of the *English* bordering upon *Scotland*, who were most of them Papists . . .

'Of these things she informed the King of *Scots* and advised him to suppresse those *Scottish* Noblemen betimes, and to exercise his royal authority against his seditious subjects.'[7]

As will be seen in perusing Kyd's letters, these interesting documents are more revelatory of Kyd's state of mind than they are of Marlowe's. The dark despair of his mood colours and distorts almost everything he says. The whole tenor of his writing is to whiten himself and blacken Marlowe; in the deep recesses of his mind lurks fear, in his heart envy and injustice rankle. Just as Frizer was in the dock, so Kyd finds himself a man accused, and unjustly. His desperate determination is to 'Liue & shake the vyper of my hand into the fier'.

In his second unsigned letter, which was evidently in reply to a request from Sir John Puckering to provide further information concerning Marlowe's atheist associates, he hedges cautiously, regretting that he can 'but particulariz fewe in the respect of them that kept him greater company'; having previously mentioned '*Harriot, Warner, Royden* and some stationers in Paules churchyard', he mentions Royden a second time, in order to present him in a treasonable light, and concentrates instead on listing again the scurrilous denunciations he had furnished to Baines.

It is only possible here to state the evidence and to indicate its contradictory and intrinsically unreliable nature. That Kyd's testimony is not to be taken at face value is emphasised by Dr. Boas: 'In his feverish anxiety to clear himself of this deadlier charge [i.e. of atheism] Kyd does not hesitate to minimize the extent of his association with Marlowe and to defame his character.'[8] Nevertheless, in their final verdict, scholars have been influenced to a considerable extent by Kyd's statements concerning Marlowe's character, simply because they have seen in these a corroboration of Frizer's account of Marlowe's behaviour in the quarrel over 'le recknynge'. Charles Norman writes: 'We learn from the records of his life that he was quick to grasp sword, voice turning ugly and provocative, fist clenched for threat of striking; that he was a scorner of the unlearned, a scholar and a blasphemer.'[9] Yet this portrait is furnished by the evidence of two suspect witnesses, and by them only. If Kyd's statements are seen as a reflection of the Deptford story, being his use of the after-knowledge of these happenings to further his own ends, it is no longer possible to take them as independent evidence. We are then left with Frizer, backed by his two equally suspect witnesses, as our sole source for this detrimental assessment. And it is self-evident that he had excellent reasons for lying.

Kyd, of course, hearing of Marlowe's end, would doubtless have believed every word of the story, since he was in a mood to think nothing but evil of Marlowe. He would obviously have felt quite justified in quoting it to help his case with Sir John. He did so with a vengeance and with a subtlety designed to take the Lord Keeper in. He may, by the way, have taken us in as well.

It remains for us to look at the whole evidence of Marlowe's life and achievements, not merely one aspect of it. If Kyd and Frizer were speaking the truth, we are left with a concept of Marlowe as a schizophrenic personality. For how else is it possible to reconcile the man of Kyd's letters and Frizer's murderous quarrel with the poet who wrote as though he had a heart neither cruel nor intemperate, and had tasted of love and friendship:[10]

Above our life we love a steadfast friend;
Yet when a token of great worth we send,
We often kiss it, often look thereon,
And stay the messenger that would be gone.

And,

For faithful love will never turn to hate.

And,

Now are those spheres where Cupid us'd to sit,
Wounding the world with wonder and with love,
Sadly supplied with pale and ghastly death,
Whose darts do pierce the centre of my soul.

And,

Love deeply grounded, hardly is dissembled.

And,

That which hath stoop'd the chiefest of the gods,
Even from the fiery-spangled veil of heaven,
To feel the lovely warmth of shepherd's flames,
And march in cottages of strowed reeds,
Shall give the world to note, for all my birth,
That virtue solely is the sum of glory,
And fashions men of true nobility.

And,

It lies not in our power to love or hate,
For will in us is over-rul'd by fate.
When two are stript long ere the course begin,
We wish that one should lose, the other win;
And one especially do we affect
Of two gold ingots, like in each respect:
The reason no man knows; let it suffice,
What we behold is censur'd by our eyes.
Where both deliberate, the love is slight:
Who ever lov'd, that lov'd not at first sight?

And,

The man that dealeth righteously shall live.

The Tragicall Hiſtory
of the Life and Death
of Doctor FAVSTVS.

With new additions.

Written by *Ch. Marlo̱t,*

Printed at London for *Iohn Wright*, and are to be fold at his
fhop without Newgate. 1628.

Although Dr. Faustus *is full of the academic atmosphere of Marlowe's university days and reflects the inward struggle of the divinity student who dared to challenge the doctrines of the Church, it has now been assigned to a late date in the canon of Marlowe's works. It seems unlikely that it could have been written before 1592, and may have been the last play he ever completed. If this is so, it strangely and prophetically foreshadows his own tragic end.*
Both in subject-matter and in treatment it is unique among the great works of the Elizabethan age. Only Marlowe could have conceived and written it.

321

The Tragicall History of Dr. Faustus

Scenes from the production by the Old Vic 1961-2. Directed by Michael Benthall.
Photographed by Angus McBean.

CHORUS:

Now is he born, his parents base of stock,
In Germany, within a town call'd Rhodes:
Of riper years, to Wertenberg he went,
Whereas his kinsmen chiefly brought him up.
So soon he profits in divinity,
The fruitful plot of scholarism grac'd,
That shortly he was grac'd with doctor's name,
Excelling all whose sweet delight disputes
In heavenly matters of theology;

Till swoln with cunning, of a self-conceit,
His waxen wings did mount above his reach,
And melting heavens conspir'd his overthrow;
For, falling to a devilish exercise,
And glutted now with learning's golden gifts,
He surfeits upon cursed necromancy;
Nothing so sweet as magic is to him,
Which he prefers before his chiefest bliss:
And this the man that in his study sits.

This commentary is almost autobiographical, and in many ways Marlowe must have seen
his own reflection in Faustus, 'the Insatiable Speculator'. Substitute 'atheism', or what
was termed so, the result of his own insatiable thirst for knowledge, for 'necromancy',
and we have the tragedy of Marlowe.

322

FAUSTUS:
Where are you damn'd?
MEPHISTOPHILIS:
In hell.
FAUSTUS:
How comes it then that thou art out of hell?
MEPHISTOPHILIS:
Why this is hell, nor am I out of it.
Think'st thou that I, that saw the face of God,
And tasted the eternal joys of heaven,
Am not tormented with ten thousand hells,
In being depriv'd of everlasting bliss?
O, Faustus, leave these frivolous demands,
Which strike a terror to my fainting soul!

Y

FAUSTUS:

Was this the face that launch'd a thousand ships?
And burnt the topless towers of Ilium?
Sweet Helen, make me immortal with a kiss.
Her lips suck forth my soul: see where it flies!
Come, Helen, come, give me my soul again.
Here will I dwell, for heaven is in these lips,
And all is dross that is not Helena.
I will be Paris, and for love of thee,
Instead of Troy, shall Wertenberg be sack'd;
And I will combat with weak Menelaus,
And wear thy colours on my plumed crest;
Yea, I will wound Achilles in the heel,
And then return to Helen for a kiss.
O, thou art fairer than the evening air
Clad in the beauty of a thousand stars;
Brighter art thou than flaming Jupiter
When he appear'd to hapless Semele;
More lovely than the monarch of the sky
In wanton Arethusa's azur'd arms;
And none but thou shalt be my paramour!

FAUSTUS:
Ah, Faustus.
Now hast thou but one bare hour to live,
And then thou must be damn'd perpetually!
Stand still, you ever-moving spheres of heaven,
That time may cease, and midnight never come;
Fair Nature's eye, rise, rise again, and make
Perpetual day; or let this hour be but
A year, a month, a week, a natural day,
That Faustus may repent and save his soul!
O lente, lente currite, noctis equi!
The stars move still, time runs, the clock will strike,
The devil will come, and Faustus must be damn'd.
O, I'll leap up to my God!—Who pulls me down?
See, see, where Christ's blood streams in the firmament!
One drop would save my soul, half a drop: ah, my Christ!
.   .   .   .
O, it strikes, it strikes! Now, body, turn to air,
Or Lucifer will bear thee quick to hell!
O, soul, be chang'd into little water-drops,
And fall into the ocean, ne'er be found!
My God, my God, look not so fierce on me!
Adders and serpents, let me breathe a while!
Ugly hell, gape not! come not, Lucifer!
I'll burn my books!—Ah, Mephistophilis!

The fifteenth-century tower of St. Nicholas *is all that remains of the original parish church of Deptford to which the murdered body of Christopher Marlowe was brought for hasty burial in an unmarked grave on June 1, 1593, two days after his death. Tradition has it that the grave is somewhere near the north wall of the tower.*

Today the factory chimneys and cranes of Deptford's busy dockside dwarf the little church. The two skulls on the gate-posts stand as guardians of the mystery, seeming to forbid us to question the dead.

Weepe Powles, thy Tamberlaine *voutsafes to dye.*

. . . .

Is it a Dreame? or is the Highest minde
That euer haunted Powles or hunted winde,
Bereaft of that same sky-surmounting breath,
That breath that taught the Tempany to swell.
He & the Plague *contended for the game,*

The graund Dissease disdain'd his toade Conceit
And smiling at his tamberlaine contempt,
Sternely struck-home the peremptory stroke.

Gabriel Harvey: GORGON, OR THE WONDERFULL YEARE (1593)

ADAM HART (Publishers) Ltd, LONDON ENGLAND

PUBLICATIONS 1993-1994

Christopher Marlowe and Edward Alleyn

By A.D. Wraight

In 1587 the tremendous impact of TAMBURLAINE THE GREAT launched Christopher Marlowe and the young actor Edward Alleyn on a theatrical partnership that was to dominate the Elizabethan stage.

From this long-awaited study of Alleyn's theatrical career, based largely on the Alleyn Papers at Dulwich College, he emerges as a man of many parts - literally!

He was not only the greatest actor of his day, but also a minor playwright, and co-owner of the Rose Theatre with his father-in-law, Philip Henslowe.

THE ROSE Theatre takes centre stage. Recent archaeological excavation of its site has expanded our knowledge of its construction. This book re-examines the day-to-day running of the theatre, its finances, and its refurbishment in 1591-2 with a novel turret.

The hasty writing of a new play for the Rose reveals Marlowe and Alleyn *in a working relationship in the theatre,* together with Greene and Peele, which had dramatic repercussions that added fuel to Greene's long-standing hatred of Alleyn.

The relationship between Marlowe and Alleyn and the rival dramatist Robert Greene are for the first time shown in a clear light that affects significantly the vexed problem of Greene's bitter quarrel with "Shakescene" which will prove of vital interest to all students of the period.

Important, challenging, comprehensive and very readable.

UK Price £20   •   Hardback   •   520 pages   •   19 Illustrations

Oct 1993   ISBN 1-897763-00-X

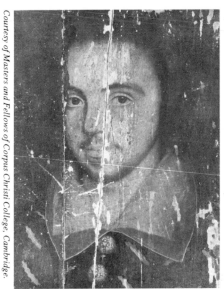

The broken portrait of Marlowe discovered 1953

Reprinted as a Tribute
for his
**QUATERCENTENARY
1593 ~ 1993**

In Search
of
Christopher
Marlowe

by
A.D. Wraight
& Virginia F. Stern

This superb pictorial biography commemmorates the great poet-dramatist, the brilliant forerunner of Shakespeare, who was murdered at Deptford in 1593 when he was aged only 29.

"In Search of Christopher Marlowe brings together everything that is known or conjectured about Marlowe from his birth to his murder . . charmingly told in prose that is just right, at times inspired. It is a superb book, poignant and intriguing."

*Eliot Fremont-Smith: **New York Times***

"A brilliant, original, and highly creative work.... the product of painstaking research - it has everything that the admirer or student of Marlowe could wish to have.... Beautifully conceived and exquisitely put together, the fruit of a collaboration astonishing in harmony and unity."

*Bernard Grebanier: **Saturday Review***

"Lavishly illustrated definitive work for ail Literary Collections."

*Frank M. Jones: **Library Journal***

UK Price £15 • High quality limpbound • 390 pages • 300 photographs
Feb 1993   248mm x 184mm   ISBN 1-897763-03-4

Forthcoming in 1994

Christopher Marlowe & The Armada

By A.D Wraight

Recent research on Christopher Marlowe reveals the exciting evidence of his participation in the greatest naval campaign of our history.

As an important intelligence agent, Marlowe was sent to assess the volatile situation in France, whether the Catholic Holy League was planning to join King Philip's 'Great Enterprise' against England. Picked up off the coast of Brittany at the last minute by Captain Fenner's ship, the *Nonpareille,* they sailed to join Drake's squadron at Plymouth.

The seal of confirmation is contained in the Armada report written for Lord Admiral Howard for presentation to Sir Francis Walsingham. This unique MS is shown to be in Marlowe's hand. An exhaustive calligraphic comparison, letter by letter, with the extant folio Leaf of Marlowe's *The Massacre at Paris* in the Folger Library establishes that the two hands are identical.

Marlowe's Armada experience is dramatically reflected in his 'Armada' play, *Edward the Third*, with the young Edward Alleyn playing the Black Prince.

This apocryphal play, attributed by some to Shakespeare, is identified as Marlowe's first English history play which launched the tremendous vogue for English historical drama (over 200 plays) dating precisely from 1588.

Marlowe was ever the great innovator of dramatic forms, and in this book he is once more revealed as the young genius consciously perfecting his art.

UK Price £25 • **Hardback** • **400 pages** • **Illustrated**

Publication Autumn 1994   SBN 1-897763-04-2

TO THE IMMORTAL MEMORY OF
CHRISTOPHER MARLOWE
WHO MET A TRAGIC DEATH
NEAR THIS SPOT ON THE 30th
MAY 1593, THIS TABLET IS ERECTED
IN 1957 BY THE ASSOCIATION
OF MEN OF KENT AND KENTISH
MEN TO REPLACE AN EARLIER
MEMORIAL UNVEILED BY
SIR FRANK BENSON ON THE
3rd JUNE 1919 AND DESTROYED
BY ENEMY ACTION IN 1940

Cut is the branch that might have grown full straight

The memorial to Marlowe in Deptford Parish Church was destroyed by bombs and resurrected by his countrymen. It is for posterity to resurrect his memory from the dust of the years and the slanders of his own superstitious age when Marlowe stood as one of the 'happy few' in the vanguard of the struggle to free men's minds from the trammels of mediævalism, and restore to him the place he rightly deserves as dramatist, poet and thinker.

> Cut is the branch that might have grown full straight,
> And burned is Apollo's laurel-bough,
> That sometime grew within this learned man.

DR. FAUSTUS, the Epilogue

Encomia

From his contemporaries:

George Peele:
'*Unhappy in thine end,*
Marley, the Muses Darling, for thy verse
Fit to write passions for the souls below.'

Edward Blount:
'*the impression of the man, that hath beene deare vnto us,*
liuing an after life in our memory'

Thomas Thorpe:
'*that pure, Elementall wit Chr. Marlow*'

Robert Greene:
'*Thou famous gracer of Tragedians*'

Michael Drayton:
'*Neat Marlowe, bathed in the Thespian springs,*
Had in him those brave translunary things
That the first poets had; his raptures were
All ayre and fire, which made his verses cleere;
For that fine madness still he did retaine,
Which rightly should possesse a poet's braine.'

John Marston:
'*Kinde Kit Marlowe*'

Henry Petowe:
'*Marlo admir'd, whose honey-flowing vaine*
No English writer can as yet attaine;
Whose name in Fame's immortall treasurie
Truth shall record to endles memorie;

.   .   .   .   .

Live still in heaven thy soule, thy fame on earth!
Thou dead, of Marlos Hero findes a dearth.
Weep, aged Tellus! all on earth complaine!
Thy chief-borne faire hath lost her faire againe:
Her faire in this is lost, that Marlo's want
Inforceth Hero's faire be wondrous scant.
Oh, had that king of poets breathed longer,
Then had faire beautie's fort been much more stronger!
His goulden pen had clos'd her so about,
No bastard aeglet's quill, the world throughout,

Had been of force to marre what he had made;
For why they were not expert in that trade.
What mortall soule with Marlo might contend,
That could 'gainst reason force him stoope or bend?
Whose silver-charming toung mov'd such delight,
That men would shun their sleepe in still dark night
To meditate upon his goulden lynes,
His rare conceits, and sweete-according rymes.
But Marloe, still admir'd Marlo's gon
To live with beautie in Elyzium.

. . . .

There ever live the prince of poetrie,
Live with the living in Eternitie.'

Thomas Nashe:
'Let me see, hath any bodie in Yarmouth heard of Leander and
Hero, of whome diuine Musæus *sung, and a diuiner Muse than him,*
Kit Marlow?'

Thomas Heywood:
'Marlo, renown'd for his rare art and wit,
Could ne'er attaine beyond the name of Kit.'

Gabriel Harvey:
'Weepe Powles, thy Tamberlain *voutsafes to dye.*

Is it a Dreame! or is the Highest Minde
That euer haunted Powles of hunted winde,
Bereaft of that same sky-surmounting breath,
That breath that taught the Tempany to swell.'

From modern critics:

Alfred, Lord Tennyson:
'If Shakespeare is the dazzling sun of this mighty period, Marlowe is certainly the morning star.'

Edward Dowden:
'If Marlowe had lived longer and accomplished the work that lay clearly before him, he would have stood beside Shakespeare.'

Charles Grant:
'Marlowe's *Dr. Faustus* was the first work which bore the unmistakable impress of that tragic power which was to find its highest embodiment in *King Lear*, *Macbeth*, *Hamlet* and *Othello*.'

John Bakeless:
'What is not apparent to the modern reader, familiar with three centuries of lyric verse, in which the lessons Marlowe had taught were applied by Shakespeare, Milton, and Keats, and a hundred others, is the amazing newness and strangeness that Marlowe's contemporaries easily discerned in his poetry.'

A. H. Bullen:
'In all literature there are few figures more attractive, and few more exalted, than this of the young poet who swept from the English stage the tatters of barbarism, and habited Tragedy in stately robes; who was the first to conceive largely, and exhibit souls struggling in the bonds of circumstance.'

Algernon Charles Swinburne:
'Of English blank verse, one of the few highest forms of verbal harmony, or poetic expression, Marlowe was the absolute and divine creator. By mere dint of original and god-like instinct he discovered and called it into life; and at his untimely and

329

unhappy death, more lamentable to us all than any other on record except Shelley's, he left the marvellous instrument of his invention so nearly perfect that Shakespeare first and afterwards Milton came to learn of him before they could vary or improve on it. In the changes rung by them on the keys first tuned by Marlowe we retrace a remembrance of the touches of his hand; in his own cadences we catch not a note of any other man's.'

Michael Poirier:
'Marlowe is one of the poets who have most nobly expressed that thirst for the infinite which haunts the human soul.'

William Allan Neilson:
'In the vastness and intensity of his imagination, the splendid dignity of his verse, and the dazzling brilliance of his poetry, Marlowe exhibited the greatest genius that had appeared in the English drama.'

Algernon Charles Swinburne:
'Marlowe is the greatest discoverer, the most daring pioneer, in all our poetic literature. Before Marlowe there was no genuine blank verse and genuine tragedy in our language. After his arrival the way was prepared, the path made straight for Shakespeare.'

Thomas M. Parrott:
'Without Marlowe there would never have been the William Shakespeare we know.

Edward Phillips:
'Christopher Marlowe, a kind of second Shakespeare.'

THE CANON OF MARLOWE'S WORKS
Tilte-pages from Marlowe's nine published works written before the age of thirty years. Apocryphal works attributed to him include the history plays, The True Tragedy of Richard Duke of York, *and* The First Part of the Contention between the Two Famous Houses of York and Lancaster, *and* The Troublesome Reign of King John, *and the domestic tragedy* Arden of Faversham, *which on both topographical as well as internal evidence is attributable to Marlowe rather than to Kyd. He may have collaborated with Peele and Kyd in such plays as* Solyman and Perseda, *and* The Spanish Tragedy. *Of shorter lyric poems, only* The Passionate Shepherd *is definitely known to be from his pen.*

330

ALL
OVIDS ELEGIES:
3 BOOKES.
By C. M.
Epigrams by J. D.
At Middleborough.

LVCANS
FIRST BOOKE
TRANSLATED LINE
FOR LINE, BY CHR.
MARLOW.

AT LONDON,
Printed by P. Short, and are to be sold by Walter
Burre at the Signe of the Flower de Luce in
Paules Churchyard, 1600.

THE
Tragedie of Dido
Queene of Carthage:
Played by the Children of her
Maiesties Chappell.
Written by Christopher Marlowe, and
Thomas Nash. Gent.

Actors
Iupiter,   Aescanius,
Ganimed,   Dido,
Venus,   Anna,
Cupid,   Achates,
Iuno,   Ilioneus,
Mercurie or   Iarbus,
Hermes,   Cloanthes,
Aeneas,   Sergestus.

AT LONDON,
Printed by the Widdowe Orwin, for Thomas Woodcocke, and
are to be solde at his shop, in Paules Church-yeard, at
the signe of the blacke Beare. 1594.

Tamburlaine
the Great.
Who, from a Scythian Shephearde,
by his rare and woonderfull Conquests,
became a most puissant and migh-
tye Monarque.
And (for his tyranny, and terrour in
Warre) was tearmed,
The scourge of God.

Devided into two Tragicall Discourses, as they were sundrie times
shewed vpon Stages in the Citie
of London.

By the right honorable the Lord
Admyrall, his seruantes.

Now first, and newlie published.

LONDON.
Printed by Richard Ihones: at the signe
of the Rose and Crowne neere Hol-
borne Bridge. 1590.

The Famous
TRAGEDY
OF
THE RICH IEVV
OF MALTA.

AS IT WAS PLAYD
BEFORE THE KING AND
QVEENE, IN HIS MAJESTIES
Theatre at White-Hall, by her Majesties
Servants at the Cock-pit.

Written by CHRISTOPHER MARLO.

LONDON;
Printed by I. B. for Nicholas Vavasour, and are to be sold
at his Shop in the Inner-Temple, neere the
Church. 1633.

THE
MASSACRE
AT PARIS:
With the Death of the Duke
of Guise.

As it was plaide by the right honourable the
Lord high Admerall his Servants.

Written by Christopher Marlo.

AT LONDON
Printed by E. A. for Edward White, dwelling neere
the little North doore of S. Paules
Church, at the signe of
the Gun.

The troublesome
raigne and lamentable death of
Edward the second, King of
England: with the tragicall
fall of proud Mortimer:

As it was sundrie times publiquely acted
in the honourable citie of London, by the
right honourable the Earle of Pem-
brooke his seruantes.

Written by Chri. Marlow Gent.

Imprinted at London for William Iones,
dwelling neere Holbourne conduit, at the
signe of the Gunne. 1594.

THE
TRAGICALL
History of D. Faustus.

As it hath bene Acted by the Right
Honorable the Earle of Nottingham his seruants.

Written by Ch. Marl.

LONDON.
Printed by V. S. for Thomas Bushell. 1604.

HERO
AND
LEANDER.
By Christopher Marlo.

LONDON,
Printed by Adam Islip,
for Edward Blunt.
1598.

The Morning Star

'The star that Marlowe sang into our skies,
With mouth of gold, and morning in his eyes'.
                                        Swinburne

It is perhaps fitting that the most appreciative of the early critics of Marlowe should have been a poet, Algernon Charles Swinburne, with whom the 20th century reassessment of Marlowe may be said to begin, in conjunction with the editing of his works and the publication of his biography by C. F. Tucker Brooke and by J. H. Ingram. In comparing Marlowe with his contemporaries Greene and Peele, Swinburne wrote: 'These three gifted men have been bracketed together by his critics for 300 years. But Marlowe differs from such people, not in degree, but in kind; not as an eagle differs from wrens and tit-mice, but as an eagle differs from frogs and tadpoles.' Comparing Marlowe, on the other hand, with his true successors, Shakespeare and Milton, he wrote: '[Marlowe] first, and he alone, gave wings to English poetry . . . among all English poets he was the first full-grown man, the first among us of their kind.'[1]

Swinburne thus placed him in the hierarchy of the truly great, the first genius of his kind, the 'morning star' of a line of lyric poets of the highest calibre. This has been conceded by others since, though more cautiously, since the critics of Marlowe have usually also doubled as the critics of Shakespeare, and have therefore laboured in the shadow cast by the more splendid light of Marlowe's great successor, and this, it would seem, has made the task difficult. But before we attempt to analyse this problem it is necessary to establish what exactly was so remarkable about Marlowe's genius.

Swinburne has stated it: '[Marlowe] began his career by a double and incomparable achievement; the invention of English blank verse, and the creation of English tragedy.'[2] This is not too much to claim, and in this assessment Swinburne is by no means alone. As Professor Bakeless has pointed out, 'the amazing newness and strangeness' of Marlowe's poetic drama was immediately striking to his contemporaries, if it is less so to us who have heard the strains of Shakespeare, Milton, Keats and a hundred others who came after.[3] The appearance of *Tamburlaine* made Norton and Sackville's *Gorboduc*, the first English drama to be written entirely in blank verse, as out-of-date as last year's fashions.

Nowhere is there to be found a more brilliantly concise assessment of Marlowe's development of the medium of English blank verse than in Professor M. R. Ridley's introduction to his edition of Marlowe's works for the Everyman Library, which has been used throughout this book for the purpose of quotations from Marlowe. Ridley effectively answers the question, What was it that Marlowe did? As he points out, it is a matter that has been subject to a certain amount of misstatement:

> 'A tacit line of argument seems to be as follows: *Gorboduc* is very monotonous; *Gorboduc* is heavily end-stopped; *Tamburlaine* is much less monotonous than *Gorboduc*. All three premises may be readily granted; but we are then presented with the quite fallacious conclusion, stated or implied, that *Tamburlaine* is therefore less heavily end-stopped than *Gorboduc*, and that Marlowe's chief contribution to blank verse is that, even as early as *Tamburlaine*, he reduced the amount of end-stopping. Marlowe in fact did nothing of the kind. If anyone will take the slightest trouble to take three passages of say twenty lines apiece at random from each play, he is likely to find that (though the monotonous regularity of *Gorboduc* sometimes seduces one into making a pause where no pause should be) the passages from *Tamburlaine* are more, not less, heavily end-stopped than those from *Gorboduc*. Marlowe's revolution was much more fundamental and vital. It concerned, not end-stopping, but the internal structure of the single line.'[4]

The writers of *Gorboduc*, in abandoning the rhymed decasyllabon and quatrain in favour of blank verse, had followed Surrey in adopting the five-metre line for blank verse in their adaptation of the classic medium of Greek tragedy, the twelve-syllable Iambic trimeter, to the less staccato English language. But so different is English from Greek that even this modification did not get over the difficulties, and instead of producing a rich and flexible medium they ended up with a tediously monotonous repetition of five equal stresses to each line ($\cdot$ — $\cdot$ — $\cdot$ — $\cdot$ — $\cdot$ —) only very occasionally substituting spondee for iamb, and with every line end-stopped. Here is a sampling of this kind of writing from *Gorboduc*:

> *Such is in man the greedy mind to reign,*
> *So great is his desire to climb aloft,*
> *In worldly stage the stateliest parts to bear,*
> *That faith and justice, and all kindly love,*
> *Do yield unto desire of sovereignty,*
> *Where equal state doth raise an equal hope*
> *To win the thing that either would attain.*

Compare this with:

> *He that with shepherds and a little spoil*
> *Durst, in disdain of wrong and tyranny,*

333

Defend his freedom 'gainst a monarchy,
What will he do supported by a king,
Leading a troop of gentlemen and lords,
And stuff'd with treasure for his highest thought!

In this passage, chosen at random from Marlowe's *Tamburlaine*, only the last of the six lines is anything approaching the conventional conception of a blank-verse line with five regular iambics. In the passage from *Gorboduc*, again chosen at random, the two young lawyers, Norton and Sackville, who wrote it for performance at the Christmas festivities of the Inner Temple in 1561/2, took their model so seriously that every one of the seven lines in the passage follows the same pattern of five regular iambics. This did not make their blank verse better than Marlowe's, in fact the contrary is quite obviously true. In Marlowe it would be hard to find anywhere seven consecutive lines repeating the regular pattern, while in *Gorboduc* one may search through an entire page before one finds even one variation such as a spondee.

As the musician learns to play his instrument and vary the tempo, as well as the pianissimo or fortissimo and the quality of his playing, so Marlowe learned to develop his use of the internal variations of his poetic line, using also feminine endings more frequently to vary the end-stopping of his blank verse. There can be no doubt that his was an exceptionally sensitive musical ear. Professor Ridley draws our attention to

'two consecutive lines which illustrate the delicate skill with which Marlowe can play variations:

Clad in the beauty of a thousand stars,
Brighter art thou than flaming Jupiter.

Each line begins with a trochee, and each has four stresses, the incidence of the first two of which is identical; but because of the slight pause after "thou", while there is no pause after the first syllable of "beauty", and of the differing distribution of the third and fourth stresses, the effect of the two lines is subtly but manifestly different.'

He then goes on to demonstrate Marlowe's ultimate achievement:

'Finally, in Faustus' last terrific speech there is a line which shows how far Marlowe now knew he could push freedom without its becoming unmetrical licence:
See, see, where Christ's blood streams in the firmament.

Five heavy stresses crowded into the first six syllables; and yet that is unmistakably an English blank-verse line, and a wonderful one. It is Marlowe's greatest gift to the poets, his fellow countrymen, who came after him, that he learned to write lines like those himself and so made possible the writing of others like . . .

O dark, dark, dark, amid the blaze of noon,
Irrecoverably dark, total eclipse.'[5]

In discussing Marlowe's development it is necessary to remember that he stands in relation to the later works of Shakespeare as the 'young Shakespeare', for had he never lived Shakespeare would inevitably have had to make for himself all those experiments in his medium which Marlowe forefashioned and which we can trace with breathless wonder in his works, marvelling at each new development of his burgeoning genius. It was in this pioneering labour that much of his creative energy was being consumed, and the critic of Marlowe who forgets this is likely to be waylaid into making odious comparisons.

It has frequently been suggested that although Marlowe was a great poet he was not a great dramatist, and that his characterisation is weak. The danger here is that his works are studied too often at the scholar's desk, and rarely seen in performance. Those who have played in Marlowe productions, even in such disparaged pieces as *The Massacre at Paris*, but half of which survives in the truncated version of Edward White, will not feel inclined to agree. *The Massacre* is full of brilliant little vignettes in which characters are on stage often for a few minutes only before being murdered, yet with a few lines to say they establish themselves as individuals. It is not overwritten, for we obviously have an abbreviated text to work from in this case, but characterisation is there, and it is strongly presented.[6] The same may be said of every one of his plays. They would not have been such successes on the Elizabethan stage if characterisation had been weak. Because Marlowe does not always write in a long speaking part for the actor does not mean that he supplies no character. On the contrary, this argues how well he understands the actor's art. He is a master of sketching in a character with a few deft lines. To take the worst example again, in the abbreviated text of *The Massacre*, of the three murderers, who have scarcely more than a couple of lines each, the Third Murderer is definitely very different in character from the other two:

> FIRST MURDERER:
> *Fear him, said you? tush, were he here, we would kill him presently.*
> SEC. MURD.:
> *O, that his heart were leaping in my hand!*

Not so the Third Murderer. He says only,

> *But when will he come, that we may murder him?*

and this is the man who then gives the game away to the Duke of Guise and warns him to fly for his life. In this same play, the Friar, who has a dozen lines, is already a strongly drawn character. No dramatist who is weak in his characterisation would be capable of sketching in a character with such economy of writing.

Tamburlaine is judged by scholars as a long epic poem about the chief character, but in performance it is full of dramatic incident, with touches of wit and

335

humour and depths of characterisation one had hardly suspected. Even when Marlowe writes little, he provides enough to give the actor a handle to work with, and throughout this, his first major work, he shows that he has the instinct for theatrical effect which lies at the heart of the true dramatist.

Michel Poirier, in his *Christopher Marlowe* (1951), wrongly assesses Marlowe as a poet first and a dramatist second, claiming that his chief weakness as a dramatist is that he 'projects his own personality into this or that fictitious hero' to the detriment of dramatic values. This may be true of the early Marlowe, but it is at this stage in particular that allowance must be made for the infantile state in which the drama existed at the beginning of Marlowe's career. Marlowe had first to re-create the dramatic idiom in a new form. Considering the condition in which he found it, it would have been surprising if he had not made some mistakes in his first attempts to stage effective plays of the new hybrid form of his own invention. Poirier himself notes the difficulties:

> 'let us only remember the condition of the English drama as depicted by Sidney in his *Defence of Poesie* written a few years before Marlowe began his career. On one side there existed a popular type of play, derived from miracle plays and moralities, without either rules or artistic values; on the other side a literary production fostered by the *literati*, but devoid of inspiration and caviare to the general. Thus it looked as if the literary drama and the popular drama were to diverge and to become sterilized, the former because too far removed from actual life, the latter because far too removed from art.'[7]

Marlowe achieved this synthesis because he bestrode both worlds; his humble origins combined with his university education to give him an insight of peculiar breadth. At the same time his art gave him the power to lift the drama to new heights on the wings of poetry. This in itself was a double achievement stamped with the audacity of genius. In the circumstances Marlowe had far more to learn about the stage and its possibilities than he had about writing poetry. It is not to be expected that he would master this new medium with one leap, but this is in effect what is sometimes demanded of him. Poirier, however, makes a concession to latent dramatic powers in Marlowe:

> 'Even so it is necessary to distinguish between what he could not and what he did not intend to do. For instance, the weakness of his characterisation is due far less to the playwright's incapacity than to his very personal conception of the drama. . . . His *Edward II* is proof that he is able, when he likes, to create an objective character living a life of his own[8] (i.e. as opposed to a larger-than-life figure who is the mouthpiece of the author's mind, characters who 'are poets like himself in their language, and still more in their yearning after beauty'[9]).

One might go further and say that it was poetry which made Marlowe a dramatist, as it made Bruno a philosopher. For while large tracts of *Tamburlaine* are indeed magnificent poetic rant, they are still imbued with drama. They remain material which the actor can 'put across', as Alleyn had found, and

336

as Guthrie and Wolfit have rediscovered. This was the fertile seed from which Shakespearean drama proliferated. But this final emergence from poet to dramatist, as far as Marlowe was concerned, was with *Edward II*. With this play Shakespearean tragedy had arrived, and it is self-evident that the distance travelled between *Tamburlaine* and *Edward II* could only have been covered by a man who possessed the essential attributes of a dramatist.

Whilst he was a poet at heart, Marlowe, the dramatist, wrote to satisfy his public—a public which craved spectacle and the vicarious thrill of blood, horror and cruelty, and was accustomed to crude stage presentation and the sights of public execution. Marlowe first educated them to better things. Even in *Tamburlaine*, which is else filled with the bloodlust that surrounded his Canterbury childhood spent near the bull-baiting yard, he extols 'sweet mercy', commends 'virtue solely as the sum of glory', and curses the man 'that first invented war'. It is in the play's loveliest lyric passages on beauty that we feel the true Marlowe is speaking rather than in Tamburlaine's bombastic thunder, whose 'high astounding terms' are the poetic expression of every young man's boasting.

Marlowe's plays, like most Elizabethan dramas, have a preponderance of male parts. It has sometimes been said that Marlowe did not like the female sex, and that his characterisation of women is poor. The latter can easily be shown to be false, the former is not so easily answered. This touches on the vexed question of Marlowe's attitude towards women. Two statements constituting documentary evidence, quoted in an earlier chapter, require further comment. Baines' Note accuses Marlowe of holding the opinion 'That all they that loue not *Tobacco* & Boies were fooles', and Kyd echoes this in his second letter when he writes of Marlowe that 'He would report St John to be our savior Christes *Alexis* I cover it with reverence and trembling that is that Christ did loue him with an extraordinary loue'. These are seemingly allusions to a homosexual tendency in Marlowe, and it has been argued by some that this is supported by the rerferences to such associations in his writings, even though these are all drawn from either classical or historic sources.

The theme of *Edward II*'s love for Piers Gaveston is drawn from history, as is the hint of such a relationship between Henry III (Anjou) and Epernoun in *The Massacre at Paris*. On the other hand, we are not particularly invited to sympathise with Edward, who is shown to be a very foolish man; and the Guise's retort, when bidden to salute Henry's 'lovely minions', could hardly be more scornful.

> *I love your minions! dote on them yourself;*
> *I know none else but holds them in disgrace.*

The question, always difficult to answer with Marlowe, is: is this Marlowe the dramatist portraying life and people as they are, or is this the opinion of Marlowe the man? The opening scene in *Dido*, showing Jupiter dandling Ganymede, and the pursuit of Leander as he swims the Hellespont by Nepture in

Hero and Leander, may also be seen as reflections of Marlowe's classical reading. These are not autobiographical writings as Shakespeare's *Sonnets* are. Yet such accusations against Shakespeare are more often vehemently denied than upheld.

On the other hand, Marlowe's handling of women is exquisitely tender and full of understanding. His portrait of Hero, 'so young, so gentle, and so debonair', could not be more sympathetically drawn, and his revelation of true love between a boy and girl from its virgin beginnings,

> *He touch'd her hand: in touching it she trembled:*
> *Love deeply grounded, hardly is dissembled,*

to its sensual climax at the end of the second sestiad is beautifully conceived. In contrast to the gentle Hero, Marlowe tosses in a delightful description of the country maid,

> *Whose careless hair, instead of pearl t' adorn it,*
> *Glister'd with dew*

whom the god Hermes pursues with hot love in one of the poem's classical digressions from the main story. This sophisticated wench is not prepared to sell her honour for anything less than a sip of the nectar of the gods which bestows immortal youth. 'All women are ambitious naturally,' remarks Marlowe.

Marlowe's *Dido*, his first dramatic essay as far as we know, attempts the characterisation of a woman in a 'star role', and from a student pen it is a remarkable achievement. His portrayal of the queen who in her passionate intensity lives and dies for love presages the full-length portrait of Cleopatra by Shakespeare. Dido is all woman, and the part offers a tremendous opportunity to the actress. Isabella in *Edward II* is no less a creature of flesh and blood, and no painted puppet. She moves us in her forlorn abandonment by Edward, whose selfishness and heartlessness towards her are well established. In the early scenes it is Isabella who wins our sympathy by her pathetic loyalty to Edward, and only her utter frustration finally drives her into Mortimer's arms and turns her into a fiend. *Tamburlaine*, too, is graced with some splendid women: Zenocrate, Zabina, and Olympia—patrician ladies, the last two, who know how to die when faced with dishonour. But Zenocrate, 'lovelier than the love of Jove', is at least half-sister to Dido and falls hopelessly in love with her captor. In *The Jew of Malta* Marlowe introduces two of his most felicitous female creations in the Jew's daughter Abigail and the artful courtezan Bellamira, who is worthy of a study to herself. The mutilated text of *The Massacre at Paris* affords one of the most delightful scenes in Marlowe—the Duchess of Guise writing her love-letter to her secret lover, at which task she is discovered by her husband. Into this one brief scene Marlowe packs a perfect little portrait of a French court lady entangled in her amours. Marlowe has also shown us what he could do with old women in his sketch of the nurse in *Dido*, an endearing old hag who comes out of the same rag-bag as Juliette's old nurse.

One may regret that *Dr. Faustus* lacks a single real woman's part, except for the brief dumb vision of Helen. Yet somehow the play is not unbalanced by this. Helen, the eternal woman, epitomizes Marlowe's yearning for beauty, and perhaps also for a realisation of love which was beyond him, but which attracted and haunted him.

Marlowe's atheism, which Baines and Kyd so bitterly attested, may similarly be reflected in the challenging cry of Orcanes, the Natolian king in *Tamburlaine*:

> *Then, if there be a Christ, as Christians say*
> *But in their deeds deny him for their Christ,*
>
> . . . .
>
> *Thou, Christ, that art esteem'd omnipotent,*
> *If thou wilt prove thyself a perfect God,*
> *Worthy the worship of all faithful hearts,*
> *Be now reveng'd upon this traitor's soul.*

Tamburlaine then flings the same challenge at Mahomet, the god of the Turks against whom he makes war, and in revenge burns their sacred books:

> *Now Mahomet, if thou have any power,*
> *Come down thyself and work a miracle:*
> *Thou art not worthy to be worshipped*
> *That suffer'st flames of fire to burn the writ*
> *Wherein the sum of thy religion rests:*
> *Why send'st thou not a furious whirlwind down,*
>
> . . . .
>
> *Well, soldiers, Mahomet remains in hell;*
> *He cannot hear the voice of Tamburlaine:*
> *Seek out another godhead to adore;*
> *The God that sits in heaven, if any god,*
> *For he is God alone, and none but he.*

That little phrase, 'if any god', betrays a doubting mind, perhaps even one ready to take the step over the brink into atheism, or agnosticism; while the challenge to Christ's divinity put into the mouth of Orcanes may be seen as a reflection of the Arrian heresy which questioned the divinity of Christ while upholding that of the supreme Deity.

Against these outbursts of the young Marlowe we have to balance the testimony of what was probably his last work, *Dr. Faustus*, in many ways his most autobiographical play. To what extent Faustus' passionate rejection of Divinity for the practice of necromancy reflects Marlowe's own choice in finally discarding a career in holy orders for literature and drama, it is not possible to say. The play contains echoes of Cambridge discourses, and Faustus' tormenting dilemma seems to bear the authentic ring of deeply felt personal experience. In it one feels that Marlowe has battled his way through the disbelief that assailed him in his youth and brought him to the verge of atheism, back to the

z

recognition of God's omnipotence that had never really left him. Ralegh also seems to have made this pilgrimage, at one time daring to question orthodox beliefs to the uttermost, and then resolving his doubts in a genuinely personal religious conviction.

In the case of a dramatist it is almost impossible to separate the personal autobiographical element in his writing from his identification of a character with its dramatic involvement in the play. Marlowe adheres so closely to his sources, moreover, that these must also be allowed to bear witness in any attempted assessment of how much his text reflects Marlowe, the man, and how much of it is the dramatist of his source material.

It is not within the scope of this biography to attempt such an assessment in detail, but Marlowe's brilliance as a dramatist should warn us that the task of discovering him behind the façade of his creations is harder than has sometimes been too confidently maintained.

The Machiavellian element in Marlowe has also come under fire. Philip Henderson's attitude may stand as typical of a certain aspect of criticism. Contrasting Marlowe's 'lack of human feeling' with Shakespeare's 'humanity', he writes (concerning the contested authorship of *Henry VI*): 'the second part is consistent in tone, and this tone we associate with Marlowe—cold clarity of intellect and a corresponding lack of human feeling'. Yet in the next instant he has to admit that Shakespeare's Richard III 'is not only a Machiavel, he has the special brand of grim humour of Marlowe's heroes', and thereupon he comments: 'but this is no more than to show how much Shakespeare was under Marlowe's influence at this time, and . . . *we recognise that Shakespeare was simply making use of the dramatic idiom of his age*'.[10] (My italics.) What is recognised for Shakespeare is, apparently, not recognised for Marlowe. Yet the two men were exactly contemporaneous in age, and a less prejudiced deduction would acknowledge the truism: had Shakespeare's life been cut short leaving only *Titus Andronicus* and *Richard III* as his bequests to posterity, the 'humanity' for which he is acclaimed would be no more apparent to us from these early works than from those of Marlowe at the same age.

The vexed problem of Marlowe's tremendous influence on Shakespeare is never more acutely brought to the fore than when such a work of disputed authorship as *Henry VI* is discussed. Dr. Allison Gaw, whose work has already been widely quoted, percipiently points out that 'there is here great danger of arguing in a circle—of assigning the finest passages to Shakespeare and then finding little worthy of the genius of Marlowe in what is left'.

The subconscious impulse to credit everything that is admirable to Shakespeare, because he has by now become a national legend rather than a historical figure (and a legend does not have to bow to historical or literary evidence), has bedevilled unbiased criticism of Marlowe. Wherever the paths of the two meet, the tendency is to push Marlowe to the wall, or simply not to find it possible to credit him with the ability to have written such a passage. Even that most sober critic, Dr. Boas, was not entirely free from the effects of the legend. He finds it 'difficult, on the face of it, to associate with the author of *Tamburlaine*, at any period of his career, the couplet (i. 167–8):

> *It lies not in our power to love, or hate,*
> *For will in us is over-rul'd by fate.*[11]

Yet there is no disputing that the above lines were written by Marlowe. Again, when acclaiming the beautifully drawn picture of Hero's surrender in love to Leander, he exclaims:

'It is an exquisite vignette, rare in Marlowe, of nature in a peaceful, gentle mood, fit background to the maiden who is herself so "whist and still".'
Finally, in dealing with *Edward II*, Boas writes:

'Mortimer's final speech, perhaps the noblest in the play,

> *Farewell, fair queen, weep not for Mortimer,*
> *That scorns the world, and, as a traveller,*
> *Goes to discover countries yet unknown,*

was recollected by Shakespeare in *Hamlet*, and expresses a philosophical self-possession we had hardly suspected.'[12]

Marlowe no sooner reveals a new development of his genius, than we have to rub our eyes and find it hard to believe. There is a tendency to take one aspect of his youthful work, a phase of his development, and to label this as 'the essential Marlowe'. Nothing is more typical of great genius than sudden, and immeasurable, leaps of development, but in Marlowe's case his genius must be typed and labelled, for fear it might somehow succeed in approximating Shakespeare's and rub some of the lustre off the legend. The two men shared their birth year, but must not be allowed to share their genius; yet it would seem that a very remarkable star was in the ascendant in that year.

In dealing with a highly gifted man it is always dangerous to set limits and say 'This he could not have written'. Who would suspect in the early works of Beethoven the potential for the tremendous development of the *Ninth Symphony*—or that the author of *The Two Gentlemen of Verona* would one day write *King Lear*?

Finally, it must be noted that the very fragmentary nature of Marlowe's work as it has come down to us makes it difficult to estimate him as he deserves. As far as we know, nothing has survived in manuscript apart from one leaf of *The Massacre at Paris*, and this has already revealed a speech of the Guise two and a half times as long as that given in the octavo edition of the printed version. Elizabethan plays perished wholesale. Thomas Heywood claims that he had a hand in at least two hundred dramas. Of his works, in part or whole, only one-tenth have survived. We may be grateful that Shakespeare's works were collected in the First Folio. Marlowe was less fortunate. As Charles Norman has remarked, 'his books had all but disappeared'. We have only mutilated copies of *Dr. Faustus*, *The Jew of Malta* and *The Massacre at Paris*, all either grossly curtailed or altered by other hands. Of his great works only

Nature, that fram'd us of four elements
Warring within our breasts for regiment,
Doth teach us all to have aspiring minds;
Our souls, whose faculties can comprehend
The wondrous architecture of the world,
And measure every wandering planet's course,
Still climbing after knowledge infinite,
And always moving as the restless spheres,
Will us to wear ourselves, and never rest,
Until we reach the ripest fruit of all,
That perfect bliss and sole felicity,
The sweet fruition of an earthly crown.

TAMBURLAINE THE GREAT, Part i. ii, vii.

342

Tamburlaine and *Edward II* have survived in what we may take to be their original form.

Edward II, considered by some to be Marlowe's most mature work, has drawn eulogies from such perceptive and diverse critics as Charles Lamb and Berthold Brecht. The former testified that the last scene had the power to move pity and terror beyond any play he had ever seen; the latter was inspired to translate *Edward II* into German. Charles Norman has written of Marlowe's superb achievement in this, the first great historical tragedy of the English stage:

> 'Much that Shakespeare was to do is found in *Edward II* in epitome, and all of it is shadowed forth in verse not even he surpassed—the steady revelation of great spirits in opposition, like planets tugging in their orbits; the searching soliloquy, and the close-packed, intense lines. Rash and intemperate Marlowe may have appeared to some, but on the evidence of this play something serene and deeply felt in him was gathering into beauty for a second harvest.'[13]

Though Norman, with other critics, sees Marlowe the man as 'rash and intemperate', like all those who come into contact with his works, he perceives that there is also 'something else'. 'In dealing with a poet', he writes, 'a chronology of violence may be less biographical than certain lines.'[14] In attempting to probe the enigma of Marlowe it is, perhaps, legitimate to balance the poet's own words, his writings, against the word of Frizer and Kyd—to argue backwards from the writings of the man, as has been done on countless occasions by the biographers of Shakespeare.

It is this apparent 'chronology of violence', in what was admittedly a violent age, and the taint of 'atheism' that have cast a murky fog around Marlowe, obscuring him even to this day; while the radiant achievement of the mature Shakespeare has shed such a backward glow upon the man that he remains the blue-eyed boy of his biographers no matter what he does: whether he sells a load of stone to Stratford corporation, sues a man for a paltry debt, or is arraigned by Privy Council order against grain hoarders in time of famine as one 'more lyke unto wolves than men'. Conversely, the picture of Marlowe as an atheist, a blasphemer, a man frequently in trouble with the law, has coloured the appraisal of his works. Partly the tendency to minimise his genius must be seen as evidence of a lurking fear lest his greatness too nearly touch Shakespeare with an imputation of plagiarism. With such inverted arguments is Shakespeare condoned and Marlowe denigrated.

It is time to redress the balance. By a careful reappraisal of Marlowe, as a man who was an exemplar of the English Renaissance in his life and liable with his compeers, Dante, Galileo and Bruno in Italy, and Ralegh in his own circle, 'to suffer the slings and arrows of outrageous fortune', as well as of his works, by regarding these as dramas to be performed, it is possible to see how truly great, as a thinker, a poet and a dramatist, he was; and to understand how much our national literature may have lost in the untimely eclipse of his superb original genius.

Select Bibliography

General Reference

(*Biographies, Critical Works & other General References*)

Bakeless, John.　　　*The Tragicall History of Christopher Marlowe*. Cambridge: Harvard Univ. Press, 1942.

Boas, Frederick.　　　*Christopher Marlowe*. Oxford: Clarendon Press, 1940.

Brooke, Tucker.　　　*The Life of Marlowe*. London: Methuen, 1930.

Cambridge Modern History. Vol. I (*The Renaissance*). London: Macmillan, 1902.

Camden, William.　　　*A Complete History of England*. London: Thomas Harper for Benjamin Fisher, 1635.

Henderson, Philip.　　　*Christopher Marlowe*. London: Longmans Green, 1952.

Hoffman, Calvin.　　　*The Murder of the Man Who Was Shakespeare*. New York: Grosset & Dunlap, 1960.

Ingram, John H.　　　*Christopher Marlowe and his Associates*. London: Richards, 1904.

Kocher, Paul.　　　*Christopher Marlowe, A Study of His Thought, Learning and Character*. New York: Russell & Russell, 1962.

Levin, Harry.　　　*The Overreacher*. Cambridge: Harvard Univ. Press, 1952.

Marlowe, Christopher.　　　*Works*. Ed. Tucker Brooke. Oxford: Clarendon Press, 1910.

Marlowe, Christopher.　　　*Works*. Everyman Edition. London: J. M. Dent, 1955.

Norman, Charles.　　　*The Muses' Darling*. New York: Macmillan, 1960.

Poirier, Michel.　　　*Christopher Marlowe*. London: Chatto & Windus, 1951.

Robertson, J. M.　　　*Marlowe, A Conspectus*. London: Routledge, 1931.

Saintsbury, George.　　　*A History of Elizabethan Literature*. London: Macmillan, 1898.

Shakespeare's England. Oxford: Clarendon Press, 1926.

Symonds, J. A.　　　*Shakespeare's Predecessors*. New York: Scribners, 1900.

Wilson, F. P.　　　*Marlowe and the Early Shakespeare*. Oxford: Clarendon Press, 1953.

Part I: Canterbury

Church, Richard.　　　*A Portrait of Canterbury*. London: Hutchinson, 1953.

Cowper, J. M. (ed.).　　　*Intrantes: List of Persons admitted to live and trade within the city of Canterbury, from 1392–1502*. Canterbury: Cross & Jackman, 1904.

Cowper, J. M. (ed.).　　　*The Register Booke of the Parish of St. George the Martyr, within the citie of Canterburie, of christenings, mariages and burials, 1538–1800*. Canterbury: Cross & Jackman, 1891.

Cowper, J. M. (ed.).　　　*Roll of Freemen of the City of Canterbury, 1392–1800*. Canterbury: privately printed, 1903.

Edwards, D. I.　　　*A History of the King's School, Canterbury*. London: Faber & Faber, 1957.

Frere, W. H. (ed.).　　　*Registrum Matthei Parker A.D. 1559–1575*. Transcribed by E. M. Thompson. The Canterbury and York Society, Oxford Univ. Press (3 vols.), 1928–1933.

Hasted, Edward.   *History and Topographical Survey of the County of Kent.* Ed. Henry H. Drake, Vols. III & IV. Canterbury: Simmons & Kirkby, 1790–1799.

Lea, Henry J. (ed.).   *Prerogative Court of Canterbury (Abstracts of Wills, Register Soame, 1620).* Boston, Massachusetts: New-England Historic Genealogical Society, 1904.

Mann, James G.   *Canterbury. The Times of Edward the Black Prince.* Canterbury: The Friends of Canterbury Cathedral, 1954.

Nichols, John.   *Progresses and Public Processions of Queen Elizabeth.* London: J. Nichols (3 vols. and Vol. IV, pt. 1), 1788–1821.

Routledge, Charles.   *Canterbury.* Kent Archaeological Society, 1858.

Part II: Cambridge to Rheims

Boas, Frederick.   *Sir Philip Sidney.* London: Staples Press, 1955.

Brodrick, James.   *The Progress of the Jesuits 1556–1579.* New York & London: Longmans Green, 1947.

Burgon, J. W.   *Life and Times of Sir Thomas Gresham.* London: Rbt. Jennings, 1839.

Carleton, George.   *A Thankful Remembrance of Gods Mercie.* London: printed by I.D. for R. Mylebourne & H. Robinson, 1625.

Catalogue of the First Exhibition of University and College Portraits Held in the Fitzwilliam Museum, May 1884. (Cambridge Antiquarian Society.)

Cooper, Thompson.   *Athenae Cantabrigenses.* Cambridge: Deighton Bell, Macmillan (3 vols.), 1858–1913.

Cooper, William D.   *Notices of Anthony Babington.* Reprinted from the 'Reliquary', No. VIII, April 1862. Sheffield: James Gilbert, 1862.

Costello, William T.   *The Scholastic Curriculum at Early 17th Century Cambridge.* Cambridge, Mass.: Harvard Univ. Press, 1958.

Dasent, John R. (ed.).   *Acts of the Privy Council.* Vols. XV and XXIV. London: Her Majesty's Stationery Office, 1897.

Digges, Dudley.   *The Compleat Ambassador.* London: Tho. Newcombe for Gabriel Bedell & Tho. Collins, 1655.

Heywood, James (ed.).   *Statutes of Q. Elizabeth for the University of Cambridge* (trans. from Latin originals). London: William Clowes, 1838–1840.

Heywood, Thomas.   *An Apology for Actors.* 1612.

Hollande, Maurice.   *Trésors de Reims.* Ed. by Michaus. Reims, 1961.

Hume, Martin.   *The Great Lord Burghley.* London: James Nisbet, 1898.

Kempe, William.   *A Dutiful Invective against the Treason of Ballard and Babington.* London: (B.L.) R. Jones, 1587.

Lamb, John.   *Master's History of the College of Corpus Christi and the Blessed Virgin Mary.* London: John Murray, 1831.

Masters, Robert.   *History of Corpus Christi College.* Cambridge: J. Bentham, 1755.

Read, Conyers.   *Mr. Secretary Walsingham and the Policy of Queen Elizabeth.* Oxford: Clarendon Press, 1925.

Sarazin, Charles.   *Les Jesuites à Reims.* Paris: Monce et Cie, 1922.

Seaton, Ethel.   'Fresh Sources for Marlowe', *Review of English Studies.* Oct., 1929.

Smith, Alan G. C. G.   *The Babington Plot.* London: Macmillan, 1936.

Smith, G. C. Moore.   *College Plays performed in the University of Cambridge.* Cambridge Univ. Press, 1923.

Smith, G. C. Moore.   'Marlowe at Cambridge', *Modern Languages Review*, Jan., 1909.

Stokes, Henry P.   *Ceremonies of the University of Cambridge.* Cambridge Univ. Press, 1927.

Stokes, Henry P.   *Corpus Christi.* University of Cambridge College Histories, 1898.

Strype, John.   *The Life and Acts of Matthew Parker.* London: John Wyat, 1711.

Tanner, J. R. (ed.).   *Historical Register of the University of Cambridge to the year 1910.* Cambridge Univ. Press, 1913.

Venn, John.   *Alumni Cantabrigiensis.* Cambridge Univ. Press, 1922–29.

Venn, John.   *Book of Matriculations and Degrees &c. 1544–1659.* Cambridge Univ. Press, 1913.

Venn, John.   *Grace book Delta, containing the records of the University of Cambridge for the years 1542–1589.* Cambridge Univ. Press, 1911.

Part III: London

Adams, Joseph Q.   *Shakespearean Playhouses.* London: Constable, 1920.

Aubrey, John.   *Brief Lives.* Oxford: Clarendon Press, 1898.

Boulting, William.   *Giordano Bruno, His Life, Thought and Martyrdom.* London: Kegan Paul, 1916.

Collier, John Payne.   *Alleyn Papers.* London: Shakespeare Society, 1843.

Eccles, Mark.   *Christopher Marlowe in London.* Cambridge, Mass.: Harvard Univ. Press, 1934.

Furnivall, F. J.   *Harrison's Description of England.* Ed. from the editions of Holinshed's Chronicles, 1577–87. London: The New Shakespeare Society, N. Trubner (3 vols.), 1878.

Harrison, G. B.   *Elizabethan Journal.* New York: Richard Smith, 1931.

Hutton, Luke.   *Blacke Dogge of Newgate.* London: (B.L.) G. Simson and W. White, 1600.

Nicoll, Allardyce.   *The Elizabethans.* Cambridge Univ. Press, 1957.

Seaton, Ethel.   'Marlowe's Map', *Essays and Studies*, 10, pp. 13–35. 1924.

Stopes, Charlotte.   *Life of Henry, Third Earl of Southampton, Shakespeare's Patron.* Cambridge Univ. Press, 1922.

Stow, John.   *A Survey of London.* London: (B.L.) J. Wolfe, 1598.

Thompson, Edward.   *Sir Walter Ralegh, Last of the Elizabethans.* London: Macmillan, 1935.

Watson, Thomas.   *Amintae Gaudia.* William Ponsonby, 1592.

Watson, Thomas.   *An Eglogue upon the Death of the Rt. Hon. Sir Fran. Walsingham.* London: Robt. Robinson, 1590.

Watson, Thomas.   *Meliboeus.* London: Rbt. Robinson, 1590.

Wilson, John Dover.   *Life in Shakespeare's England.* London: Penguin Books, 1930.

Wood, Anthony à.   *Athenae Oxoniensis.* London: Tho. Bennett, 1691–2.

Grafton Regis & Lamport Hall

Edmonds, Charles (ed.).   *Isham Reprints.* William Shakespeare. *Venus and Adonis*, 1599; *The Passionate Pilgrim*, 1599; *Epigrammes by Sir John Davies & Certain of Ovid's Elegies translated by Christopher Marlowe.* London: 1870.

Kay, Thomas.   *The Story of the Grafton Portrait.* London: Partridge, 1914.

Stopes, Charlotte.   Letter to *Times Literary Supplement*, Nov. 4, 1915.

School of Night

Bradbrook, Muriel.   *The School of Night.* Cambridge Univ. Press, 1936.

Bruno, Giordano.   *Gesammelte Werke.* Trans. by Ludwig Kahlen. Leipzig, 1904–1909.

Buckley, George T.   *Atheism in the English Renaissance.* Univ. of Chicago Press, 1933.

Chapman, George.   *Works.* Ed. by C. Algernon Swinburne and Richard Herne. London: Chatto & Windus (3 vols.), 1874.

Clark, Eleanor G.   *Ralegh and Marlowe.* New York: Fordham Univ. Press, 1941.

Hakluyt, Richard. *The Principal Navigations, Voyages, & Discoveries, etc.* London: G. Bishop & R. Newberie, Deputies to C. Barker, 1589.

Hakluyt, Richard. *Original Writings & Correspondence of the Two Richard Hakluyts.* Ed. E. G. K. Taylor. London: Hakluyt Society, Series II, 1935.

Hariot, Thomas. *A briefe and true report of the new found land of Virginia.* London, 1588.

Irwin, Margaret. *That Great Lucifer, A Portrait of Sir Walter Ralegh.* London: Chatto & Windus, 1960.

LeFranc, Abel. *Sous Le Masque de William Shakespeare.*

Memoirs of the Stanley Family. Manchester, 1767.

Peele, George. *The Honour of the Garter.* London: (f) Widowe Charlewood. J. Busbie, 1593.

Peele, George. *The Merrie Conceited Jest of George Peele, Gent.* London: (B.L.f) G.P. for F. Faulkner, 1627.

Pemberton, Henry. *Shakespeare and Sir Walter Raleigh.* London: Lippincott, 1914.

Raleigh, Sir Walter. *Scepticks or Speculations.* London: W. Bentley, 1651.

Raleigh, Sir Walter. *Works*, Vol. III. Ed. by Oldys & Birch. Oxford Univ. Press (8 vols.), 1829.

Raleigh, Sir Walter. *Writings and Letters of Sir Walter Raleigh.* Ed. by A. B. Grosart. London: Elliot Stock, 1892.

Singer, Dorothea W. *Giordano Bruno, His Life and Thought.* New York: Henry Schuman, 1950.

Singer, Dorothea W. *The Cosmology of Giordano Bruno (1548–1600).* Reprinted from *Isis*, 1941.

Stevens, Henry N. *Thomas Hariot and his Associates.* London: privately printed, 1900.

Swinburne, A. C. 'Christopher Marlowe in Relation to Greene, Peele, and Lodge', in *Letters on the Elizabethan Dramatists.* London: 1914.

Titherley, A. M. *Shakespeare's Identity. William Stanley, Earl of Derby.* Winchester: The Wykeham Press, 1952.

White, John. *True Pictures and Fashions of the People of Virginia.* Frankfurt: (f) I. Wechel for T. de Bry, 1590.

Controversy in Literary London

Adams, Joseph Q. *Shakespearean Playhouses.* London: Constable, 1920.

Chambers, E. K. *The Elizabethan Stage.* Oxford: Clarendon Press (4 vols.), 1923.

Chettle, Henry. *Kind-hart's Dreame.* London: W. Wright, 1592.

Chubb, Thomas. *Aretino, Scourge of Princes.* New York: Reynal & Hitchcock, 1940.

Collier, J. P. (ed.). *Memoirs of Edward Alleyn.* London: Shakespeare Society, 1841.

Gaw, Allison. *The Origin and Development of 1 Henry VI.* Univ. of Southern Californian Studies, 1926, Serial No. 1.

Greene, Robert. *Groatsworth of Witte, etc.* London: W. Wright, 1592.

Greene, Robert. *Life and complete Works of Robert Greene.* Ed. by A. B. Grosart. London: The Huth Library, 1881–86.

Henslowe, Philip. *Diary from 1591 to 1609.* Ed. by Walter Greg. London: A. H. Bullen, 1908.

Hutton, Edward. *Pietro Aretino.* London: Constable, 1922.

Nashe, Thomas. *Works.* Ed. by R. B. McKerrow. London: A. H. Bullen (5 vols.), 1904–10.

Sanders, Chauncey. *Robert Greene and the Harveys.* Indiana Univ. Studies, 1931.

Schrickx, W. *William Shakespeare's Early Contemporaries.* Antwerp: Nederlansche Boekhandel, 1956.

Thorndike, A. H. *Shakespeare's Theatre.* New York: Macmillan, 1916.

Walker, Leslie. *The Discoveries of Nicole Machiavelli.* Kegan Paul, 1950.

Calligraphy

Adams, Joseph Q.   'Massacre at Paris Leaf'. *The Library*, XIV, March 1934.

Brown, J. J.   'The Detection of Faked Literary MSS'. *The Book Collector*, Spring, 1953.

Tannenbaum, S. A.   *The Handwriting of the Renaissance*. New York: Columbia Univ. Press, 1930.

Tannenbaum, S. A.   *The Booke of Sir Thomas More*. New York: The Tenny Press, 1929.

Tannenbaum, S. A.   *Shakesperian Scraps, and other Elizabethan Fragments*. New York: Columbia Univ. Press, 1933.

Part IV: Scadbury

Barnard, Etwell.   *The Sheldons*. Cambridge Univ. Press, 1936.

Chapman, George.   *Hero and Leander, continuation of the Poem with Marlowe's two sestiads*. London: Felix Kingston, 1598.

Kellwaye, Simon.   *A Defensative against the Plague*. London, 1593.

Webb, Edward A., Miller, G. W., & Beckwith, J.   *History of Chislehurst*. London: George Allen, 1899.

Whitaker, Mildred.   *A History of the Shelton Family*. St. Louis, Mo.: Mound City Press, 1941.

Winter, Carl.   *Elizabethan Miniatures*. Penguin Books, 1953.

Part V. Deptford

Boas, Frederick S.   'Richard Baines, informer', *Nineteenth Century*, 112: 742–751. December, 1932.

Brown, Ford K.   'Marlowe and Kyd', *Times Literary Supplement*, 20: 355. June 2, 1921.

De Kalb, Eugenie.   'Death of Marlowe', *Times Literary Supplement*, 24: 351. May 21, 1925.

De Kalb, Eugenie.   'Robert Poley's movements as a Messenger of the Court', *Review of English Studies*, 9: 13–18. January, 1933.

Fitzroy, Almeric.   *The History of the Privy Council*. London: John Murray, 1928.

Hall, Edgar Vine.   'Christopher Marlowe's Death at Deptford Strand, 1593. Wills of Jurors at the Inquest and some other Wills'. *Testamentary Papers III*. London: Mitchell, Hughes and Clarke, 1937.

Hotson, J. Leslie.   *The Death of Christopher Marlowe*. London: Nonesuch Press, 1925.

Percy, E. S. C.   *Privy Council under the Tudors*. Oxford: B. H. Blackwell, 1907.

Seaton, Ethel.   'Marlowe, Robert Poley and the Tippings', *Review of English Studies*. July, 1929.

Southernden, John Burn.   *The Star Chamber*. London: J. Russell Smith, 1870.

Tannenbaum, S. A.   *The Assassination of Christopher Marlowe*. Connecticut: Shoe String Press, 1962.

MSS. referred to in the text are not included in the above.

Appendix

'vile hereticall Conceiptes
denyinge the deity of Jhesus
Christ our Savior fownd
emongest the papers of Thos
kydd prisoner
Which he affirmeth that he had ffrom Marlowe.'

Harl. 6848, Folio 189v.

In the Registrum Parvum, *or college admission book of Corpus Christi, Marlin is listed among the pensioners as 27th among the 28 entries for the second term of the year ending March 1580–1.*

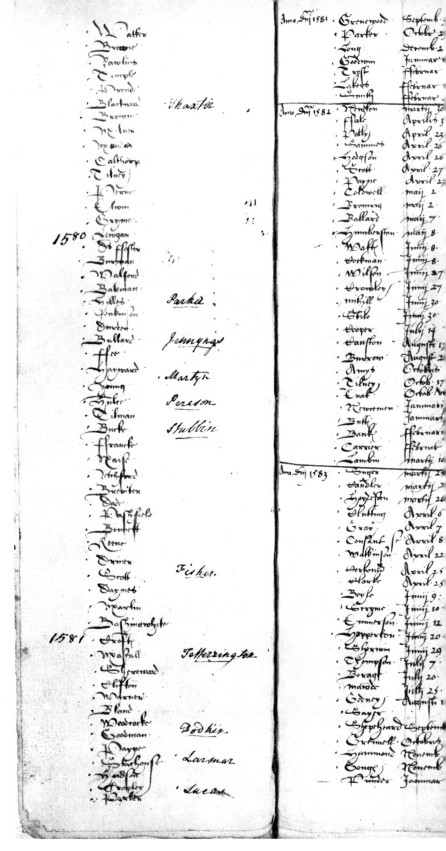

A page from the 1580 *Corpus Christi* Buttery *Book showing one of Marlowe's first purchases of beverages at Cambridge for four pence and a subsequent purchase of some item for sixpence. In the Buttery book some items are superscribed* promi, *i.e. steward, and some* co(quus) *i.e. cook. The former evidently denotes beverage purchases, the latter food. Marlowe's entry reads:*

promi
Marlin   iiij^d   vj^d

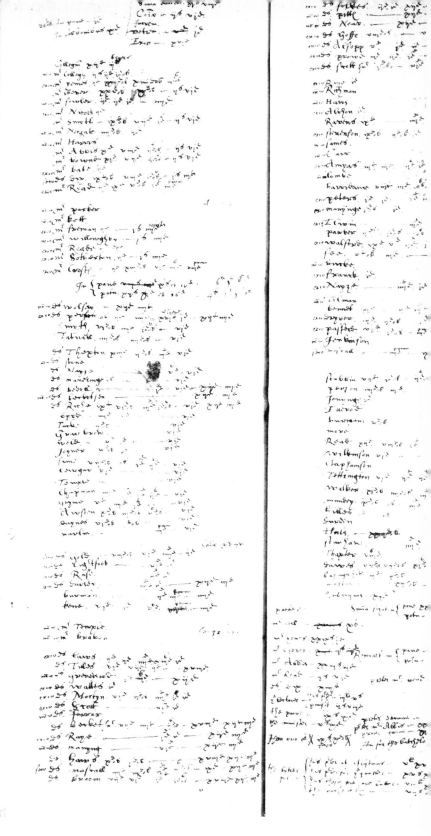

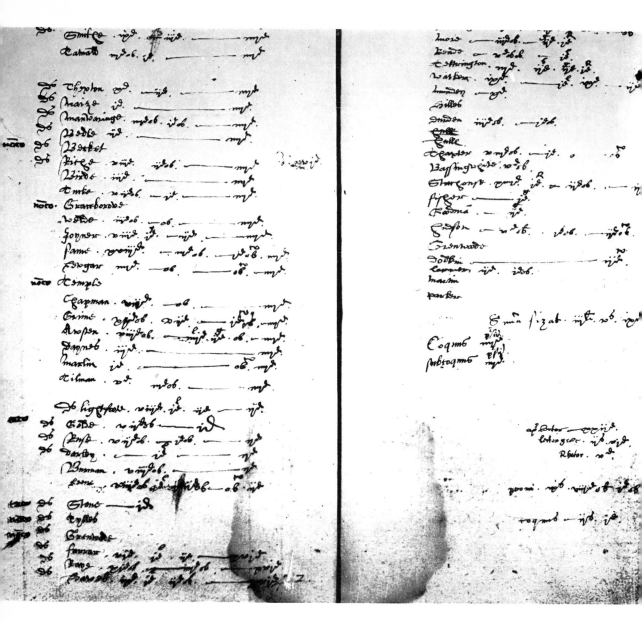

Portion of a leaf from the Corpus Christi BUTTERY BOOK showing student expenditures for beverages and food during the week of September 9, 1582. Having been given an Archbishop Parker scholarship, Marlowe was entitled to a regular allowance of one shilling weekly. Here (as 'Marlin' slightly below the centre of this excerpt in the left-hand column) he is listed as having made a purchase of one penny for a beverage, and a half-penny and fourpence for food.

(Courtesy of Corpus Christi College, Cambridge)

352

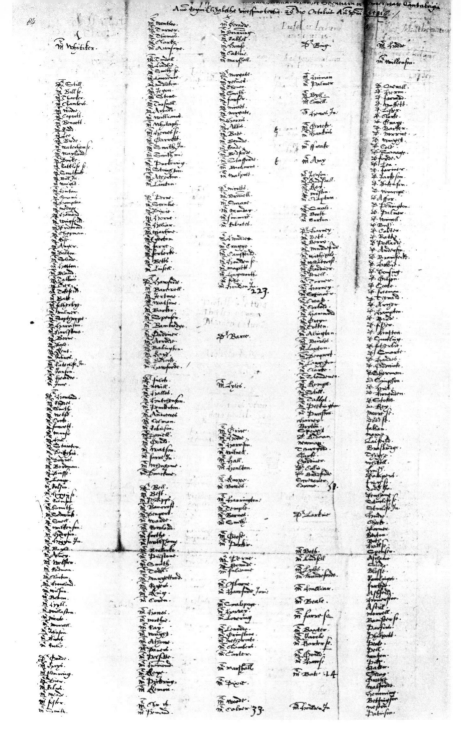

FIRST PAGE of the CAMBRIDGE LISTING (Lansdowne MS. 33, f. 84) showing its departments, professors, readers, and students on October 29, 1581. This document is headed *Nomina Professorum et Auditorum omnium artium et scientarum in Universitate Cantabrigia.* Its third page, which contains Marlowe's name, is described in the picture caption on page 54. The leaf shown above is the first part of this listing. It begins with the departments requiring highest academic standing: Theology, Hebrew, Law, Medicine, Philosophy (for graduate students). Then follows Mathematics in the right-hand column, continued in a long listing on the ensuing page.

353

Remembraunces of wordes & matters against Ric Cholmeley.

(Courtesy of British Museum: Harleian MS. 6848, f. 190, recto and verso)

That hee speaketh in generall all evill of the Counsell; sayenge that they are all Atheistes & Machiavillians, especially my Lord Admirall

That hee made certen libellious verses in Comendacen of papistes & Seminary priestes very greately inveighinge againste the State, amonge wch lynes this was one, Nor may the Prince deny the Papall Crowne

That hee had a certen booke (as hee saieth) deliverd him by Sr Robt Cecill of whom hee geveth very scandalous reporte, that hee should invite him to consider thereof & to frame verses & libells in Comendacen of constant Priests & vertuous Recusants, this booke is in Custodue & is called an Epistle of Comforte & is printed at Paris.

That he railes at Mr Topcliffe & hath written another libell Ioyntlye againste Sr Francis Drake & Iustice younge whom hee saieth hee will Couple vp together because hee hateth them alike

That when the muteny happened after the Portingale voyage in the Strand hee said that hee repented him of nothinge more then that hee had not killed my Lord Threasorer wth his owne handes sayenge that hee could not have Done god better service, this was spoken in the hearinge of Franncis Clerke & many other Souldieurs

That hee saieth hee doeth entirely hate the Lord Chamberleyn & hath good cause to so doe.

That he saieth & verely beleveth that one Marlowe is able to showe more sounde reasons for Atheisme then any devine in Englande is able to geve to prove devinitie & that Marloe tolde him that hee hath read the Atheist lecture to S^r walter Raliegh & others.

That he saieth that hee hath certen men corrupted by his p[er]suasions who wilbee ready at all tymes & for all causes to sweare whatsoever seemeth good to him, Amonge whom is one Henry younge & Iasp[er] Borage & others

That hee so highly esteemeth his owne witt & Iudgement that hee saieth that noman are sooner devyned & abused then the Counsell themselves

That hee can goe beyonde & Cosen them as hee liste & that if hee make any Complainte in behalfe of the Queene hee shall not onely bee pri[va]tely heard & enterteyned, but hee will so vrge the Counsell for money that wth out hee have what hee liste hee will Doe nothinge

That beinge imployed by some of her ma^tys prevy Counsaile for the apprehension of Papists & other dangerous men hee vsed he saieth to take money of them & would lett them passe in spighte of the Counsell.

That he saieth that william Parry was hanged drawen & quartered but in Ieste that hee was a grosse Asse overreached by Cunninge, & that in trueth hee now meante to kill the Queene more then himselfe had.

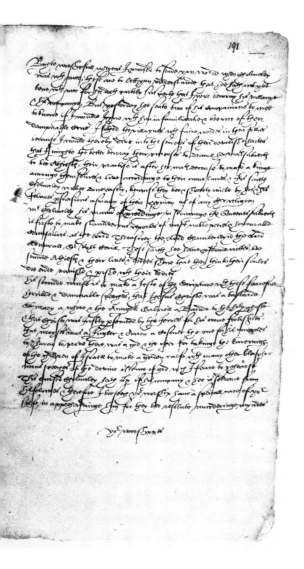

(Courtesy of the British Museum· Harl. MS. 6848, f. 191)

Righte worshypfull whereas I promised to sende you worde when Cholmeley was wth mee; these are to lett you vnderstande that hee hath not yet bene wth mee for hee doeth partely suspecte that I will bewray his villanye & his companye. But yesterday hee sente two of his Companions to mee to knowe if I would Ioyne wth him in familiarertie & becom of there damnable Crewe. I sothed the villaynes wth faire wordes in there follies because I would thereby dive into the secretes of their develishe hartes that I mighte the better bewray their purposes to Drawe her ma^{tys} subiects to bee Athiests, their practise is after her ma^{tys} Decease to make a Kinge amonge themselves & live accordinge to their owne lawes, & this saieth Cholmeley wilbee Done easely because they bee & shortely wilbe by his & his felowes p[er]suasions as many of their opynion as of any other religion. Mr Cholmeley his maner of p[ro]ceedinge in scorninge the Queenes subiects is firste to make slanderous reportes of most noble peeres & honorable Counsailors, as the Lord Threaseror the Lord Chamberleyn the Lord Admirall, Sr Robt Cecill, these saieth hee haue p[ro]founde witnes bee sounde Athiests & their lives & deedes showe that they thinke their soules doe ende vanishe & p[er]iske wth their bodies.

His seconde course is to make a Ieste of the Scripture wth these fearefull horrible & damnable speeches, that Ihesus Christe was a bastarde St Mary a whore & the Anngell Gabriell a Bawde to the holy ghoste & that Christe was Iustly p[er]secuted by the Iewes for his owne foolishnes that Moyses was a Iugler & Aaron a Cosoner the one for his miracles to Pharao to prove there was a god, & the other for takinge the Earerings of the children of Israell to make a golden calfe wth many other blasphemous speeches of the devine essence of god wth I feare to rehearse This Cursed Cholmeley hath Lx of his company & hee is seldome from his felowes & therefore I beeseech yor worship haue a speciall care of yor selfe in apprehendinge him for they bee resolute murderinge myndes

yor worshyppes

The Atheist indictment against Richard Cholmley prepared by an anonymous informer quotes the same stock-in-trade charges as were made by Baines against Marlowe. Cholmley provided the only documented evidence linking Marlowe's name with Sir Walter Ralegh when he stated that Marlowe had read the 'Athesit lecture', probably a discussion based on John Proctor's treatise (*The Fal of the Late Arrian*) to Sir Walter Ralegh and others of his circle.

AA

INGRAM FRIZER PARDON (Patent Rolls 1401, 33, 34)

The Latin document which granted a pardon to Frizer is today reposing in London's Public Record Office in the middle of one of the lengthy parchment rolls of Elizabeth's day. The stitching shown occurs at intervals throughout the roll to interlace the various sections of parchment. The pardon repeats most of the words of the Inquisition shown on page 293, omitting only that Frizer made no attempt to escape and that the jury was not cognizant of the amount of property. The document concludes with Elizabeth's pardon to Ingram Frizer for the breach of peace in the death of Christopher Morley, and is signed by the Queen at Kewe on the 28th of June, 1593. Frizer was thus given his liberty within less than a month after the murder at Deptford.

Notes—References

NOTE TO STUDENTS

The texts of quotations from original works printed in this book do not in every case reproduce the spellings of the 16th-century texts quoted. Elizabethan imprints vary considerably from each other in their renderings, slight variations existing even in copies of the same edition. The following references to the sources used are intended to direct the student to where these can be found, but do not indicate that the original spelling of the work referred to is given. All transcriptions accompanying the documents photographically reproduced are the author's transcripts from the actual documents shown and these are given in the original spellings.

Part 1. Canterbury, 1564-1580.

Page Note

2 1 Register of Baptisms of St. George the Martyr, now in the Archives of the Cathedral Chapter Library.

2 2 Boas in his *Christopher Marlowe* (1940) also notes these, Chap. I, p. 1. See Roll of the Freemen of the City of Canterbury, A.D. 1392 to 1800, transcribed from the City Chamberlains' Accounts by Joseph Meadows Cowper (1903).

3 3 John Bakeless: 'Marlowe and his Father' in *T.L.S.*, Jan. 2, 1937.

3 4 See Dr. Urry's forthcoming book on the Marlowes in Canterbury.

6 5 Hasted's *Kent*, Vol. IV, p. 419.

8 6 Hasted, op. cit., p. 433.

13 7 Cf. Shakespeare in *King Lear* upon the death of Cordelia when he develops this Marlovian 'trick' to final perfection:

    Lear: No, no, no life!
        Why should a dog, a horse, a rat have life,
        And thou no breath at all? Thou'lt come no more,
        Never, never, never, never, never.
        Pray you undo this button.

21 8 Hasted, op. cit., p. 639.

23 9 Nicholl's *Progresses of Queen Elizabeth*, Vol. I, p. 342.

26 10 A ship called *The Flying Dragon* was in and out of Dover harbour during the 1560s according to Dr. Urry. See his forthcoming book on the Marlowes in Canterbury.

29 11 Nicholl, op. cit., p. 345.

32 12 Hasted, op. cit., p. 425.

33 13 Hasted, op. cit., p. 421.

35 14 Hasted gives the statistics, op. cit., p. 421.

35 15 Acts of the Privy Council, XVIII, p. 262, ed. Dasent (1899). See S. P. Dom. Eliz. 229/12, 230/24, 82, for charges brought by Sir Thomas Perrot against Sir Roger Manwood in Dec. 1589.

36 16 Hasted, op. cit., Vol. III, p. 595.

36 17 Hasted, op. cit., Vol. III, p. 598.

36 18 Hasted, op. cit., Vol. IV, p. 566.

36 19 Hasted, op. cit., Vol. IV, p. 524.

36 20 Hasted, op. cit., Vol. IV, p. 527.

Page Note

38   I   Chap. XXVII of the 1541 Statutes. See A. F. Leach's *Educational Charters and Documents* (1911), pp. 452–469.

40   2   D. L. Edwards, *A History of the King's School, Canterbury* (1957), p. 66.

40   3   Edwards, op. cit., p. 66.

41   4   See C. E. Woodruff and H. J. Cape, *Schola Regia Cantuariensis*, pp. 79–80.

Part II. Cambridge, 1580-1587.

54   I   See Philip Henderson, *Christopher Marlowe* (1952), p. 10.

54   2   *Indenture* between John Parker and Corpus Christi College concerning Archbishop Parker's scholarship, in MSS. of C.C.C. *Statuta*, discovered by John Bakeless. See also Strype's *Life of Parker* (1831), III, p. 386, f. 2.

54   3   See G. C. Moore Smith's researches on the C.C.C. Accounts books in *M.L.R.*, Jan. 1909, supplemented by Bakeless, *The Tragicall History of Christopher Marlowe*, pp. 47–49.

55   4   H. P. Stokes, *Corpus Christi* (1898), p. 69, in the series 'University of Cambridge College Histories'.

55   5   Thomas Lever's 'Sermon' as quoted by Strype, *Eccles. Mem.*, Vol. XI, p. 424. See also J. H. Ingram, *Christopher Marlowe and his Associates* (1904), p. 68. I am indebted to Ingram's book for the very full account he gives of the university life and curriculum in Elizabethan Cambridge.

55   6   Gabriel Harvey's Letter to Edmund Spenser, 1579. *The Works of Gabriel Harvey*, ed. A. B. Grosart, Vol. I, pp. 137–8.

59   7   Burton, *David's Evidence* (1596); Stokes, op. cit., p. 84.

QUOD ME NUTRIT ME DESTRUIT

64   I   This suggestion was put forward by the architect in charge of the repairs for the Master's Lodge at Corpus Christi, Mr. Donovan Purcell, M.A., F.R.I.B.A., of Purcell & Johnson, Chartered Architects, 64 Bethel St., Norwich, who so kindly furnished replies to my enquiries concerning the work then carried out. A box-fender construction was removed at the time.

66   2   I am indebted to Dr. J. P. T. Bury, then Acting Librarian at Corpus Christi, for his interest in furthering enquiries for me, and to Dr. J. P. C. Roach, Bursar to the College, for giving me what information was then available concerning the sudden reappearance of the portrait.

67   3   See Calvin Hoffman's *The Murder of the Man who was Shakespeare* (1960), Grosset & Dunlap, paperback ed., pp. 242–244.

68   4   This heraldic device and motto appear in *Les Devises Heroique de M. C. Paradin* (1563) and in the English version of 1591. Both Marlowe and Shakespeare seem to have been interested in Paradin's work.

68   5   Hoffman first drew attention to the interesting parallels in the Shakespeare quotations and the motto on the Corpus Christi portrait. Op. cit., p. 240.

70   6   Boas, op. cit., pp. 14–15.

71   7   The collection of 16th- and 17th-century portraits now in the new Master's Lodge are believed to have formerly hung in the old Master's Lodge, formerly Matthew Parker's residence, which is where Copcott would have dwelt.

          *   *   *

76   8   William Harrison, *The Description of Britaine*, in Raphael Holinshed's *Chronicles* (1587). See F. J. Furnivall's ed. of *Harrison's Description of England* (1878), Part I, pp. 77–8.

80   9   Ingram quotes this story in *Christopher Marlowe and his Associates*, giving the source as H. P. Stokes' 'An Interrupted Performance' in *The Benedict*, Lent Term, 1899, pp. 3–8.

81   10   Photograph from the production of *Dido Queen of Carthage* by Michael Ferguson who directed this first revival of the play since Marlowe's day in August 1959, when it was performed at the Questors Theatre in Ealing, London. A second revival was staged by the Marlowe Society in London in 1964 in honour of Marlowe's quatercentenary.

85   11   See J. H. Ingram, op. cit., pp. 64–92.

86   12   Marlowe's translation of Lucan's *Pharsalia*, 1, 567.

86   13   Boas, op. cit., p. 14.

88   14   Privy Council Registers, Elizabeth, vi, 381 b, Public Record Office. Dr. Hotson first identified the 'Christofer Morley' of this letter as Christophere Marlowe, the poet, as distinct from a contemporary Christopher Morley of Trinity College, Cambridge, who became a seminary priest. See Hotson's *The Death of Christopher Marlowe* (1925), pp. 57–64, in which this important fact is established. The members of the Privy Council who testified to Kit's 'good service' were: the *Lord Archbishop* (Whitgift), *Lord Chancelor* (Sir Christopher Hatton), *Lord Threasurer* (Lord Burghley), *Lord Chamberlaine* (Lord Hunsdon), *Mr. Comptroler* (Sir James Crofts).

THE QUEEN'S SECRET AGENT

92   1   Burgon, *Life and Times of Sir Thomas Gresham*, i, 95n.

92   2   Lloyd's *State-Worthies* (1670), p. 516.

92   3   Philip Henderson, op. cit., p. 24, mentions this, giving as his only source Michel Poirier, *Christopher Marlowe*, p. 25.

96   4   See Bakeless, *The Tragicall History of Christopher Marlowe*, Vol. I, pp. 161–2, for interesting details of Thomas Walsingham's career in espionage. Thomas' older brother, Guldeford, had also been employed as an agent in 1578. It was evidently a family concern.

96   5   Sir Francis Walsingham's London residence was situated in Seething Lane, near the Monument.

96   6   Eugenie de Kalb, 'Robert Poley's Movements as a Messenger of the Court, 1588 to 1601', in *R.E.S.*, Jan. 1933, pp. 13–18.

Part III. London, 1587-1593.

THE CITY

105   1   The translation is taken from W. B. Rye's *England as seen by Foreigners* (1865).

106   2   Map of Moorfields, 1599. I am indebted to Mr. Tom Miles for drawing my attention to this fascinating map of the Norton Folgate district in which Marlowe was living, which was only discovered in 1962. M. R. Holmes, Curator of the London Museum, has presented his researches most excitingly in his *Moorfields in 1599* (published by H.M. Stationery Office, 1963). However, he fails to mention Marlowe's connection with the district shown. Eccles notes (*Christopher Marlowe in London*, 1934, p. 159) that Watson was evidently residing in St. Helen's, Bishopsgate, where he was tutor to William Cornwallis' son, in 1587, when Marlowe first arrived in London. Two years later they are both living in the suburbs just without Bishopsgate. Robert Greene was buried in the 'New-Churchyard neere Bedlam' (Harvey's *Foure Letters*) shown on the map, and his mistress, the sister of 'Cutting Ball', lived with their bastard son, Fortunatas Greene, at Shoreditch. Another of Marlowe's cronies, Robert Poley, also lived in Shoreditch. The district is thus redolent with Marlowe connections, as well as those of Shakespeare.

THE BRADLEY AFFRAY

117   1   See Mark Eccles' *Christopher Marlowe in London*, 1934, for the full account and documentation of this important discovery.

Documents: Middlesex Sessions Roll 284, 1 October, 31 Elizabeth (1589), translated and summarized by J. C. Jeaffreson in his *Middlesex County Records* (1886), i, 189; concerning Marlowe's sureties for his appearance to answer charges at the next sessions for Newgate; Public Records Office, *Chancery Miscellanea*, Bundle 68, file 12, no. 362, for writ and return into Chancery of the Gaol Delivery at Newgate, quoting the Coroner's inquisition on William Bradley; and Watson's Pardon in the Patent Rolls, 32 Elizabeth, part 4, C 66/1340.

117   2   George Orrell has been identified by Mark Eccles. (See Eccles, op. cit., pp. 62–4.) Orrell's belligerent character later found its satisfaction in military service abroad, where he became 'Captain Orrell, a tall man, a follower of Lord Monteagle' (*Calendar of State Papers relating to Ireland, 1601/3* (1912), p. 113). He also played a prominent part in the skirmishes during the Essex rebellion when 'he did run and leap in the forefront with Sir Christopher Blunt and Mr. Bushell, their weapons drawn, crying, "Saw, saw, saw, saw, saw, tray, tray"', and it was noted that he held 'his neck awry'. (Letter from William Reynolds to Cecil: Historical MSS. Commission, *Calendar of the MSS. at Hatfield House*, XI (1906), 46 of p. 44 and XIV (1923), 171.)

117   3   This record was discovered by J. L. Hotson in the Queen's Bench Controlment Rolls, P.R.O., K.B. 29/226, membrane 119, and is quoted by Eccles, op. cit., p. 57.

117   4   Quoted verbatim in the Inquisition.

118   5   This 18th-century street map was kindly loaned for this publication by Mr. Tom Miles.

119   6   Dr. Eccles' discovery of Marlowe's recognizance in the Middlesex Guildhall, London (Middx. Sessions, Roll 284), has corrected the error of ten days in the date (Sept. 28 instead of 18) regarding the Bradley/Watson affray repeated by the Chancery records and the Pardon.

120   7   See p. 127 for the Epitaph and a translation.

121   8   Middx. Sessions, Roll 309, no. 13, entry May 9, 1592: 'Christofer Marle his Recognizance'. For the full account of this interesting find see Eccles, op. cit., pp. 104–9. Charles Norman, *The Muses' Darling*, p. 138, gives an English translation of the document.

121   9   Tucker Brooke, followed by J. L. Hotson, first identified these sureties. See Hotson's 'Marlowe among the Church-Wardens', *The Atlantic Monthly*, July 1926. See also Eccles, op. cit., Chap. IV, pp. 69–101.

121   10   Boas, op. cit., pp. 105–7.

121   11   Bakeless puts the point of view: 'That these two reputable businessmen were willing to be sureties for the godless playwright speaks fairly well for his character; and that so poor a bondsman as Rowland that was acceptable to the authorities at all may mean either that they regarded Marlowe himself as prosperous enough to make possible a levy of forty pounds; or else that they did not regard the murder charge very seriously, or even that official influences were again at work on Marlowe's behalf.' *The Tragicall History of Christopher Marlowe*, Vol. I, p. 103.

121   12   See Richard Baines' Note, p. 309.

122   13   Eccles, 'Marlowe in Newgate' in *T.L.S.*, September 6, 1934.

123   14   For full details of this episode see Dr. Urry's forthcoming book on the Marlowes in Canterbury. William Urry's researches in the archives there have disclosed Kit's presence in Canterbury in the autumn of 1592 when he was involved in a fight with William Corkine, a tailor and part-time musician at the Cathedral, who was probably the father of William Corkine, the lutenist, who so delightfully set to music Marlowe's 'Come Live with Me and be My Love'. The duel was not a fatal one, and it is nice to know that Corkine and Marlowe were happily reconciled at the end of the story.

Page	Note	
123	1	Eccles, *Christopher Marlowe in London*, p. 129.
124	2	The English translation of Watson's Latin dedication (which is in verse) is here quoted from Dr. Eccles, who first published an English rendering of part of this work in *Christopher Marlowe in London*, pp. 130–1.
124	3	Entry: '15 die D. Watonus Parisios hinc abiit' on October, 1576, and in May, 1577, '15 die Mr. Tho. Watsonus e Parisiis huc revertitur et post aliquot dies ad nostra communia est admissus' (*Calendar of State Papers, Foreign Series, of the Reign of Elizabeth*, 1575–77 (1880), p. 567; 1579–1580, pp. 219, 251). See Eccles, op. cit., p. 137.
127	4	See Eccles, op. cit., Chap. IX, 'A Dedication by Marlowe'.
128	5	The translation of Marlowe's Latin *Dedication* is here given according to the rendering by Dr. Eccles, who first published an English version, op. cit., p. 166, and drew attention to this dedication.

THE SCHOOL OF NIGHT

132	1	J. H. Ingram, op. cit., pp. 91–2.
133	2	John Aubrey, *Lives of Eminent Men* (1813), ed. Andrew Clark, Vol. II, p. 513.
134	3	Sir Robert Naunton, *Fragmenta Regalia* (1641), pp. 33, 35.
135	4	Eleanor Grace Clark, *Ralegh and Marlowe* (1941), p. 229, requoted from Oldys, p. 33.
137	5	Op. cit., p. 265.
139	6	Op. cit., p. 269.
139	7	Aubrey, op. cit., Vol. II, p. 368.
141	8	Hariot's MSS. are in the British Museum in the Egremont Collection, Addit. MSS. 6782–9, and Harleian MSS. 6001–2, 6083.
141	9	Discovered by Baron Zach at Petworth Place beneath a pile of shabby accounts in 1784. See Henry Stevens, *Thomas Hariot and his Associates* (1900), for his comments on this.
147	10	William Sanderson, a wealthy London merchant who married Ralegh's niece, also contributed to financing the Virginia voyage of 1584, and became one of Raleigh's staunchest supporters in all his colonising ventures.
150	11	See Hakluyt Society's Publications, iii (1848), Introduction, p. xxix.
151	12	Hariot's Will is published by Henry Stevens, op. cit., in the Appendix. Torporley was entrusted with the task of posthumously editing Hariot's voluminous MSS. which he began, and after Torporley's death Sir. Tho. Aylesbury and Walter Warher saw Hariot's treatise on algebra through the press.
151	13	Eleanor Grace Clark, op. cit., p. 279.
151	14	Aubrey tells us: 'He [Hariot] made a philosophicall Theologie, wherein he cast off the Old Testament, and then the New would (consequently) have no foundation. He was a Deist. His doctrine he taught to Sʳ Walter Raleigh, Henry Earle of Northumberland, and some others' (Aubrey, op. cit., Vol. II, p. 369). The 'others' evidently included Marlowe.
152	15	Charles Norman gives a very full quotation of the proceedings at Cerne Abbas in his *The Muses' Darling* (1947), pp. 211–17.
152	16	Aubrey, op. cit., Vol. II, p. 519.

Robert Parsons, a Jesuit pamphleteer, accused Ralegh of atheism in his *Responsio ad Elizabethae edictum* (1592). The English version gives:
'Of Sir Walter Rawleys school of Atheisme by the waye, & of the Coniurer that is Master thereof, and of the diligence vsed to get yong gentlemen of this schoole, where in both Moyses, & our Sauior, the olde and the new Testaments are iested at, and the schollers taughte, among other thinges, to spell God backwarde!'
It would be as unjust to believe that Ralegh really indulged in this kind

of nonsense, as it is to credit Marlowe with the blasphemies later alleged by the informer Baines. If we had Marlowe's accredited treatise on the Trinity, probably this would compare most interestingly with Ralegh's *Treatise on the Soul*, and reveal Marlowe as a philosophical thinker on religion. Hariot (who is evidently referred to as the 'Coniurer' above) must also be seen in the same light regarding his rationalisation of religion.

153 17 *The Works of Sir Walter Ralegh, Knt.*, ed. Oldys and Birch (1829), Vol. VIII, pp. 573–83.

156 18 Nashe, *Have with you to Saffron-Walden* (1596), from *Works*, ed. R. B. McKerrow, III, p. 80.

160 19 Quoted by E. G. Clark in *Ralegh and Marlowe*, p. 266.

162 20 William Camden, *Annales* (3rd ed., 1635), p. 423.

164 21 Quoted by Dorothea Singer, *Giordano Bruno, His Life and Thought* (1950), p. 25.

166 22 This description is rendered in the translation by William Boulting in his *Giordano Bruno, His Life, Thought and Martyrdom* (1916), p. 112. Other translations form the First and Second Dialogue (except where otherwise stated) are retranslated from the German of Ludwig Kahlen, *Giordano Bruno, Gesammelte Werke* (1904–1909).

168 23 Matthew Gwinne was an Oxford don of St. John's College, a Welshman whose acquaintance Bruno first made at Oxford. He is probably the 'Mr. Guin' of this story.

169 24 Translation from Boulting, op. cit., p. 111.

170 25 From the Third Dialogue as translated by Dorothea Singer, op. cit., pp. 302–3.

171 26 Stevens, op. cit., p. 117, prints this letter (B.M. Addit. MS. 6789).

172 27 Dorothea Singer, *The Cosmology of Giordano Bruno (1548–1600)*, p. 196. This paper was read before the International Congress of the History of Science, Prague, 1938, and published in 1941. Singer's works on Bruno have proved an invaluable source for this chapter.

172 28 Ibid, p. 193. From *De Immenso et Innumerabilis*, Lib. I, cap. 7.

172 29 Singer, *Giordano Bruno, His Life and Thought*, p. 61. (From *De Immenso et Innumerabilis*, Lib. II, cap. 12.)

173 30 Bruno was facing his judges in Rome for the first time on May 26, 1592, almost exactly one year before Marlowe's tragedy.

173 31 Singer, op. cit., p. 229. (From the Introductory Epistle to *De Immenso et Innumerabilis*.)

173 32 Singer, op. cit., p. 61.

173 33 From the translation by William Boulting of the third Sonnet in the Introduction to *De Immenso et Innumerabilibus*, op. cit., p. 139.

174 34 Singer, *Giordano Bruno, His Life and Thought*, p. 4.

174 35 E. G. Clark, op. cit., p. 280.

174 36 Singer, op. cit., p. 248. Translation of the second Sonnet in the Introduction to *De Immenso et Innumerabilibus*.

MARLOWE AND THE STATIONERS

176 1 'The Waterman' from Sir Thomas Overbury's *Characters* (1614–16).

177 2 Kyd's Letter to Sir John Puckering. See p. 315.

179 3 From the Quarto edition of *Hero and Leander* by Adam Islip in the Folger Shakespeare Library, the single surviving copy of Blount's 1598 publication of Marlowe's two sestiads without Chapman's continuation of the poem.

CONTROVERSY IN LITERARY LONDON

181 1 The D.N.B. quotes this giving Thomas Nashe's *Lenten Stuffe* (1599), v. 241, as source, but this appears to be an error.

181 2 Thomas Nashe, *Have with You to Saffron-Walden*, from *Works*, ed. R. B. McKerrow, III, p. 127.

181 3 Nashe states that he had 'not trauaild far'. See McKerrow's 'Introduction' to his edition of Nashe's *Works* (1910) for discussion of how far this might have been. I am inclined to agree with McKerrow that he probably did not reach Italy, as some writers have assumed.

182 4 Richard Harvey entered Pembroke Hall in 1575, graduating B.A. in 1577/8 and M.A. in 1581, whereupon he was elected a fellow of his college and seems to have remained at the university for some years after, so that Marlowe would doubtless have known of him there, as Nashe certainly did. Both the Harveys were conspicuous at Cambridge.

182 5 Nashe's *Have with You to Saffron-Walden,* from *Works,* ed. R. B. McKerrow, III, p. 85.

184 6 See Nashe's *Strange Newes,* op. cit., I, pp. 287–8.

184 7 Epistle to the Reader, *Christs Teares over Ierusalem* (1593), op. cit., II, p. 12.

184 8 Gabriel Harvey, *New Letter of Notable Contents* (1593), C. 4v.

184 9 Transcript of the Stationers' Register, ed. Arber, iii, p. 677.

184 10 Thomas Middleton, *The Ant and the Nightingale* (1604).

185 11 Nashe's 'Preface' to Greene's *Menaphon* (1589), from *Works,* ed. McKerrow, IV, p. 311. McKerrow doubts that these jibes are intended for Marlowe since Nashe claimed that he 'neuer abusd Marloe . . . nor anie that vsde me like a friend'. But that was long after. In 1589 Nashe was at the beginning of his literary career, and closely associated with Greene, who leaves us in no doubt as to his opinions of Marlowe's literary efforts. Nashe's address 'To the Gentleman Readers of Both Vniuersities' is a general tirade against 'Rhetoritians' and 'vaine glorious Tragedians' who 'embowell the clowdes in a speach of comparison: thinking themselues more than initiated in poets immortalitie, if they but once get *Boreas* by the beard, and the heauenly Bull by the deaw-lap'. Marlowe's fondness for references to Boreas in *Tamburlaine* is particularly striking. Since *Tamburlaine* was the play of the moment which was resounding with such eclat, it seems obvious that Nashe was referring to this when he wrote: 'How is it, then, our drowping wits should so wonder at an exquisite line, that was his Masters day-labour?' With Marlowe he also taunts Kyd, whose *Spanish Tragedy* had likewise made a recent 'hit' through the London 'Stage-mans throate'.

185 12 Preface 'To the Reader', *Christs Teares over Ierusalem* (1594), from *Works,* ed. McKerrow, II, p. 180.

185 13 Dekker, *Newes from Hell* (1606).

185 14 'The Choosing of Valentines' by Thomas Nashe (possibly written for the Earl of Southampton?) in Inner Temple MS. 538. This is printed in McKerrow's edition of Nashe's *Works,* III. Harvey comments on Nashe's 'idle vanityes' and 'filthy Rymes', though his own verses are not exactly a model of propriety. (See *Pierce's Supererogation,* 1593.)

ROBERTO GREENE AND THE ACTOR MANAGER OF THE ROSE

187 1 Greene's *Perimedes the Blacke-Smith* (1588), letter 'To the Gentlemen Readers'. This appears to refer either to Marlowe's saucy Prologue to *Tamburlaine* or some other lines not now in the printed edition. Greene writes: 'I keepe my old course, to palter vp something in Prose, vsing mine old poesie still, *Omne tulit punctum,* although latelye two Gentlemen Poets, made two mad men of Rome beate it out of their paper bucklers: & had it in derision, for that I could not make my verses iet vpon the stage in tragicall buskins, euerie word filling the mouth like the faburden of Bo-Bell, daring God out of heauen with that Atheist *Tamburlan* or blaspheming with the mad preest of the sonne: but let me rather pocket vp the Asse of *Diogenes:* then wantonlye set out such impious instances of intollerable poetrie: such mad and scoffing poets, that haue propheticall spirits, as bred of *Merlins race* . . .' (Greene's *Works,* ed. A. B. Grosart, Vol. VII, pp. 8–9, Huth

Library, 1881–6). Greene could not leave Marlowe alone, and attacks him again in his *Farewell to Folly* (1591) when he calls him a 'propheticall full mouth' that was 'a Cobblers eldest sonne' and boasts that his own works were proving so popular that the pedlar 'found them too dear for his pack, and was fain to bargain for the life of *Tamburlaine* to wrap up his sweet powders in those unsauoury papers'. Harvey indeed refers to Greene as one 'tormented with other mens felicitie' (*Foure Letters*).

189 2 See Letter from Gabriel Harvey to Spenser, quoted p. 55.

191 3 This view was also upheld by Ralegh, whose political and religious attitude is closely reflected by Marlowe. Ralegh wrote: 'History doth plainly tell us, that that furious war (which broke out in France) in the reign of Francis II, and which occasioned most barbarous murders, devastations, and such other calamities (which are the most common products of civil commotions, and by continuing nearly forty years had reduced France to the last misery), was begun and carried on by some few great men of ambitious and turbulent spirits, *deluding the people with the cloak and mask of religion* to gain their assistance to what they did more especially aim at.' (My italics.) With a clear eye he saw Protestants and Catholics alike resorting to religious slogans to further their own ends. 'It is plain that the admiral Coligny advised the Prince of Conde to side with the Huguenots, not only out of love to their persuasion, but to gain a party, and be made thereby the stronger.' Thus he exposes Conde, the Huguenot hero, and with equal candour condemns the Catholic zealots: 'Neither can any man think that the papists, out of the principle of the Christian religion, which enjoins us to be meek and charitable, did in a few days' space cut the throats of nearly thirty thousand Protestants in France. . . .' (From *The Works of Sir Walter Ralegh, Kt.*, Oxford, 1829, Vol. VII, p. 284.)

194 4 F. E. Halliday, *A Shakespeare Companion, 1550–1950*, pp. 162–3.

196 5 Allison Gaw, *The Origin and Development of 1, Henry VI* (1926), pp. 75–6.

197 6 Ivor Brown, *Shakespeare* (1949), p. 157.

198 7 Allison Gaw, op. cit., p. 143.

199 8 Ibid, p. 144.

200 9 Ibid, p. 54.

200 10 Ibid, pp. 57–8.

201 11 Ibid, p. 59.

202 12 Nashe in his *Pierce Penilesse* (1592) is (if the arguments put forward hold) referring to the play written by his friends Marlowe, Greene and Peele.

203 13 Allison Gaw, op. cit., p. 84.

203 14 Ibid, p. 60.

203 15 Ibid, p. 61. The foregoing arguments in this chapter constitute little more than a summary of Dr. Gaw's brilliant book. The conclusions concerning Edward Alleyn's part in *harey the vj* are my own.

204 16 Ibid, p. 83.

205 17 Dr. Gaw writes (op. cit., pp. 414–24): 'C's treatment of his sources . . . is distinctive. While none of the other collaborators hesitate to adapt and add to the historical facts freely in order to obtain dramatic effects, no one so extravagantly wrests history as C. . . . In order to obtain the effect of Joan in the turret with the flaming signal (III, ii, 1–32) he combines details from the English capture of Evreux by stratagem, transferred from the English to the French credit, with the story of the cresset of light at the time of the French capture of Le Mans (in Holinshed twenty-one pages distant) and applies both to a wholly fictitious capture and recapture of Rouen. . . . Stylistically also C stands apart: he makes Joan speak of "*the* Talbot", address the French king and nobles as "your honors", and use the odd phrase "unto Parisward"; he employs the Latinisms "Talbotites", "extirped" and "expulsed" . . . and his versification is markedly alliterative.'

206 18 At the end of his tale Greene informs the reader of so much: [Roberto's] 'life in most parts agreeing with mine . . . hereafter suppose me the saide *Roberto*'.

210 19 Gaw, op. cit., p. 151.

210 20 Op. cit., p. 168.

213 21 Nashe, *Have with You to Saffron-Walden*, from *Works*, ed. McKerrow, III, p. 131.

TWO PORTRAITS

218 1 *The Connoisseur*, February 1909, p. 100, questioning the attribution to Shakespeare, remarks: 'Is it credible that an obscure youth, occupied in a vocation more or less inglorious, should have been honoured by a painter of ability in a manner usually reserved for men and women of position or established reputation?'

220 2 Thomas Kay, *The Grafton Portrait of Shakespeare* (1914), p. 70.

221 3 Ibid, p. 73.

221 4 Ibid, p. 43.

223 5 The discovery at Lamport Hall of two copies of the 1598 *Hero and Leander* and of other rare Elizabethan volumes was reported by Sir Charles Edmonds in the *Gentleman's Magazine*, 1867, Vol. IV.

MARLOWE'S MANUSCRIPT: A COMPARISON OF CALLIGRAPHY

227 1 Boas, *Christopher Marlowe* (1940) prints the two versions of this scene from *The Massacre at Paris*. See also J. Q. Adams, 'Massacre at Paris Leaf' in *The Library*, XIV, March 1934.

232 2 S. A. Tannenbaun, *The Booke of Sir Thomas Moore* (1927), Chap. VII, p. 59, for the identification of Chettle's and Heywood's holographs.

KYD AND THE BOOK OF SIR THOMAS MORE

235 1 *Acts of the Privy Council*, ed. Dasent, Vol. XXIV, p. 222.

236 2 B.M. Harl. MS. 7368. Reproduced in *The Booke of Sir Thomas More*, Malone Society Reprint (1911), Sig. A.

236 3 'The Booke of Sir Thomas More' (Harleian MS. 7368) was investigated by Sir Edward Maunde Thompson, then Director and Principal Librarian of the British Museum, who attempted to prove, on palæographic grounds, that the handwriting of the three folio pages which constitute the revised insurrection scene in the MS. is identical with that of the seven signatures of William Shakespeare (*Shakespeare's Handwriting: A Study*, pp. ix, 63, Clarendon Press, Oxford, 1916). A. W. Pollard commented: 'Sir E. M. Thompson's arguments were respectfully received and there was a general acknowledgment by reviewers of the exceptional skill with which the scanty evidence was marshalled and analysed. . . . Thoroughly to test the conclusions reached requires not only some preliminary knowledge, but much patient investigation and a gift of palæographic vision of a very unusual kind.' (Introduction, p. 11, in *Shakespeare's Hand in the Play of Sir Thomas More*, Cambridge University Press, 1923, by A. W. Pollard, Sir E. Maunde Thompson, J. Dover Wilson, R. W. Chambers, and W. W. Greg.) Dr. S. A. Tannenbaum subsequently proceeded to demolish the arguments put forward by these scholars (*The Booke of Sir Thomas Moore*, Tenny Press, New York, 1927). He summarizes his findings thus: 'On the basis of Shakespeare's extant seven autographs the test of handwriting is at present overwhelmingly against the assumption that he wrote those three pages' (p. 69). Tannenbaum suggests Peele or Marlowe as a more likely author; but the discovery of Marlowe's signature, and the comparison with this and the Folio Leaf of *The Massacre at Paris*, has convinced the authors of the present work that it certainly was not Marlowe. The bold loop of the 'h' in particular, as well as formation of other letters, and the pen-pressure of the

writing designated hand D in 'The Booke of Sir Thomas More', does not correspond with Marlowe's autograph. Peele's hand only survives in the italic style, so that no comparison can be made for attributing this to him. The question, therefore, remains open, but attribution to Shakespeare is by no means established, and should perhaps be treated with caution.

237 4 G. B. Harrison, *The Elizabethan Journals* (revised ed. 1938), p. 238.

238 5 See Boas' chapter on 'Cholmley, Raleigh and Marlowe' in his *Christopher Marlowe* (1940), p. 255. It is to Cholmley we owe the final evidence linking Marlowe with Sir Walter Ralegh and his School of Night. One of the charges against Cholmley was that 'Hee saieth & verely beleueth that one Marlowe is able to shewe more sounde reasons for Atheisme than any devine in Englande is able to geue to prove devinitie & that Marloe tolde him that hee hath read the Atheist lecture to Sʳ Walter Raliegh & others.' See document in Appendix, p. 354.

239 6 Dr. S. A. Tannenbaum, *The Booke of Sir Thomas Moore* (1927), p. 101.

Part IV. Scadbury, 1593

POETIC INTERLUDE

244 1 Boas, *Christopher Marlowe*, p. 235.

THOMAS WALSINGHAM

249 1 The wills are reproduced in the Appendix of E. A. Webb's *History of Chislehurst* (1899).

250 2 Nicholl's *Progresses of Elizabeth*, Vol. II, p. 20. Lady Walsingham Senior was Ursula, the widow of Sir Francis Walsingham.

250 3 *State Papers*, 6 Cecil, S.P.D. 1597, p. 471.

257 4 For reproduction of this list from the family archives we are indebted to Major J. Marsham Townshend.

LADY AUDREY WALSINGHAM

261 1 Nicholl's *Progresses of Elizabeth*, Vol. III, p. 591.

263 2 See *Calendar of Proceedings of the Committee for Compounding*, 28 Nov., 1651, p. 511.

263 3 E. G. Clark's *Ralegh and Marlowe*, p. 281.

PEDIGREE OF THE WALSINGHAMS

281 1 The will of Thomas Walsingham III (Inq. P.M. 26 Eliz. pt. i, no. 38) states: 'I will the same Dame Anne Gray, my wyfe [i.e. his second wife, who survived him] all such goodes, juylles and plate as she brought vnto me, & all suche stuf of hers as she brought remaining at the Blacke Fryers or ellswhere . . .' Perhaps this was where the Walsinghams' London house stood, thus not far from the Earl of Northumberland's residence at Blackfriars, which would have been handy for Marlowe.

281 2 From the Baptismal Register of St. Nicholas, Chislehurst, in the possession of the Rector of Chislehurst.

282 3 E. A. Webb's *History of Chislehurst*, p. 34.

282 4 Chan. Inq. P.M. Ser. 2, Vol. 226, no. 181 in the Public Record Office.

Part V. Deptford, 1593

289 1 The identities of the sixteen jurors have been established by the researches of Dr. Hotson (see *The Death of Christopher Marlowe*, p. 38) and added to by E. Vine Hall, *Testamentary Papers*, iii (1937). See also Boas, *Christopher Marlowe*, pp. 271–2. I am also indebted to Miss Elizabeth Vaux for the loan of her notes from her current researches on the Balls of Deptford.

THE DEATH OF CHRISTOPHER MARLOWE

Page Note

291　1　See Boas, *Christopher Marlowe*, pp. 125 and 268.

291　2　His name is given as ffrezer in the burial register of St. Nicholas, Deptford. See Hotson's researches on the origin of the name in his *The Death of Christopher Marlowe* (1925), pp. 20–22.

291　3　Philip Stubbes, *The Anatomie of abuses* (1583), sig. C2, recto and verso.

292　4　Gavin Thurston, Secretary of the Society of Coroners of England and Wales, has recently conducted a comparison of Elizabethan inquisitions and has established this fact. (From a lecture delivered to the Marlowe Society, May 1963.)

295　5　J. L. Hotson, op. cit., p. 40.

295　6　John Bakeless, *The Tragicall History of Christopher Marlowe*, Vol. I, p. 158.

296　7　Charles Norman, *The Muses' Darling* (1947), p. 207.

296　8　Eugenie de Kalb, 'Death of Marlowe' in *T.L.S.*, 21 May, 1925.

296　9　S. A. Tannenbaum, *The Assassination of Christopher Marlowe* (New York, 1928).

296　10　Frizer's Pardon was discovered by Hotson, who gives this translation (op. cit., p. 37). The document is reproduced in the Appendix of this volume, p. 356.

297　11　See Hotson, op. cit., pp. 42–9, for a full account of this fascinating case which was also uncovered by Hotson.

298　12　Hotson gives a transcript of the case of Woodleff v. Frizer in the Appendix of his book (op. cit., pp. 69–73).

298　13　See Hotson, op. cit., pp. 49–51, for cases of leases in reversion to Lady Walsingham involving Frizer.

299　14　Boas, op. cit., pp. 268–9.

299　15　Ibid, p. 269.

300　16　Ethel Seaton, 'Robert Poley's Ciphers', in *R.E.S.*, April 1931, with facsimile of a cipher from *State Papers*, 106, Vol. II, in P.R.O.

300　17　See Boas, op. cit., pp. 265–6.

300　18　Ibid, p. 275, and Eugenie de Kalb, 'Robert Poley's Movements as a Messenger of the Court, 1558 to 1601', in *R.E.S.*, January 1933, pp. 13–18.

300　19　Ethel Seaton, 'Marlowe, Robert Poley, and the Tippings', in *R.E.S.*, Oct. 1929. See also Boas, p. 273.

301　20　See Boas, p. 268. Letter of Sir Robert Cecil to Sir T. Heneage dated May 25, 1592, in *State Papers* (Dom) Eliz., Vol. CCXLII, no. 25.

301　21　S. A. Tannenbaum, *The Assassination of Christopher Marlowe*, p. 36.

301　22　Ibid, p. 37.

302　23　Eugenie de Kalb, 'Death of Marlowe', in *T.L.S.*, 21 May 1925.

302　24　Boas, p. 276.

303　25　Ibid, p. 351.

303　26　Calvin Hoffman, *The Murder of the Man who was Shakespeare* (New York, 1955), pp. 76–98.

306　27　J. L. Hotson, *The First Night of Twelfth Night* (1954), p. 65.

MARLOWE VILIFIED

308　1　Charles Norman, *The Muses' Darling*, Chap. XXVIII, p. 243.

310　2　Boas, *Christopher Marlowe*, p. 242.

311　3　Charles Norman, op. cit., p. 220.

311　4　Nashe's Preface to Greene's *Menaphon* (1589), from *Works*, ed. McKerrow, IV, p. 311.

313　5　The translations of Kyd's Latin quotations are all given according to Charles Norman's excellent renderings in *The Muses' Darling*, Chap. XXV.

317　6　Op. cit., p. 222.

319　7　William Camden's *Annals* (3rd ed., 1635), p. 417.

319　8　Boas, op. cit., p. 242.

Page Note

319 9 Charles Norman, op. cit., 'Foreword', p. xiv.

320 10 Professor Bakeless makes a most relevant comment: 'There was always a strong temptation to credit the Puritans because they were so definite in their charges and so picturesque in stating them; whereas the quite different picture of the dramatist which can be drawn from the casual but usually friendly references of his contemporaries in literary and theatrical London is less arresting. From them we get the same picture of brilliant impassioned youth that is so clearly implicit in the plays and poems. Though it is dangerous to seek anything save the most general outlines of a dramatist's opinions and personality in his work—since the best dramatist is he who most entirely veils himself in the characters he creates—such a general impression is at least no bad confirmation of the verdict of his fellows. Marlowe's fellows in the Elizabethan theatre usually describe for us a winning, talented, impetuous youth.' (*The Tragicall History of Christopher Marlowe*, Vol. I, p. 150.)

THE MORNING STAR

332 1 Algernon Charles Swinburne, 'Christopher Marlowe in relation to Greene, Peele and Lodge', in *Letters on the Elizabethan Dramatists* (London, 1910).

332 2 Ibid.

332 3 See also Bakeless' masterly analysis of Marlowe's development of English blank verse in *The Tragicall History of Dr. Faustus*, Vol. II, Chap. XV, 'The Mighty Line'. Bakeless qualifies Swinburne's claim, certainly, by pointing out that other writers had employed 'the various devices whose skilful use gave his [Marlowe's] verse much of its melody'. But he adds: 'Marlowe is the first writer of really great blank verse in English, the first that can possibly be called the "mighty line"' (p. 179).

333 4 Introduction to *Marlowe's Plays and Poems*, Everyman Library (revised ed., 1955), p. xiii.

335 5 Ibid, pp. xv–xvi.

335 6 *The Massacre at Paris* was performed for the first time since Marlowe's day on January 30, 1963, in a production by Michael Ferguson for the Marlowe Society at the Chanticleer Theatre, London, to mark the 370th anniversary of the first night of this play on January 30, 1593, when it was first put on by Henslowe at the Rose. On that day he marked the play in his diary 'ne' (new).

336 7 Michel Poirier, *Christopher Marlowe* (1951), p. 205.

336 8 Ibid, p. 207.

336 9 Ibid, p. 204.

340 10 Philip Henderson, *Christopher Marlowe* (1952), p. 151.

341 11 Boas, *Christopher Marlowe*, p. 230.

341 12 Ibid.

343 13 Charles Norman, *The Muses' Darling*, p. 175.

343 14 Ibid, 'Foreword', p. xiv.

Index

Figures in italics refer to illustrations.

Trinidad, 148
Troublesome Reign of King John, The, 330
True Tragedy of Richard, Duke of York; The, 195–6, 198, 202, 203, 330
Turkish Affairs Familiarly Known, 86
Tyler, Frank W., 228

Urry, Dr. William, v–vii, xi; on the marriage of Marlowe's parents, 3, 25; in the bombing of Canterbury, 4; on John Marlowe, 5; on Marlowe's duel at Canterbury, 123; on the Collier Leaf, 227

Valenciano, Aida, C., 232
Vann, Elizabeth, ix
Vaughan, William, on Marlowe, 307
Venus and Adonis, copy at Lamport Hall, 222–3; compared with *Hero and Leander*, 283
Vickers, John, 114, 116
Virginia, 142

Walker, Adrian, juror at Marlowe's inquest 290
Walpole, Sir Hugh, 30
Walsingham family, *280*, 281–2
Walsingham, Lady Audrey, dedication of *Hero and Leander* to, 223; date of marriage, 250–51, 260–61; family background, 259–60; at Court, 261–3; relations with Cecil, 263
Walsingham, Dorothy, 249–50
Walsingham, Sir Edmund, 105, 249, 250
Walsingham, Edmund II, 103, 249
Walsingham, Frances, *see* Sidney, Frances
Walsingham, Sir Francis, his espionage system, 35, 86, 90, 92, 95, 218–19; relations with Marlowe, 35–6, 70, 92, 95, 96; portrait and signature, *94*; deals with the Babington plot, 96, 98; friend of Watson, 123; death and Watson's eclogue, 125–6; Hakluyt's dedication to, 149–50
Walsingham, Geoffrey, 249
Walsingham, Margaret, 249
Walsingham, Thomas I, 249
Walsingham, Thomas II, 249
Walsingham, Sir Thomas III, 103, 249
Walsingham, Sir Thomas IV, relations with Marlowe, 70, 86, 283, 284–5; during the Babington plot, 96; his inheritance in London, 103; in

Watson's *Meliboeus*, 125–6; possibly in the School of Night, 143, 145; during the Armada, 219; succession to Scadbury, 249; date of marriage, 250–51, 260–61; in the family pedigree, 281–2; in relation to Marlowe's death, 296–7, 303–4
Walsingham, Sir Thomas V, 251, 252
Warner, Walter, 139, 146, 151
Warner, William, 104, 146, 147, 157 (caption)
Warton, Thomas, 185
Waterhouse, Jack, ix
Watson, Thomas, under the patronage of Sir F. Walsingham, 86; at Douai, 90; lodges with Marlowe, 104; in the affray with Bradley, 117–23; studies abroad, 123–4; works and influence, 125; madrigals, *124*, 125; tributes at his death, 126; his *Amyntae Gaudia*, 126–7, *128*; tribute by Harrington, 160; disciple of Bruno, 171
Webb, E. A., on Scadbury and the Walsinghams, 254, 281, 282
Webster, John, 157 (caption)
White, Edward, 224
White, John, journeys to and drawings of Virginia, 142, *143*, *144*, 145, 258; brings back an Indian, 145
Whitgift, John, Archbishop, orders the burning of books, 224; in the Star Chamber, 235; portrait, *294*
Whitiker, M., 60
Wilkenson, Professor, 60
William the Englishman, 13
Winston on Tees, 219, 220
Wodehouse, Mary, 259, 260
Wolfe, John, 123
Wolfit, Sir Donald, as Tamburlaine, *114*, *116*
Wolley, Sir John, 285
Wolsey, Cardinal, 8
Woman Killed with Kindness, quoted, 304
Wood, Anthony à, on Watson, 123; on Hariot, 141; on Marlowe, 307
Woodleffe, Drew, 297–8
Woodward, Joan, 113
Wotton, Dean, 40
Wotton, Edward, 110
Wright, W. S., ix
Wylde, Stephen, 118
Wyngaerde, Anthonis van den, 106